# HELD TOGETHER BY PINS

# HELD TOGETHER BY PINS

## Liberal Democracy under Siege in Africa

Tatah Mentan

### Africa World Press, Inc.

P.O. Box 1892
Trenton, NJ 08607

P.O. Box 48
Asmara, ERITREA

# Africa World Press, Inc.

P.O. Box 1892　　　　　　P.O. Box 48
Trenton, NJ 08607　　　　Asmara, ERITREA

Book and cover design: Saverance Publishing Services

Library of Congress Cataloging-in-Publication Data

Mentan, Tatah, 1948-
 Held together by pins : liberal democracy under siege in Africa / Tatah Mentan.
   p. cm.
 Includes index.
 ISBN 1-59221-520-3 (cloth) -- ISBN 1-59221-521-1 (pbk.)
 1. Democracy--Africa. 2. Liberalism--Africa. I. Title.

JQ1879.A15M46 2007
320.96--dc22
                      2006039298

To the victims of the "popular struggles for democracy" in Africa

# Table of Contents

# Acknowledgements

I am pleased to acknowledge the huge debt of gratitude owed to those who helped me prepare this book: my sponsor Scholar Rescue Fund director, Robert Quinn, without whose encouragement and constant support this idea of the book might never have come to fruition; Illinois Wesleyan University, whose host services gave the initial impetus to this idea; my research and teaching associates, Professors Tom Griffiths, Irving Epstein, Rebecca Gearhart, Frank Boyd, and William Munro, for their enormous assistance and undying concern. My thanks also go to Sarah Willcox and Carla Stuart for their devoted services to Scholars at Risk like me; to Katie Chase who also deserves my appreciation for pruning through the text, and searching for sources above and beyond the call of her duty; to Professor John Mukum Mbaku for "making it happen," by transforming the manuscript to a book; to Dr. Sammy M. Ngum for footing the bills; and, finally, to my family, for their patience and understanding throughout this undertaking.

# Preface

"Democrazy? Dem all crazy, what a crazy demonstration!" fumed late Fela Ani-kulapo Kuti of Nigeria when asked what he thought of elections in Africa. Such outrage didn't stop the drum-beating and chanting musician from running for the presidency of the Federal Republic of Nigeria or to participate in the "crazy demonstration." However, concerns about democratization in Africa today center both on the threat of authoritarian regression, as well as on the depth, quality, fairness, and completeness of democratization thus far.

But, what, indeed, is Africa—a continent so torn and convulsed by crises? Africa is the world's abandoned continent fraught with multiple contradictions. It is one of the richest, if not the richest, continent in natural resources. Yet Africans range among the poorest people on earth. Of its total population of some 800 million, over 300 million survive on incomes that are barely above abject poverty level. Yet of the US$80 billion of private foreign direct investment in the developing world in 1994, only $4.5 billion went to Africa. Despite more than a decade of structural adjustment programs, average income per head at $520 is still below the level of 1975. Seven out of ten Africans live in rural areas and depend on small-scale farming and local supply industries for work. Six out of ten African women are illiterate, and the primary school system still reaches less than two- thirds of African girls. Some thirty percent of African children under the age of five are below the weight they should have reached for their future healthy development.

Women make up a particularly vulnerable group in the labor market in Africa. They have been hard hit by the deteriorating economic situation and the impact of structural adjustment programs and devaluations. The majority of women still work in subsistence agriculture, often unremunerated. They are used to working long hours with little improvement in productivity or technology. The small minority of women working in the modern sector, often in public services, have been particularly affected by layoffs following restructuring or privatization. The combination of rural and urban poverty and lack of opportunities has led to an intensification of the already existing disparities between women and men and to large numbers of women being forced to take up informal sector activities in order to survive.

African cities are expanding at 6 percent per year, which is the fastest urban growth rate in the world. Poor farmers, who with their families make up over 80 percent of the total numbers living in extreme poverty, are still moving in vast numbers to the burgeoning shantytowns that surround most cities. Many are migrating across national borders to do so. The jobs they find are almost all in the informal sector following the cutback of employment in the public sector and in the few large commercial, often state-owned, enterprises. Two-thirds of all urban workers are in the informal sector and urban unemployment has doubled since the 1970s to reach between 15 and 20 percent. Real wages in manufacturing have fallen sharply during the 1980s with an average annual decline of 12 percent recorded in 15 countries for which the International Labor Organization has reliable data. Current structural adjustment policies are failing to meet basic human needs or reduce the burden of debt and thus have not put Africa on to a path of sustainable economic growth.

Against this bleak economic background, the newly established democracies face enormous problems in containing the tensions that threaten their survival. The most optimistic forecasts for the recovery of the African economy suggest that the total numbers living in poverty will not start to fall until well into the twenty-first century. During that period, 60 million young African men and women will have begun the frustrating task of looking for some means of sustaining themselves. HIV/AIDS will have infected 20 million and at least four times that number will have died of preventable diseases. On top of that, food shortage in Africa was projected to more than triple by the year 2000. There is a clear danger that further progress toward building democratic institutions may be arrested amid a slide into large-scale social dislocations and a reversion to the corruption and repressive rule that has held back development for so long.

Given the bleak economic situation, does democracy have a future in Africa? This book argues that the urgency of democratization in African debate flows from the desperate condition of the mass of Africans, and from the fact that "democratization" has in essence replaced Marxism as both explanatory device and panacea while being appropriated as a goal and tool by foreign policy agendas in league with a growing local parasitic transnational capitalist class.

My goal in writing *Held Together By Pins: Liberal Democracy under Siege in Africa* is to produce an intellectually challenging text that at the same time would be accessible and engaging to students, scholars, and political practitioners. The more common approach has been to emphasize one or the other of these dimensions of threats to democracy. Some texts have done well by sacrificing rigor in the name of user-friendliness. But although such books sometimes keep readers happy, they often fail to prepare them for critical thinking about democracy in Africa.

Other texts have succeeded by sacrificing accessibility in the name of rigor, where rigor is all too often taken to mean mathematical density. These books overwhelm many readers, and even those few who become adept at solving well-posed political problems are often baffled by questions drawn from everyday contexts. I have always believed that a text could at once be rigorous *and* user-friendly.

I wrote this book with the conviction that the teaching of democratization and the teaching of African political economy are complements, not substitutes. Students who learn only about the democratization process rarely seem to develop any real affection for our discipline, and even more rarely do they acquire that distinctive mindset we call "thinking like an historical materialist." By contrast, students who develop dialectical materialist intuition are stimulated to think more deeply about the driving forces of the history of Africa's democratization and to find more interesting ways to apply them. Most important, they usually end up liking this critical mode of analysis.

Chapter 1

# Introduction

*There is no opposition in heaven. God himself does not want opposition—that is why he chased Satan away. Why should Kamuzu have opposition?*

(Decalo, 1992: 10)

In "A Narrow Victory—Ike Oguine's View from the South—Malawi, Democracy in Africa," *New Internationalist* (NI), November, 2002, the author wrote:

> Recently the Malawian Parliament, by only three votes, defeated an attempt by President Bakili Muluzi to change the country's constitution. The change would have allowed Muluzi to run for a third term in office. Many Africans far beyond Malawi's borders were jubilant. Letters poured into the Africa Service of the BBC, ironically one of the liveliest pan-African forums around, congratulating Malawians for successfully resisting the return of the Life-President Syndrome that has so terribly scarred Africa.

Many opposition politicians had agreed to vote for the amendment sought by Muluzi's political party. With their votes it had seemed that the president would have no difficulty in getting rid of the constitutional restriction on his running for a third term. However, a broad coalition of forces, including former cabinet ministers, church, and nongovernmental organizations (NGOs), mounted a determined campaign against the amendment and managed to win enough parliamentary support to defeat it. Though the battle is by no means over, as Muluzi's supporters say, they will try again. However, the victory won at least so far by Malawian pro-democracy forces was indeed significant. It is yet another indication that the democratic coalitions, which in the 1990s ended decades of autocratic rule in many African countries, will do everything they can to protect their hard-won gains. These democratic forces recognize that the struggle does not end when the autocrat is forced to give up power; it only enters a new phase.

From fighting bare-knuckled dictatorships (and in many cases making incredible sacrifices), the struggle has shifted to guarding the new processes of democracy from the rampaging ambitions of political leaders. In Zambia, a coalition similar to Malawi's was successful in preventing President Frederick Chiluba from changing the constitution to allow him to run for a third term in office. Across Africa there are many other examples of groups in recently redemocratized countries that are not just trying to protect democratic institutions but striving to make them more participatory and responsive. Even as the world was praising Sierra Leonean relatively free and fair elections that followed years of savage and fratricidal civil war, for example, NGOs in the country were ringing alarm bells. What the outside world saw as a move toward democracy, Sierra Leonian democratic activists saw as a potential return to the past, where two insensitive and corrupt political parties held sway. They feared a return to mass discontent, widespread bitterness, and civil conflict. Labor unions such as Nigerian Labor Congress (NLC) and the Congress of South African Trade Unions (COSATU) are further examples: rank-and-file trade-union groups resisting in their countries the application of one-size-fits-all economic policies fashioned in Washington.

Enforcing constitutional term limits, seeking to broaden democratic participation, and challenging market fundamentalism are all important in themselves. But it is perhaps even more important that these various struggles are revitalizing democratic debate in societies that have been under repressive rule for a very long time. They are ensuring that our new democracies do not lapse into complacency, do not become nice curtains to be displayed to the world while power elites continue to transact business as usual among themselves.

Of course there are still too many countries in Africa where the journey away from autocracy has not even begun. The *NI*, in its August edition of 2002 (No. 348), reported that out of 53 nations in Africa only 21 are electoral democracies. The rest range from Somalia, which for many years has remained a "failed state" paralyzed by interclan conflict, to Egypt, which has a national parliament of sorts but where a system of secretive military courts hands out summary (in)justice to opponents of the government. Recent peace agreements in the Democratic Republic of Congo (DRC) and Sudan hold out some hope that the wars in those countries may be brought to an end soon. However, if the fate of past agreements is anything to go by, any such hope must be cautious indeed. And until these and other bitter civil wars can be brought to an end, the struggle for democracy in many parts of Africa will remain on hold.

Recent trends toward dynastic succession and *coups d'état* in Togo and Mauritania respectively are eloquent testimonies. With a combination of savage brutality and extreme wiliness, Africa's longest surviving autocrat, Togolese President Gnassingbé Eyadema, frustrated years of struggle to hold free and fair elections in his country. In 1998, independent civil-rights groups reported that the bodies of several of his political opponents had washed up along Togolese beautiful beaches and in neighboring Benin. They were reported killed by the Eyadema security forces for protesting against fraudulent elections he had organized. Not long after that French President Jacques Réné Chirac paid a visit to Eyadema and large posters of the two aging politicos beaming at each other dotted the streets of Lomé, Togolese capital. Even a brutalized people could not help but seethe in anger.

Gnassingbé Eyadema died of a heart attack on Saturday, February 5, 2005, ending his ruthless reign as the longest-serving African ruler after 38 years. The Togolese military took immediate control, closing the national borders and naming the son of the deceased, Faure Gnassingbé, president. It ignored a succession plan written into the Togolese constitution that would have elevated the speaker of parliament, who was in Europe at the time, to the presidency and required elections within 60 days. Parliament on Sunday, February 6, 2005, overwhelmingly ratified the dynastic ascension of Gnassingbé by changing the constitution to allow him to serve out his father's term, which was to have ended in 2008.

According to a *Reuters* report on Wednesday August 3, 2005, the Mauritanina military toppled the twenty year regime of President Maaouya Ould Sid'Ahmed Taya, who was on a visit to Saudi Arabia to attend the funeral of Saudi Arabia's King Fahd in Riyadh. A communiqué signed by the Military Council for Justice and Democracy said the coup was aimed at "putting an end to the regime's despotic practices." The statement, relased by official state media, said the council would rule Mauritania for a transitional period not exceeding two years "during which real democratic institutions would be created."

However, hundreds of Mauritanians took to the streets of the capital city of Nouakchott, shouting and honking car horns in celebration after the army announced it had seized power. Convoys of vehicles with people hanging out the sides shouting "Praise Be to God" and making victory signs paraded down one main avenue. The Spokesman for UN Secretary-General Kofi Annan condemned the *coup d'état* and called for the restoration of constitutional order and underlined the need for the full respect for human rights and the rule of law. The African Union also condemned the coup. But Ould Sid'Hamed Taya had long faced growing opposition from Islamists unhappy with his closeness to Israel, black ethnicities in the south who accuse him of favoring the Arab elite, and generally by advocates for democracy and human rights. For now, however, Mauritania remains a one-party state. The country continues to experience ethnic tensions between its black population and the Maur (Arab-Berber) populace.

So it is certain that several grim battles lie ahead in the struggle for democracy in Africa. Heavy sacrifices will continue to be required of people who have already given so much, while a cynical or largely inattentive world offers at best formulaic noises. Nevertheless, the message from Malawi is a positive one: When the autocrat is finally defeated, a façade of electoral democracy to satisfy the formal requirements of aid donors will not be acceptable, nor will regression to constitutional autocracy. African democrats want the real thing and will fight very hard for it.

## CHALLENGES

On April 25, 2002, UN Secretary-General Kofi Annan spoke to a capacity crowd at the Kennedy School of Government's ARCO Forum. He said emphatically that "No amount of aid, no degree of diplomacy, can produce lasting progress if it is not rooted in legitimate, rule bound institutions responsive and accountable to the people." To Annan, the spread of liberal democracy offers Africa its best hope for recovery. It is a truism that a river of ink has already flowed in debates over the prospects for liberal democracy in Africa. But there is sharp disagreement as to why. In fact, most observers take a dim view of the chances of liberal democracy in Africa's immediate future.

The reasons are not far to seek. Strong leaders buy off dissent; in Algeria, for example, Islamists with impressive public support deride democracy; culturally embedded patterns of patronage undermine popular participation in politics; civil society is weak and easily manipulated; and globalization has besieged the process of democratization and reduced it to mere voting for tyrants, killers and pillagers. In such conflictive conditions the authoritarian temptation will resurface again as the imposition of structural adjustment programs (SAPs) will require political surrender to the dictates of international financiers, rule through decrees, and the autocratic style of local technocrats educated in the dogmatism of the World Bank (WB) and the International Monetary Fund (IMF). As William Robinson has explained (1996: 375):

> International] agencies are secretive, anti-democratic, and dictatorial in the imposition of their policies, with absolutely no accountability to the mass publics to which under polyarchic systems states are ostensibly accountable. New institutions required for the management of globalized production have come into being ... but they are even less democratic and less accountable than nation-states. These institutions have usurped the functions of economic management from the public sphere ... and transferred them to their own private and almost secretive spheres.

Throughout the continent, international financial institutions and other foreign donors and their representatives have persistently threatened to withdraw their support if African institutions and politicians fail to submit to the stringent requirements of the sapping SAPs. This is the process that transforms state administrators into "the pimps of global capitalism" (Robinson, 1996: 374). It generates popular cynicism and discontent and undermines any genuine democratic prospect. Each of these points has merit. Nonetheless, the pressures for change are formidable, and African rulers who are intent on survival may find political reform irresistible. A democratic Africa may be long in coming. However, there is good reason to believe that the continent stands on the brink of a momentous era of change.

One of the most obvious indicators is the dramatic picture of rapid population growth and growing citizen demands in Africa. Aggregate rates of natural increase, though high in comparison to the remainder of the world, are often dwarfed by poverty, urban population growth, and HIV/AIDS. Even providing primary education poses an extraordinary challenge, especially in the less wealthy states, where schools are already inadequate. Unemployment and underemployment are high, and will only grow. At the same time, literacy has steadily increased in the continent, and while female literacy rates lag considerably behind those for males, the changes over time are quite striking. Rising female literacy rates portend declining birth rates, but the effects will not be felt for decades. In the intervening years, women will enter the workforce in greater numbers, further increasing demands for job creation.

## CRACKS IN THE MONOLITH

The media's role in the conduct of multiparty politics is important because freedom of expression is a vital condition for *free and fair* elections. In the past, personal rulers built their personality cult using state-owned and state-controlled media, mainly the radio and sometimes television. The print media are often confined to towns and this is linked to low levels of literacy and income. The media thus operated under strict state control with journalists, editors, and writers as opinion formers living under the fearsome shadow of the Orwellian Big Brother. Today the situation is quite different.

The proliferation of printing companies and corner-shop photocopy machines ensures that people have more to read than government-dominated newspapers. Popularly oriented political tracts and religious pamphlets are readily available from street vendors. Villagers and city dwellers traveling across borders in search of work return with fresh images that often reflect poorly on the quality of life at home. Equally important, labor migrants have earned the money to support protest movements and collective self help organizations. Though government ineptitude, unresponsiveness, and corruption are a given, complaints about government abuses of power—corruption and nepotism, torture and mistreatment of prisoners—are increasingly common. Although many citizens, given government intolerance for dissent, choose to remain mute, the resultant cynicism further erodes support for government.

Obviously, liberal democracy is not a necessary outcome of political reform. Nor will all efforts to make the political system more efficient or more responsive succeed. Reform does, however, imply an increase in the accountability and responsiveness of those who rule and, therefore, will necessarily involve limits to power as well as the application of the rule of law. In other words, reform entails political liberalization.

For example, the cooperation framework adopted in 2000 between the European Union and 77 countries in Africa, the Caribbean, and the Pacific (ACP) identified political dialogue and governance conditionality as the core strategies for promoting democracy and anchoring the rule of law in developing countries. There are mechanisms for suspending aid on political grounds, originally introduced in 1995. What are the policies and strategies of the European Community aimed at responding to the crises of governance and preventing conflict in ACP states? How easy is the combination of democracy assistance and governance conditionality to prevent democratic regression in politically fragile countries by reviewing the European Community's response to crises of governance in Niger, Côte d'Ivoire, and others? Can offering appropriate responses to abrupt interruptions in democratization processes, traditional forms of political conditionality, prove adequate for responding to the gradual corrosion of governance and the decay of democracy? Furthermore, does conducting structured political dialogue not put more demands on the management of aid, as it converts foreign aid into a highly political endeavor?

On June 9, 2004, Roger Bate wrote in *Business Day* (South Africa) that "Africa Cannot Afford Regression to Big Man Leaders." He continued "Africa's despots are saber- rattling again. Last week Namibian President Sam Nujoma called white people 'snakes,' and then Robert Mugabe, Zimbabwe's disgraceful dictator, called the almost saintly Archbishop Desmond Tutu an 'evil and embittered little bishop.'"

After reading write-ups like this one, some questions readily spring to one's mind:

1. Why such contradictory cynicism and concern for democratization in Africa?
2. Why such iron determination to achieve democracy in Africa?
3. Whose democracy? For what Africa?

## CRUEL REALITIES OF PSEUDOELECTIONS

Most African governments have opted for the symbols of liberal democracy, not the substance. Even so, that autocrats choose to go through the motions is instructive; while they may deride the suitability of liberal democracy for the continent, they concede the universality of democratic symbols. Observers are not fooled by displays of pseudoparticipation any more than the African people are. When Tunisian President Zine al-Abidine Ben Ali won a plebiscite in 1994 with 99.3 percent, or when disdained candidates were declared winners in Moroccan parliamentary elections in 1993, few voters confused what was happening with liberal democracy. Indeed, many African elections are so blatantly manipulated that most people simply conclude that it is better not to vote. In Egypt's 1990 parliamentary elections, fewer than 10 percent of eligible voters actually cast ballots in many Cairo districts. And given the chance, voters have shown ingenuity in thwarting rigged elections. In the Moroccan elections, the number two vote winner often was the null ballot; voters paid to vote for the pro-government candidate simply put nothing into the ballot box.

In much of the rest of Africa, the story is one of conducting problematic *mutipati* (as they would say in Malawi) elections without initiating substantive changes to the leadership or to the polity. When changes seem imminent, political protagonists refuse to accept the outcome as *fair*. The case of Angola is instructive as the country switched to civil war shortly after multiparty elections that were supervised by "international observers" who applauded the outcome as "free and fair."

A kind of multiparty fatigue led people to question the relevance of multi-party politics in the African setting. Eritrean President Isayas Afewerki is forth-right in arguing that "We do not want any absolute or childish democracy, and neither do we advocate European or US-style democracy which would not be suitable for our society, because these were established in circumstances differ-ent from what we have gone through .... We now need a political climate which will guarantee stability and the reconstruction process" (Salih, 1999: 139).

In power since the new state of Eritrea was created in 1993 and for more than two decades as the leader of the fighting front that delivered independence, Eritrea's president is skeptical if any party will be in a position to maintain both stability and reconstruction. Yet the new country's constitution espouses multi-party liberal democracy.

Given freely contested elections, the incumbents would win few votes. Governments have grossly overestimated their popularity, with unsettling results. In Algeria the ruling National Liberation Front (FLN) designed an elec-tion, replete with gerrymandered districts, that was calculated to produce an overwhelming victory. Instead, in the first round of parliamentary elections in December 1991, the FLN won 15 seats while the opposition Islamic Salvation Front (FIS) won 188 out of the 430 total seats. The FLN design worked quite well but not for the intended beneficiary. With 48 percent of the total national vote in the first round of balloting, the FIS was positioned to win a large major-ity in parliament in the second round. For many of the Algerian voters, the FIS was not the Islamist party; it was a credible opposing voice to a discredited ruling clique.

The Algerian example illustrates the importance of carefully designed elec-toral mechanisms, not to deny the venting of opposition voices but to avoid overstating the popularity of the government or its opponents. Thus, any serious discussion of political reform must pay attention to different techniques of orga-nizing balloting. In Algeria a proportional system would have assured the FIS the major voice in parliament, but would have precluded a situation in which it could have easily mustered the two-thirds vote necessary to amend the Algerian constitution. Moreover, if a proportional system had been in use, voters might well have thrown their support to smaller opposition parties. In the winner-take-all system that was used, a vote for a small party, no matter how articulate its leadership or compelling its program was a wasted vote.

The January 1992 coup in Algeria marked not only the end of the dramatic experiment in political reform in the country, but also the end of a period of experimental reform in the Maghreb (Arab North Africa). Following the FIS electoral victories, many North African elites lost their enthusiasm for reform, and certainly for democratization. In Tunisia and in Egypt, Ben Ali and Hosni Mubarak suddenly found a middle-class constituency urging caution rather than demanding a more open system.

Skeptics, more taken with the frailty of civil society than with its potential, have learned the wrong lesson from recent experiments in democratization.

There is no question that civil society lacks the power to confront existing regimes in African states; but the oppositional power of civil society has generally been exaggerated throughout the world.

Nonetheless, when the state opens up public space, the blossoming of civil society, even if inchoate, is impressive, as was seen in Algeria. Given the opportunity to mature, these organizations not only lend vitality to experiments in open government but serve as counterweights to populist movements such as the Islamists or ethnicists. Civil society will not mature overnight, however, which is why the project of reform must be seen as a gradualist endeavor.

As for the Algerian Islamic Salvation Front (FIS), the radicalizing effect of the coup was both predictable and tragic. But the violent behavior of the FIS—when denied the fruits of its earned electoral victory—cannot be extrapolated backward to predict how it might have behaved had it been allowed to assume legislative power. Algerian descent into civil war has certainly illustrated that the logic of violence is an unlikely cure for the problems dogging Middle Eastern and North African states. The Algerian army is a professional, well-trained body, yet it has been unable to impose its will on the country. And recent government actions indicate that a dialogue between the FIS and the government may well be in the offing.

For the Islamists, the decision to participate in elections is almost always contentious. Time and again, there is a tendency to arrive at a decision to split the Islamist movement, though not into equal parts. Hardliners portray such a decision as a sellout, saying state-dominated elections are meaningless and worse, a case of playing into the hands of the rulers. Moderates, consistently bringing a majority with them, argue for a gradualist approach, and seize on the legitimacy that comes from competing. Not surprisingly, the decision to exclude the Islamists from elections usually, though not always, solidifies and radicalizes the Islamist opposition, submerging hardliner-moderate distinctions. There are exceptions, as in Tunisia, where the proscribed al-Nahda Islamists has, under the leadership of Rashid Ghannoushi, been remarkably restrained despite the inclusionist position of Ben Ali's government. More important, the process of inclusion promotes pragmatism and moderation; service in government and inclusionary politics tend to reduce radicalism (Putnam, 1993).

Of course, we do not yet have an example of Islamists successfully gaining power through the electoral process. Allusions to the Sudan, where an Islamist government came to power through a coup are not instructive. The dynamics of the violent seizure of power and incremental political reform have little in common. Reform implies accommodation and compromise, while revolution is synonymous with the subjugation, or even eradication, of adversaries.

Those who oppose the electoral participation of Islamists point to the Islamists' positions on women, minorities, and others. These are not trivial concerns, but to begin with the proposition that Islamicists' values preclude any form of participation in the political process is self-defeating and a recipe for confrontation. Values bend in the face of necessity. That is an empirical fact.

Guarantees are essential to address the justified fears of minorities and others who see Islamism as a fundamental threat. This also means that human rights and other watchdog organizations must be given political space to develop and for the fetters on civil society to be removed. The legacy of authoritarianism cannot be reversed overnight, but unless governments take gradual steps to open up public space and permit civil society to develop, then only the rulers and the Islamists will be left in stark confrontation. At that point, the example of the genocide in the Darfur region of Sudan becomes strikingly relevant.

The war in Sudan is complex. Alliances are made and unmade. All sides practice a policy of divide-and-rule. All abuse human rights. The war is better understood as a number of interlocking civil wars, where southerner is set against southerner and northerner against northerner as well as northerner against southerner. Yet there is one constant issue which underlies both the current conflict and the earlier civil war that began before independence in the mid-1950s and lasted until 1972.

This *casus belli* is the enduring economic and cultural gap between the Muslim, Arab inhabitants of the central, riverine provinces, whose elites have controlled the state since independence, and the non-Arab, largely non-Muslim peoples of the South—of which the Nuer and the Dinka are two among many. Northerners have consistently discriminated against southerners on grounds of ethnicity and religion; and the southern region has been marginalized in economic development. Many other parts of Sudan have suffered from this hegemony of the center. These are notably the western provinces (the majority of whose inhabitants are Muslim but not Arab). However, it is the southerners who have suffered most. Thus it was southerners who, in the 1950s and again in the 1980s, took up arms against the government.

The war is not just about control of natural resources or access to state power, although these are important factors. There is a conflict over the nature of the state itself. The ruling elites in Khartoum view Sudan as a Muslim country and an integral part of the Arab world. Their opponents, not only southerners, see it as a multi-religious, multi-ethnic, multilingual state, one in which Arabs (though not Muslims) are a minority. Today many southerners embrace a more radical solution: they see the establishment of a separate southern state as the only solution to this seemingly intractable divergence of views. This notion is implacably opposed by most Northern Sudanese and by nearly all neighboring countries, particularly Egypt. The Radical Islamic factor has been condemned as being historically at the base of the problem.

The Coalition for the Defense of Human Rights, representing minority religious and ethnic communities from around the world, called upon the World Conference Against Racism, Racial Discrimination, Xenophobia and Related Intolerance, meeting on September 8, 2001, in Durban, South Africa, to address and condemn the ideology of Radical Islamism—a deviation from Islam—as intolerant, xenophobic, racist, supremacist, discriminatory, anti-democratic, and genocidal. In Sudan, this deviation is exemplified by Radical Islamism's culture of animosity and destruction and the victims of this oppressive ideology of hate toward religious minorities of all beliefs, races, and nationalities are witnessed by the genocide in the Darfur region (Online at http://www.dhimmi.com).

The Conference recognized that Radical Islamism is a totalitarian movement aimed at establishing a worldwide Radical Islamist state that would:

1. Divide Humanity into two groups: those defined as righteous Muslims or infidels; Support religious wars against non-Islamist Muslims and non-Muslim infidels worldwide;

2. Establish an Apartheid-like regime similar to those in Afghanistan, Iran, Pakistan, Saudi Arabia, and Sudan, to subjugate and control infidels;

3. Legitimize and extend human rights abuses—including slavery—on a massive scale; Employ a global economic resource (oil) as a weapon against non-Muslim nations in the service of its goals. To that end, the Conference recognized the following historical facts and warned against future threats of Radical Islamism:

## (I) Radical Islamism Sanctions War through Its Radicalized Version of a World Religion.

(A) Jihad, or Holy War, is a religiously sanctioned call for individual and collective violence made by Radical Islamists against "infidels" worldwide. In the past, the concept of Jihad was responsible for many of the greatest tragedies in human history. For over thirteen centuries, millions of human lives have been sacrificed by Jihad campaigns around the world. Now, inspired and organized by the Supremacist ideology of Radical Islamism, Jihad again threatens millions of individuals across the globe.

(B) Fatah, or military conquest, is the employment of Jihad for imperial expansion and colonization of non-Islamic lands. Radical Islamists believe that Fatah is as legitimate today as when the concept gave rise to a series of invasions of countries outside Islam's original birthplace in the Arabian Peninsula.

Historically, Fatah was employed repeatedly over the centuries and included the unprovoked invasions known as Ghazwas by Arab Muslims beginning in 636 AD/CE. These invasions aimed to capture and dominate the Dar al-Harb and impose the religion, and in many areas the language and culture, of the Arab Muslims on their captive subjects. Radical Islamists today wish to re-institutionalize the Ghazwas, thereby re-connecting themselves to a nostalgic, "heroic" past. If successful, they will have reconstituted the world's longest ongoing campaign of imperialist aggression.

### History's Three Regional Jihads

In the 7th Century following the establishment of a government under the Caliph or supreme Muslim religious leader in the Arabian Peninsula, Arab Muslim armies conquered Syria, Palestine, and Mesopotamia, and imposed their rule over the indigenous Christian Armenians, Arameans, Assyrians, Syriacs,

Chaldeans, and Jews. Coptic Christian Egypt, Nubian Northern Sudan, Berber Cyrenaica (Libya) and Numedia (Algeria) also were then conquered followed by Spain, southern France, and Sicily. The Arab Muslim armies also invaded Persia and Central Asia reaching as far as India. In all of these lands, an Islamic state was established against the will of the native populations and imposed by Arab governors under the Caliph.

A second Fatah was launched from the 11th to the 17th century when Turkish Muslim warriors stormed and conquered Christian Armenia, Byzantium, Greece, the Balkans, and parts of eastern and central Europe, up to the gates of Vienna. Meanwhile a third unprovoked Fatah caused the subjugation of Hindu and Buddhist India. The Fatah was a planned and organized movement to subdue cultures, and destroy them as a prelude to replacing them with a new foreign religious culture. Today, Radical Islamists wish to revive the Fatah on a global scale.

## (II) The Adepts of Radical Islamism Subscribe to an Anachronistic and Widely Discredited Version of a Universal, Monotheistic Faith, Islam That Is a Source of Inspiration to Hundreds of Millions of Muslims Worldwide.

(A) Radical Islamists believe in a 1400 year-old religious concept that divides the world into two zones: Dar al-Islam: the realm of peace and Dar al-harb: the realm of war. The former is a zone that is ruled by Islamic states which are worthy of full peace, while the latter is ruled by infidels who inhabit a zone of war, susceptible to Islamic subjugation. Radical Islamists promote a religious worldwide confrontation between the two zones that grants legitimacy to imperial conquest, colonialism, slavery, ethnic cleansing, suppression of liberties, forced religious conversion, and Jihad or Holy War.

(B) Radical Islamists also believe in the 1400 year-old concept of Ridda which holds that a natural born or converted Muslim may not convert or revert to another religion. Today, in many countries ruled or influenced by the Radical Islamist version of Koranic Law, there exists a religiously sanctioned death penalty for those who may decide to change their religion.

## (III) Radical Islamism Imposes an Inferior Status on All Non-Muslims and the Special Subservient Status of *Dhimmi* for "the People of the Book"—Jews and Christians.

In the 7th century, the Caliph *Umar* imposed this *Dhimmi* status on conquered populations under his rule. Christians, Jews, and others were forced to accept Al-Shurut al-Umariya, or Umar's conditions, a system of restrictions designed to shame and despoil non-Muslim subjects. *Dhimmi* peoples had to relinquish their land, were forced to pay a special "protection" tax (*dhimma*) or face death, wear distinctive clothing, and were banned from most government positions.

Today in Sudan, Radical Islamists seek to reimpose this state-sanctioned discrimination, calling it an effort to "protect" minorities. In reality, such measures are always part of an effort to enforce assimilation, conversion, and to annihilate the identity of others. The example of Afganistan, where the Hindu minority is forced to wear distinctive clothing to mark them as infidels, is among the most well known.

In areas throughout the Islamic world, Radical Islamists use repression and violence against infidel minorities. In Egypt, Radical Islamists persecute the Copts; in Sudan, the Radical Islamist regime massacres and enslaves the Dinkas, both Christian and traditionalist; in Lebanon, Radical Islamists terrorize the Christians; in Nigeria, they butchered Biafran Ibos and oppress the Christians. In Iraq and Syria, alleged secular radical regimes that are governed by Arab nationalist ideologies and penetrated by Jihadic norms suppress native Christian cultures. In Iran, they persecute Christians and Bahais; in Kashmir, they wage a terrorist war against the Hindu minority; in the southern Philippines, they terrorize Catholics and kidnap foreigners; in East Timor, they have endorsed the regime's attempts at ethnic cleansing against Christians; in Indonesia, they routinely assault the native Christians, particularly in the Moluccas.

## (IV) Radical Islamists Seek to Establish the Supremacy of Their Version of Islam over All Other Faiths: the "Global Jihad"

Guided by a deviated interpretation of Islam, the Radical Islamists believe that they will rule the world because of their conviction in the superiority of their religion. Their propaganda mirrors such beliefs as in the Middle East, where they call for the takeover of secular governments in Muslim countries, the destruction of Israel, and the elimination of Christians in Lebanon and South Sudan. In Africa, they call for the conversion to Islam of Black Africa. In Russia, they call for the violent secession of Chechnya, and Dagestan. In Pakistan, they promote Jihad to sever the multi-ethnic province of Kashmir from India. In China, they call for the creation of an Islamic state in Xinjiang. In South East Asia, they support the elimination of East Timor, the destruction of Christian and Chinese minorities in Indonesia, the establishment of a Radical Islamist state in the South Philippines. In Europe, they encourage Radical Islamist separatism in Bosnia and Kosovo, and now in Macedonia. In America and Europe, they have taken over the leadership of the growing Muslim communities to radicalize them and pave the way for Radical Islamist political action in the service of a global Jihad. In every instance, their message is carefully tuned to promote the legitimization of Jihad movements by the international community. To accelerate that goal the Radical Islamists of today are planning, and implementing a Jihad to re-establish the universal Caliphate.

## (V) Radical Islamists Abuse Human Rights in Their Home Countries

Racial Islamists reject political pluralism, democracy, and fundamental human freedoms in their home countries and abroad. Wherever possible, they use existing freedoms to reach power and then physically eliminate or subdue their opposition. Radical Islamists prohibit or have eliminated political freedoms in Afganistan, Iran, Saudi Arabia, and Sudan, and plan on eliminating those freedoms enjoyed in other countries as they come to dominate them.

Similarly, Radical Islamists do not tolerate religious freedom, or regimes that permit religious equality. In Saudi Arabia, state law forbids non-Muslims to practice their faith. In Afghanistan, Iran, Sudan, and Egypt, non-Muslims are discriminated against in varying degrees. Much like Dhimmis, women under Radical Islamist regimes and throughout the Muslim world live as an inferior class of citizens. Such regimes promote gender discrimination against women, theologically, ideologically, socially, politically and economically. From Afghanistan to Morocco, women suffer dearly at different levels and in different contexts. Women, who have unequal legal rights, are abused through systematic social discrimination, psychological oppression. Female genital mutilation (FGM) and honor killings are among the most well-known depravations suffered by women in many countries.

Radical Islamists proclaim the equality of races under Islam, but have established a form of religious racism wherever they expanded. They have developed the concept of the "*Umma*"—the "religious nation"—from which non-Muslims are excluded as a whole. Hence, religion to Radical Islamists is not just a faith held by some citizens and not others; it is an absolute demarcation, dividing superior from inferior human beings. To Radical Islamists, religion is akin to race in any racist system as it sets up an exclusive, superior category of human beings with rights to dominate the others. Within this system, Arab Radical Islamists advocate an Arab Caliph, the Arabic language as the sacred language, and regard other Muslims, especially those of African origin, as inferior. The Radical Islamists' distaste for Africans is rooted in the Arab Muslim participation in the enslavement of Africans, a practice that dates back to the 7th Century AD/CE. Arab-Islamist raids into Africa since the conquest of Egypt have ravaged Africa, uprooted tens of millions of men, women and children, destroying countless families. It contributed to the European slave trade from Africa to the Americas from the 17th century. The Arab enslavement of Africans over the centuries remains active today in Sudan.

## (VI) Radical Islamists Deny Their Crimes against Humanity

While other cultures, movements and religions have acknowledged and sometimes apologized for past racist practices, the Radical Islamists refuse to admit the historical crimes they, and their predecessors, have perpetrated since the 7th century and refuse to acknowledge that those crimes are still being perpetrated today.

In the areas under their control the Sudanese Radical Islamists write revisionist histories of their actions, denying the identity and history of the nations they have subjugated and burying the evidence of the Jihad that they waged against native peoples. In the West, they fund educational programs aimed at erasing their crimes from history. Radical Islamists are penetrating the public educational systems to impose their view of their victims' world with the unwitting assistance of their victims. In this way, they obliterate the violent and racist nature of their predecessors' actions and prepare for their return to absolute power, decreed by their beliefs.

Several decades of impunity, misrule, and of course bad governance exemplified by personal rule and ruthless dictatorships left most African states politically demobilized and economically decapitated. The immiserized population remains ravaged by poverty, illiteracy, and disease. Regrettably, Africa is saddled with the highest stock of the world's poorest people, and now the rampaging HIV/AIDS pandemic. The debilitating poverty of the people accentuated by the economic crisis seems to have provided a basis and, indeed, a common platform in their demand for democratic change. Thus the struggle for democratization in Africa has relevance not only in liberalizing the political arena and achieving civil and political liberties, but also to ensure better living standards and social welfare for the African people (Adejumobi, 1996; Mamdani, 1987; Lisulo, 1991). However, the extent to which the current liberal democratic project—with its frailties, uncertainties, and sometimes reversals—could usher in a viable democracy and ensure good governance, particularly in the 21st century, remains an issue of conjecture. In other words, what is the future of liberal democracy and good governance in Africa?

During the last two decades of the 20th century, Africa set forth on a Western-style democratic adventure without precedent in its history. This gave cause for hope. Nevertheless, it is only natural to wonder about the sustainability and the quality of the democracies that have emerged in Africa. What we call democracies today in Africa is held together by pins. This may sound very pessimistic. But the precarious nature of African democracies testifies to this assertion.

The events behind the gloomy mood are manifold and complex according to the nature of the hybrid regime. African regimes can be divided into four fluid categories. First are a handful of states with strong and potentially enduring commitments to both free-market economies and democratic governance but that are not yet consolidated democracies. In this category are Benin, Botswana, Mali, Madagascar, Mauritius, Namibia, and South Africa. Second are those that have demonstrated a modest to strong commitment to macroeconomic reform and have embarked on democratic transitions by holding multiparty elections or have carried out a significant degree of political liberalization. Included in this group are Burkino Faso, Côte d'Ivoire, Kenya, Malawi, Mozambique, Senegal, Tanzania, Uganda, and Zambia. Third are those that have embraced macroeconomic reform but seek to promote development without democracy. In this group are Burundi, Ethiopia, Eritrea, Gabon, Gambia, Niger, and Rwanda. Fourth are those that either resist both economic reform and democratic rule or are unable to exercise authority across their territory due to civil war, erosion of state authority, or state collapse. In this group are Angola, Cameroon, Congo, Nigeria, Sierra Leone, Somalia, and Sudan.

A new generation of African leaders backed by highly trained and (un)disciplined armies has assumed power in some countries. The most assertive of these new leaders are former warlords or guerrilla commanders who developed their character and worldview as their movements defeated foreign-supported, postcolonial despots in drawn-out struggles. While highly nationalistic, these leaders once flirted with Marxism, organizing along democratic-centralist lines and planning to nationalize their economies on grabbing power. Today they are pragmatists, favoring free markets and insisting that corruption, not class difference, is the greatest threat to national development. Steeped in the values of secular nationalism, each has sought to incorporate disenfranchised ethnic and religious groups. Yet not one of these leaders can easily be called democratic. Each still rules as a recycled *de facto* one-party ruling and rigging autocrat.

The mixed record of democratization in Africa includes the emergence of a large number of hybrid regimes of the DRC, Uganda, and Rwanda in Africa's Great Lakes and Eritrea, Ethiopia at the Horn of the continent committed to effective governance and real economic development but not Western-style democracy. Lately, the focus has been on the leaders who have come to power in the Horn such as Meles Zenawi of Ethiopia, Isaias Afwerki of Eritrea and Yoweri Museveni of Uganda, and Paul Kagame of Rwanda.

Although we have regular elections, some 600 million human beings—half of the region's population—are living and dying in poverty. Almost 300 million exist in abject poverty and extreme misery. There are children of a lesser God, virtually excluded from the political system and condemned to a short and brutish existence. These millions of poverty-stricken humans are a constant reminder that Africa's fundamental dilemmas are yet to be resolved. Neither globalization, nor economic growth, nor democratic institutions will represent lasting solutions to Africa if Africans do not adopt a new ethical stance and a historical objectivity that its people have previously lacked.

Are these trends a sign that the oscillations between democracy and authoritarianism that plagued the region for most of the 20th century are continuing into the 21st century? The argument of this book is that democracy in Africa is under siege which makes any democratization precarious. This precariousness lies not in a dramatic wave of coups and a return to military rule, but in a steady, creeping deterioration of the quality of democracy. The objective of this book is therefore to analyze threats or challenges to the quality of liberal democracy according to the following hypotheses:

- Democracy may be threatened when power is centralized in the executive branch of government. Lawless executives, especially when they are popular and backed by the military, can destroy democratic institutions. Moreover, when the executive acts illegally it turns the military into a deliberative institution. This is the main source of impunity and the single greatest threat to the rule of law in Africa.
- Democracy may be threatened when the rule of law is undermined. Judicial subordination turns judges into pawns in a political chessboard, and

weakens the constitutional basis of the democratic state. A vital element of democratic government is the ability of citizens to oversee political authorities. Social movements are beginning to emerge around the issues of police abuse (which in countries like Nigeria has reached epidemic proportions) and crime.

- Democracy requires respect for basic rights and freedoms, and is threatened whenever they are violated. In a number of African countries the state is unable to provide protection for basic rights and freedoms including due process of law, access to justice, respect for religious freedom and tolerance, or even the minimal educational levels necessary to enjoy these rights and freedoms.

Modern democracies are systems of political representation and citizenship. Yet there has been an observable weakening of parties, legislatures, and other representative institutions in Africa. We need to explore the relationship between party systems and social actors, as well as the historical and gendered nature of citizenship in the continent.

One of the biggest challenges facing African democracies is to include indigenous peoples. Yet we know little about indigenous community organizations and identities, and the relationship between these communities, the state, and other social actors—including, for example, NGOs. Can indigenous communities achieve representation, political autonomy and recognition within the framework of the liberal rights, identities, and citizenship norms established by new democratic states?

## BETWEEN STABILITY AND CRISES

The key question is whether African governments really wish to reform. The evidence is not altogether encouraging. In March 1994, the Egyptian Muslim Brotherhood issued a memorandum accepting multiparty competition and the values of a pluralist society. The document is a significant deviation from the teachings of the late Hasan al-Banna, the founder and "supreme guide" of the Brotherhood. The memorandum was virtually ignored by the government. The "national dialogue" President Hosni Mubarak convened in June was more like a company meeting than a serious attempt to talk about political reform.

In Egypt, government response to opposition or potential opposition ranges from cooptation, subversion, and imitation to manipulation, domination, and emasculation. When nongovernmental organizations are gaining support, it is not uncommon for the government to create its own lookalike NGO or alter the rules governing them. Thus in Egypt the government has changed the electoral rules in professional syndicates (*niqabat*) to thwart Islamist electoral victories. In Sudan the ruling junta moved aggressively to put Islamists in leadership positions in the independent-minded syndicates (Norton, 1994 and 1995).

The Islamist opposition is often too strong to be eradicated, yet too weak to topple the state through direct action. In some countries such as Egypt, an impasse has been reached. This offers two possibilities: sinking deeper into the mire of obduracy or bridging the impasse through dialogue and compromise. President Mubarak has chosen the former course, arguing that distinctions between moderate and extremist Islamists are unjustified. Egypt's first contested presidential elections on September 7, 2005, were marred by low voter turnout and allegations of fraud. But President Hosni Mubarak scored a very comfortable lead over his closest challengers Ayman Nour and Noman Gomaa of radical Islamist sympathies. In other settings, the second course has been taken, with instructive results.

The pressures for political reform are being felt across the African continent. This is not to argue that ruling autocrats are contemplating retirement cottages. Those who rule do not savor conceding power. The Eyademas, Biyas, Bongos, Mugabes, Mubaraks, and others are witness to this proposition. Nonetheless, sharing power through inclusionary reform is a means of preserving some power. Even in Libya, Muammar Qaddafi, has been moving along the path of reform. Strategies of inclusion will obviously vary, and reverses are to be expected. The path of reform is strewn with risks for the present leaders and for the opposition, as well as for outside players. Nonetheless, if the perils of reform invite anxiety, the dangers of clinging to the authoritarian status quo are even more unsettling.

In sub-Saharan Africa, two decades after Africa began returning from authoritarian rule to western-style democracy, public opinion in the region remains conflicted and ambivalent. Some countries—South Africa, Ghana, Kenya, Benin and, to some extent, Senegal—manifest levels of support for democracy, satisfaction with democratic functioning, and institutional trust comparable to those in the stable democracies of Europe. At the same time, the other countries since 1990 show much more tentative patterns of democratic commitment, and a few may even be said to suffer at present from a crisis in public attitudes toward democracy.

In most of Africa, majorities of the public accept democracy as the best form of government, but in many countries there are also sizable pockets of authoritarian sentiment. Most African publics are also skeptical—if not actively cynical—about key institutions of democracy, and Africans manifest some of the lowest levels of interpersonal trust observed anywhere in the world.

The picture that emerges from the latest situation on democracy in Africa is thus a mixed one. The initial euphoria evoked by democratic change has long since disappeared. There was, no doubt, too much enthusiasm on the part of analysts at the beginning of this wave of democratic change in Africa. The difficulties in the way of democratic consolidation were not sufficiently conceptualized and appreciated. A few countries have made progress toward consolidation, but others have regressed.

What is most striking, perhaps, is the relative stability of public attitudes and values over the past few years in Africa. Many countries in the region are far from showing sufficient changes in their political and social culture to indicate movement toward consolidation of democratic gains. In a few countries, such as Sudan, Nigeria, Egypt, Algeria, and Zimbabwe, the most recent facts indicate that democracy is in serious difficulty. In most of the rest of the region, democracy is suspended somewhere between stability and crisis. In fact, democracy is held together by pins. It is neither consolidated nor in imminent danger. For these countries, the problem is not so much the threat of renewed authoritarianism but the existence of distinct, and in some ways diminished, forms of democracy.

We shall thus problematize the issues of democracy and good governance in Africa and analyze their future prospects, especially in the 21st century. Liberal democracy and good governance as well as market reforms are the new puzzle words on the global agenda. Indeed, the three issues appear to be organically linked in the present context to the hegemony of the liberal capitalist ideology in the international arena.

However, there are inherent problems and contradictions in the nature of the domestic and international political economies of African states. These problems and contradictions may significantly vitiate or undermine the "democracy-good governance" project in the continent. Thus, evolving liberal democracy and good governance in Africa will require the discipline of the state, the reconstitution of politics, the animation of the civil society and its democratic potentials, readjustment in economic policy and agenda from the fundamentalist market orthodoxy, resolving the military question, and engendering some relative reordering of economic and power relations within the global environment.

## PRESSURES FOR CHANGE

A constitution is an important social and political contract as it allows judgment by "the people." Yet the contract that existed in post independence Africa was the one received from the colonial era. It was not consummated through public debate; it was done through secret dealings. Now the very stuff of politics or the negotiation over the distribution of resources in society has turned out to be more a matter of coercion than consent. Because coercion breeds resistance, violence and military threat remain ever present in African politics. Violent transfer of power is becoming the norm, each generation demonizing the past and the forced agreement of its predecessors.

Côte d'Ivoire that is still suffering from the violent transfer of power from General Robert Guei to President Laurent Gbagbo is not alone in this practice. For example, the civil war in Côte d'Ivoire started in September 2002 and has led to the de facto partition of the country between the North and the Centre controlled by the rebellion of the New Forces of Guillaume Soro and the South held by the National Armed Forces of Côte d'Ivoire (FANCI), loyal to President Laurent Gbagbo. It entered a new phase at the beginning of November 2004, when the French army destroyed the FANCI's air force. The eloquent lesson here is that those who seize power by force of arms and are using terror to hang on to it would tend to survive. Liberal democracy cannot be part of such a brute force deal. And the power-hungry African officers are not in short supply to deliver the brute force.

With few exceptions, the officer corps in Africa represents a crucial base of regime support, and officers have benefited handsomely from fat defense budgets and the associated privileges and perks. There is no doubt that any attempt to cut real spending on the military will be met by firm uniformed resistance. In fact, the initiation of reform projects that shortchange military spending could provoke military intervention to forestall the process of democratization. Even efforts to pull defense budgets into the limelight could cause a protective military reaction. In Egypt, for instance, the military budget is protected from public scrutiny or even nominal legislative oversight.

Thinking of Africa as a single region has always presented an analytic challenge. Now that superpower rivalries no longer mask the Cold War conflict, subregional conflicts have become more obvious, as well as more divisive. New sources of regional turmoil emanate from attempts by hegemons to interdict reform in a neighboring state. The role Rwanda and Uganda play in the DRC civil war is instructive; informed reports underscore the deep involvement of these countries in fomenting the fighting with frequent incursions into the torn DRC in "search and kill" of Rwandan *Interahamwe genocidaires.*

The end of the Cold War also deprives many African states of the automatic support of a superpower sponsor. In Ethiopia, for example, there is little doubt that Soviet upbraiding of Mengistu Haile Mariam during the Eritrean-Ethiopian war was a decisive turning point. No longer able to bank on Soviet largesse, Mengistu was brought cheek to jowl with the imperative of coming to terms with Eritrean rebels and, hence, the United States. He escaped to Zimbabwe.

No doubt there will be financial sweeteners in any regional peace package, but these sweeteners are more likely to be one-time payments rather than aid programs. In the case of Egypt, it is plain that U.S. aid allows the government to hold off on reform. It is precisely in those states that have contemplated financial disaster where experiments in democratization have occurred. Thus Algeria was on the brink of insolvency when its reform programs were launched. In short, the prospect of financial collapse mightily concentrates the mind on reform as a means of dissipating public disaffection and anger, and sharing the blame for the pain of economic restructuring.

Societal pressures for change should not be minimized in those states that do not stand on the brink of fiscal disaster. It has become customary for Western creditors, including the World Bank and the IMF, to emphasize dual reforms, namely, economic liberalization and "good governance." It remains important and useful that political reform is seen as a vital condition for economic reform. While political reform in the direction of democratization is a prerequisite to human development and accountability, the vital issues that need reckoning are the background to these reforms.

This is particularly the case since a country's political and economic transition is a function of its history, culture, tradition, and economic development. Most African countries rely on the production and export of raw materials and cash crops; they are also extremely susceptible to natural hazards and external shocks. They face unfavorable terms of trade and protectionist measures from industrialized countries. Many depend on foreign aid, and some on food handouts. Foreign investment is limited to a few countries and selected sectors such as mining and extractive industries. Political instability and unfavorable policies mean that Africa's share of foreign direct investment has been one of the least compared to other developing countries (see UNCTAD, 1999).

## TIMELINESS

The topic of democracy under siege is timely from a policy perspective and relevant to the central debate on democratization and democratic consolidation in Africa today.

There is widespread disillusionment that accompanies the creeping erosion of the quality of democracy in Africa.

Six mechanisms have laid siege on the democratic processes in the continent: the centralization of executive power, resurgence of the military as a political actor, the lack of rule of law, weak representative institutions, social exclusion, and corporate imperialism. These siege instruments can be traced to structural, cultural, and institutional conditions, as well as pressures from global capitalism. Structurally, Africa is one of the most unequal regions of the world. Culturally, many African societies are hybrids of colonial European, Arabic, and native African traditions. Institutionally, weak African states have inhibited citizenship and legal protection for civil and human rights. There is nothing to defend and promote democracy by means of such instruments as a functional Democracy Charter for Africa.

## LITERATURE REVIEW

Much scholarly work has been done on democratization in Africa. Professor Ben O. Nwabueze's book, *Democratisation* (1993), is the best place to begin for a wide-ranging and textured examination of democratization. "Democratisation is not only a concept, nor is it synonymous with mul ti-partyism," Nwabueze writes, "it is also concerned with certain conditions of things, conditions such as a virile civil society, a democratic society, a free society, a just society, equal treatment of all citizens by the state, an ordered, stable society, a society infused with the spirit of liberty, democracy, justice and equality." The stated thesis of Nwabueze's book is that democratization, "in the fullest sense of the term, requires that the society, the economy, politics, the constitution of the state, the electoral system and the practice of government be democratised" (p. ix).

The essays in *Popular Struggles for Democracy in Africa* (Nyong'o, 1987) deepen the theoretical and analytical study of democratization with contributions on aspects of the broad theme of "the state, development, and participatory democracy" in Africa by Mahmood Mamdani, Harry Goulbourne, and other leading African scholars. Case studies are presented of some African states limping on the path to democracy. "However repressive regimes have been in Africa," editor Peter Anyang' Nyong'o concludes, "and however successful they might have been in defeating popular attempts at democratic change...the people's impulse to struggle for freedom and social justice can never completely die" (p. 24).

The link between popular struggles and the building of democracy in Africa is developed further in two additional collections of studies. The first is a highly recommended anthology of 626 pages compiled by Mahmood Mamdani and Ernest Wamba-dia-Wamba, *African Studies in Social Movements and Democracy* (1996). The 15 studies in the book emerged from an 8-year-long (1985-93) "continental dialogue" sponsored by CODESRIA (Council for the Development of Social Science Research in Africa). The second collection, entitled *Democracy, Civil Society and the State* (Sachikonye, 1995) analyzes social movements and democratic initiatives in the Southern Africa region. Most of the material in the above-mentioned publications concentrates on democratization in sub-Saharan Africa.

The scholarly papers presented in *Rules and Rights in the Middle East: Democracy, Law, and Society* (Goldberg et al., 1993) extend the study of democratic structures and processes to include North Africa (the Maghreb). In what is advertised to be "the first sustained look at democracy and democratic movements in the Middle East," contributors analyze the practice of electoral democracy in t he Arab East and North Africa and speculate about the prospects for broader democratization in the region.

Two issues of *Middle East Report,* the bimonthly publication of the Middle East Research and Information Project (Washington, D.C.), explore broadened understandings of democracy in North Africa and the Arab East: "Democracy in the Arab World," no. 174 (January/February 1992), and "Islam, the State and Democracy," no. 179 (November/December 1992).

The *Review of African Political Economy* (London: Routledge) has carried a number of stimulating articles on democracy in North *and* sub-Saharan Africa in recent years. See, particularly, "Democracy and Development," no. 49 (Winter 1990), "Surviving Democracy?" no. 54 (July 1992), and "Democracy, Civil Society and NGOs," no. 55 (November 1992).

The following books examine selected issues related to democracy in Africa:

*Democracy and Human Rights in Developing Countries* (Arat, 1991) explores the theme of social and economic rights as integral elements in democratic societies.

The academic conference papers reproduced in *Democracy and Pluralism in Africa* (Ronen, 1986) offer a variety of perspectives on the problems facing democracy and pluralism in Africa.

Ethnicity and democracy is the topical concern of two booklets in the Occasional Monograph series published by the Centre for Advanced Social Science (Lagos): *Ethnicity and its Management in Africa: The Democratization Link* (Osaghae, 1994) and *Ethnicity and Democracy in Africa: Intervening Variables* (Nnoli, 1994).

The chapters in *Democracy and Socialism in Africa* (Cohen and Goulbourne, 1991) focus on what the editors identify as "the burning political and social issue facing the [African] continent in the 1990s": the relationship between democracy and socialism.

Convinced that "no society qualifies as democratic, representative, and progressive until there is free and voluntary participation of all its citizens in all spheres of life" 11 Kenyan women scholars and writers examine the "structural constraints" that have kept women from participating fully and meaningfully in Kenyan society. See their essays in *Democratic Change in Africa: Women's Perspective* (Kabira et al., 1993).

Several books examine the nature and role of the state as this entity relates to democracy and citizen exercise of political power in Africa. See, among others, *The African State in Transition* (Ergas, 1987); *Government and Politics in Africa* (Tordoff, 1993); *Political Domination in Africa: Reflections on the Limits of Power* (Chabal, 1986); *The Precarious Balance: State and Society in Africa* (Rothchild and Chazan, 1988); *The State in Africa: The Politics of the Belly* (Bayart, 1993); and *State Building and Democracy in Southern Africa: A Comparative Study of Botswana, South Africa, and Zimbabwe* ( du Toit, 1995).

The role of the media in the democratic process is examined in a 20-page booklet in the Seminar Paper Series published by SAPES Trust in Harare, Zimbabwe: *Media and Democracy: Theories and Principles with Reference to an African Context* (Ronning, 1994). Studies of democratic processes in individual African nations are found in: *Democracy: The Challenge of Change* (Chiluba, 1995)—Zambia; Political *Parties and Democracy in Tanzania* (Mmuya and Chaligha, 1994); Liberalization *and Politics: The 1990 Election in Tanzania* (Mukandala and Othman, 1994).

Botswana is an emerging exception to the generalizations on the process of democratization in Africa. "At a time when Africa's dismal economic performance and political corruption and mismanagement have given rise to a new intellectual movement called Afropessimism," Professor Stephen John Stedman writes, "...Botswana stands out as an example of economic development, functioning governance, and multiparty, liberal democracy." Writing further in his introduction to *Botswana: The Political Economy of Democratic Development* (Stedman, 1993) Professor Stedman explains: "[Botswana] is...a country akin to Switzerland, an exception that confounds generalizations, but whose very exceptionality prompts analysts to see it as a hopeful model for other societies" (p. 1). The ten essays in the book by Stedman present the analyses of African scholars from Botswana, Germany, and the United States on Botswana's political system and, more generally, on the nature of "good governance in Africa and its relationship to democracy and development" (p. 1).

These works notwithstanding, a belief, called afropessimism (Bayart, 1993) has become commonplace in Africa today. Afropessimism about democratization has become a common belief because initial election observer missions failed to obtain adequate outcomes. They declared faulty elections as "a step in the right direction" (Abbink and Hesseling, 2000: 2). Part of the problem was that external observers had unclear mandates and ambiguous standards and methodology. Additionally, donor states may have their own realpolitik interests and, thus, they may care more about their particular concerns than the long-term prospects for democracy. Finally, the "free and fair" qualification is meaningless so long as it does not engage the broader problems of democracy, equality, and justice (ibid: 8).

O.Van Cranenburgh in his "Power and Competition: the Institutional Context of African Multi-party Politics" in *African Political Parties: Evolution, Institionalisation and Governance*" discussed the theoretical relationship between multiparty politics and democracy. Of course, multiparty elections are part of routine political practice everywhere in the West. The author criticized, quite rightly, the reductionist and elitist view that multiparty elections are the necessary and sufficient condition for democracy. The picture is more complex than that and the totality of problems should be taken into account, presumably with an interdisciplinary approach that gives fair coverage of historical, political, and cultural issues. The search for mirror images after imposing Western features on non-Western settings is bound to backfire. A working paradigm requires certain grounds to explain a social, political, and economic reality. A Western multiparty system presumes the existence of, among other things, a modern capitalist industrial state, a fully functioning civil society, and a free press.

"Organic" constitutions that are grounded on the soil need to clearly define the powers, rights, and responsibilities of all involved. The social contract is such that parties, both in opposition and in power, understand and abide by the rules. For many African states, this contract was handed down at the time of decolonization and it is incompatible with the values and belief systems of the people and thus poorly understood by them. In the realm of society, the sponsored democracy seeks the "civil" society. That, however, is not the same as Goran Hyden's "uncaptured peasantry" (1986: 677) or Mahmood Mamdani's "decentralized despotism" (1996) where the subjects are "trapped in a non-racial version of apartheid." It is a fact of life that in Africa, rural societies account for the largest portion both in population size and in terms of economic activity. This obviously does not conform to the expectations of technologically advanced countries. The focus on literati society is not surprising looking at the evolution of Western, liberal democracy. But when the rural world is left out of oppositional politics, it does not augur well with the spirit of democratization. There is another, yet more important dimension: economic activity. Most countries in Africa are characterized by monoeconomic structures, producing and exporting a select few agricultural or mining products. More important, where the state is the focus for shrinking economic resources, the premium on losing and winning power becomes hugely expensive.

All this happens in an African setting where heterogeneity is the norm. O. Van Cranenburgh (2003) sees the "consociational or consensus model of democracy" to be "increasingly relevant" (Abbink and Hesseling, 2000: 26). In addition, Ellis (2000) in "Elections in Africa in historical context" is adamant that the sovereignty of the popular will, tested most obviously through general elections, was replacing all other principles of sovereignty throughout the world. Indeed, it is crucial to any country that wished to develop (cited in ibid: 39). Consequently, rather than focusing on fundamental political reforms, democratization was narrowly construed, making it unsurprising that elections failed to bring increased power sharing or greater economic prosperity (ibid: 43).

The issue does not end with the nature of the postcolonial state, which remains colonial in its adherence to generally anti-democratic and repressive measures and attitudes. Van Kessel queries the goals, rules, roles, and responsibility of election observers, as well as those of the donor countries. Donors who sponsor election observation are concerned more with political stability than democratization. Hence, the right approach would be for them to send peace monitors rather than election observers.

Ted Gurr (1970) argues that it is part of a human being's constitution that if frustration, dissatisfaction, and grievances are sufficiently prolonged or sharply felt, aggression is quite likely, if not certain, to occur. Whereas democracy must begin with the process of democratization, the sudden introduction of multiparty elections may lead to protests, rebellions, and regime-orchestrated violence, as occurred in countries such as Rwanda, Burundi, Nigeria, Kenya, Ethiopia, and others. Gurr grapples with the fact that even in the West, where democracy implied representation, accountability and participation, the Westminster-style "winner takes all" model produces a "single party government as a result of multiparty elections" (p. 86). Given the widespread dissatisfaction with the experience of multiparty democracy in Africa, the question remains. If multiparty politics are problematic in Africa, what alternatives are there?

In an attempt to answer the preceding question, M. Doornbos recommends that the Ugandan no-party system "introduced by the [National Revolutionary Movement] in 1986 is quite novel for Africa or anywhere for that matter" (Abbink and Hesseling, ibid: 109). The substance of the no-party alternative lies in competing individual candidates vying for votes as individuals and not as members of a party. Skepticism, at best, is the feeling about copying any social models that were developed for certain circumstances that may not exist in other places, times, and conditions. The Ugandan practice has its own political and historical background. Uganda, which is a country greatly haunted by its turbulent past, is quite different from its immediate neighbor, Kenya, which does not see it fit to dismantle the entrenched Kenya African National Union (KANU) one party system.

Ethnicity is another issue multiparty democracy has to contend with since African ethnicity, as a form of nationalism, has not been accorded sufficient attention. Most of the time, it attracts negative attention from both academic and media outlets. Neglected are the analyses of why it is resilient. It is a realty in Africa, as Timothy Shaw persuasively argued (1986: 587-605), as well as the positive side of ethnicity. Conforming to the existing approach, Kenya's political system is characterized by "ethnic voting" as illustrated in the 1992 election results being along ethnoterritorial boundaries (Abbink and Hesseling, op. cit.: 128). Mention is made of ethnic clashes and manipulations and division of opposition largely along ethnic lines.

Looking into Ethiopia, Abbink goes beyond the watered-down declarations of "free and fair." The narration of "Democracy and ethnicity: The Ethiopian approach" may sound more than novel where "ethnicity… has made its entry in the official political discourse of Ethiopia and perhaps indeed of Africa" (ibid: 152). To critical students of Ethiopian historiography, the events of the late 19th century— the conquest and the imperial expansion to the south that resulted in the formation of modern-day Ethiopia—largely explains the revolutionary declarations of the Derg military rule that ended in 1991 and the Ethiopian People's Revolutionary Democratic Front (EPRDF) rebel army rule that replaced it. For the latter, the organization of elections meant the organization of its victory.

Those concerned less with democratization and more with "strategic geopolitical motives" could easily understand what was really happening. One could find moral relief by comparing the new arrangement "with the worst cases as Liberia, Sierra Leone, Rwanda and Sudan" (ibid: 171-172). The EPRDF was also accorded with another exotic notion of "ethnic federalism" and the most revolutionary constitution on earth, a contract that neither the citizens nor the subjects have the will and the capacity to put into practice. The views of protagonists vary. For some, the post-1991 order represents nothing but the extension of the old system with new methods of divide and rule; for others the semblance of language and cultural barriers constitute nothing but an "ethnic apartheid." This dark side is apparent to everyone except those who want to believe that democracy is flourishing in the middle of the city, Addis Ababa.

Thus the secrets of multiparty democracy know no bounds. R. van Dijk (1999) provides the anthropological slant to the secret worlds of culture, including the political culture. He notes that "the cultural implications of the imposition of democratic procedures and their monitoring" are often overlooked (ibid: 181). Many observers take for granted the development of the Western nation-state in Africa. But the realties in Africa do not guarantee such assumptions. That is why, in Malawi, for example, the secrets of *muttiparti*, as they know it locally, needed to be told by the young cadres that it was not "just another party." The new converts explain to the elderly that it is an alternative to Hastings Banda, who also used *Nyau* secret society as a means of oppression and repression.

To the international observers the idea of *Nyau* secret society inspecting and monitoring the ballot boxes by "placing magic eyes in polling booths" in the villages is secret in itself (ibid.: 198). For they lacked "knowledge of the local culture" and time "to prepare themselves" (ibid: 203). For Mali, the new democracy was a "process of the democratization of access to the financial resources either of the state or of foreign aid" (ibid: 245-46). The role of observers in this instance "appears as without any real influence on the democratization process in the country" (ibid: 250). Here as elsewhere in Africa, Lange notes: "Is not a kind of consensus ... being constructed between African leaders and Western leaders, ready to accommodate regular and free elections which they have no real political stakes, lack financial transparency on party finances and electoral campaigns, and which also are increasingly held in the absence of the voters" (cited in ibid: 251)?

The policy and practice of international election observation in Africa faces tremendous problems stemming from the mandate and the role as well as the organization and execution of election observation. One problem for the observers is acting as arbiters whose values and standards may differ from those held in the country in which they are stationed. The other related point is the issue of sovereignty and involvement in the political process. The masses who protested against bad governance in the early 1990s are now facing even more difficult times, because what they obtained is multiparty politics, rather than democracy, participation, accountability, and representation.

In sum, one would conclude that due to the imperfect packaging and delivery, multiparty democracy is becoming increasingly unsalable. The level of apathy is powerful enough to question the motives behind a very restricted aspect of democracy, multiparty election, and its observation. Undermined are the cultural and economic, historical, and political underpinnings of a particular slant of the global project coming from a single direction. Corruption, incumbency, nepotism, unrealistic promises and intimidation are often still regarded as vital tools for acquiring and maintaining power. This is perhaps the most unfortunate legacy of colonial rule stretched to 21st century Africa.

This unfortunate legacy explains why the unrestructured postcolonial African state has failed in its developmental and democratizing mission. Why the state spoils everything it touches is because of: (1) its excessive and counterproductive intervention in political and economic processes; (2) its overbureaucratization and excessive size; (3) the domination of its apparatuses by patrimonial clientelist networks; (4) an urban coalition that orients the state against the rural sector; (5) its monopolization of the main economic levers of society with the resultant proliferation of rent-seeking activities; and,(6) its overcentralization that has discouraged local initiative in both economic development and democratic participation.

# WHY A POLITICAL ANALYSIS?

The personal happiness of mankind depends in no small degree on what government does or does not do. This dependence of man on political decisions and actions of government compels him to know that he has a considerable stake in how government works. Through the study of politics, man becomes aware of his dependence on the political system wherever he is. His awareness also makes him better equipped to determine when to support and when to oppose policy options of government.

The 1960s were characterized by the great hope of seeing an irreversible process of development launched throughout independent African states. But the present age is one of disillusionment. Development has broken down. Its theoretical underpinnings are in crisis. And its ideology is now in doubt. There is general agreement on failure in Africa. Opinions are more varied in regard to Asia and Latin America. An examination of the economic successes of the newly industrializing countries, such as South Korea, Brazil and India, compel one to conclude that the only possible development is one that intelligently succumbs to the increasing worldwide expansion of all economies on earth. That is, these examples should be followed and the illusions of alternative paths to the transnational model abandoned. The explanation here is that socialism is itself in crisis in the countries of the East. Third World countries that look to them for inspiration and the socialist countries themselves are obliged to yield to revisionism and seek reintegration in the expansion of a world economy.

This book intends to analyze Africa's failure to evolve its own democratic patterns from a political standpoint, for discussion of the options in the framework of electoral or macroeconomic schema provides no more than commonplace and foreseeable findings. This work aims higher and integrates in the discussion all the economic, political, social and cultural facets of Africa's democracy problem. At the same time the book fits these facets into an African local framework that takes account of interaction on a global scale.

For instance, capitalist globalization, especially in its present form, makes the practice of even liberal democracy increasingly problematic in Africa. This is simply because huge transnational corporations are able to make resource allocation decisions that cannot be controlled by even the most powerful liberal democratic African government. That is, no matter what popular mandate such a government may have, there is little it can do to control the global decisions of the major corporations. Indeed, most liberal democratic governments are at the service of the global capitalist system, whose prosperity is seen as a prerequisite to national economic health. The question is: which nation? The answer can definitely not yet point to an African one.

It is understandable therefore that the ambition to make a political analysis comes up against major theoretical difficulties. Social reality as a whole has three facets: economic, political, and cultural. The economic aspect is perhaps the best known as Africa wobbles from economic crisis to solutions that don't solve any of its problems. In this field, conventional economics has forged tools of immediate analysis and with greater or lesser success of management of an advanced capitalist society. Historical materialism has sought to plunge deeper and has often succeeded in illuminating the character and extent of social struggles underlying the economic choices.

The field of power and politics at the global level is relatively unknown. And eclecticism in the theories advanced shows the inadequate scientific mastery of African reality. Functional political thought, like its former or recent ingredients (geopolitics, systems analysis, etc.) may sometimes be of immediate use in shaping strategies but remains conceptually impoverished and does not warrant the status of a critical theory.

It is true that historical materialism provides a hypothesis as to the organic relationship between the material base and the political superstructure (African economies and the practice of liberal democracy). The hypothesis is fruitful if it is not too crudely interpreted. The Marxist schools, however, have not conceptualized the issue of power and politics (modes of domination) as they have the categories (modes of production). The propositions in this direction, by Freudian Marxists for example, have the undoubted merit of drawing attention to neglected aspects of the issue but have not yet produced an overall conceptual framework. The field of politics lies virtually fallow.

It is not by chance that the first chapter of Volume One of *Capital* includes the section entitled "The Fetishism of Commodities and the Secret thereof." Karl Marx intends to unveil the mysteries of capitalist society. And this is the reason why it appears to us as directly governed by economics, in the forefront of the social scene and the determinant of the other social dimensions that seem then to accommodate to its demands. Economic alienation thus defines the essence of the ideology of capitalism. Conversely, precapitalist class societies are governed by politics, which takes the forefront and provide the constraints that other aspects of the social reality—including political and economic life—seem bound to obey.

There is nothing analogous to the clockwork precision with which the economic operation of capitalism, even at a global level, has been described. Marxism has not provided a theory of politics for precapitalist or underdeveloped society like Africa (and hence a theory of politics in general) as it has provided a theory of capitalist economics. At best there are concrete analyses of the relationship of politics and economics in Marxian political writings devoted particularly to the vicissitudes of France, not of Africa. These writings highlight the degree of the autonomy of politics in these circumstances and especially the conflict that may arise between the logic of power and that of capitalist (mis)management.

As for the cultural dimension, it is an even more complex mystery. Even empirical observation of this aspect of reality (of religious faiths for example) has so far yielded no more than intuitive forays. This explains why discussion of the cultural dimensions of African political history remains imbued with culturalism (folklorism) or the tendency to treat cultural characteristics as transhistorical constants. Furthermore, culture has no generally accepted boundaries, since its definition depends precisely on the underlying theory of the social dynamic that is being followed. This culture may be called global culture or global village. According to the observer in any pursuit of common ingredients in the social evolution of all peoples or conversely a rejection of such inquiry, emphasis will be placed on the analogous and shared characteristics of seemingly diverse African cultures or alternatively on the particular and specific.

Finally, in such circumstances the mode of articulation of these three dimensions of the overall social reality remains virtually unknown. This ignorance is in regard to its operative dynamic as soon as the search goes beyond a posterior explanation or too broad an abstraction. It could be just an assertion of a determination "in the last analysis" by the material base or the "decisive" force of macroeconomic strategic models. Furthermore, so long as there is no significant advance in this area, the debate will continue to be encumbered by emotional responses, romantic visions, and scholastic prejudices of all hues.

The analysis of the failure of economic and democratic development in Africa offered here must, therefore, explain the hypotheses on which it is based, particularly those concerning the theory of state and nation, the theory of interstate systems, and state and transnational capitalism. Similarly, it must add historical profundity and a cultural dimension to the consideration of the contemporary crisis of capitalism and its attendant liberal democratic (under)development in Africa.

## References

Abbink, Jon and Gerti Hesseling (eds.). 2000. *Election Observation and Democratization in Africa,* New York: St. Martin's Press.

Adejumobi, S. 1996. "International Civil Society and the Challenge of Development and Democracy in Africa," *21st Century Trust News and Journal* (March), 15-17.

Arat, Z. F. 1991. *Democracy and Human Rights in Developing Societies.* Boulder: Lynne Rienner.

Bayart, Jean-François. 1993. *The State in Africa: The Politics of the Belly.* London: Longman.

Chabal, P. ed. 1986. *Political Domination in Africa: Reflections on the Limits of Power.* Cambridge: Cambridge University Press.

Chiluba, F. 1995. *Democracy: The Challenge of Change.* Oxford: African Books Collective.

Cohen, R. and H. Goulbourne, (eds.). 1991. *Democracy and Socialism in Africa.* Boulder, CO: Westview Press.

Decalo, Samuel. 1992. The Process, Prospects and Constraints of Democratisation in Africa. *African Affairs,* 91, 7-35.

Ellis, Stephen. 2000. Elections in Africa in historical context. In *Election Observation and Democratization in Africa,* ed. Jon Abbink and Gerti Hesseling, 37-49. Houndmills and New York: Macmillan and St. Martin's Press.

Ergas, Zaki. ed. 1987. "The State as Lame Leviathan: The Patrimonial-Administrative State in Africa," in *African State in Transition,* London: Macmillan.

du Toit, Pierre .1995. *State Building and Democracy in Southern Africa: A Comparative Study of Botswana, South Africa and Zimbabwe*. Pretoria: HSRC Publishers.

Goldberg, E., R. Kasaba, and J. Migdal eds. 1993. *Rules and Rights in the Middle East: Democracy, Law and Society*. Seattle: University of Washington Press.

Gurr, Ted R. 1970. *Why Men Rebel?* Princeton, NJ: Princeton University Press.

Hyden, Goran. 1986. "The Anomaly of the African Peasantry" *Development and Change* 17, 677-705.

Kabira, W. and Nzioki, E. 1993. *Democratic Change in Africa: Women's Perspective*. Nairobi: AAWORD/ACTS.

Lisulo, D. M.1991. "Presentation" in Africa Leadership Forum, (ed), *Democracy in Africa*. Ota: Africa Leadership Forum.

Mamdani, M. 1987. "Contradictory Class Perspectives on the Question of Democracy: The Case of Uganda" in Peter Anyang N'yongo', ed. *Popular Struggles for Democracy in Africa*. London: Zed Books

Mamdani, Mahmood, and Ernest, Wamba-dia-Wamba (eds.). 1995. *African Studies in Social Movements and Democracy*. Dakar: CODESRIA.

Mamdani, Mahmood. 1996. *Citizen and Subject: Contemporary Africa and the Legacy of Late Colonialism*, Princeton, NJ: Princeton University Press.

Mmuya, Max and Amon Chaligha. 1994. *Political Parties and Democracy in Tanzania*, Dar-es Salaam: University Press.

Mukandala, R.S. & Othman, H. ed. 1994. *Liberalization and Politics: the 1990 Elections in Tanzania*, Department of Political Science and Public Administration University of Dar es Salaam. Online at: www.udsm.ac.tz/pospa/courses/ps226.htm

Nnoli, Okwudiba. 1994. *Ethnicity and Democracy in Africa: Intervening Variables*. Lagos: Malthouse Press.

Norton, Augustus R. ed. 1994 and 1995. *Civil Society in the Middle East,* two vols. (Leiden: E. J. Brill).

Nwabueze, Ben O. 1993. *Democratisation*. Ibadan: Spectrum

Nyong'o, P.A. ed. 1987. *Popular Struggles for Democracy in Africa*. Tokyo: United Nations University.

Osaghae, E. 1994. *Ethnicity and Its Management in Africa: The Democratization Link*. CASS Occasional Monograph, No. 2, Lagos: Malthouse Press.

Putnam, R.D. 1993. *Making Democracy Work: Civic Traditions in Modern Italy*. Cambridge, MA: Harvard University Press.

Robinson, William I., 1996. *Promoting Polyarchy*, Cambridge: Cambridge University Press.

Ronen, D. 1986. *Democracy and Pluralism in Africa*. Boulder, CO: Lynne Rienner Publishers, Inc.

Ronning, Helge. 1994. Seminar Paper Series published by SAPES Trust in Harare, Zimbabwe: *Media and Democracy: Theories and Principles with Reference to an African Context*.

Rothchild, Donald and Naomi Chazan. 1988. *The Precarious Balance: State and Society in Africa*. Boulder, CO: Westview Press.

Sachikonye, L. 1995. *Democracy, Civil Society and the State: Social Movements in Southern Africa*. Harare: SAPES Trust.

Shaw, Timothy.1986. "Ethnicity as the Resilient Paradigm for Africa: From the 1960s to the 1980s," *Development and Change* 17: 587-605.

Stedman, S. J. ed. 1993. Botswana: The Political Economy of Democratic Development. Boulder, CO: Lynne Rienner.

Salih, Mohammed. 1999. "Horn of Africa: Security in the new World Order" in *Globalization, Human Security and the African Experience* Caroline Thomas and Peter Wilkin (eds.). Boulder:CO: Lynne Reinner.

Tordoff, W. 1993. *Government and Politics in Africa.*London: MacMillan.

UNCTAD. 1999. *Foreign Direct Investment in Africa: Performance and Potential.* UNCTAD/ITE/ IIT/Misc. 15. New York: United Nations.

Van Cranenburgh, O. 2003. "Power and Competition: The Institutional Context of African Multi-party Politics" in M Salih, ed *African Political Parties: Evolution, Institutionalisation and Governance.* London: Pluto Press.

_____. 2000. "Elections and Democracy in Africa: the role of international observation," and "Election Observation: Policies of the Netherlands Government," both chapters in *Election Observation and Democratization in Africa.* London: MacMillan.

van Dijk, R. A. 1999. "The Pentecostal Gift" in R. Fardon, W. M. J. van Binsbergen and R. A. van Dijk (eds.) *Modernity on a Shoestring.* Leiden: EIDOS .

# Chapter 2

# Democracy under Siege in Africa: Theoretical Considerations

Democracy may be a word familiar to most people. But it is a concept still misunderstood and misused in a time when totalitarian regimes and military dictatorships alike have attempted to claim popular support by pinning democratic labels upon themselves. The simple fact is that political symbols, rituals, mythologies, and traditions serve the same kind of veiling function. Where ordinary veils smooth rough edges, mask wrinkles, and highlight the best features of a body, political veils gloss over historical details or aspects of the political apparatus, offering instead an idealized image of the system or a stylized representation of a civic virtue.

In fact, modern liberal states are marked by the use of political veils as a specific style of politics that recognizes the force of veils and intentionally uses them for political purposes. Because veils always imply some degree of concealment of the "truth" behind them, we are left skeptical of how they can be acceptable given traditional liberal commitments to transparency. Yet the power of the democratic idea has also evoked some of the most profound and moving expressions of human will and intellect in history. It has been so from Pericles in ancient Athens to Vaclav Havel in the crumbled Czech Republic, from Thomas Jefferson during Declaration of Independence in 1776 to last speeches of Andrei Sakharov in 1989.

In the 1960s French writer René Dumont in his book *False Start in Africa* (1988) lamented post colonial African failure to yield development. Today, a similar judgment might not be out of place. The first postindependence wave of democratization in Africa has failed woefully to produce substantive and sustainable democratic institutions. UN Secretary General Kofi Annan explained that,

In the 1960s, the newly independent African states inherited those colonial boundaries, together with the challenge that legacy posed to their territorial integrity and to their attempts to achieve national unity. Too often, however, the necessary building of national unity was pursued through heavy centralization of political and economic power and the suppression of political pluralism. Predictably, political monopolies often led to corruption, nepotism, complacency and the abuse of power (UN Report, April 16, 1998: 2).

Democracy is more than a set of constitutional rules, procedures, and elections that determine how a government functions. In a democracy, government is only one element coexisting in a social fabric of many and varied institutions, political parties, organizations, and associations. This diversity is called pluralism, and it assumes that the many organized groups and institutions in a democratic society do not depend upon government for their existence, legitimacy, or authority.

Democracy is about political choice fostered by meaningful political competition. In a democracy all partisan interests and ideological flavors have a chance to make their case to the electorate. A well-functioning democracy does not guarantee success in the political (or economic) marketplace. Rather, it does assure that everyone should potentially be capable of securing elected office.

Democracy has two basic defining characteristics: representation and rule of law. Representation exists in degrees and differences among democracies on this score seem to depend on a number of things. The most common seem to be the identities of the groups excluded from the voting franchise, the method of selecting leaders, and the transparency of government decisions. The rule of law means blindness among those who enforce and administer the law to such individual characteristics as the identity of the relatives and friends, religion, ethnicity, physical appearance, place of birth, wealth, willingness and ability to pay bribes, willingness and ability to coerce, and others. The rule of law also exists in degrees. Of special significance, administration and enforcement of some laws are likely to be more impartial than those of others. The reality is that the traditional liberal requirement of rational deliberation in democracy defines an overly expansive space of reasoned debate and political thinking. This requirement leaves no room for the ways in which seemingly autonomous individuals are actually encumbered as persons found in specific cultural contexts based on seemingly irrational aspects of life.

## TYPES OF DEMOCRACY

**Procedural democracy** is common in the United States of America. The key feature of procedural democracies is that much greater attention and importance is attached to the rules and procedures by which decisions are reached than to the particular decision itself. Political rights such as the right to vote, freedom of speech and assembly, right of privacy and travel are far more important than economic rights.

**Substantive democracy** prevailed in the now defunct Soviet Union from 1917 to 1991. The key feature of substantive democracies is that the focus is on the fairness or justice of governmental decisions and actions, but the process by which they are reached is not a major consideration. Political rights are far less important than economic rights such as the right to housing, education, medical care, income security, and so on.

## TWO DISTINCT KINDS OF DUE PROCESS

**Substantive due process** is concerned with limitations on the power or authority of governmental legislative bodies to abridge the life, liberty, or property interests of any person. Put differently, does the government have the power to enact this particular law, rule, or standard of conduct? The U.S. Constitution contains numerous limitations on the power of government to interfere with individual rights (i.e., the Bill of Rights). Substantive due process today is used to invalidate government actions interfering with individual freedoms when no more specific constitutional ground can be found (examples: marriage, procreation, abortion, interstate travel).

**Procedural due process**, on the other hand, is concerned with the processes governmental bodies and officials must follow in administering or enforcing any law or rule that has the effect of abridging the life, liberty, or property interests of a person as well. There are fewer explicit procedural restrictions contained in the U.S. Constitution because the Framers could not anticipate all the ways in which governmental officials might abuse power. However, some procedural rules are expressly included:

1. Right Against Unreasonable Searches and Seizures
2. Presentment to and Indictment by Grand Jury
3. Right Against Double Jeopardy
4. Right Against Self-Incrimination
5. Right Against Excessive Bail
6. Right to Speedy and Fair Trial by Impartial Jury
7. Right of Confrontation
8. Right of Compulsory Process
9. Right to Counsel
10. Right to Jury Trial in Civil Cases

According to Robert Dahl (1989: 221), three essential conditions must exist for a multiparty democracy to function: (1) extensive competition by contestants including individuals, groups, or parties for government; (2) political participation that provides the choice for the electorate to select candidates in free and fair elections; and (3) civil and political liberties that enable citizens to express themselves without fear of punishment.

One of the determinants of liberal democracy is procedural due process. Indeed, procedural due process,

> has three basic senses in contemporary usage: (1) a form of government in which the right to make political decisions is exercised directly by the whole body of citizens, acting under procedures of majority rule, usually known as direct democracy; (2) a form of government in which the citizens exercise the same right not in person but through representatives chosen by and responsible to them, known as representative democracy; and (3) a form of gov-

ernment, usually a representative democracy, in which the powers of the majority are exercised within a framework of constitutional restraints designed to guarantee all citizens the enjoyment of certain individual or collective rights, such as freedom of speech and religion, known as liberal, or constitutional, democracy.

Deliberative democracy is more valuable than non deliberative democracy in part because deliberation makes a positive difference in the quality of outcomes. Democrats therefore need to support the social conditions that conduce to more and better deliberation: a good educational system, a responsible media, a robust set of secondary associations, and political institutions that encourage deliberation over time. Deliberation over time—what I call "reiterated deliberation"—contains the means of its own correction. Majorities are obligated to offer reasons to dissenting minorities; minorities are given a fair chance of persuading majorities of the justice of their position. A bad decision is more readily exposed and corrected during the next round of deliberation and decision making.

Deliberative democracy is more acceptable because it speaks to our ever increasing need for more mutual and moral understanding in the conduct of our increasingly mutual affairs. The need is greater today, in our interdependent and diverse societies, than it has ever been before. We should not be surprised therefore if deliberative democracy becomes an increasingly popular conception of politics and if democracy spreads even further across the globe, putting nondemocratic forms of government and nondeliberative forms of democracy increasingly on the defensive. Deliberative democracy is an aspiration that speaks to our capacity to live together with mutual respect amid ongoing disagreement. Deliberative or "consensual democracy" is what Africa practiced before European colonialism.

## DEMOCRACY UNDER SIEGE IN AFRICA

Pretensions apart, liberal democracy is not alive and well in Africa. The type of democracy that has emerged in Africa from authoritarianism since the 1980s is best defined as procedural. A procedural democracy is essentially a competition of parties in an electoral system. An electoral-based definition of democracy assumes that process is at the core of its legitimacy. The electoral definition emerged where the purpose of establishing representative institutions was taken for granted. Those using this definition did not deem it a problem that corrupt elites might use electoral procedures to maintain themselves in power against the best interests of the people.

In the 1990s there were signs of authoritarian recidivism. But if we use electoral contest as a measure, these years were a period of democratic renewal (Bratton and van de Walle, 1997). Nonetheless, it has become trite to point to the "fallacy of electoralism" (Schmitter and Karl, 1991). The assumption is that elections are a sufficient measure of democracy. However, if we view democracy as a system that institutionalizes universal adult participation in public decision making, civil liberties, and the resolution of conflicts within a common political space by peaceful political contest and accommodation, Africa's formal democratization has, as Richard Joseph (1998) has argued, in most cases proved illusory. Popular participation in decisionmaking and control over elected officials is very weak. In fact, in many cases, rulers present a façade of democracy while denying civil liberties to their opponents and dissenting citizens. Autocrats near and sundry, old and new have proved adept at using electoral contests to legitimize undemocratic regimes.

It has been argued that only low-intensity democracy exists in Africa. That is, there is an emphasis on human rights to the detriment of other practices such as one-man/one-vote. Paul Nkwi notes (http://www.unesco.org/most/wsfnkwi. doc) that this is not a new phenomenon as the term low-intensity democracy was coined following the observation of practices in Central America. Why?

## Tyranny of Imposed Globalization

Global political and economic interaction is not all that new. Ancient Rome controlled and economically integrated most of the Western world, while China ruled the Far East. Beginning with the 15th century, Spain, Portugal, France, England, and the Netherlands created worldwide empires in which goods, people, and ideas flowed almost freely. Economic factors came first then, as they largely do today. Spices and sugar were the touchstones. In order to keep control of the small East Indian spice isle of Banda, the Dutch were happy to cede Manhattan to English rule. The French were just as willing to let the English keep Canada as long as France could hold on to the West Indian sugar island of Guadeloupe. Crops were diffused globally; the slave trade moved millions across oceans; indeed the Chinese demand for silver largely financed the Spanish slave trade. Ideas moved globally as well—Christianity, capitalism, and, eventually, even electoral democracy.

The same circumstances that led to the introduction of this practice of using electoral contests to legitimize autocratic regimes in Central America have been replicated in Africa with the imposed structural adjustment programs. Most parastatal companies created under the *dirigistic state* in Africa are being ceded to Western companies, which put an emphasis on political stability. After some observation, African profiteers argue that political stability for these companies means dealing only with the incumbent governments. Given this emphasis and the tendency of these companies to networks which play a crucial role in determining the foreign policies of their various countries, it is not surprising that most Western countries have also tended to deemphasize the practice of democracy. Rather, they tend to emphasize stability and human rights, which they see as non-innocuous to the detriment of concepts such as one-man/ one-vote. The case of the Congo, where Elf Aquitaine determined France's policy in the 1990s by helping Sassou Nguesso to shoot his way back to power using his *Cobra militia* begins to illustrate this preference for stability over democracy with its headaches. Similarly, it has been argued that Charles

Pasqua caused France to support Paul Biya in presidential elections in Cameroon in 1992 despite his defeat at the polls. Not only was the latter seen as one of their "boys" who would protect their interests in their hunting ground( "chasse gardée") but his main opponent, Fru Ndi, was an Anglophone who was seen as the personae responsible for promoting the boycott of French goods in the struggle for democratization in the early 1990s.

The procedural definition of democracy does not therefore exclude the corrupt democratic regime. As long as a country is able to hold elections it is still considered a democracy, whether the government is corrupt or not. Advocates of the procedural definition do not necessarily believe that corruption can not be avoided in an electoral system, nor do they address the issue that the electoral system can be used to maintain corrupt elites. Yet when corruption assists elites to manipulate the electoral system, then accountability, the very purpose of the electoral system, is nullified. In order to eliminate false claims of democracy, the understanding of the democratic regime needs to be extended beyond the procedural definition. It should take into account the potential symbiotic relationship between ruling elites, organized crime, and the globalized financial criminal syndicates.

## Concept of a Democratic Republic

Classic considerations of republican theory deal with the problems of holding power in check, with democracy as only one component of a limited, or constitutionalist, regime. The democratic republic has traditionally been the principal model of the mixed regime designed to deal with the corruption of rulers and ruled. There have been two types of mixed regimes. One type, the classical mixed regime, is historically composed of monarchical, aristocratic, and popular elements. The Roman republic, according to the description given by Polybius, was a working model. The executive power was held by two consuls who administrated the state and had the power to declare war. The aristocratic senate held the purse strings, and the popular assemblies were the source of rewards and punishments. The other type, the modem mixed regime, is composed of executive, legislative, and judicial powers. Both types of mixed regimes seek to prevent corruption, tyranny, and abuse of power. They do not rely exclusively on the electoral process to maintain the integrity and balance of the regime. The modern mixed regime adds interinstitutional accountability to electoral accountability.

The writings of Niccolo Machiavelli and Alexis de Tocqueville are particularly instructive regarding the institutional and cultural components necessary for a republic respectful of political accountability. According to both Machiavelli and Tocqueville, the maintenance of the republican regime is the underlying purpose of the democratic process. In the classic Machiavellian formulation, the republic was designed to avoid tyranny at home and the loss of autonomy abroad. The republic, as a mixed regime in the Machiavellian (1908) sense, merges the principles of monarchy, aristocracy, and democracy in a form of checks and balances to prevent tyranny, degeneracy, and external domination. In its modern functional form, the republic separates the executive, legislative, and judicial functions of the state to accomplish the same purposes. Classically, the democratic processes served to promote domestic freedom and provide the popular loyalty the state needed to defend itself from its foreign enemies. It did not address the possible loss of state autonomy because of transnational free market economic interests.

The free market is not only economically destabilizing; perhaps more important, it is socially destabilizing as well. But the problem is not only with the speed of destabilization and destruction. The often involuntary nature as the creative destruction of the free market spreads from the economy to the community and the family. A primary negative consequence of globalization has been to increase economic inequality, both on a world scale and within nations. The inequalities engendered by globalization domestically are even more blatant internationally. In Africa, the situation is worse.

Procedural democracy alone does not accomplish the objectives of true democratization, which requires additional institutional and civic cultural safeguards. A regime that includes constitutionally protected checks and balances and a moral civic culture deals most effectively with the challenges of narcostatization. Such a regime emphasizes the governmental and cultural components of an effective anti-drug-trafficking policy. The regime must also support mechanisms to control the transnational economic environment.

The democratic component of the republican regime both obliges and allows the people to agree on what is just and unjust in their culture and provides the common standards that hold the representatives of the people accountable. It also provides principles for the community whereby the people may accomplish much of their social, economic, spiritual, and governance needs without relying on an intrusive permanent state bureaucracy. An independent and self-reliant society, a mixed political structure, and mechanisms of transnational economic accountability are the essential ingredients of the modern democratization process. Yet a counter civic culture may subvert the process of democratization and assist the process of narcostatization by supporting the consumption of mind-altering substances.

## Narcostatization and Anocratization of Democracy

The process of narcostatization may occur in stable or consolidated democracies, in transitional democracies, and in autocracies. Wherever it occurs, it undermines widespread democratic peace. If autocracy and democracy are at the opposite ends of a continuum, then the anocratic regime that possesses a mixture of democratic and autocratic features lies in the middle of that continuum. One definition of anocracy describes it as an uninstitutionalized state where the patterns of political competition cause the executive leaders to be constantly imperiled by rivals (Gurr, 1974: 1487). The anocratic state, Gurr wrote, has minimal functions, an uninstitutionalized pattern of political competition, and executive leaders constantly imperiled by rival leaders. The anocratic state is an intermediate state where elites maintain themselves in power despite the existence of democratic procedures.

Anocratizing is the process whereby either an autocratic state or a democratic state becomes an anocratic state. An anocratic state has the procedural features of democracy while retaining the features of an autocracy, where the ruling elite face no accountability. Consequently, anocratizing may apply to an autocracy where electoral and competitive features are allegedly in place. It may also apply to a democracy where existing procedural democratic features are undermined. Democratizing takes place when an autocratic or anocratic system makes its ruling elements accountable. Autocratizing takes place when even the façades of democratic procedures are being eliminated.

Edward D. Mansfield and Jack Snyder (1995: 9) have differentiated democratizing and autocratizing features as follows: "We consider states to be democratizing if, during a given period of time, they change from autocracy to either anocracy or democracy, or if they change from anocracy to democracy. Conversely, states are autocratizing if they change from democracy to autocracy or anocracy or from anocracy to autocracy." However, the single term anocratizing is used here for all processes toward the anocratic state, whether from a democracy or an autocracy. Democratizing is used only to describe a process toward democracy, and autocratizing a process toward autocracy. Likewise, the term anocratization is used here to describe the false democratization process of an autocracy and the reversal process of a consolidated democracy. As a state anocratizes, it is removed from inclusion in the democratic peace thesis, for conflict is likely to occur where democracies are in fact anocracies.

Currently, narcostatization appears to be the most common process facilitating the anocratization of a democracy, an autocracy, or an autocracy in transition to a democracy. Where there is narcostatization, what may appear to be a democratizing state producing peace will actually be an anocratizing state producing conflict. According to *Africa Confidential* (Britain) (42, no. 14, July 2001) and *World Policy Institute* (U.S.) ( July-August 2001), elections and democratization efforts in many Central African countries--including Cameroon, Chad, Gabon, Republic of Congo (ROC) and Sao Tomé and Príncipe–have not produced accountable, transparent governments.

In other countries in the region, notably Democratic Republic of Congo (DRC), Rwanda, and Burundi, chronic political instability has continued to breed corruption. Corruption within the civil service of countries in the region is attributable to both greed and poverty among employees in government and the private sector. In those countries that have been part of the recent boom in oil exploration in Central Africa—notably Chad and Equatorial Guinea, but also Cameroon, Gabon, ROC, and São Tomé and Príncipe—the revenues flowing to the governments have opened huge opportunities for corruption. In the DRC, valuable mineral resources provided the incentive for international companies to deal with rebels, with revenues transferred into personal bank accounts that were used to purchase more arms to sustain the war. Indeed, in Congo, for instance, Sassou Nguesso used war to oust the legitimate government of Pascal Lissouba. And since war begets war, the chances of sustaining democratic practice in this environment are rather slim.

## Legitimacy and Corruption

The criminalization of the state, or narcostatization, allows the value-free definition of democracy to obscure the reality of whom or what truly controls political power. Narcostatization insulates elected officials from accountability and thereby undermines the democratic checks on the abuses of power.

The legitimacy of a political system is justified to the degree it prevents the abuse of power. When a political system abuses power, no matter what its institutional form, it loses legitimacy, or the right to be obeyed by the population. Where power is used to corrupt and abuse the citizens, no matter what the institutional label, that government is unaccountable. This is how political corruption could produce tyranny through the unaccountable use of power. For instance, not even the advent of pluralist democracy has solved the problem of political accountability (Nkwi, ibid.). Cases of election rigging can be catalogued from Zimbabwe, where Robert Mugabe and his ZANU-PF deprived the Movement for Democratic Change of its victory in the polls, to Cameroon, where the results of elections have been known to be declared well in advance of the counting. However, the regimes born of these elections are conscious of the fact that they can suffer from a legitimacy deficit because they are not representative.

With a view to redressing this situation, the unrepresentative regimes have unilaterally crafted mechanisms that are meant to confer them with a mantle of legitimacy. Clear evidence of this is the National Elections Observatory in Cameroon. Among the obnoxious provisions of this law is the fact that the president is granted the prerogative of naming all the members of the Election Observatory. No doubt, this automatically erodes the consensual basis of democracy and by that token also prepares the ground for future contestation of election results with attendant murdering of political opponents.

If narcostatization distorts the concept of the public good and prevents accountability to the electorate, then the concept of the republican state, which is explicitly designed to check the abuses of power of those democratically elected, is subverted. The complex institutional nature of the republican regime stresses the purpose of the electoral component of selecting representatives and holding them accountable. Democracy, as well, calls for effective offsetting structures of government (checks and balances) that compel those elected to be responsible and honest while holding public trust. The democratic method is not the goal in and of itself. The accountability of leaders takes precedence over the method of choosing them. Procedures must neither disguise elitism nor substitute for genuine accountability.

Corruption and the criminalization of the state necessarily challenge a value-free, purposeless definition of democracy. Modern American political science focuses on a value-free, or scientistic, approach to democracy that attempts to exclude normative criteria. Dwight Waldo (1956: 21-22) defines scientific political science as an attempt to avoid all "oughts," care in the formulation of hypothesis, preoccupation with fashioning political models, meticulous attention to "research design," use of quantification where possible, concern for leaving a trail that can be followed—"replication"—and caution in conclusions drawn from particular studies of an ever-growing establishment of generalizations.

This definition of a scientific political science undergirds the predominant perception of democracy in contemporary political science and is called the "procedural" definition of democracy. It stresses the processes of democracy in order to make the analysis independent of any value judgments about democracy. A majority of American political scientists probably agree with the procedural definition of democracy. Joseph Schumpeter (1947: 269) defines democracy as "that institutional arrangement for arriving at political decisions in which individuals acquire the power to decide by means of a competitive struggle for the people's vote."

Samuel P. Huntington supports the definition given by Schumpeter. Both men consider a minimal and procedural definition the basis for generalizing about democracy. Huntington (1971: 7) writes that his study "defines a twentieth century political system as democratic to the extent that its most powerful collective decision-makers are selected through fair, honest and periodic elections in which candidates clearly compete for votes and in which virtually all the adult population is eligible to vote."

The strictly procedural Schumpeter-Huntington definition is operationalized in books on democracy and polyarchy by Robert Dahl, which he defines as inclusive participatory regimes based on party alternation or contestation. According to the participation concept of Dahl (1971: 6-7), "Democracy provides opportunities for (1) effective participation, (2) equality in voting, (3) gaining enlightened understanding, (4) exercising final control by the people over the agenda, and (5) inclusion of adults." The political institutional procedures that are necessary to pursue these goals are: "(1) elected officials, (2) free, fair and frequent elections, (3) freedom of expression, (4) alternative sources of information, (5) associational autonomy, and (6) inclusive citizenship."

The procedural definition is defended on the grounds of its utility and the inadequacy of its alternatives. Dahl (ibid: 31-32) argues, "Even one who held the extreme position that a shift from hegemony to polyarchy is never desirable would want to understand, I should think, the conditions required to prevent such a change. In this sense, the analysis is intended to be independent of my commitments or biases in favor of polyarchy." Although Dahl admits to a bias in favor of polyarchy, he does not assume "that a shift from hegemony [a dominant power] towards polyarchy is invariably desirable" (ibid.).

Anocracy embraces both competitive oligarchies and inclusive hegemonies that are democratizing. Competitive forms and participation may exist in anocracies, but the reality is of a preponderant executive power that is not fully accountable. The concept given by Huntington that could be useful is similar but goes somewhat further. He recognizes that the procedural definition may require some refinements. Anticipating criticisms of his definition—such that governments may be "inefficient, corrupt, short-sighted, irresponsible, dominated by special interests, and incapable of adopting policies demanded by the public good"—he asserts that these "qualities may make such governments undesirable but they do not make them undemocratic"(Huntington, 1971: 10). He goes on to argue that democracy is just one public virtue and not the only one. For him, the relationship of democracy to other public virtues and vices "can only be understood if democracy is clearly distinguished from other characteristics of political systems" (ibid.).

Besides the utility of this justification for the non-normative definition of democracy, the Schumpeter approach is bolstered by the alleged inadequacy of the alternative classic definition. Schumpeter (1947: 250-52) defines the classical theory as "that institutional arrangement for arriving at political decisions which realizes the common good by making the public itself decide issues through the elections of individuals who are to assemble in order to carry out its will." Schumpeter asserts that there is no such thing as "a uniquely determined common good that all people could agree on or be made to agree on by the force of rational argument." The justification for this assertion is (1) "that to different individuals and groups the common good is bound to mean different things" and (2) that even if a definite common good proved acceptable to all "this would not imply equally definite answers to individual issues." He concludes that the force of these two propositions means the concept of the will of the people vanishes.

The stress on procedure in Schumpeter debunks classical theory and transforms democratic theory into an emphasis on the competition between elites. Democracy as a procedural system means that the people at regular intervals "have the opportunity of accepting or refusing the men who are to rule them" (ibid: 285). This definition suggests a comparison with the concept of the ruling class by Gaetano Mosca. The acceptance of proceduralism to establish a ruling-class definition of democracy requires that elite be able to persist in government independently of the existence of contestation and inclusive participation. Mosca (1939: 50) notes that "in all societies ...two classes of people appear —a class that rules and a class that is ruled." He continues,

> What happens in other forms of government—namely, that an organized minority imposes its will on the disorganized majority—happens also and to perfection, whatever the appearance to the contrary, under the representative system. When we say that the voters 'chose' their representative we are using a language that is very

inexact. The truth is that the representative has himself elected by the voters (ibid: 154).

Antielitist theorists have charged that American political scientists accept an elitist theory of democracy. Giovanni Sartori (1987: 56-63) has been identified by some as holding such a view, and his early writings on democratic theory have been cited as evidence. But in his later writings, Sartori explicitly denied having an elitist theory. He charged the so-called antielitist theorists with being the true elitists. His analysis of the antielitist critique makes clear that, in his view, the procedural definition depends on norms principally to avoid tyranny or unaccountability. He asserted that the procedural definition must not be seen as having an exclusively participatory function but also, and equally, a selective function. This function is critical because the purpose, as his discussion of the founding of America pointed out, is to prevent tyranny.

Despite the alleged moral neutrality of the procedural definition and its apparent bias toward elites, political scientists such as Sartori brought back into the discussion of democracy the purpose of elections. In actual circumstances, those who apply the procedural definition as an operationalizing device have had to modify their stance.

Authors attempting to deal with transitions and consolidations from authoritarian regimes (or in the terminology of Dahl, "closed hegemonies") have had to come up with a number of variations for labeling regimes that include both contestation and inclusive participation.

For example, scholars, particularly those dealing with Latin America, who use the procedural definition of democracy, agree that democracy can "best be defined and applied in terms of the procedural criteria that Robert Dahl ...has specified." They observe that "no real world regime fits the ideal type perfectly," and they are concerned that democracy may be little more than a *façade* behind which a privileged economic elite dominates and exploits the popular classes (Burton, Gunther, and Higley, 1992: 1).

As a result, empirical scholars of politics do not espouse a simple distinction between democratic and undemocratic regimes. Instead, they introduce different stages in the democratic process and identify the possibilities for reversal. These modifications do not break completely with other procedural definitions, nor do they alter the elitist nature of the procedural approach: "A key to the stability and survival of democratic regimes is, in our view, the establishment of substantial consensus among the elites concerning rules of the democratic political game and the worth of democratic institutions"(ibid: 3).

Other scholars, say of Latin America, have also made the effort to distinguish between transitions from authoritarian rule to the consolidation of a democratic regime. They believe the minimal and procedural definition of democracy should apply only to the transition phase, from autocracy or authoritarianism to the installation of democratic procedures. Mainwaring, O'Donnell, and Valenzuela (1992: 5) argue that the second transition, the transition to a consolidated democracy, "raises problems that are broader than those that pertain in a strict sense to the transformation of a political regime." They consider the second transition to the consolidation phase to be precarious.

Valenzuela (1992: 62-68) identifies four perverse institutions and deems a consolidated democracy one in which these elements are absent:

1. Tutelary powers, the principal example of which is the military.
2. Reserved domains, or areas of authority in policy that are excluded from the control of elected officials.
3. Discrimination in the electoral process, where significant sectors of the population are either grossly over- or underrepresented.
4. Noncentrality of elections, or the situation where elections are not the only means to constitute governments.

Interestingly, the discussion of elites and democratic consolidations in the context of the procedural definition of democracy raises the problem that the electoral definition of democracy is not sufficient. For Michael Burton, Richard Gunther, and John Higley (1992) elite unity is necessary, and for Valenzuela the absence of perverse institutionality is necessary.

Although the market economy may hasten the transition and consolidation process, the corruption or criminalization of the market economy may be exploited by elites. Funds supplied by corrupt elements allow corrupt elites to become independent of legitimate financial interests and defeat the candidates with legitimate interests and support. In these circumstances, democratic procedures disguise their unaccountability to the public. This unaccountability is furthered by the globalization of the financial capitalist economy. With the rise of corrupt political regimes, the transnational capitalist economy has become increasingly excluded from the control of legitimately elected officials.

The very idea of consent becomes problematic as soon as governing elites are seen as being able to insulate themselves from accountability because of global interconnectedness, which gives inordinate economic power to a national ruling class. David Held (1992: 197) pioneered the theoretical implications of this problem when he wrote, "Nations are heralding democracy at the very moment at which changes in the international order are compromising the viability of the independent democratic nation-state."

Even a cursory examination of the regimes that have been classified as "democratic" indicates a wide range of institutional framework. Students of democracy search for the institutional form of democratic government that provides the most stability. This search presupposes that democracy is a good form of government, based on the principle of accountability. Excluding the concept of corruption from their study of democracy, procedural democratic theorists ask the following questions about a supposed democracy:

1. What conditions increase or decrease the chances of democratizing a hegemonic regime?

2. What factors increase or decrease the chances of public contestation?
3. What factors support or retard participation?

In order to cope with narcostatization as the principal means for defeating accountability in a globalized economy, however, the normative implications of corruption must be incorporated in a theory of democracy. The description which Schumpeter ascribes to classical theory fails to incorporate how corruption may defeat the essential accountability of democracy (its legitimacy), while maintaining the external form of democracy. It becomes essential that the democratic procedures produce accountability and prevent tyranny. At the same time, the existence of the procedures themselves does not guarantee accountability if a certain degree of corruption exists.

## Democratic Republicanism as Alternative to Procedural Democracy

The alternative to procedural democracy is democratic republicanism (Tocqueville, 1972), which explicitly grapples with the problem of corruption by seeking to prevent decay and abuse of power by politicians. Democratic republicanism provides an alternative foundation for democratic theory by focusing on how power may be abused and how the process of accountability may be corrupted. Democratic republicanism is historically based on the mixed regime that highlights the responsibility of the people to maintain accountability.

The norms of the democratic republic were developed to address the problems of tyranny, to provide independence for the state vis-à-vis other states, and to promote liberty within the state. Democratic republicanism considers participation a phenomenon of a disciplined people, seeks to avoid electoral despotism, supports a mixed regime, and fears the corruption of the public and the public servants. This book seeks to reach beyond the classical theoretical concerns of democratic republicanism, to add to those the challenges that arise from the globalization of the world economy and the threat of corruption in Africa hiding behind the shield of democracy.

## Militarized Ethnokleptocracy

One of the major challenges to liberal democracy and well-being in Africa is the legacy of its military history. For instance, in the Central African countries, which were torn by war in the 1970s, 1980s, and 1990s, peace agreements have been signed and democratic institutions are in place in some countries. However, the weapons from those wars have remained in the hands of soldiers and rebels or been sold on the street, contributing to atrocious levels of violent crime. Many Central Africans feel a greater fear for their safety today than they did during the years of the wars. Ethnic political entrepreneurs seize such opportunities of fear to build personal militias for their safety as they bleed the national treasuries dry. It is in the thick of this confusion that they practice militarized graft.

Ethnicity is not a backward or primordial phenomenon. Rather, it is a social construct created by rational human beings at specific times in their history. And ethnicity is created for specific purposes and is adapted and changed to fit changing needs. Ethnic consciousness has a strong correlation with the anxiety that often accompanies periods of change like democratization in Africa. During periods of change, ethnic mobilization is most likely to be volatile or conflictual. It may even become very violent or militarized.

Nonetheless, ethnicity often provides a means to retain one's dignity and survive in hostile environments where one's culture, language, and beliefs are constantly denigrated. Each of these groups may become more cohesive due to their anxieties about their place in the new dispensation, especially when one attempts to assess the changes and adaptations, using factors such as electoral behavior.

The reemergence of multiparty politics in Africa in the 1990s ignited serious political power struggles between stakeholders. Power brokers preyed on their ethnic identities and differences to gain political leverage. The deeply ingrained pattern of social inequality and exclusion within African societies surfaced. The overall syndrome of systematic exclusion from livelihood resources (jobs, security, freedom, and land), exclusion from public welfare schemes, from political participation, and, more so, from the state as a collective social and cultural construct had reared its ugly head during the single-party days. This time, the syndrome exploded in violent clashes for political inclusion to share the spoils of political office before doomsday comes. Many textbook examples abound: in Kenya between the Kikuyus and the people of Migori District of Nyanza Province in 1997, the civil wars in Somalia, Sudan, Ethiopia, Angola, the Congos, Sierra Leone, Burundi, Rwanda, just to cite a few, are violent crises due to the politicization and misuse of ethnic identities and disparities by those in possession of military and political power (Nyang'Oro, 1993). Here, only political ethnicity counts when it comes to grabbing power and its spoils.

Political ethnicity assumes that ethnicity is a total identity and that ethnic diversity is the ultimate political horizon. From this perspective, space is ethnicized and self-determination means ethnic government. Ethnicized territory and political institutions are made to coincide to such an extent that political boundaries must also be ethnic boundaries, thus hardening ethnic identities. Accordingly, political representation is not a question of a politics of ideas and interests but a matter of being represented by ethnic kinsfolk. In this practice lurks the notion of ethnic purity insofar as it posits that representation has legitimacy only if there is an ethnic identity between the electorate and the elected. One may call this ethnic fundamentalism or ethnic purism, but whatever one calls it, it is a principle that inevitably leads to the creation of ethnic-bound institutions. It gives primacy to ethnic political parties and makes an ethnic territorial imperative the basis for creating states. The outcome is an ethnic-based society and the legalization of ethnic secession. In a nutshell, ethnicity is destiny according to political ethnicity. "It is our turn" to "chop," as they say in Cameroon. And armed militias come up to protect our "chop". The rise of ethnic killers as the *Interahamwe* in Rwanda or the *Janjaweed* in Sudan demonstrates how bloody the protection of ethnic "chop" could cost a nation in human lives and property.

Civic ethnicity is despised as pure politically irrelevant. The reason is that civic ethnicity recognizes what political ethnicity denies: that people have multiple identities that allow them to think, live, and act beyond their ethnic identity. Civic ethnicity does not consider ethnic diversity as the ultimate horizon of politics. By making membership a voluntary act that in no way infringes on other social identities because civic ethnic associations make ethnicity a partial identity, comfortably articulated with other identities. Civic ethnicity is thus compatible with the democratic idea that politics is a legitimate quest for unity within complexity and that its objective is, in a multiethnic society, the construction of a "transethnic we" in a context of ethnic diversity.

In addition, civic ethnicity contributes profoundly to the creation of a democratic culture in at least three ways. First, when one becomes a voluntary member of a civic ethnic association, one moves from an ascriptive to a freely chosen self-description; one asserts oneself as a self-defining individual—a necessary condition for democracy—and works for an association without denying one's other identities. Second, civic ethnic associations contribute powerfully to a deeper understanding of one's own culture and history, creating therefore a sense of self-worth, a quality fundamental for democracy. Third, civic ethnic associations, in promoting the cultural development of their ethnic identities, educate others about these cultures and thus break down the walls of ignorance and bias that separate one group from the other, a condition essential for the development of a democratic culture in Africa. Civic ethnic associations educate people and give Africa the moral density, the cultural unity, and social capital that democracy needs to become the natural inclination of the continent.

## STRUCTURE, CULTURE, AND INSTITUTIONS

Current obstacles to democracy seem innocuous compared with the political dynamics that brought about the collapse of democratic regimes in Africa in the period following independence. Yet the confluence of these dangers creates unfavorable conditions that imperil the quality of democratic life in substantial parts of the region. Moreover, they are persistent and insidious dangers because they are rooted in enduring features of African social structure, culture, and institutions.

### Structure

African democracies are different from those of other regions of the world because the structural and historical conditions in which they emerged were different. To give a specific example, Africa is the region of the world where wealth is most unequally distributed. Economic growth over the past decade has not overcome the "pathology of inequality" (Korzeniewicz and Smith, 2000: 7-54).

Inequality is inimical to the long-term survival of democracy for three reasons. First, lack of growth threatens all political systems, democracies included, and high levels of inequality can threaten sustained economic growth. Second, inequality can undermine the positive effects that growth would otherwise have on stabilizing democracy (Muller, 1997). Military coups become less common as per capita income rises, but this positive effect of growth can be diminished by inequality. Thus, Africa is at greater risk of the erosion of democracy than would be predicted by its level of economic development. Finally, a wide range of undemocratic practices and institutions—clientelism, populism, corruption, and paternalism—are engendered or abetted by both inequitable income and lack of equitable access to state services (health, education, justice). For instance, "Inequality's pernicious undermining of democratic aspirations, institutions, and rules is the greatest threat facing democracy in the Americas today," avers Terry Lynn Karl (2000: 149-56).

## Culture

African societies are cultural hybrids that combine colonial European, Arabic, and Native African traditions. The superimposition of liberal political institutions on hybrid cultures often has unexpected consequences. For example, in Africa, liberalism is historically associated with authoritarianism and the expropriation of communal lands. Thus, the oft-heard objection that those African democracies are "illiberal" needs to be qualified by an appreciation of the distinctive experience with liberalism in the region. The cultural baggage of competitive individualism may make liberal democracy unattractive to indigenous peoples for whom individual rights—especially the right to private property in land—have often threatened customary rights, cultural survival, and material welfare.

If members of indigenous communities tend to abstain from voting in Liberia, or support rebellion in Sierra Leone, Angola, and Sudan, this should lead us not to conclude that they are "antimodern," a conclusion that invariably leads to disastrous policy implications, but rather encourage us to examine how democratic institutions could be made more congruent with local habits, customs, and mores. By the same token, notions of an idealized consensus within indigenous communities may be as fallacious as the presumption that indigenous mobilizations will always support democratization.

The popular uprising against former President Charles Taylor in Liberia, for example, was the result of a convergence between the military intelligentsia and the indigenous leaders who had developed links with the army. Public exasperation with Charles Taylor led to a coalition of strange bedfellows. For some, the fight against social inequality and the quest for better integration of the indigenous people in the Liberian political system was primary; for others the main goal was to improve conditions for the military and the performance of the executive. The complexity of these issues was dramatized by the collapse of post-Taylor talks between indigenous leaders and the Liberian government after the former demanded amnesty for the rebels involved in the uprising.

## Institutions

Democracy can be viewed as a system of elections in which political leaders compete for votes. However, democracy-as-elections works only when voters are citizens. In other words, elections in the absence of the full set of rights, obligations, and freedoms associated with citizenship are likely to produce results quite different from those in which citizenship is secure. The state is the ultimate guarantor of citizenship rights. Without a state there are no citizens, and without citizens there can be no democracy.

The typical historical sequence of institutional development in Africa involved the creation of oligarchic states that provided the initial (highly exclusionary) foundations of the rule of law during the colonial era. However, the mobilization of the popular sectors by populist leaders against colonialism led to the political inclusion of the popular sectors in ways that violated the rule of law, and this often prompted highly repressive, authoritarian responses from those who inherited power from withdrawing colonialists. Either Ghana in the days of Kwame Nkrumah or Uganda in those of Milton Obote is an important exemplar of this historical sequence, precisely because otherwise they enjoyed conditions propitious to the development of democracy and strong legal institutions.

The internal differentiation of the state and the separation of powers is required to depoliticize and rationalize law. This same process creates civil society by limiting state power and guaranteeing the autonomy of the social realm. Under these conditions, the extension of citizenship further reinforces the legal state, expands the scope of rights, and enhances the autonomy of pluralism in society. The African pattern has followed a different logic. For example, the oligarchic state in Ghana was selective in its reliance on constitutional principles, and when it broke down in the 1960s and 1970s a radical majoritarianism emerged under the leadership of former President Jerry John Rawlings. This majoritarian tendency became even more clearly vocal with the rise and consolidation of Rawling's revolution in the 1980s and 1990s.

In Nigeria, General Sani Abacha attempted to deconstitutionalize political life, and eliminate legislative and judicial autonomy in favor of centralized executive power, had disastrous but predictable consequences. As in Argentina "The violation of the principle of the separation of powers was followed by repeated curtailment of fundamental rights" (Peruzzotti, 1997: 94-103). Although the cycles of populism and authoritarian repression have abated, populism and authoritarian leadership styles have reemerged in new guises. As Michael Shifter notes in the *Los Angeles Times* of January 16, 2000, the winning formula for seizing power in Africa or Latin America today is: "Challenge the political establishment, eschew party attachments and ideological labels, espouse direct contact with the people; and use simple language and be authoritative (if not authoritarian)." Contemporary populists, including those who implement neoliberal policies, remain prisoners of this pattern.

The Musevenis are living examples. Why? The bipolar international political system promptly ended in the 1990s. Its end set the stage for a new international political system with new sets of demands: democracy, freedom of the press, freedom of expression, and economic reforms. Since then, democratic and economic reforms are stagnant or nonexistent on the African continent. The promised economic reforms of the 1990s continue to elude the continent while the surge in despotism, corruption, military gangsterism and fratricidal wars continue unabated in countries like the Sudan, Uganda, the DRC, and so on. These ills and the evanescent presence of political oppositions and democratic institutions have made the continent unattractive to potential investors. Political and economic problems are immense.

But the solutions to Africa's problems are long term, thus incisive leadership with the right implements and resolve are needed to strategize and extricate the continent from political conundrum. To succeed, African leaders need to take democratization which is the catalyst of political and economic reforms seriously. Rather, many have taken advantage of the gullibility of the masses to insulate themselves and stymie all democratic reforms in the continent. Some, like Museveni, have introduced a strange and psychologically demented political philosophy latent with militarism known as "The Movement." Under his self-driven political philosophy, opposition political gathering is limited to five persons, and a political party (no parties exist under "The Movement") can not challenge President Museveni in a presidential election. The system has kept President Museveni and his cohorts in power for more than one dozen years. This is no democracy. It is totalitarianism in disguise. And this totalitarianism subjugates and dehumanizes the sovereign people of Uganda.

In sum, democracy in Africa is held together by pins. Many factors have besieged this wave of democratization—domestic and external to Africa. Opportunities for democratic movements around Africa abound. But paradoxically at the same time, these opportunities produce unprecedented threats and challenges: ethnic and communal hatreds, growing disparity between the have and have-nots, transnational crime syndicates, renegade classes and states, and the challenges, sometimes perplexing, of globalization. Can the emerging African democracies handle these threats and challenges without eroding civil liberties, the very foundation on which democracy is built? Or is the new model the semiauthoritarian one? Answers to these questions can be obtained only by dissecting the factors that have laid siege to democracy in Africa.

## References

Bratton, Michael and Nicolas van de Walle. 1997. *Democratic Experiments in Africa: Regime Transitions in Comparative Perspective*. Cambridge: Cambridge University Press.

Burton, M., Richard Gunther, and John Higley. 1992. "Introduction: Elite Transformations and Democratic Regimes," in John Higley and Richard Gunther, (eds.), *Elites and Democratic Consolidation in Latin America and Southern Europe*. Cambridge: Cambridge University Press.

Dahl, R.A. 1971. *Polyarchy: Participation and Opposition*. New Haven, CT: Yale University Press.

Dahl, R.A. 1989. *Democracy and its Critics*. New Haven, CT.: Yale University. Available online at: http://www.eb.com:180/cgi-in/g?DocF=micro/164/95.html.

Dumont, René. 1988. *False Start in Africa* (London: Earthscan).

Gurr, T.R. 1974. "Persistence and Change in Political Systems, 1800 - 1971," *American Political Science Review*, 68, 4: pp.1482-1582.

Held, D. 1992. "Democracy" in Scot Mainwaring et al.(eds.), *Issues in Democratic Consolidation: The New South American Democracies in Comparative Perspective*. Notre Dame, IN.: University of Notre Dame Press.

Huntington, S. 1971. *The Third Wave*. Norman: University of Oklahoma Press.

Richard, Joseph. 1998. "Africa, 1990-1997: From Abertura to Closure," *Journal of Democracy*, 9. 2: 3-17.

Karl, T.L. 2000. "Economic Inequality and Democratic Instability," *Journal of Democracy*, 11, 1: 149-156.

Korzeniewicz, R.P. and William C. Smith. 2000. "Poverty, Inequality, and Growth in Latin America," *Latin American Research Review*, 35, 3: 7-54.

Machiavelli, N. 1908. *The Prince*, ed. W. K. Marriott. London: J. M. Dent and Sons.

Mainwaring, S., Guillermo O'Donnell, and J. Samuel Valenzuela (eds.). 1992. *Issues in Democratic Consolidation: The New South American Democracies in Comparative Perspective*. Notre Dame, Ind.: University of Notre Dame Press.

Mansfield, E.D. and Jack Snyder. 1995. "Democratization and the Danger of War," *International Security*, 20, 1: 162-198.

Mosca, G. 1939. *The Ruling Class*. New York: McGraw-Hill.

Muller, E. 1997. "Economic Determinants of Democracy" in Manus I. Midlarsky (ed.), *Inequality, Democracy, and Economic Development*. Cambridge: Cambridge University Press.

Nyang'Oro, Julius E. (ed). 1993. *Discourse on Democracy: Africa, in Comparative Perspective*. London: Oxford African Books Collective Ltd.

Peruzzotti, E. 1997. "Civil Society and the Modern Constitutional Complex: The Argentine Experience," *Constellations*, 4,1: 94-103.

Sartori, Giovanni. 1987. *The Theory of Democracy Revisited*. New Jersey: Chatham House Publishers.

Schmitter, Philippe and Karl, Terry.1991. "What Democracy Is ... And Is Not," *Journal of Democracy* 2, 3: 75-78.

Schumpeter, J. 1947. *Capitalism, Socialism and Democracy*. New York: Harper & Brothers.

Tocqueville, Alexis de. 1972. *Democracy in America*, Vol. 1. New York: Vintage Books.

Valenzuela, J. S. 1992. "Democratic Consolidation in Post-Transitional Settings: Notion, Process, and Facilitating Conditions," in Scot Mainwaring et al.(eds.), *Issues in Democratic Consolidation: The New South American Democracies in Comparative Perspective*. Notre Dame, IN: University of Notre Dame Press, pp. 62-68.

Waldo, D. 1956. *Political Science in America*. Paris: Unesco.

# Chapter 3

# Democracy in Africa: Revisiting the Precolonial Past

Democracy is not the only trade in town. But, as a system, democracy possesses better mechanisms to handle human nature. Its strength lies in the principle of people's participation in their governance (Mbaku, 2000). Democratic solutions promote a search for balance of power among different branches of a government. While the formalization of the rules of interaction eases conflict resolution, the transparency of the democratic system increases trust and accommodation. This means group identities and cultures face lower threat. Wider participation of the people also gives a chance for higher quality of leadership. The system is likely to produce supportive elements such as a responsive state, civil society, and expanding educational and economic opportunities. Democratic systems tend to be responsive to the collective needs of society due to periodic changes in governments and personalities. That is, in order to win periodic votes, democratic governments pay attention to diverse interests of their constituents. When the ruled are dissatisfied with the rulers, the latter are peacefully replaced through free and fair elections. When political regimes block such a mechanism, replacement takes violent forms (Fortman, 2000: 78-79). It also means that when people cannot change the rulers peacefully, they invoke different social and political options.

These grand designs and pious hopes of democracy are getting further and further away from realization in Africa of the 21st century. There is evidently inadequate consensus on democratic norms and values. There is also insufficient counterpressure from civil society. And this democratic deficiency enables political regimes to fail to give adequate heed to elite abuse, ethnic fears of majoritarian tyranny, corruption, and legitimate group demand for political and social rights. Even with competitive multiparty elections, the possibility remains that political and ethnic minorities are excluded from the political process and face an insecure future (Rothchild, 2000: 11). Why?

The desirability of democracy and its principles are not contested, not even in Africa. However, problems arise from the imposition of specific political and social models on different contexts. Moreover, minimizing democracy to multiparty elections does disservice to democratization. The theoretical and historical foundation of competitive politics is understandable in the West, but it cannot be taken for granted in Africa today. For example, while elections of a sort have existed in many African countries since independence, they merely served as mechanisms to confirm political facts than to remove incumbent regimes. Sham elections whose outcomes were known well before the voting served as mechanisms for legitimizing existing repressive rule or as an institutional façade to attract foreign aid. Similarly the electoral campaigns since the 1990s failed to bring increased power-sharing or greater economic prosperity (Ellis, 2000: 43). Multiparty elections also failed to address the nature of the state, which is undemocratic and repressive in its modus operandi, causing civil strife here and there all over the continent.

In fact, this grim situation is worrying to everybody. And the observation of the possibility of reconstructing African democracy given by a social anthropologist, Asmarom Legesse, cannot be bypassed in this day and age:

> The study of an indigenous African democracy is a very worthwhile enterprise, because it is a rich source of ideas that can inspire and inform constitutional thinkers in Africa. On that foundation of historic and ethnographical knowledge, we can build genuinely African democratic constitutions that differ from the borrowed constitutions of today – alien constitutions people do not care about and will not defend when they are violated (Legesse, 2000: xi).

Scholars have not sat idly as Africa drifts in the whirlwind of democratization. For instance, some scholars hold that democracy can thrive in Africa only if it is grounded in the communal egalitarian values of the precolonial past. This means indigenous models of governance (Ayittey, 1991, 1992; Owusu, 1992) must be incorporated into whatever innovations are sought after. Others believe very strongly that European colonization bestowed on Africa the gifts of "good governance" and "civilization." According to this school of thought, Africa's salvation lies in renewed Western political tutelage and economic benevolence. Thus, Ali Mazrui (1992) has called for the recolonization of the continent. Ignoring the structural distortions caused by colonization these scholars, African or Western, compete in coining the worst epithets—"failed," "collapsed," "weak," "marginalized states"—to describe the postcolonial state in Africa (Diamond, 1987; Bratton and Van de Walle, 1994; Zartman, 1995; Zeleza and Ogot, 1988).

## LAMENTING AFRICA'S PRECOLONIAL NORMS

The concept of democracy is not alien to Africa. Africa's own past perceptions and practices of democracy were rooted in consensus and inclusion. Precolonial African societies had traditional checks and balances, and consultative decision making as the following quote attests:

> Traditional African political systems were infused with democratic values. They were invariably patrimonial, and consciousness was communal; everything was everybody's business, engendering a strong emphasis on participation. Standards of accountability were even stricter than in Western societies. Chiefs were answerable

54

not only for their own actions but for natural catastrophes such as famine, epidemics, floods, and drought. In the event of such disasters, chiefs could be required to go into exile or "asked to die" (Ake, 1993b: 72).

In precolonial times, there had been African societies that understood and adhered to the rituals and structures of democratic dispensation. One characteristic of these societies is the devolution of power down to the local units, for instance, territorial divisions, clans, lineages, and extended families, with an individual as a vital member of the community. These political systems were structured in a hierarchy in which the basic unit was the family, extended to the levels of lineage, the clan, on to territorially defined entities. In this participatory system of governance, decisions were generally reached by consensus and broad-based consultation through group representation at various levels.

Indeed, Africa in the precolonial era was endowed with traditional institutions in which leadership was based on the wise use, distribution, and management of power. Though this system of government was deemed "primitive" and dictatorial by colonialists, it worked and did enshrine democratic attributes like consensus, accountability, and transparency.

In addition, duty in precolonial Africa was sacred as opposed to confrontational human rights. The African society has historically been built on the notion of duty. This is not unique. Other developing societies, such as some in Asia, have had similar experiences. In general, rights, in contrast to duties, are aggressive and assertive. Duties, on the other hand, call for modesty and humility, yet at the same time realizing the importance of coexistence. In many cases, rights are egocentric and tend to be jettisoned by surrogate activists in pursuit of their own selfish ends at the expense of the common good. To this end, the pursuit of anarchy is often disguised as an act of human rights. But this view does not exonerate society from the obligation to respect and uphold the rights of its citizens. Indeed, the view does not call for a conservative and reactionary culture. Rather, duties and rights pinned down both the African state and the individual as far as civic responsibilities were concerned.

Generally, the concept of duty requires an individual to place the common good before individual satisfaction. This is how the precolonial African society was modeled. Those who went against these norms were seen as outcasts, and this explains why for a long time African communities farmed and harvested in groups. It was done for the common good of the extended family. The point being made here is not to revert to the old norms upon which the African society was based. Rather, the argument, which is a challenge to human rights scholars and activists who have advanced Eurocentric notions of human rights in Africa, is that we should deconstruct the Western myth of human rights and permit Africans to rediscover their ideal versions of democracy and human rights. In this respect, the dialectical law of negation of the negation calls us to revisit the historical context within which democracy and human rights are conceived

(Online: http://www.murdoch.edu.au/elaw/issues/v7n4/mwenda74_notes. html - n14 ).

The concept of duty, which is modeled after the old traditional African society, presents some difficulties because we are faced with many overenlarged and oppressive African state bureaucracies. The concept of duty does not therefore capture the civic obligations of the African state, although it would work well with individual citizens. To overcome this weakness, Africa must move ahead and consider the notion of responsibility as a basis upon which social order should be constructed. The state owes social, political, and economic responsibilities to its citizens and, in this respect, the rule of law must be observed and constitutional restraints placed on arbitrary powers of the state (Shivji, 1991).

Equally, the individual owes responsibilities toward the state to refrain from prejudicial acts or omissions such as subversive maneuvers. Thus the notion of responsibility is more attractive than that of duty because it is wider in scope and has its pedigree in the moral and ethical domains. By contrast, the notion of duty is rigidly sourced from the legal domain, and for it to be effective it must be judicially enforceable and justiciable. Responsibilities, on the other hand, need not necessarily be judicially enforceable or justiciable. Responsibilities, generally, capture the very ethos upon which the common good of society is based. We know that often the state can show that it has no duties toward the well-being of the individual if that individual lets himself down. But at the same time, we know that there is an element of social responsibility for the state to provide social welfare for pensioners, and to provide education and much more for its citizens (Mwenda and Owusu, 1999).

Once we move away from the aggressive agenda of human rights, which is often confrontational against the state and places no major responsibilities on the individual, yet requiring the all-embracing and oppressive postcolonial African state to observe the rights of its citizens, we can avoid confrontational means to restoring social order. It is important to note that the state machinery of many postcolonial African states is visibly and notoriously oppressive. It is therefore not easy to subject such a powerfully coercive state system to the "human rights" agenda. By contrast, it would serve strategically useful purposes to place emphasis on an enforceable and well-respected bill of responsibilities for both the state and the individual.

The traditional African society, whose value system is still notable in the contemporary modern African society, was not developed on capitalist *laissez-faire* values of aggression and individualism. The African society, evolving through different socioeconomic formations, has often shown greater tendencies toward communitarianism, with values and ethos of the common good embedded in social responsibilities of the state and the individual. It is, indeed, futile to attempt to view the concept of human rights in Africa in isolation from the level of development of the continent. Even from the perspective of historical materialism, it could be argued that the Western capitalist system as we know it today developed from a feudal system. But Africa has stagnated somewhere in between the feudal and capitalist systems. We cannot therefore impose a capitalist human rights superstructure on a continent that is not fully capitalist.

Economically speaking, the material bases of most African societies have not even developed to levels that can sustain aggressive individualism. There is still a sense of collective and communal responsibilities in many parts of the African society. Therefore, the concept of human rights, which is deeply underscored by the philosophy of individualism, would not find the same attraction and support in such a community than the concept of responsibilities. But that is not to say there is nothing progressive in Western capitalist values. There are elements that are progressive in both the traditional African setup and the Western capitalist system. What is important therefore is to identify and rationally stitch together into one fabric, and in a pragmatic way, such progressive-looking constitutional elements.

## REVISITING AFRICA'S DEMOCRATIC PAST

Traditional African societies have been divided into two broad categories, namely, those that had very highly centralized authority and leadership under kings or powerful chiefs and those that had decentralized authority and leadership, where small chiefs ruled over small clans or lineages. Anthropologists have referred to the first category as primitive states and to the second as stateless or acephalous societies (Fortes and Prichard, 1950: 5).

A case like that of Buganda in Uganda could be very instructive to this survey. The Buganda had an absolute monarch because directly under the king (who was also a hereditary ruler), there were heads of clans, chiefs, and sub-chiefs all the way down the hierarchy to the extended family. The council of heads of clans under the king acted as the parliament and lower down were the chiefs at the various levels of society; all of them assisted in the social and political administration of society. Because of the structure just outlined, traditional Buganda society had a political organization of society.

The major concern of social and political philosophy in traditional African societies then was one of reconciling individual interests and those of society. The relationship between the individual and society was as significant, where man saw himself first and foremost as an individual in society. His whole being was because society was. Mbiti summarizes that position as follows: "I am because we are and because we are therefore I am" (1969: 214). The individual in Africa was therefore so intertwined in the affairs of society that it was only natural that a way had to be sought to relate the individual to society.

### Monarchical Type of Government

The hereditary nature of the kings and their quasidivine origins is of philosophical interest. Kings were viewed as semidivine human beings with semidivine origins. This divine attribute had two major implications:

## 1. Authority

Because kings were believed to be semidivine entities, their power and authority, though never absolute, was never questioned publicly. This practice was true in Buganda as well as in many other African societies like Botswana.

Writing generally about kingship in Africa, J.S. Mbiti made the following observation: where these rulers are found, they are not simply political heads: they are the mystical and religious heads, the divine symbol of the health and welfare of the people. The individual as such may not have outstanding talents or abilities but their office is the link between human rule and spiritual government. They are therefore, divine or sacral rulers, the shadow or reflection of the rule of God in the universe. People regard them as the viceroys of God on earth (ibid: 182).

On the part of the kings their position meant that they had moral and social obligations to behave benevolently to their subjects, who, after all, were God-given to them and whose presence justified the existence of kings. Kings were seen as the axis of legal and moral norms, holding people together in a political community, which was at the same time a religious community. Kings were the force of mythical values. All these points imbued kings with authority unquestioned by anybody in their kingdoms.

## 2. Transfer of Power

Owing to their semidivine origins, traditional Buganda experienced a smooth transfer of power—a fact that was of considerable social and political significance. The reins of power automatically were passed on to the male son of the king who had been born with the symbols of divine authority. Moreover, this succession took place after the death of the incumbent. It is important to note that power in traditional Buganda society did not derive from any written constitutions, but solely from the fact that one had been born with the symbols of power recognized by tradition.

The traditional theory and practice contrasts very sharply with current theory and practice, where whoever qualifies as a citizen qualifies also for the highest office in the land. This open-door policy has led to a "legitimization crisis" à la Habermas, namely, a situation in which people withdraw from the government the support it needs for its continued survival and existence. Legitimation crises can be due to several reasons, but more often than not because the subjects have questioned the credentials, origins, and sources of the authority of their leaders. Writing about a postindependence leader in Africa, S.R. Karugire (1980: 190) states that the person concerned did not come to power "because of any particular advantage, his choice had largely been a matter of chance. It was not on account of his longer experience in politics, proven qualities of statesmanship or charismatic leadership that he was chosen."

This quotation is relevant because on closer analysis what is said about present-day leaders-- namely, their lack of experience, ascent to power by chance, and others-- was true also of the kings. Kings did not have any experience, nor did they have such glaring charismatic qualities. Why then did they not face legitimization crises? The quasidivine origins of the power of the kings made the subjects obey them. Authority and power derived from God could not be questioned. This authority system is the very factor that seems lacking in the current African political leaderships.

## Consensus as a Traditional Form of Democracy

Can one really talk of democracy in a monarchical government? There was always room for debate, critical discussions, and often outright rejection of what the king otherwise wanted, in short, there was room for consensus formation. The monarch ruled through a council of heads of clans and there were many types of council heads, subheads, and chiefs at the various levels of society. After every debate a consensus had to be reached. Consensus was very central to the operation of democracy and justice in traditional Buganda society, for example.

If after deliberations the heads of clans reached a consensus it would be taboo on the part of the monarch to reject or oppose what the clan leaders had agreed upon. That would spell disaster. In spite of his semidivine origins, the monarch avoided working autocratically. It is noteworthy that the king rarely took part in the deliberations himself, the rationale being that the monarch should not prejudice the proceedings of the debate. Democracy demanded that the king execute what had been arrived at without his contribution. If the king had anything to contribute he would present it through one of his closest councilors, who would then pass it on for discussion and eventual consensus formation.

Consensus formation was carried out at the highest level, as well as at the various levels in the structure of society down to the extended family. In the formation of consensus at the highest level one can see a form of representative democracy. Though heads of clans were not elected representatives of the people, it was clear that every Muganda belonged to at least one of the 52 clans. These clan heads formed the consensus on which the Buganda was governed. The fact that kings worked on the basis of consensus from among their citizens points to an open outlook in governance in spite of monarchism.

The concept of a veto was alien to traditional African society; any application of it would have spelled disaster. Today, political decisions have come to be the result of compromise between powerful interest groups, like labor organizations, trade unions, and the like, rather than the outcome of rational discussions or agreements. In fact, in certain cases decisions have been expressions of the whims and caprices of an individual leader. In traditional African society there was room for reasoned arguments and respect for agreed consensus.

However, there were often cases of discrepancies between the theory and the practice. Although the rule of the king was supposed to follow the consensus, there were often glaring instances in which kings infringed upon the unwritten constitutional rights of the people. Whenever that happened, it always led to popular disapproval and civil disobedience. One feature stood out very markedly, however, namely that in cases of civil disobedience or rebellion, the aim and result was always to change the personnel of office and never to abolish the office. Whenever citizens rebelled against the monarch, they did so only in defense of the values (traditional values) that they felt the king had violated by his malpractices. Organized force was used in traditional society, but the aims were always territorial expansion. Armies were externally directed. They were never used in solving internal conflicts by brute force.

## Political Parties as Negation of Consensus Formation

Political parties have come to the scene with many promises, but at the same time many inherent problems that stem simply from the fact that they are political organizations. Political parties have been responsible for the rejection of the traditional concept of consensus due mainly to two considerations: their undemocratic nature and their corrupting influences. The party system destroys consensus and, thus, democracy, by denying the individual any significant opportunity for effective political action.

With the rise of the party system, the party replaces the "people" with "citizens" as the dominating factor in democracy. It follows that the candidates proposed by each party no longer appear as individual men of flesh and blood as from the ethnic setup in the case of elders or clan leaders knowledgeable about the societal norms and values. What we have with political parties are party members clad with party robes and party membership cards. With the massive help of the party machine, party members try to win votes by appealing to their base instincts and sentiments; driven to frenzy, the electorate, in turn, is not always so discriminative.

Finally, those who are elected are representatives not really of the people, but of the party that has become an abstract concept. Party members do not have loyalty to the people whom they are supposed to represent as is understood by the principles of political delegation. Rather, their loyalty is to the party that ensured their success in the elections. In such a fluid situation of shifting loyalties, where is there room for consensus formation? But political parties have come with yet another problem. Any party worth the name will try to come to power in order to implement its programs. In order to come to power and retain it, political parties have had to resort to Machiavellian principles.

Acting upon the time-honored dictum that the end justifies the means, political parties in the modern state have become unscrupulous about the means, thereby draining all ethical considerations from political theory and practice. Whereas ethical considerations had been a key feature of traditional political theory and practice, parties in the modern state will use any means, fair or foul, to get power and keep it. Traditional values that have been thrown overboard had guided consensus formation in the past. What we have nowadays are materialistic considerations that foster the welfare not of society, but of individuals.

## Personal Rule

Traditional Africa was characterized by personal rule, whereby the king knew personally all his senior officials. That situation was due to the small size of the ethnic group. This made for possible social interaction with a great number of the people. The so-called personal rule of the king in traditional Africa was a manifestation of his humaneness rather than his overbearing power.

Though rejected in the modern state because social interaction fosters corruption and tribalism, the phenomenon of personal rule of the king remains very much a feature of African society today. Owing to the development of political parties we find that in elections, the electorate delegates its power to the representatives. But not every party member has power in the party hierarchy. Only a few members at the top really wield power, even the parties that command the majority and therefore form the government. They are ruled by a handful of men at the top of the party in question. The powerful party bosses, as a matter of fact, personalize power, and whoever wants favors will try to come under their sway. Consequently, personal rule, after having been rejected, makes its return into the political arena of modern states.

## Justice as Fairness

Justice in traditional African society was justice as fairness. A practice is deemed fair when it is in conformity with the principles that those who participate in it could propose or acknowledge before one another. Justice as fairness can be appreciated very easily given the small size of the tribes where many people stayed together in extended families and many people knew one another.

Justice followed not an elaborate canon of laws, but societal norms. To illustrate the point: if a young woman for some reason ran away from her husband and returned to her father, say after a quarrel, the traditional concept of justice demanded that before passing justice in favor or against anybody, both sides had to be listened to. Even here, consensus was very central. Judgment could be given only after the elders from both sides had met and come to a consensus.

Three features emerge about the traditional conception of justice:

1. The offender had a right to be heard. This right, which is enshrined in modern constitutions, is not an exclusive concern of modern society, but goes back to the traditional African society as well.

2. Because justice was always given by the elders in the extended family, it was always given promptly. "Justice delayed is justice denied" seems to be an exclusive problem of modern society. These two points are of considerable importance when one realizes that according to modern constitutions we have a right to be heard, but that this right has to be realized through a whole institution of the law courts and a legal system involving lawyers and other officials. Because all this has to be paid for, in cases where the citizen is unable to pay, the right is denied. Then, too, the modern state has witnessed an unprecedented incidence of "popular justice." This phrase is now very commonly used in law

enforcement agencies, the administration of justice, discussions, publications, and in society generally.

Popular justice may be defined as what is fair in the eyes of the public regarding a given case or in general (Kakooza, 1989: 6). It may now be asked, why has popular justice become a common feature of modern social life? The answer seems to be that in the modern state justice is dispensed from a distance by the police, the civil administration, and law enforcement agencies, all of which are centralized and generally located at a distance. As a result the practice of popular justice has to be seen against a background of justice delayed.

There were areas of patent injustice in precolonial Africa as well; here I am referring, for example, to cases of witch-hunting where those accused of sorcery were expelled from villages and often killed. To traditional man that was seen as justice. What would have constituted an injustice would have been to let a sorcerer go unpunished, for traditional man saw those who practiced witchcraft, evil magic, and sorcery as the very incarnation of moral evil. Their activities were directed to the destruction of social relationships and society; justice demanded that they be punished. Often punishment would be payment of fines, after which the member would be allowed back into the mainstream of society.

3. A third feature of the traditional conception of justice was that its administration had to be based upon a consensus. The widespread application of the methodology of consensus as a way of coming to decisions implicitly points to an awareness in traditional minds of the possibility of a dictator emerging and imposing his will on the rest of society. Consensus can be seen as an implicit safeguard against dictators infringing on the unwritten constitutional rights of the people.

How did a political structure lacking elaborately organized law enforcement agencies ensure that decisions arrived at by consensus became binding? This point was raised also by Hobbes who argued that "just and unjust presuppose a coercive power capable of enforcing obligations" (quoted in Edwards, 1973: 300). The question how, in the African context, did society ensure that everybody abided by the decisions brings us to another important feature of traditional African society, namely, taboo.

## Taboo in Traditional Africa

Taboo is defined in the dictionary as an act or thing that religion or custom regards as forbidden. Nabakwe (1988: 4) has argued that the African mind uses the term taboo "to mean an attitude against what is regarded as bad or wrong." Now, in traditional Africa, consensus operated in such a way that if the elders of the community agreed to an issue, the offender had to obey whether he liked it or not.

The taboo system here dictated the social and moral roles, and was as binding on the king as on the common citizen. The taboo system enforced social sanctions, rejection of which would bring ostracism, death by curse, deprivation, and so on. Nabakwe points out that ostracism was "a more severe punishment than being in jail because a man and his tribe are inseparable. A man under curse is no man. Yet all those things may come to pass because of the break of taboo norms" (ibid.: 2). What made the taboo so forceful is that it was viewed as an unwritten moral imperative, a supreme good, adherence to which would enhance individual happiness and welfare and make him a fully integrated member of society. Taboo therefore was deeply rooted in consensus.

## Equality and Freedom

The concept of equality as we know it today-- namely, equality in view of our common humanity or because we are all sons of God-- does not seem to have struck the traditional mind of, say, a Muganda. There were distinctions drawn between the royals, *abalangira,* chiefs, *abaami,* and commoners, *abakopi.* Hence, through hard work and diligence a commoner (*omukopi*) could become a chief, and a chief could enter the royal family through marriage. It follows therefore that behind the apparent inequality in traditional Buganda there was always the equality of opportunity to join other classes of higher distinction.

What is important about equality in traditional Buganda society is that, regardless of class, every citizen of the tribe was free to contribute to consensus formation. Consensus formation was not an exclusive right of clan heads and chiefs. The people of lower classes were always conscious of their civil rights and always attempted to exercise them. The point made by M. Fortes and Evans Prichard goes to the heart of the matter: "The structure of an African state implies that kings and chiefs rule by consent. Those ruled by a king are fully aware of the duties he owes to them, as they are of the duties they owe to him, and are able to exert pressure to make him discharge these duties"(1950: 9).

That position marks a sharp contrast of the traditional African to the modern social/political structure, where owing to the emergence of political parties, only the ruling party can influence decisions. In the social organization of the tribe everybody, at whatever level, was free to talk. People "talk till they agree" (Nyerere, 1969: 104), which is what consensus and democracy in tribal society was all about.

## Conflict Resolution

Conflict resolution in indigenous African communities follows more or less standard procedures. In my home, Oku, Cameroon, I was exposed to conflict resolution of a very peaceful type. Before any kind of meeting takes place between the parties involved in a conflict and the person or persons chosen to deal with the case, the matter is discussed with everyone involved separately. In the case of personal conflicts between community members, this would include their respective kin groups. In the case of conflicts that affect the whole community, a wider consultation would take place. It is only after this consultation takes place that there is a formal meeting between those involved and the person(s) asked to deal with the dispute.

Community authorities or others asked to resolve conflicts usually act more as mediators than as judges who impose solutions. In those cases in which kinsmen and neighbors are the disputants, social pressure may influence the form of resolution. Overtly the nature of this pressure is simply discussion and argument, in which everyone who cares to contribute to its resolution is allowed to voice his views fully. The authority is frequently involved in this kind of proceeding, also airing his opinions, solutions, or "reasonable man" arguments.

However, underneath the discussion and the attempt to reach consensus among the parties, there seems to be a threat that if voluntary compromise is not attained, relationships of the parties may be disrupted or damaged. As kinsmen, especially, are aware of the degree of their interdependency, the threat of a break in normal peaceful relations is a factor to be carefully weighed against the value of "winning" a particular dispute.

## PEOPLE'S POWER, NOT MAJORITY TYRANNY

Today, according to David Held, democracy is defined in terms "of a number of liberal and liberal democratic tenets" (1995: 15). These tenets, he asserts, include "the centrality in principle of an impersonal structure of public power, of a constitution to help and safeguard rights, and a diversity of power centers within and outside the state, including the institutional fora to promote open discussion and deliberation among alternative viewpoints and programmes."

Traditional African political systems were based primarily on kinship guided almost entirely by oral tradition and a body of unwritten conventions. It thus did not lack the core ingredients of a democratic order as identified by Held. Scholars, Africans and non-Africans alike, have delineated the elements of African traditional democratic order.

First, power was derived from the people for whom it is held in trust. According to William Abraham, this condition of democratic governance was, in the case of the Akans of Ghana, safeguarded by the provision for the removal of rulers, and the grounds for such removal. Although the power of the king was hereditary, he could be removed on a number of grounds. Among these grounds are: self-opinionation, oppression and arbitrariness in governance, corruption, neglect of state affairs, and others (Abraham, 1962: 77-78).

These grounds were stated in the charter of leadership that defined the contract between the king and his people (Taban, 1997: 20-22). These were thus, in traditional society, elements of a regime of checks and balances meant to ensure that the king did not become authoritarian in his rule. These autochthonous forms of local self-government have been systematically eroded since the beginning of colonial rule. This process continued in the unitarist states after independence. Large parts of the population, however, still identify themselves with their traditional leaders.

Second is the feature of the African democratic order that relies on dialogue and consultation as a means of decision making. K.A. Busia expresses this aspect of the African democratic order when he writes thus:

When a Council, each member of which was the representative of a lineage, met to discuss matters affecting the whole community, it had always to grapple with the problem of representing sectional and common interests. In order to do this, the members had to talk things over; they had to listen to all different points of view. So strong was the value of solidarity that the chief aim of the counsellors was to reach unanimity, and they talked until this was achieved (1967.28).

In the case of the Ibos in southern Nigeria, Nwala writes:

Unanimity and all the rigorous processes and compromises ... that lead to it are all efforts made to contain the wishes of the majority as well as those of the minority. In short, they are designed to arrive at what may be abstractly called "the general will of the people of the community" (1985: 168).

Here, then, is another feature of the African traditional democratic system: decision making was based on consensus rather than on majority tyranny.

To this day, Botswana stands out in the history of Africa as a model of democracy. Despite the hopeless socioeconomic state at its independence, Botswana has defied the Liberal theory and burgeoned into a stable and economically productive nation. From their earliest history, the Tswana tribes developed sound institutions with limits on power. Throughout the colonial period, these institutions were preserved, largely unmodified. At independence, both traditional authority and Western democratic rule were united in the politics and leadership of Seretse Khama in Botswana. Through his policies, the military was subjugated and the government firmly established its legitimacy. The liberal theory of democracy has proved insufficient to explain the democratic success in Botswana. Wealth was not the catalyst for democracy, but rather effective institutions and history. The tribal institutions provided a foundation of legitimacy on which democracy could be built. However, this legitimacy was formed over the course of nearly three centuries. It began at the lowest levels and slowly grew to the national level as conditions permitted. In Botswana, the liberal theory played out in reverse: Democratic stability fostered a positive environment for substantial and rapid socioeconomic growth. Why is the political success of Botswana important? The implications of its democratic success maintain significant bearing on the current struggle for democracy in Africa. The continent is still as politically chaotic as ever. In the past decade, the world has witnessed a number of African democracies fall, including the Gambia in 1994 (N'Diaye, 2001: 71), and many nations are now in dire political instability, such as the Democratic Republic of Congo. All the nations of Africa should consider the institutions and policies that have made Botswana a political paragon. Perhaps Botswana can provide both hopeful inspiration and practical methodology for creating stable democracy in Africa.

Botswana is a shining gem among the war-torn and economically devastated nations of Africa. From its birth in 1966 to the present, Botswana has held six competitive democratic elections, which gives it the honor of being the "longest surviving multiparty democracy in Africa" (ibid: 71). Furthermore, its effective institutions of private property have allowed its economy to grow at an average rate of over 7 percent annually (Acemoglu, Johnson and Robinson, 2002: 1-2; the World Bank Group Countries (2003): Botswana). Clearly, Botswana is a democratic success and an outstanding exception to the liberal theory.

As a historical review, the Republic of Botswana gained its independence from the British Empire on September30, 1966, under the leadership of Sir Seretse Khama. It was formerly Bechuanaland, a British protectorate established in 1885, which was indirectly ruled from Mafeking, South Africa. The imperial administration worked with the Dikgosi (kings) of the various Tswana tribes, preserving the integrity of the tribal institutions for the most part. In this way, the new independent government was built on existing traditional political structures (N'Diaye, op.cit: 69). These tribal political institutions emphasized broad participation and limited the power of leaders (Acemoglu et al., 2002: 3). These precolonial institutions had a profound impact on the political stability of the new republic.

How did Botswana establish a legitimate and stable democracy based on its precolonial traditional democratic institutions? The people of the modern Tswana tribes (known collectively as the Batswana) are descended from immigrants who came from present day South Africa in the 18th century. They share a common cultural and linguistic heritage with the modern Basotho, who live in Lesotho. They subdued the indigenous San tribe and assimilated them into the Tswana. By the beginning of the 19th century, the Tswana had organized themselves into eight distinct groups: Bangwato, Batawana, Bangwaketse, Bakwena, Balete, Bakgatla, Barolong, and Batlokwa (ibid: 9). Before proceeding with the political institutions, it is critical at this point to discuss the distinction between ethnicity and tribe in Botswana.

While the synonymous usage of these terms is common, especially in relation to Africa, they do in fact represent separate concepts of social organization. "People of the same tribe do not necessarily belong to the same ethnic group, and different members of a single ethnic group belong to different tribes, or to no tribe at all" (Wiseman, 1990: 36-37). In Botswana, a tribe is a political grouping of those who claim allegiance to a given chief. Examples of such tribes are the eight mentioned above. Ethnicity, on the other hand, is defined in terms of birth, not political allegiance. The primary ethnic group in Botswana is the Tswana. Although it so happens that all the tribal chiefs are members of the Tswana ethnic group, every tribe includes many people, even a majority in some cases, who come from any number of different ethnic backgrounds, such as Kalanga, Bayei, Ndebele, and Herero. In this way, the tribes are multiethnic and the ethnic groups are multitribal. The eight political tribes can be referred to colllectively as the "Tswana tribes."

Several characteristics of the Tswana tribal political and economic institutions are noteworthy and have bearing on Botswana's later success. The central political figure was the Dikgosi, the chief or king, who reserved the power to allocate land for residence and agriculture. Tribal land, however, was not owned solely by the chief but was collectively owned by the tribe. By contrast, cattle were private property and were owned principally by the chief and other members of the aristocracy (N'Diaye, 2001: 69; Acemoglu et al., 2002: 10).

The chief ruled through a hierarchical bureaucracy composed of relatives, officials and ward supervisors. In addition to this hierarchy, there was the *kgotla*. While this served as the king's court, it was also a public assembly of adult males who discussed public issues. In this forum, commoners could voice their complaints against the king. Thus, the *kgotla* provided an effective means of limiting the chief's power (ibid: 10).

## The Limited Influence of Colonialism on Botswana's Political Institutions

As political and economic structures were taking shape at the local level among the Batswana, outside forces were beginning to stir the political cauldron on a much larger scale. In the early nineteenth century, the Batswana were thrown into turmoil as foreign powers began to invade their tribal territories. The period from 1818 into the 1830s in southern Africa, referred to as the *difaqane*, was marked by the militaristic expansion of the Zulu kingdom led by Shaka. An unprecedented degree of cooperation was required in order for the Tswana tribes to withstand the onslaught (ibid: 11).

In the 1830s, the Zulu hostility gave way to another threat: European colonialism. It was not the first time that the Batswana had come in contact with Europeans. As far back as 1805 the Batswana had engaged in trade with Europeans in South Africa (ibid.). Furthermore, the London Missionary Society (LMS) had worked in Botswana since 1817. David Livingstone trekked throughout the region in the 1840s. In fact, Khama III, chief of the Bangwato tribe, converted to Christianity in 1860. While interaction with Europeans was nothing new, it now represented a real threat. The Afrikaners continued to encroach upon Tswana territory until they were halted by the Tswana victory at Dimawe in 1852. These early conflicts with the Boers caused extensive cooperation among the Tswana tribes. This unity would have a profound impact on the people of Botswana, which was to lay the foundations for a future Republic of Botswana.

In an ironic turn of events, the Batswana appealed to a European power, the British, in order to procure protection from the Boers. Though the Batswana made the first of these pleas in 1853, Britain ignored them for another three and a half decades, despite the fact that the LMS had taken up the cause. In the minds of the British, Botswana lacked any strategic value (ibid: 12). It was merely a "worthless strip of land" (Wiseman, 1990: 38).

Then the situation changed. Diamonds and gold were discovered in South Africa, in 1867 and 1884-1885 respectively. Germany jumped at the chance to control a part of the region and seized South West Africa (present-day Namibia) in 1884. Following the Berlin Conference in that same year, the scramble for Africa was formally declared. Britain suddenly realized the strategic position of the Tswana territory, which acted as a buffer between German South West Africa and the Boer territories. As previously mentioned, the British created the Bechuanaland Protectorate in 1885. This protectorate was remotely administered from Mafeking, South Africa (Acemoglu et al., 2002: 12).

The conditions under which the British annexed the Bechuanaland protectorate have great bearing on the political institutions of Botswana. Because the British assumed control of the Protectorate merely as a buffer territory, they only sought to keep out foreign powers and preserve the road into the interior. It was not intended to be colonized by the British (ibid.: 13). As Wiseman observed, "Considering the reluctance with which Britain involved itself in the area, it is hardly surprising that the British were disinclined to commit themselves to any great expense in administration of the territory" (Wiseman,1990: 38-39). Therefore, the imperial administration did little to create new political structures.

Rather, administrative rule was founded on preexisting tribal political structures, whereby chiefs maintained a large degree of autonomy (N'Diaye, 2001: 69; Wiseman, 1990: 39). Even when the British changed their policy in 1932 and attempted to establish ultimate authority over the Tswana chiefs, their plans were thwarted by unified Tswana legal opposition and the onset of the World War II (Acemoglu et al., 2002: 14). Thus, the political institutions of Botswana remained essentially unchanged throughout the period of British colonialism.

## Independence and the Centralization of Political Authority

After World War II, it seemed increasingly impractical for the British to merge the Bechuanaland Protectorate with South Africa, thus acquiring greater political control (ibid.: 14). While this notion was not officially abandoned until 1963 (Wiseman, 1990: 38), the "winds of change" were sweeping through Africa in the late 1950s and early 1960s, and colonial powers were beginning to move their controlled lands towards independence (N'Diaye, 2001: 69-70).

For Botswana, independence was on the horizon. With independence in sight, Seretse Khama emerged as the preeminent political figure in Botswana. In fact, he is even called the "founding father" of Botswana. Khama was the heir to the throne of the Bangwato, the largest Tswana tribe. In 1925 his father Sekgoma II died, leaving Seretse as the recognized chief of the Bangwato at the age of four. Due to his young age, tribal authorities designated Tshekedi Khama, his uncle, to act as regent on his behalf until he came of age (Wiseman, 1990: 39).

His privileged birth afforded Seretse Khama the opportunity of a formal education. He completed a B.A. at Fort Hare University in South Africa, an institution designated for blacks only. Khama then pursued further study in England at Balliol College, Oxford, and studied law at the Inns of Court (ibid.). Despite his success, trouble was brewing.

In 1948 Sir Seretse Khama married Ruth Williams, an Englishwoman whom he had met while studying in Britain (Acemoglu et al., 2002: 14). The interracial marriage enraged the South Africans, whose Afrikaner Nationalist party had instituted severe segregation policies. While Khama was able to win the support of Tshekedi and the other Bangwato royals in 1949, the British, caving to South African pressure, took severe action against him. Khama was barred from returning to the protectorate, and later he was stripped of his legal right to the chieftainship (Wiseman, 1990: 39-40). In 1956, Seretse and Tshekidi renounced their claims to the throne of the Bangwato (Acemoglu et al., 2002: 14).

Finally, clear of British legal restrictions, Seretse Khama returned to the protectorate to participate at the forefront of the movements toward self governance. Khama became involved in the Joint Advisory Council, which the British had formed in 1951 from the union of both European and African councils. In 1960 the British created the Legislative Council and the first political party, the Bechuanaland Peoples' Party, which was later renamed the Botswana Peoples' Party (BPP). The BPP advocated a radically anti-colonial platform and appealed to the narrow strata of urban groups and workers. In response to this party, Seretse Khama formed the Bechuanaland Democratic Party (later rename the Botswana Democratic Party, BDP). The BDP appealed to the rising educated elite and the tribal chiefs. Here the significance of Seretse Khama's unique political position comes to light. On the one hand, he was the traditional leader of the largest Tswana tribe, and thus he inherited the political authority, loyalty, and legitimacy inherent in the tribal system. On the other hand, he had received a distinguished European education, and thus he was respected by the educated elite. In this arrangement, the BDP, headed by Khama, wielded broadly based and deeply rooted political power (Acemoglu et al., 2002: 14).

The scene was set for independence with Seretse Khama leading the way. The BDP easily won the first election in 1965, and in September 1966 the independent Republic of Botswana was born, with Seretse Khama as its first president and the BDP with a significant majority in the National Assembly, the parliament (Acemoglu et al., 2002: 15; Wiseman, 1990: 40). Khama now sought to create a strong central government by gradually reducing the political authority of the tribal chiefs. The House of Chiefs was created in the constitution, and served to give the eight tribal chiefs representation.

However, Khama "ensured that the House of Chiefs became a talking shop that gave the chiefs no real power over legislation" (Acemoglu et al., 2002: 16). Khama took away the chiefs' right to allocate land and gave the central government the power to remove a chief. Through this process of centralization, Khama had consolidated and institutionalized political power into a stable democratic government.

## Protecting Civilian Control of the Military

Since the independence of most African states in the 1960s and 1970s, nation after nation has fallen prey to military coups and subsequent oppression under military regimes. At the time of the independence of Botswana in 1966, governments in Ghana, Central African Republic, Burundi, Upper Volta

(Burkina Faso), and Nigeria had already been overthrown by military insurrections, and more were to follow close behind (N'Diaye, 2001: 71). A serious issue facing President Khama was how to protect civilian-controlled democracy from the threat of a military *coup d'état*.

To start with, Botswana took a markedly different approach to the military than most of its African contemporaries. While nearly all of the new African states created a standing army at the time of independence, Botswana did not. There were two main reasons for this. First, the new republic was in severe economic impoverishment and the creation of a military force was simply not in the budget. Second, the risks associated with a standing army at this volatile stage were very high, especially in light of the recent coups in other parts of the continent (ibid: 73). It was not until 1977 that the Botswana Defense Force (BDF) was created, after the police had a number of run-ins with Rhodesian troops at the border. Botswana had maintained a stable democracy for over a decade and was thus in a better economic position. At this point, the formation of a formal military force seemed both safe and necessary (ibid: 74-75).

From the beginning, professionalization was a primary goal for the BDF. Soon after the creation of the BDF, a number of officers (including Seretse Khama's son Ian Khama) were sent to the Sandhurst Royal Military Academy in Britain. In 1980, Botswana procured the help of the American government for military education and training. Later, they attained the aid of the British Special Air Services (SAS) for further training. (ibid: 76). In addition to extensive training, the military was also well cared for financially, receiving considerably higher wages than most of their African counterparts (ibid: 77).

This professionalization produced loyalty in the military, making them less likely to intervene in the government (ibid: 78). As such, the military views the government as a legitimate authority, so much so in fact, there have never been any mutinies, conspiracies or coup attempts against the government in Botswana (ibid: 80). As Richard Sklar observed, the military "has never threatened the civilian and constitutional order" (quoted in ibid: 81).

## Consensus and Nonparty Polity

The tendency nowadays is to replace the one-party system with a multiparty one based on majority rule. However, for Kwasi Wiredu, it is doubtful that this system is meeting the democratic aspirations of the people or generates those conditions in which the "unhappy conflicts that have bedeviled African life into our times 'can be resolved'" (see Oladipo, 1996: 44-45). One of the reasons for skepticism regarding the potential of the multiparty system to meet African democratic aspirations, according to Wiredu, is that it has the tendency "to place any one group of persons consistently in the position of the minority" (ibid.) This situation easily generates disaffection in society.

Another problem with the multiparty system is that it is one in which the party that wins the majority of seats or greatest proportion of votes, if the system in force is one of proportional representation, is invested with governmental power. This makes the struggle for power to be fierce and confrontational. Thus, rather than promote consensus and cooperation, the multiparty system generates conflict and disaffection. The unsuitability of this kind of party system for multiethnic societies, particularly those in Africa in which the search for community is still at a nascent stage, should not be difficult to see.

Thus the heralded forms of democracy based on the principle of majority rule are flawed. The alternative to them, of course, may not necessarily be the one-party system. The alternative is to build on the potential for democracy based on consensus that we find in some African traditional political systems, for example, the Ashanti system. Some aspects of this system make it a better option for Africa than the system of majoritarian democracy that is now en vogue.

In a consensus system, the voluntary acquiescence of the minority with respect to a given issue would normally be necessary for the adoption of a decision. For one thing, the traditional African system was based on consensus not only in the choice of representatives, but also in the making of decisions. There were no political parties, defined as organizations of people of similar tendencies and aspirations with the sole aim of gaining power for the implementation of their policies. This made it possible for all concerned to participate in power and reduced the potential for conflict that electoral competition under multiparty rule offers. In short, government under this system was a coalition of citizens whose right of representation was respected.

For another, this nonparty alternative, modified to suit prevailing conditions in Africa, which the nonparty alternative that the Ashanti system, like many other African traditional systems, provides the potential to secure for us in Africa a political dispensation under which governments are not formed by parties but by the consensus of electoral representative.

*To what extent is the traditional model of democracy adequate for our time?*

It should be noted, very quickly, that the ideological legitimating of the traditional political order is no longer adequate for present-day Africa. The traditional sociopolitical order was legitimized by what T.U. Nwala called a "mythical charter." This charter, which, according to Nwala, was in "the history and ideology of the traditional community" stressed the "descent (of the people) from a founding father, and the inevitable role of the gods of the community in its founding and perfection" (1985: 167). But given the negation of the moral autonomy of the traditional community and the emergence of new sociopolitical structures in Africa, this charter of legitimation would have to be replaced with a constitution.

It is noteworthy, however, that for a constitution to perform its noble role as the foundation or basis of order in society, the processes leading to its promulgation would have to be all-inclusive, giving every individual, group, or interest in society the opportunity to participate in deciding what the founding charter of the society should be. The role of dialogue in this process cannot be overemphasized. It is the only means through which a rational, noncoercive harmonization of views on the basic rules and procedures for regulating the affairs of the society can be achieved. Thus the ideological legitimating of the traditional sociopolitical order is no longer adequate for contemporary pluralist African society whose values and belief systems have been penetrated and convulsed by the capitalist socioeconomic formations of greed, exploitation, and class divisions. Also inadequate is the emphasis on the clan as a basis of leadership, an arrangement that required "the establishment of a hierarchy of clans." It does not require much reflection to see that this arrangement has become anachronistic. The modern society is a cosmopolitan society in which people with different cultural, socio-historical backgrounds coexist. Hence, there is the crying need for the democratization of leadership and governance in a manner that allows all citizens to become "equal members of a single political community" (Mamdani, 1998: 14).

This raises another crucial question: How can we reconcile the claim of democracy briefly highlighted in the above paragraph with that of justice? This question arises with respect to African multiethnic states in which, to use the words of Mahmood Mamdani, "the minority fears democracy; the majority fears justice" (ibid: 11). This issue is at the core of many of the conflicts that have been tearing many African countries apart.

It should be noted, however, that the tension between democracy and justice has arisen, partly because the dominant conception of democracy in Africa today is the majoritarian one. This conception, in practice, creates a situation in which some people are consistently in the minority. It is this kind of situation that the traditional African consensual model of democracy sought to prevent. But, how can this model be rendered functional in a new Africa in which "the moral autonomy of the traditional community" has been negated?

To address this question, we need to spell out the kinds of structures that would be required to make a consensual model of democracy work in Africa today. In this regard, what is required is a kind of political arrangement in which power is sufficiently decentralized to allow for a significant degree of regional and local autonomy in African multiethnic states. This kind of arrangement would allow for political representation to be structured along lines that would allow each ethnic group to develop according to its values, culture, historical experience, and aspirations. Also, it would prevent a situation in which some people see themselves as permanent outsiders to the state (Awolowo, 1966).

The point here is this: Any program of social transformation— which would succeed in addressing the question of how Africans can develop and maintain viable social orders within which individuals can exercise their rights, perform their obligations, and realize their genuine human potentials—has to contend with the problem of the entrenchment of ethnic/clan consciousness in most African societies. What is required in this respect is not to obliterate this consciousness or pretend that it is not important. What is required is the construction of political systems within which this aspect of our social experience can be accommodated in a manner that does not threaten social cohesion. The consensual nonparty model of democracy and a structure of political power, which guarantees considerable autonomy to the nationalities in Africa's multi-ethnic states, seems to be the best in the present circumstances.

In sum, many African scholars and politicians (Simiyu, 1988: 49-54) have portrayed the African societies before colonialism as harmonious, undifferentiated entities enjoying democratic tranquilities. For example, Julius Nyerere (1969: introduction) bases his view on this as he points out that the traditional African family was the most satisfactory institution for all its members. He argues that despite all the variations and some exceptions where the institutions of domestic slavery existed, African family life was everywhere based on certain practices and attitudes that together mean basic equality, freedom, and unity.

Indeed, these are some of the tenets of a democratic system. For Nyerere (ibid.), the political authority in this traditional setup was based on democracy and free discussion among the elders: "They talk until they agree." This free discussion was the "very essence of African democracy" to use Nyerere's own words. These were political systems which cherished and practiced "government by discussion." Property ownership was also governed by the same egalitarian principles and no individual hoarded wealth while others starved in poverty. There were no exploiting classes. African traditional life was a socialist one, Nyerere argues. He further argues that inequality set in only with the advent of the capitalist money economy during colonialism when this delightful harmony of egalitarianism was disrupted.

Jomo Kenyatta, writing as far back as 1938, was even more forthright about the existence of democracy among his Kikuyu people and, by extension, among all African traditional societies before the advent of colonialism. In his words: "before the coming of the Europeans, the Kikuyu had a democratic regime." According to Kenyatta (1965: 50), originally the Kikuyu had a monarchy. The monarchy was vested in a tyrannical sovereign who was overthrown in a people's revolution. This people's revolution held a representative council where a democratic constitution based on the following principles was drawn: freedom of land acquisition; equality among the members of the tribe who had the right after initiation to take part in the government, and regular elections. This democratic government was vested in the Council of Elders (*Kiama*) who had passed the stage of warriors—that is, those who had attained the age of 40 years and above. It was this that was supposedly destroyed by European colonialism.

However, other scholars, foreign and African, especially anthropologists and historians, have described African social and political institutions before the advent of colonialism either as detached observers or more important with that sympathy that betrayed the same assumption that the nature of African traditional governments and social systems was egalitarian and democratic. As was argued by Fortes and Evans-Pritchard (1990, passim): "It is possible that groups are more easily welded into a military political system without the essence of classes, the closer they are to one another in culture." The argument here is that it is quite elusive to try to prove as a bottom line that democracy existed in these societies before the coming of colonialism. Indeed, what comes out of a careful analysis of the political institution and mechanisms of the precolonial African societies is a mixture of democratic practices on the one hand and aristocratic, autocratic, and/or militaristic practices, with varying degrees of deposition, on the other. Agreeably, many precolonial African regimes were certainly authoritarian, such as those of the emperors of Ethiopia, the Kabakas of Uganda, and Shaka the Zulu chief. However, Botswana's relative success in incorporating the traditional *kgotla*, or system of elders, into a modern constitution is a clear testimony of original African democracy. The new constitutions of Ghana and South Africa, for example, have incorporated significant roles for the traditional authorities, thus, recognizing the democratic values of the African traditional systems that have always existed.

However, a sober conclusion to this argument is that when colonialism came to Africa, it did not find a pure democratic tradition and base, as others have argued, but, rather, various mixtures of rudimentary democratic institutions and despotism. Some of the institutions ranged from wild ones and hardly noticeable models as in the so-called acephalous societies, to quite brutal ones in the highly centralized states that tended to deny any democratic practices.

Colonialism, on the other hand, unleashed such violence, discrimination, and exploitation that Africans, young and old, educated and uneducated, soon forgot the violence and undemocratic practices of their traditional rulers. Therefore, the past could have been portrayed as a bygone world of bliss, harmony, and democracy

To a very large extent there has been a break from the traditional practices and the social political philosophy of African society. The breaks have been due to several causes:

1. Colonialism and Neocolonialism: These have been responsible for wholesale transplantation to Africa of political and social models. Witness the proliferation of political parties and parliamentary democracy that has taken the place of consensus of the traditional African society. Party politics is not as such adverse to consensus. Nevertheless, the inner dynamics of party politics are such that the conditions of consensus formation have little chance to survive because the values that guided consensus formation in African pre-colonial society are largely ignored.

2. Economics: The economic restructuring of the newly emerged states of Africa may have a far more serious impact on the political and social philosophy of the continent than colonialism and neocolonialism. It is an open question whether the economics of the modern states are not themselves so many forms of recolonization. What can be said with certainty, however, is that in the pre-colonial structure economic considerations, though important, were not so overriding in the social and political realm. In the structures of an economics of scarcity, the toll on democracy cannot be over-emphasized. Walter O. Oyugi argues that "indeed the whole idea of democracy does not make sense where a peoples' major preoccupation is survival" (Oyugi and Gitonga, 1987: 109).

One would hasten to add here that the economic struggle now is more intense than ever before, given the growing populations and diminishing resources.

3. Pluralism: The problem of shifting away from homogenous societies to heterogeneous societies. In the traditional setup, Buganda or Ashanti was a homogenous entity with a uniform culture and language: The ethnic group had its centralized leadership under the monarch. In the nation-state, we find bundled together tribes of different, often opposed, cultures. The mingling of formerly highly centralized societies with the formerly stateless societies is bound to cause some conflict, and any understanding of present turmoil in Africa must bear this in mind. A new national political culture needs to blend many traditional and current trends of democratic thought.

Africa's struggles for independence relegated these institutions to oblivion, and what emerged was a "nationalist leadership" void of any traditional historical roots and whose ultimate goal was to remove the colonialists, not promoting democracy. A viable adaption and transformation of this African democratic heritage could have helped to consolidate the continent's multicultural societies. The central task in this process would lie in the reconciliation of democracy and justice via the establishment of a typically African consensus-oriented dialogue for decision making, a constitutional legitimization of the role of competing ethnic groups, and a decentralization of political power, so that local and regional autonomy becomes possible.

## References

Abbink, Jon and Gerti Hesseling, (eds.). 2000. *Election Observation and Democratization in Africa*. New York: St. Martin's Press.

Abraham, William. 1962. *The Mind of Africa*. London: Weidenfeld & Nicolson.

Acemoglu, Daron, Simon Johnson, and James A. Robinson. 2002. "An African Success Story: Botswana." *CEPR Discussion Paper Series*. File URL: http://www.cepr.org/pubs/dps/DP3219.asp

Achebe, Chinua. 1967. *A Man of the People*. Garden City, New York: Anchor Books.

Agyeman, Opoku. 2001. *Africa's Persistent Vulnerable Link to Global Politics*. San Jose, CA: University of California Press.

Ake, Claude. 1993a. "The Unique Case of African Democracy." *International Affairs*, 69, 2: 239-244.

_____. 1993b. "Rethinking African Democracy" In Larry Diamond and Marc F. Plattner (eds.) *The Global Resurgence of Democracy*. Baltimore: The Johns Hopkins University Press.

_____.1996. *Democracy and Development in Africa*. Washington, DC: Brookings Institution.

Awolowo, Obafemi. 1966. *Thoughts on the Nigerian Constitution*. Ibadan: Oxford University Press.

Ayittey, G.B.N. 1991. *Indigenous African Institutions*. Ardsley-on-Hudson, NY: Transaction Publishers.

Ayittey, G.B.N. 1992. "Africa in the Postcommunist World," *Problems of Communism*, vol. 41, pp. 207-17.

Bathily, Abdoulaye. 1994. "The West African state in historical perspective." In *Between State and Civil Society in Africa*. ed. Eghosa Osaghae (ed.), Dakar: Council for the Development of Social Science Research in Africa.

Bayart, Jean-François. 1993. *The State in Africa: The Politics of the Belly*. London: Longman.

Berman, Bruce. 1998. "Ethnicity, Patronage and the African State: The Politics of Uncivil Nationalism." *African Affairs* 97, 388: 305-341.

Bhagwati, Jagdish. 1966. *The economics of underdeveloped countries*. London: Weidenfeld and Nicholson.

_____. 1995. "Democracy and Development: New Thinking on an Old Question." Rajiv Gandhi Memorial Lecture. New Delhi: Rajiv Gandhi Foundation.

Bratton, M. and N. Van de Walle. 1994. "Neopatrimonial Regimes and Political Transition in Africa," *World Politics*, 46, 4: 453-89.

Bratton, Michael. 1998. "Second elections in Africa," *Journal of Democracy* 9, 3: 51-66.

Busia, K.A.1967. *Africa in Search of Democracy*. London: Routledge & Kegan Paul.

Carnenburgh, O. van. 2000. "Democratization in Africa: The role of Election Observation." In *Election Observation and Democratization in Africa*. Jon Abbink and Gerti Hesseling (eds.), 21-36. New York: St. Martin's Press.

Chabal, Patrick and Jean-Pascal Daloz. 1999. *Africa Works: Disorder as Political Instrument*. Oxford and Bloomington: International African Institute, James Currey, and Indiana University Press.

Chazan, Naomi. 1990. "Africa's Democratic Challenge: Strengthening Civil Society and the State," *World Policy Journal,* 9, 2: 279-307.

Daddieh, Cyril. 2001. "Beyond Governance and Democratization in Africa: Toward State Building for Sustainable Human Development."[Online]http://www.kzoo.edu/africa/SUSFINAL2.html ( July29, 2001).

Dahl, A. 1971. *Polyarchy: Participation and Opposition*. New Haven, CT: Yale University Press.

Dahl, Robert. 1989. *Democracy and Its Critics.* New Haven: Yale University Press.

Decalo, Samuel. 1992. "The Process, Prospects and Constraints of Democratisation in Africa." *African Affairs*, 91: 7-35.

Diamond, L. 1987. "Class Formation in the Swollen African State," *Journal of Modern African Studies*, 25, 4: 567-97.

_____. 1989. "Beyond Autocracy: Prospects for Democracy in Africa." *Beyond Autocracy in Africa*. Atlanta: Carter Centre for Emory University.

Doornbos, M. 2000. "African Multi-partyism and the Quest for Democratic Alternatives: Ugandan Elections Past and Present. In *Election Observation and Democratization in Africa*, Jon Abbink and Gerti Hesseling,(eds.) 99-121. New York: St. Martin's Press.

Dumont, René. 1962. *False Start in Afric* a. Paris: Edition de Seuil.

Edwards, P. ed. 1973. *The Encyclopedia of Philosophy*, Vol.V, New York: AMS Press

Ekeh, Peter. 1990. "Social Anthropology and Two Contrasting Uses of Tribalism in Africa," *Comparative Study in Society and History,* 32, 4: 660-700.

Ellis, Stephen. 2000. "Elections in Africa in Historical Context." In *Election Observation and Democratization in Africa*. Jon Abbink and Gerti Hesseling ( eds.): 37-49. New York: St. Martin's Press.

Foeken, D. and T. Dietz. 2000. "Of Ethnicity, Manipulation and Observation: The 1992 and 1997 Election in Kenya." In *Election Observation and Democratization in Africa*, Jon Abbink and Gerti Hesseling (eds.): 122-149. New York: St. Martin's Press

Fortes, M. and Evans Prichard (eds.). 1950. *African Political Systems*. London: Oxford Univ. Press.

Fortman, B. de Gaay. 2000. "Elections and Civil Strife: Some Implications for International Election Observation." In *Election Observation and Democratization in Africa*, ed. Jon Abbink and Gerti Hesseling (eds.): 76-98. New York: St. Martin's Press.

Fukuyama, F. 1989. "The End of History. " In *National Interest*, No. 16 (Summer): 3-18.

Galbraith, John. 1994. *The World Economy Since the War*. London: Sinclair-Stevenson.

Gurr, Ted. 1970. *Why Men Rebel*. Princeton: Princeton University Press.

____. 1993. "Why Minorities Rebel: A global Analysis of Communal Mobilization and Conflict since 1945." *International Political Science Review*, 14, 2: 161-201.

Hameso, Seyoum. 1997a. *Ethnicity in Africa: Towards a Positive Approach*. London: TSC Publications.

____. 1997b. *Ethnicity and Nationalism in Africa*. New York: Nova Science Publishers.

____. 2001. *Development, State and Society: Theories and Practice in Contemporary Africa*. New York: Authors Choice Press.

Held, David. 1995. *Democracy and the Global Order: From the Modern State to Cosmopolitan Governance*. London: Polity Press.

Horowitz, Donald. 1985. *Ethnic Groups in Conflict*. Berkeley: University of California Press.

____. 1991. *A Democratic South Africa? Constitutional Engineering in a Divided Society*. Berkeley: University of California Press.

Human Rights Watch. 1999. *Hostile to Democracy: The Movement System and Political Repression in Uganda*. New York: Human Rights Watch, August.

____. 2001. "Uganda: Not a Level Playing Field." Online http://www.hrw.org/reports/2001/uganda/uganda0301.PDF.

Huntington, Samuel and Joan Nelson. 1978. *No Easy Choices*. Cambridge, MA: Harvard University Press.

Kakooza, J. 1989. "Criminology as Viewed from Human Rights Violation" presented at the Uganda Human Rights Activists Seminar on Human Rights. Kampala: Makerere University.

Karugire, S. R. 1980. *A Political History of Uganda*. Nairobi: Heinemann Educational Books.

Kenyatta, J. 1965. *Facing Mount Kenya*. London: Vintage Books.

Legesse, Asmarom. 2000. *Oromo Democracy: An Indigenous African Political System*. New Jersey and Asmara: The Red Sea Press.

Mamdani, Mahmood.1998. "When Does a Settler Become a Native? Reflections on the Colonial Roots of Citizenship in Equatorial and South Africa." Text of an Inaugural Lecture as A.C. Jordan Professor of African Studies, University of Cape Town, May 13, 1998.

Mazrui, A. 1992. "The Impact of Global Changes on Academic Freedom in Africa: A Preliminary Assessment," CODESRIA Symposium on Academic Freedom, Research, and Special Responsibilities of the Intellectual in Africa, Kampala, Uganda.

Mbaku, John. 2000. "Governance, Wealth Creation, and Development in Africa: The Challenges and the Prospects." *African Studies Quarterly, 4*, 2: 1. On-line, http://web.africa.ufl.edu/asq/v4/v4i2a3.htm, (December 30, 2000).

Mbembe, Achille. 2001. *"On the Postcolony," Studies on the History of Society and Culture*, 41. Berkeley: University of California Press.

Mbiti, J. S. 1969. *African Religions and Philosophy*. London: Heinemann.

Mwenda, K. K. and Owusu, G.S. (eds.). 1999. "Human Rights Law in Context: The Case of Ghana," The Review of the African Commission on Human and Peoples' Rights, 8, Part 1. Online: http://www.murdoch.edu.au/elaw/issues/v7n4/mwenda74_notes.html - n16.

Nabakwe, W. M. 1988. "Social and Moral Responsibility within African Traditional Context." The First International Regional Conference in Philosophy, Mombasa, May 23-27, 1988.

The National Summit on Africa. 1998. "Democracy and human rights," Thematic Working Paper Series.

N'Diaye, Boubacar. 2001. *The Challenge of Institutionalizing Civilian Control*. Lanham, MD: Lexington Books.

Nwala, T.U.1985. *Igbo Philosophy*. London: Lantern Books.

Nyerere, J. 1969. *On Socialism*. Dar-es-Salaam: Oxford University Press.

Oladipo, Olusegun. 1996. *Philosophy and the African Experience: The Contributions of Kwasi Wiredu*. Ibadan: Hope Publications.

Olakunle, George. 2000. "African Politics, African literatures: Thoughts on Mahmood Mamdani's Citizen and Subject and Wole Soyinka's The Open Sore of a Continent." *West Africa Review* 2, 1. On-line, http://www.icaap.org/iuicode?101.2.1.3, (February 4, 2001).

Owusu, M. 1992. "Democracy and Africa – A View from the Village," *Journal of Modern African Studies*, 30: 369-96

Oyugi, W. O. and A. Gitonga. 1987. *Democratic Theory and Practice in Africa*. Nairobi: Heinemann.

Rothchild, Donald. 1995. "Ethnic Bargain and Sate Breakdown in Africa." *Nationalism and Ethnic Politics* 1, 1: 54-72.

_____. 2000. "Liberalism, Democracy and Conflict Management: The African Experience" *Facing Ethnic Conflicts: Perspectives from Research and Policy-making*, Center for Development Research, Bonn, Germany. December 14-16.

Salih, Mohammed. 1999. "Horn of Africa: Security in the new World Order." In *Globalization, Human Security and the African Experience*, Caroline Thomas and Peter Wilkin (eds.). Boulder, CO: Lynne Rienner, p.139.

Schumpeter, Joseph. 1994. [1942] *Capitalism, Socialism and Democracy*. London: Routledge.

Shaw, Timothy. 1986. "Ethnicity as the Resilient Paradigm for Africa: From the 1960s to the 1980s." *Development and Change,* 17: 587-605.

Shivji, I.G. (ed.). 1991. *State and Constitutionalism: An African Debate on Democracy.* Harare: SAPES Books. Available online at: http://www.murdoch.edu.au/elaw/issues/v7n4/mwenda74_notes.html - n15).

Simiyu, V.G. 1988. "The Democratic Myth in the African Traditional Societies." In *Democratic Theory and Practice in Africa.* Walter O. Oyugi et. al. (eds.). Portsmouth, NH: Heinemann.

Skinner, Elliott. 2000. "African Governance and Political Cultures." *Global Bioethnics,* 13, 1-2: 55-62, March-June.

Snyder, Jack. 2000. *From Voting to Violence: Democratization and Nationalist Conflict.* New York: Norton.

Taban Lo Liyong .1997. For a delightful poetic reconstruction of this charter in the poem entitled "The Magnum Akan Magna Carta," see his collection: *Homage to Onyame.* Lagos: Malthouse.

Talbott, Strobe. 2000. "Self-determination in an Interdependent World." *Foreign Policy,* 118 (Spring): 152-163.

Throup, David and Charles Hornsby. 1998. *Multi-party Politics in Kenya: The Kenyatta and Moi States and the Triumph of the System in the 1992 Election.* Oxford: James Currey.

Tronvoll, K. and O. Aadland. 1994. *The Process of Democratisation in Ethiopia – An Expression of Popular Participation or Political Resistance?* Oslo: Norwegian Institute of Human Rights.

UNCTAD. 1999. *Foreign Direct Investment in Africa: Performance and Potential.* UNCTAD/ITE/ IIT/Misc. 15. New York, Geneva: United Nations.

Wiseman, John, 1990. *A Democracy in Black Africa.* New York: Paragon House Publishers.

The World Bank Group Countries: Botswana. *The World Bank Group.* Nov.19, 2003.

Young, Crowford. 1996. Africa: An Interim Balance Sheet. *Journal of Democracy,* 7, 3: 53-68.

Zartman, I. W. (ed.). 1995. *Collapsed States. The Disintegration and Restoration of legitimate Authority,* Boulder, CO: Lynne Rienner.

Zeleza, P.T. and B.A. Ogot. 1988. "Kenya's Road to Independence and After." In Gifford and W.R. Lewis (eds.), *Decolonisation and African Independence: The Transfer of Power 1960-1980.* New Haven, CT: Yale University Press.

# Chapter 4

# Resurgence of the Military as a Political Power Factor

The democratic political process is at best a regulated rivalry. It does not answer, even at best, to the desirable properties that price theory dictates to truly competitive markets. The effects of injustices in the political system are much graver and longer lasting than market imperfections can inflict. Political power rapidly accumulates to points of inequality by making use of the cohesive apparatus of state and its laws, and those who have gained the advantage assure themselves of a favored position.

Universal suffrage is therefore insufficient to maintain democracy, for when political parties and elections are financed not by public funds, but by private contributions, the political forum is inextricably constrained by the dominant interest. The liberty provided by the principle of participation should not be eroded by permitting those who have greater private means to use that advantage to determine and control the course of public debate. For when the less- favored members of society have been effectively prevented by their lack of means from exercising their fair degree of influence, they would withdraw into apathy and resentment.

The establishment and consolidation of democratic regimes has long been a difficult, if not elusive, challenge in Africa. In the 20th century, factors such as economic underdevelopment, poverty and inequality, and Cold War geopolitics contributed to regime instability and frequent periods of authoritarian rule. In the 1980s and 1990s, virtually all African countries made transitions to competitive electoral regimes. Can electoral democracy be sustained? Or will contemporary regimes give way to another cycle of authoritarianism? The militarization of electoral politics either through the use of militia or other violent measures has besieged the effort toward free and fair democratic competition.

The 1990s have witnessed remarkable and sweeping changes in the way African states are governed. A large number of military and one-party dictatorships have collapsed in the face of mass civil protests; and a new wave of democratization is sweeping through the continent. One of the most interesting aspects of this process is the increasing attention granted to crafting political systems that reflect the plural character of African societies. But democratization has not followed a uniform pattern, and there have been major setbacks in some countries. Problems of political instability and violence have given rise to regional security initiatives that have ambiguous implications for democratization. In certain situations, there has even been a resurgence of the military as a political force.

Despite considerable democratic progress, many African countries are now suffering an explosion of violence, rising public insecurity, and a deteriorating rule of law, much of it fueled by the mafia, the military, and police impunity. How can we reconcile this troubling situation with the transition to or consolidation of democracy? Are democratic concerns being trumped by a preoccupation with the rule of law and the militarized gang role in undermining it? How might we think about the relationship among these issues and about the problems of militarized impunity more generally, not only in scholarly terms but also with an eye to eliminating such abuses and guaranteeing both democracy and the rule of law? This militarization of democracy has led to government surveillance of individuals and organizations, and to persecution and incarceration of people without legal recourse. These are the main challenges that have put democracy in Africa under siege today, consequent upon resurgent militarization of politics (Mentan, 2004: Ch.5).

## IN THE NAME OF "GUARDIANS"

The military has had a permanent presence in African history, at least since the states were formed by European colonizers. Throughout the 20th century, the influence of the military has been decisive in shaping the political and institutional life of each of the continent's states. To a great extent, at least until the end of the 1980s, the African states were configured under the shadow of military power, whose influence became particularly strong starting in the mid-1960s, when the reign of the bureaucratic authoritarian regimes began with the Ghanaian coup of 1966 against Kwame Nkrumah.

The post-World War II period saw the rise of a type of military intimately linked to what began to be called neocolonial "rent-seeking"(Mbaku,1994), which was neither the expression of a transformation in international economic relations, nor any political and ideological program whose principal goals were the defense of democracy and the struggle against communism. That is why the history of African states is replete with instances of internal political violence, military interventions in the national political process, military dictatorships, counterinsurgency campaigns, and low-intensity warfare.

## COUPS D'ETAT

A *coup d'état* (French, *golpe de estado* in Spanish and Portuguese, and *putsch* in German, often simply called a *"coup,"* is the sudden overthrow of a government, usually done by a small group that just replaces the top power figures. It is different from a revolution, which is staged by a larger group and radically changes the political system. The term is French for "a sudden stroke, or blow, of a nation." The term **coup** can also be used in a casual sense to mean a gain in advantage of one nation or entity over another, for example, an *intelligence coup*. By analogy, the term is also applied to corporations, for instance, a *boardroom coup*.

Tactically, a coup usually involves control of some active portion of the military while neutralizing the remainder of armed services of a country. This active group captures or expels leaders, seizes physical control of important government offices, means of communication, and the physical infrastructure, such as streets and power plants. The *coup* succeeds if its opponents fail to dislodge the plotters, allowing them to consolidate their position, obtain the surrender or acquiescence of the populace and surviving armed forces, and claim legitimacy.

*Coups* typically use the power of the existing government for its own takeover. In other words, a coup consists of the infiltration of a small but critical segment of the state apparatus, which is then used to displace the government from its control of the remainder. In this sense, use of military or other organized force is not the defining feature of a *coup d'état*. Any seizure of the state apparatus by extralegal tactics may be considered a *coup*.

*Coups* have long been part of African postindependence political tradition. Samuel P. Huntington (1957) has divided coups into three types, ignoring Luttwak (1969) nonmilitary *coups*:

1. *Breakthrough coups* - in which a revolutionary army overthrows a traditional government and creates new bureaucratic elite. Breakthrough coups are generally led by noncommissioned officers (NCOs) or junior officers and only happen once. Examples include China in 1911 and Egypt in 1956.

2. *Guardian coups* - which have been described as musical chairs. The stated aim of this form of coup is to improve public order, efficiency, or to end corruption. There is usually no fundamental shift in the structure of power. Many nations with guardian coups undergo many shifts between civilian and military governments. Examples include Pakistan, Turkey, and Thailand.

3. *Veto coups* - which occur when the army vetoes mass participation and social mobilization. In these cases the army must confront and suppress large-scale and broad-based opposition and as a result they tend to be repressive and bloody. Examples include Chile in 1973 and Argentina in 1975. An abortive and botched veto coup occurred in Venezuela in 2002.

   *Coups* can also be classified by the level of the military that leads the coup. Veto coups and guardian coups tend to be led by senior officers. Breakthrough coups tend to be led by junior officers or NCOs. In cases where the coup is led by junior officers or enlisted men, the coup is also a mutiny, which can have grave implications for the organizational structure of the military.

4. There is also a category known as *bloodless coups,* in which the mere threat of violence is enough to force the current government to step aside. Bloodless coups are so called because they involve no violence and thus no bloodshed. Napoleon acceded to the power that way in 1799 (the coup of 18

Brumaire). More recently, Pervez Musharraf of Pakistan came to power in such a manner in 1999.

5. The term *self-coup is used when the current government assumes extraordinary powers not allowed by the legislation.* An example is Alberto Fujimori in Peru, who was democratically elected, but later took control of the legislative and judicial powers.

## CHRONOLOGICAL INVENTORY OF SOME COUPS D'ETAT IN AFRICA

In the Sudan, the army took over on April 6, 1985. While President Gafar Nimeiry visited Cairo, General Sewan Ali Dahab used the opportunity to seize power. Nimeiry had ruled the country for 16 years before his (mercifully) bloodless overthrow.

In Uganda, General Tito Okello overthrew President Milton Obote on August 27, 1985. Obote had returned to power in 1980, following his overthrow by military dictator Idi Amin in 1971.

In Lesotho, Prime Minister Leabua Jonathan was overthrown by Major General Lekhanya on January 20, 1986, and King Moshoeshoe II was installed as ruler.

On January 26, 1986, the National Resistance Army, led by current Ugandan President Yoweri Museveni, captured Kampala and seized power from Tito Okello who, as indicated above, had overthrown Milton Obote the previous year.

In Burundi, Colonel Jean-Baptiste Bagaza was overthrown in a military coup on September 3, 1987. He had been in power since 1976 and was in Canada at the time of the *coup*. Major Pierre Buyoya took over.

On June 30, 1989, the civilian Sudanese Government of Sadek El Mahdi was overthrown in a military coup. A military junta led by General Omar Hassan El Bashir seized power. They are still ruling to this day.

On November 6, 1990, King Moshoeshoe II of Lesotho was overthrown by the military and replaced by his son, King Letsie III.

In Mali, President Moussa Traoré was overthrown in a bloody coup on March 26, 1991. He had ruled the country since 1968.

In Sierra Leone, President Joseph Momoh, who had been in power since 1985, was overthrown on April 30, 1992 by Captain Valentine Strasser.

On July 23, 1994, President Dawda Jawara of the Gambia was overthrown by Lieutenant Yaya Jammeh.

On August 15, 1995, President Miguel Trovoada of São Tomé and Princípe was overthrown in a military *coup*. However, he managed to resume his rule on August 21, 1995, following mediation by Angola.

In the Comoros, on September 28, 1995, notorious French mercenary Bob Dénard led the overthrow of President Said Mohamed Djoar, taking him prisoner. Six days later, a French military intervention force captured the mercenaries and restored the deposed president.

In Niger, General Ibrahim Baré Mainassara overthrew civilian President Mahamane Ousmane in January 1996.

On July 25, 1996, Burundi's President Sylvestre Ntibantunganya, a Hutu, was toppled by the Tutsi-dominated army and replaced by former strongman Major Pierre Buyoya.

Apart from these "classic military coups" there were a number of other events that illustrated the nondemocratic nature of politics on the continent during this period. For example:

- the assassination of President Samuel Doe of Liberia in 1990, following massive civil unrest;
- the Hissein Habré escape from Chad in 1990, following a long-running rebellion;
- the overthrow of President Siad Barré in Somalia as a result of civil war;
- the overthrow of President Mengistu Haile Mariam of Ethiopia in 1991 as a result of civil war.

Such events illustrate the tenuous nature of attempts to establish democracy in African countries. After the coup, the military is faced with the issue of the type of government to establish. In Africa, it was common for the postcoup government to be led by a junta, a committee of the chiefs of staff of the various armed forces. A common form of African post-coup government is the revolutionary assembly, a quasilegislative body made of members elected by the army. In Pakistan, the military leader typically assumes the title of chief martial law administrator.

Generally, all African coup leaders act under the concept of *right orders*. They believe that the correct approach to government is to issue correct orders. This view of government underestimates the difficulty in implementing government policy and the amount of possible political resistance to certain orders. African military establishments have not yet admitted this concern with dictatorship rather than with democratic policy implementation.

**A military dictatorship** in the African context is a form of government wherein the political power resides within the military; it is similar but not identical to a stratocracy, *i.e.*, a state ruled directly by the military. Like all dictatorships, a military dictatorship may be official or unofficial, and as a result may not actually qualify as stratocratic. In Africa military governments more often came to be led by a single powerful autocrat. Leaders like Idi Amin, Muammar al-Qaddafi, Mobutu Sese Seko, and Gamal Abdul Nasser worked to develop personality cults and became the face of the nation inside and outside their countries.

In sum, military rule, dictatorships, and economic regression were the staple in Africa from the mid-1970s to the 1990s. After military takeovers in the early 1960s in Congo-Brazzaville, Dahomey (Benin), and Togo, the first gush of military coups in 1965-66 in Burundi, Central African Republic, Congo-Kinshasa, Ghana, Nigeria, and Upper Volta (Burkina Faso) opened the way to autocratic military rule. External involvement played a major role in such cases. Many proved disastrous from an economic and institution building point of view, as evidenced by Ethiopia (1974-91), Ghana (1966-69 and 1972-83), Mali (1968-91), Nigeria (1983-98), Somalia (1969-91), Uganda (1971-79), and Zaire (1965-97). By 1990 half of Africa's states had military or quasimilitary governments. In parallel with authoritarian military governments came a trend toward single-party rule under autocratic civilian leaders, largely pursuing interventionist economic policies, in some cases under the banners of socialism or Marxism. Especially when combined with external shocks, the resulting economic decline and politicization of the bureaucracy eroded much of what remained of institutional governance capacity and undermined many of the accomplishments of the 1960s.

African armies are not routinely cohesive. Examples of the Mobutus, Eyademas, Does, Idi Amins, and many others, demonstrate that they are far from being Westernized hierarchies intervening in the political arena for altruistic motives. Rather, they are coteries of rent-seekers or of cliques composed of ambitious officers seeking self-advancement. This observation explains why military rule in Africa has not necessarily fostered socioeconomic or political development or stability.

Many factors contribute to the maintenance of civilian control over the military in any democracy. Military professionalism might lead to acceptance of civilian control over policy, with the military effectively exercising self-constraint (Huntington, 1957). Oversight of the military and differences of opinion within the armed forces can prevent the organization necessary for intervention in politics. This is possible through dismissing officers who venture too far into politics or attempt to organize a conspiracy differentiates officers who fail to accept civilian supremacy out of the military. The presence within the military of either agents of the regime or officers who accept civilian control complicates the task of planning a *coup d'état*.

Nevertheless, a consideration of the capacity, disposition, and opportunity for armed intervention into the democratic process points to the likelihood of further coups, rebellions, and mutinies in Africa. The region faces a period of chronic instability due to famine, corruption, HIV/AIDS, and so on, in which the military is likely to be an active participant. The inhibiting factors are unlikely to be strong enough to prevent this.

The democracy and nationalities issue is left unresolved. Further coups in Africa are possible as different sections of the military, and rival chiefs, compete for control of access to wealth through grabbing political power. The planned multiparty elections are unlikely to deliver stability, given the divided nature of the indigenous national communities.

This pessimistic conclusion clearly has serious implications for the economic and political development of the continent. The instability that both brings about and is generated by coups and military intervention is also clearly detrimental for the region's economy. Evidence shows that coups reduce the per capita output in Africa. The impact on investment has even been greater. Indeed, coup-prone states have become the first "collapsed" states like the DRC in the African region.

In the context of political development, a coup or armed rebellion is at the opposite end of the spectrum from effective democratic government, or what aid donors refer to as "good governance." Whether the force is wielded by the military, police, or irregular militia, it is, at its most extreme form, politics by the bullet rather than the ballot. The lesson to date seems to be that the situation cannot be reversed by the simplistic act of insisting on good governance conditions for foreign aid. The type of democratic culture that makes military intervention unthinkable must be home grown.

Nigeria offers a very eloquent example of what bazooka democracy holds for Africa. Despite all the promises of probity, the military elite generally proved themselves more corrupt than any regime that preceded it. They take huge kickbacks on contracts and divert government funds. For example, allegations were rife about corruption and illicit enrichment by members of Ibrahim Babangida government in Nigeria. General Babangida was forced aside by the military top brass, led by General Sani Abacha, in June 1993 and an interim civilian government under Ernest Shonekan was installed. But after barely three months in office, Shonekan was overthrown by Abacha in November 1993.

Initially Abacha attempted to quell public dissatisfaction by co-opting the opposition (offering its leaders cabinet posts) and organizing a constitutional conference. It turned out to be another scam. The public viewed the Abacha constitutional conference with a massive dose of skepticism and cynicism. That the general twice postponed its opening did not help matters. A day after the conference finally began on June 27, 1994, it was adjourned for two weeks. What was the official reason? The accommodations for delegates were not ready. Moreover, the 396 delegates, who were to deliberate on the future of democracy, congregated at Abuja as "guests of the military." A fourth of their numbers (96) were nominated by General Abacha and the rest "elected" under suspiciously complex rules. Delegates were chosen by "peoples' representatives" who were themselves elected by "popular vote" on May 23, postponed from May 21. Candidates under 35 years of age were ineligible to run. In addition, a candidate had not to be "an ex-convict, must be sane, must be a fit and proper person and must not have been declared bankrupt by a court of law"—requirements that most of the ruling military elites themselves would fail to meet. Logistical problems, inadequate publicity, and apathy bedeviled the electoral exercise. There was no campaigning, no voters' register or cards. Confusion reigned. Voters did not even know whom they were voting for and for what purpose. And stunned by the annulment of June 12, elections, many chose to stay home. The general voter turnout across the country was scandalously low. More suspiciously, the constitutional conference was not sovereign.

The "Nigerian conference" was a meretricious charade that should have been dissolved. Political parties did not take part in the constitutional conference. Imagine de Klerk of South Africa banning the African National Congress and all political parties, arresting political leaders, clamping down on the news media, nominating 25 percent of the delegates to the conference, and declaring that its resolutions would not be binding on the white minority government. A Nigerian prodemocracy activist Arthur Nwankwo decried this autocratic rule,

For it was in October, 1995 that the present military dictatorship announced its transition to civil rule programme, at the end of a bazaar of mindless men and women who crafted a self perpetuating document that goes by the name of a draft constitution. Ever since then, calculated steps have been taken with fanatical commitment, unbridled enthusiasm and effusive bravado that have ensured the national descent into hell. The hell is not only physical but equally spiritual (*Post Express Wired*, June17, 1998, p.3).

On June 12, 1994, the first anniversary of the annulment, Chief Abiola belatedly declared himself "president," and was promptly arrested on charges of treason. This triggered a wave of strikes by oil workers, which disrupted oil production. The paranoid military regime unleashed a wave of brutal reprisals. Prodemocracy protesters were gunned down and political leaders of different persuasions were detained.

*The Guardian, The Concord, Newswatch,* and other newspapers were shut down and their editors arrested. And all civilians were expelled from the Provisional Ruling Council (PRC) on September 27. About 40 people, including former head of state General Olusegun Obasanjo, were arrested on trumped-up charges of plotting to overthrow the government. The irony of the charge is that it was the private press that reported rumors of an impending coup, whereupon military personnel sprang into action. These events culminated with the arrest and subsequent hanging of Ken Saro-Wiwa. General Sani Abacha ("The Butcher of Abuja") died mysteriously in June 1998. Local newspapers reported that, his wife, Maryam, was seeking political asylum in a Middle East country thought to be Lebanon. She was also reported to have inherited the vast fortunes of her husband estimated at $5 billion including an oil refinery in Brazil and had contracted a private security outfit to guard the family, whilst she assessed the situation. Ironically, Abacha was a corrupt head of state waging "a war on corruption." Following the (un)timely death of General Sani Abacha in June 1998, elections were conducted by his successor, General Abdulsalami Abubakar.

After assuming office in May 1999, President Obasanjo found the country ungovernable as elected officials were more interested in their perks and power than fixing the country's economy. A near government paralysis occurred from wrangling over distribution of power between the executive and the legislative. For 18 months (February 1999 to August 2000), Nigeria's 109 senators and 360 representatives passed just five pieces of legislation, including a budget that was held up for five months. Immediately upon taking office, the legislators voted for themselves hefty allowances, including a 5 billion naira ($50 million) furniture allowance for their official residences and offices. The impeached ex-chairman of the Senate from President Obasanjo's own People's Democrtic Party (PDP), Chuba Okadigbo, was the most predatory:

As Senate President, he controlled 24 official vehicles but ordered 8 more at a cost of $290,000. He was also found to have spent $225,000 on garden furniture for his government house, $340,000 on furniture for the house itself ($120,000 over the authorized budget); bought without authority a massive electricity generator whose price he had inflated to $135,000; and accepted a secret payment of $208,000 from public funds, whose purpose included the purchase of "Christmas gifts" (*New African*, September 2000, p. 9).

Most Nigerians would dismiss what they have as a "419 kokonut democrazy," where power was transferred from an active military general to a retired military general. Rev. Matthew Hassan Kuka, a member of the Oputa Commission set up to investigate past human rights abuses said:

You have a president who is a retired military man, a director of national security who is a retired military man, a defense minister who is a retired military man and a director of the State Security Service (SSS) or national intelligence, who is an ex-military man. Apart from the president and all the key office-holders in the land being of military background, we don't have enough elbow room to begin to talk about subordinating this system to civilian control (*The Washington Times*, November 1, 2001: A18).

On January 27, 2002, a small fire from a gas station near a central market in Lagos spread to the weapons depot at the Ikeja military base, touching off massive explosions that propelled shrapnel and shock waves for miles through the crowded slums and working-class neighborhoods that surround the base. The huge blasts sent thousands of residents fleeing in panic. Many, including children, jumped into a nearby canal, without realizing how deep it was, and drowned. The death toll from the blasts and the drowning exceeded 2,000 according to private newspapers. Residents had many reasons to be angry.

The provision of basic social services, and law and order was nonexistent. The crime rate had soared. "Some police officers had been convicted of robbery or aiding bandits over the last year" (*The New York Times*, February 3, 2002: WK6). And when these explosions occurred in January 2002, there were no fire and rescue operations because the city had no trucks. Angry residents wanted to know how and why bombs, shells, and rockets were stockpiled in a heavily populated area. They demanded that President Olusegun Obasanjo cancel a scheduled trip to the United States of America to attend the World Economic Forum in New York. He visited the devastation site to express his grief with the families of the victims. When the distressed crowd of mothers of missing children urged him to take a closer look, he reacted in anger: "Shut up! I don't really need to be here. After all, the governor of the state is here" (*The Washington Post*, February 10, 2002: A20). He later apologized, saying "he was unaware at the time that lives had been lost." "How could Obasanjo have not known that people had died?" asked Jonah Nnachi, a 22-year-old trader. "If he was a person who cared for people, he would not have said those things" (*The New York Times*, February 10, 2002: A5).

## MILITARY SPENDING AND MILITARIZATION OF AFRICA

The military budgets of African states are notoriously opaque, incomplete, and deceptive. There is no evidence that this is likely to change dramatically any time soon. During the Cold War, Africa was one of the most militarized zones in the world. The wars that raged in Sub-Saharan Africa between 1945 and 1989 were in countries such as:

Angola 1961-75, 1975-89
Burundi 1987-88
Cameroon 1955-60
Chad 1980-87
Ethiopia 1974-89, 1976-83
Ghana 1981
Guinea-Bissau 1962-74
Kenya 1952-63
Madagascar 1947-48
Mozambique 1965-75, 1981-89
Nigeria 1967-70, 1980-81, 1984
Rwanda 1956-65
Somalia 1988
Sudan 1963-72, 1984-89
Uganda 1966, 1971-78, 1978-79, 1981-87
Western Sahara 1975-87
Zaire 1960-65
Zambia 1964
Zimbabwe 1972-79, 1983

At the beginning of the 1990s, a semblance of peace and stability returned to countries that began the process of opening up the political space to more players. But coups, conflicts, and even genocide in the middle and late 1990s have undermined the gains. A peculiar feature of militarization in Africa is that the poorest countries—including Rwanda, Sierra Leone, Liberia and Somalia—are spending the most on arms and the military. With continued political uncertainty in Rwanda, Burundi, Sierra Leone, Ethiopia, Algeria, Eritrea and the Democratic Republic of Congo, military spending is likely to grow rather than decrease. Some of Africa's poorest countries tend to increase their spending on the military while cutting their spending on social welfare.

The 1990s also witnessed a strong interest in military spending in Africa by external actors, especially donors of economic aid to the continent. Three main factors accounted for this: first, the end of the Cold War allowed donors to become involved in nontraditional matters such as national security and the cost of maintaining military establishments; second, the widespread armed conflict in Africa; and third, the establishment of a linkage between good governance and development in the 1990s, which led development actors to question "excessive" or "unproductive" expenditures, such as military spending (*SIPRI Yearbook*, 2005), at the expense of the social sector and the alleviation of poverty.

The initial policy choice of donors to force a change in priorities in public-sector spending was to impose a predetermined level of military spending in recipient countries. However, this policy had the unintended consequence of increasing the secrecy surrounding military budgets in aid-dependent countries that wanted to hide the true cost of their military expenditures, and thus reduced the reliability of the military expenditure data on which donors' judgments were based.

Another deficiency of the policy of imposing a maximum level of military spending on recipient countries was that it did not take into consideration the legitimate security needs of the countries concerned. Having realized the limitations of the level approach, from 1997 on, donor countries began to discuss alternative ways of addressing the issue of excessive military spending.

By the early 2000s a new approach emerged, articulated primarily by the British Department for International Development (DFID). This approach emphasizes the process of arriving at military spending rather than the level of military spending. It also emphasizes the importance of applying sound financial management principles to the whole of the public sector, including defense. However, the process approach has not been universally accepted by donors and its details are yet to be fully understood by all donor countries.

A SIPRI (2003) study, started in 2001, has examined the processes of budgeting for the military sector in eight African countries with a view to understanding how military spending decisions are made, and how to contribute to the improvement of the processes for military sector management in these countries. The study identifies a number of challenges that must be overcome before the process approach can take root as a tool of military spending management. These challenges include the need for proper policy development in the military sector in the countries as a necessary first step toward an integrated defense planning system.

The absence of a defense policy in many of the countries hinders planning and makes budgetary allocation to defense ad hoc. The problem is partly lack of expertise and partly lack of an enabling environment. To correct this, many of the states require capacity building not just in the defense sector but also in the other policy areas with which defense interacts.

Institutions that need to be strengthened include the parliament, the ministries of finance and defense, and the audit departments. Another major challenge is the need to develop clear rules to guide the budgeting process and to specify clear roles for the various actors involved. A third major challenge is to overcome the lack of transparency in the military budgets. There is a need to have a sufficiently detailed budget that will allow for proper scrutiny of every aspect of the budget. This challenge is as much a problem of capacity as it is a result of lack of policy.

These challenges have several implications for donor countries, including a need for enhanced policy dialogue between them and recipient countries on how to correct existing deficiencies in order to boost the chances of the process approach taking firm root. Furthermore, helping to address some of the present shortcomings in the systems will require long-term commitment as opposed to the short-term initiatives donors are used to.

## MILITARIZING AFRICA FOR "PEACE, DEVELOPMENT, AND DEMOCRACY"?

Peace is a cause of democracy. The exact nature of this causation must be carefully specified, for the relationship is not at all simple and direct. First, although peace is a facilitating factor in the rise of liberal democracy, it is a permissive cause rather than an active cause. It creates a safe space for the emergence of democracy, but does not guarantee it. In fact, there are a number of cases in which autocracy developed as a result of the war-making/state-making process, yet when the autocracy established relatively defensible borders and created peace, democracy did not follow, and autocratic institutions maintained themselves for centuries. Spain and Japan, for example, established themselves in geographic positions as favorable as that of Britain, but did not liberalize until a much later date. China alternated between periods of civil war and periods of peace for thousands of years, but like Japan, retained an autocratic feudal ruling structure even during long periods of peace. Thus, although one can attribute the *rise* of autocracy in all these countries to the war-making/state-making process, it is clear that autocracy was able to *maintain* itself even under conditions of peace, an outcome that can be attributed to weaknesses in the domestic social variables for democracy in these countries.

Second, wars may have the effect of disrupting and undermining entrenched institutions in authoritarian and semidemocratic governments, providing an opening for democratic reforms, particularly if a regime loses a war. Examples of this include Germany after World War I and Argentina after the Falklands War. However, it must be noted that while particular wars may have a positive short-term disruptive effect, the stabilization of a new democratic government usually requires the institution of a long stable peace after that war. Otherwise, there is a strong possibility of a new, more vigorous authoritarianism developing. Thus, while occasional wars are not destructive to democracy, and may in some cases promote it, peace facilitates democracy in that states that experience frequent war and extended security crises will find it difficult or impossible to build stable liberal democracies.

Demilitarization for Democracy (DfD) has noted that the military's hold on political and economic power continues to undermine democratic transition in many African nations today. In a 1997 report, DfD found that 57 percent of African countries are clearly not democratic, and that the armed forces still hold substantial political and economic power in 40 of the 53 African nations. Yet from 1991 to 1995, the United States of America provided military assistance to 50 countries in Africa, 94 percent of the nations on the continent. Although military assistance to Africa began to decline in the early 1990s, more recent years have seen new increases in training and weapons exports. Between 1991 and 1998, U.S. weapons and training deliveries to Africa totaled more than $227 million.[1]

Shifting a fraction of U.S. energy that currently goes to strengthen African militaries toward nonmilitary alternatives could promote democracy, development, and peace-building. This could make a significant contribution to providing that leadership and promoting security and stability in the African region. The evidence for such thinking is abundant. In 1998 alone, Africa suffered 11 major armed conflicts, more than any other continent. For the first time since 1989, Africa is the world's most war-torn region.[2] Of late, 32 African countries have experienced violent conflict, and many of those face continuing civil war or the looming threat of renewed fighting.[3]

Ironically, most of the African countries engaged in serious conflict since the 1950s have been the recipients of U.S. weapons and training. Throughout the Cold War (1950-1989), the United States of America delivered over $1.5 billion worth of weaponry to Africa.[4] Military aid and training, covert weapons shipments, and political and financial backing poured in, as the war against communism was played out on African soil. In the process, America propped up corrupt dictators, armed some of the world's worst human rights abusers, and fueled violent conflict. In fact, many of the top U.S. arms clients of the Cold War—Liberia, Somalia, the Sudan, and Zaire (now the DRC)— have turned out to be the top basket cases of the 1990s in terms of violence, instability, and economic collapse. America offered weapons and military assistance to a repressive government with one hand while raising the other in the name of securing democracy and promoting stability. Inevitably, somewhere down the line the regime collapses. And U.S. policymakers are left struggling to rewrite their lines. Once a new government takes power, the cycle reemerges with the same old offers of U.S. military training to help "secure democracy."

Moreover, the United States has failed to acknowledge its own role in fueling conflict and undermining democratic development in Africa. A July 1999 Report by the U.S. Bureau of Intelligence and Research states clearly that "Arms transfers and trafficking and the conflicts they feed are having a devastating impact on Sub-Saharan Africa." Yet the authors fail to attribute responsibility to America for either its past or current military weapons and training exports to

Africa, explicitly leaving America out of the picture: "Arms suppliers in Western and Eastern Europe, the Middle East, North America, Latin America, and Asia have sold arms to African clients."[5] In fact, nowhere does the report mention U.S. arms transfers to the region, although more than $20 million worth of U.S. weapons and training were delivered to Africa in 1998 alone.[6] Nor is there any recognition that the hundreds of millions of dollars worth of U.S. equipment transferred to the Mobutu regime in Zaire and the late Jonas Savimbi's National Union for the Total Independence of Angola (UNITA) since the 1970s are still being utilized in current African conflicts.

Skills and equipment provided by America have strengthened the military capabilities of combatants involved in some of Africa's most violent and intractable conflicts. As to the relative importance of U.S. arms transfers to Africa, data from the most recent edition of the U.S. Arms Control and Disarmament Agency's publication, *World Military Expenditures and Arms Transfers*, ranks the United States as the second leading arms supplier to both Central Africa (behind China and ahead of France) and Southern Africa (behind Russia and tied for second with France). In contrast, the most recent data from the Congressional Research Service suggests that at best the United States ranks sixth in arms transfers to Africa for the period from 1995 to 1998, after China, Russia, the United Kingdom, France, and Italy.[7]

Any assessment of the arms flow to Africa must take account of the substantial transfers of light weaponry that are carried out beyond normal government-to-government channels. For example, as Brian Wood and Johan Peleman point out in their report, *The Arms Fixers: Controlling the Brokers and Shipping Agents*, the weapons suppliers to the perpetrators of the 1994 genocide in Rwanda included brokers and shippers in the United Kingdom, South Africa, and France, working with collaborators in Albania, Belgium, Bulgaria, Egypt, Italy, Israel, the Seychelles, and the former Zaire.[8] While the United States was not a major player in this traffic, many of its closest allies were. And the U.S. history of overt and covert weapons trafficking to the region helped nourish the informal networks that are now often the main source of supply for the world's most vicious ethnic conflicts.

For example, bordering nine other countries and rich in natural resources, Zaire has been the economic and strategic heart of Africa since it gained its independence some 40 years ago. Despite continued reports of widespread corruption and human rights abuses in Zaire, America helped build Mobutu's arsenal with a fleet of C-130 transport aircraft and a steady supply of rifles, ammunition, trucks, jeeps, patrol boats, and communications equipment. By the time the dictator was ousted in 1997, America had delivered more than $300 million (measured in constant 1998 dollars) in military hardware to Mobutu's regime. Through the International Military Education and Training (IMET) program, the United States of America also trained 1,350 of Mobutu's soldiers at a cost of more than $100 million.[9] Although Zairian forces gained a reputation for violence and repression against civilians, the State Department continued to claim IMET training served to "safeguard Zaire's internal stability and territorial integrity without threatening the security of neighboring countries."[10]

Moreover, even after the Cold War ended, America continued to provide military support to the Mobutu dictatorship. In 1991, America delivered more than $4.5 million in military hardware to Mobutu's government.[11] That same year, Congress suspended its economic assistance to Congo—not on human rights grounds, but because it had defaulted on loans provided by the U.S. government to cover its weapons purchases.[12] By that time, a hearty arsenal of deadly weaponry had already poured into the country, while Mobutu's fiscal corruption and brutal rule had incited political unrest and devastated the economy. According to the World Bank, 64.7 percent of the country's budget was reserved for Mobutu's discretionary spending in 1992; official Zaire figures put the estimate at 95 percent.[13]

In 1996-97, Laurent Desiré Kabila and his Alliance of Democratic Forces for the Liberation of Congo swept through the country and ousted President Mobutu, calling for democratic freedom under a new government. Before long, however, Kabila began his own antidemocratic crusade. Within a few short months of taking power, the new president banned political parties, suspended civil rights, and was reported to be fueling ethnic hatred. As reports of growing unrest and abuse trickled in, America held to a policy of engagement with Kabila, largely disregarding the voices of the democratic opposition and civil society groups struggling for reform within the country.

Despite the shaky future of the erstwhile left-leaning Kabila regime, American State Department officials continued to call for resumption of the IMET program (at a U.S. cost of $70,000) to support the new government in "developing an apolitical military cadre that respects human rights, the rule of law, and the concept of civilian control of the military."[14] In FY2000, the DRC received Excess Defense Articles (EDA) on a grant basis under Section 516 of the Foreign Assistance Act of 1961. The, "EDA will support a rebuilding and professionalizing of the military following years of internal strife, and assist with maintaining internal security."[15] Why providing military training and equipment to a corrupt and abusive regime would promote democracy under Kabila, after the same policy had failed miserably for decades with Mobutu, was a question U.S. policymakers should have been asking themselves.

Fighting erupted in August 1998 between the new government's forces and a coalition of Mobutu-backers and former Kabila-supporters and remained largely contained within Congolese borders. Foreign troops from at least eight other national armies were pulled into the conflict: Rwanda, Uganda, Burundi, Angola, Namibia, Sudan, Chad, and Zimbabwe have been reported in the region during the conflict, along with as many as twelve irregular, or nongovernmental, armed groups, including UNITA, the Sudanese People's Liberation Army, and the *Interhamwe* militia forces that were behind the Rwandan genocide. Rwanda, Uganda, and Burundi, as well as UNITA and other rebel forces, backed the main rebel group known as the Rally for Congolese Democracy (RCD), while

Namibia, Chad, Zimbabwe, and Angola contributed troops and hardware in support of Kabila's government forces.[16]

Other countries like Libya are reported to have arranged the transport of troops from Chad to support Kabila. Sudan has financed three Ugandan guerrilla movements and also agreed to back Kabila. The South African government provided weapons to Rwanda and maintained good relations with President Museveni of Uganda, while private mercenaries from South Africa were commissioned by Kabila.[17] The complex web of alliances has continued to evolve, with factions splitting and leaders being displaced sporadically. Not surprisingly, America has been providing weapons and training to most of the players in the Congo conflict.

In 1998 alone, U.S. weapons to Africa totaled $12.5 million, including substantial deliveries to Chad, Namibia, and Zimbabwe—all now backing Kabila. On the rebel side, Uganda had received nearly $1.5 million in weaponry since 1998 and Rwanda had been importing U.S. weapons as late as 1993 (one year before the brutal genocide erupted). U.S. military transfers in the form of direct government-to-government weapons deliveries, commercial sales, and IMET training to the states directly involved has totaled more than $125 million since the end of the Cold War.[18]

All told, the United States has helped build the arsenals of eight of the nine governments directly involved in the Congo War. In addition, some of the Rwandan forces that played a key role in toppling the regime of long-time arms client Mobutu Sese Seko in Zaire had received training from America Special Forces under the Joint Combined Exchange Training (JCET) program. The United States of America also provided an estimated $250 million in covert military assistance to UNITA's forces between 1986 and 1991,[19] and is alleged to be backing the Sudanese People's Liberation Army.

During the height of the war, the *New York Times* reported the use of U.S. communications equipment by the rebels, and small arms like the U.S.-designed M-16 combat rifle, often circulating from past wars, have been used in both combat and civilian attacks.[20] Heavier equipment and training transferred to the region by America has also likely contributed to both sides of the war. Uganda, which received just under $1 million in U.S. weapons in 1997 (up from $64,000 in 1996), boosted its total military expenditure in 1999 from $150 million to $350 million, increasing troop commitments and stockpiling tanks and anti-aircraft missiles for use against Kabila's forces. Zimbabwe and Angola—both recipients of U.S. training and equipment—also sent jets, tanks, and troops into the combat.[21]

Because many U.S.-supplied weapons have outlasted the governments and conflicts for which they were intended, yesterday's supplies are finding new uses today. A Belgian arms dealer was arrested in South Africa for selling 8,000 U.S. M-16 rifles from Vietnam War era arsenals to Kabila's forces.[22] In fact, many of the illicit arms traffickers working in Central Africa got their start as covert operators for America. Kathi Austin has documented a number of U.S.-sponsored smugglers working in the Great Lakes region of Africa, noting that "little attention is paid to how weapon suppliers fan the flames of the region's conflicts."[23] Four U.S. citizens claiming to be Christian missionaries were arrested in Zimbabwe for attempting to smuggle small arms caches—which included sniper rifles, shotguns, machine guns, firearms, telescopic sights, knives, camouflage cream, two-way radios and ammunition—across national borders.[24]

Rather than focusing greater attention on civil-society building, one of the most dramatic forms of "new partnership" undertaken by the Clinton administration was a rising wave of military training operations. As a case in point, from 1998 to 2000 America provided military training to six of the countries fighting in the DRC—Angola, Chad, Namibia, Rwanda, Uganda, and Zimbabwe.

U.S. military training takes a number of forms in Africa, including traditional International Military Education Training (IMET), Expanded IMET (E-IMET), Joint Combined Exchange Training (JCET), and more recent training under the African Crisis Response Initiative (ACRI). IMET training for Africa has floated between $4-8 million throughout the 1990s. In 1998, America provided $5.8 million in IMET training for over 400 African soldiers.[25] As Congress has cut IMET funding in recent years, however, the other programs appear to have sprouted up to fill the gaps and further strengthen military-to-military relations between the U.S. and Africa. The Department of Defense also established the Africa Center for Strategic Studies (ACSS), which allegedly provides 'academic' rather than tactical or operational instruction in "civil-military relations, national security strategy, and defense economics."[26]

JCET programs, which use special operations forces, remain exempt from congressional oversight. From 1995 to 1998 U.S. special forces conducted JCET training in at least 34 of the 53 African countries, including Namibia, Rwanda, Uganda, and Zimbabwe—all fighting in the DRC—as well as Mozambique, Côte d'Ivoire, Equatorial Guinea, Ghana, Guinea-Bissau, Malawi, Mali, Mauritania, Morocco, Senegal, Sierra Leone, Tunisia, Cameroon, Botswana.[27] Although the number of troops trained under JCET is difficult to track, at least 9,100 host-nation military personnel participated in the program worldwide in 1997.[28]

Indeed, one can comfortably conclude that U.S. promotion of human rights has been overshadowed by questions about whether Rwandan units trained by Americans later participated in atrocities in the war in Zaire. In 1997, the Department of Defense instituted the African Crisis Initiative (ACRI), a scaled-down version of the African Crisis Response Force (ACRF) that was originally proposed, and began calling for more antinarcotics operations in the region. ACRI's stated purpose is to "work in partnership with African countries to enhance their capacity to respond to humanitarian crises and peacekeeping challenges in a timely and effective manner.... to assist Africans in developing rapidly deployable, interoperable battalions from stable democratic countries."[29] However, the program has been criticized for contributing to counterinsurgency operations or conventional warfare by the trained troops and providing yet another mechanism for channeling U.S. military training and equipment to favored regimes. Some view the program as no more than an insurance policy against U.S. involvement in peacekeeping operations in the region again. Much of the training and equipment provided can also enhance their capability to engage in counterinsurgency operations or conventional warfare with other states.[30] In 1998, Ugandan troops trained under the new ACRI program were re-deployed a week later as part of a major counterinsurgency campaign against the Allied Democratic Forces in western Uganda.[31]

The Africa Center for Security Studies defines its mission as follows: to "support democratic governance in Africa by offering senior African civil and military leaders a rigorous academic and practical program in civil-military relations, national security strategy, and defense economics."[32] Critics argue that America is focusing its resources in the wrong arenas, promoting military relationships at the expense of building democracy and conflict prevention. Clarissa Kayosa, of Demilitarization for Democracy and the Year 2000 Campaign to Redirect World Military Spending to Human Development, has noted that "While many African focused organizations in the United States agree on the need for a professional, law abiding, rights respecting, civilian controlled armed forces, U.S. military training in other parts of the world, including Africa, has mixed results at best.... Africa is in a state of collapse now and what it needs is not more military assistance but more development assistance."[33]

Countries like Angola and Mozambique now report as many antipersonnel landmines buried beneath the earth as people treading it. The proliferation of small arms in Africa has become an internationally recognized crisis undermining global development and breeding a new generation of child soldiers. Yet real counteraction is not on the agenda. Military training programs continue to flourish, weapons sales to the developing world are on the rise, and small arms manufacturers are looking to increase exports worldwide.

By restricting the flow of weapons and training and increasing support for sustainable development policies, America could help create the conditions needed for peace and stability to take root. Until America is willing to serve the interests of long-term democracy, peace and stability, rather than short-term profit and politics, its Cold War policies will live on in Africa—wreaking destruction in places like the DRC, Angola, and Sierra Leone, Eritrea and Ethiopia.

## THE MILITARY FACTOR

The threat posed by the emergence of militias in Africa is both alarming and frightening. Their resurgence in African politics cannot be separated from the material conditions that bring peoples of different ethnic and political backgrounds together. These material conditions include security, social relations of production, and political power. Thus the menace of militias could be both functional and dysfunctional. No African state can pretend to ignore its existence. And unless the state refocuses its energy toward expanding the political and economic space, it will be difficult invoking and enforcing a law against their existence. While the state and the militias fight against each other national security is precarious. The way out is for the state to pursue subsistence democracy—good governance for human security.

The 1994 United Nations Development Program conceives of human security to include economic, food, health, environmental, personal, community, and political security. Human security is holistic in personification of whatever concerns human beings. This is distinct from what national security has turned out to be—solo and one-dimensional with its focus on only the state. Ideally, the social contract assumes that by national security the sovereign state is supposed to provide a holistic security for both itself and society. National security is therefore, taken to mean developmental security, which Robert McNamara (1968: 149) rightly defined as: "...Security is not hardware, though it may include it, security is not military force, though it may involve it ... security is development and without development there can be no security."

Unfortunately, the postcolonial African state has appropriated the constituents of national security and has used them from the narrow perspective of the use of force, armaments and militarization of the society. Therefore the tendency for the social contract to break down is great, as social forces begin to scramble for personal, group, and regime security. The emphasis on human security is that nonstate actors are equally relevant as the state, and without them the state cannot exist. Therefore maintaining human security is as important as ensuring the stability of the state. Claude Ake (1992) discusses the operational context of militias in African politics by pointing out that in the African situation, power is overhauled and security lies only in getting more and more power. There is hardly any restraint on the means of acquiring power, holding it or using it. Might is coexistent with right to the extent that political conflict is endemic because of the normlessness and extremist pattern of political competition. The political class operates in a state of siege and this explains why one of the paradoxes of the African social formation is that despite the monopoly of power by the state and its concentration within the state, a political order does not appear to have emerged since independence in the 1960s. Rather violence is endemic, anarchy lurks just below the surface and the political system is disarticulated as the economy and it is as fragmented as African culture.

Both governments and groups hire mercenaries to fight for their cause. However, mercenaries are emerging as a new phenomenon in Africa. They are used as militias and integrated into the cause of their employers. They are thus mercenerian-militias--groups of armed men whose purpose is both for war and money making adventurism as well as fighting a cause, which may befit them in the long run. Most of the communal conflicts in Nigeria, for example, have been sustained by mercenerian-militias. The distinguishing character of mercenerian-militias is the art of camouflaging in military uniforms. This is intended to create a false impression of the presence of federal troops, being sympathetic to the resolution of the conflict. At the end, their unsuspecting victims are killed *en masse* unless they are capable of withstanding the onslaught of the mercenerian-militias. Most of the time, they are defeated because they are not properly schooled on the topography of the area where the conflict is taking place.

Experience shows that most of the mercenerian-militias are recruited from criminal militias. Criminal militias are mostly juvenile delinquents who have been affected by social ills, either as a result of lack of parental guidance or break down of the family, economic crisis, urban decay, failing moral values, lack of economic engagement, and other social vices. Sometimes these criminal behaviors are learned in the process of interaction and association with those possessed by criminal attitudes through contacts in cinemas, peer group meetings, and the like.

In the process of identifying with criminals, an individual acquires law-violating lifestyles. Subsequently, they engage in activities that are criminalistic, like stealing, raping, arson, and fighting, among others. They also acquire weapons, and undergo training by their leaders. When trained they become militant defenders of a cause they may not totally believe in. Thereafter they easily become recruits for religious, political, ethnic, and ideological conflicts on the continent.

In Nigeria they are the Area Boys, *Yan Daba* and *Yan Banga*. In Rwanda they emerge as *Interahamwe and Maimai*. In Congo-Brazzaville we have Bernard Kolelas' *Ninja and Pascal* Lissouba's *Mambas*. There are many pockets of these mercenerian-militias and criminal militias all over Africa.

The nonstate actor militias have the primary purpose of challenging the legitimacy of the state (Elaigwu, 2002: 11) and Obasi (2002). The reasons may include, first, defending the social cultural values of the group. Second, the reason may be one of demanding a share in the economic resources of the country by violence when regular procedures have failed. Third, it could be a way of fighting to liberate themselves from political repression or marginalization, by demanding greater autonomy of political participation or by changing the political structure of governance in their favor.

In this case, sometimes, the militia becomes revolutionary by being irredentist or separatist in approach. Fourth, where government fails to provide security some groups or individuals may organize vigilantes or personal security to protect themselves and their property without recourse to due process of the law. Fifth, sometimes, too, militias are formed for the purpose of protecting the environment from degradation as well as using it as a means to take ownership of resources of which they have suffered denial.

In Africa, militias emerged as a result of the struggle of the ethnic groups, classes, and people against the colonial state. These groups and classes saw the formation of militias, commonly known as guerrilla forces, as a means toward actualizing their self-determination. This was common in Southern African counties like Zimbabwe, Angola, Namibia, and South Africa. The Africa National Congress of South Africa was a unique case of multiple ethnic associations struggling for self-determination. They raised armed liberation militias known *as Umkhonto We Sizewe,* commonly known as *MK.* Along with strikes and lockouts the militia groups began sporadic violence along with other armed groups that were fighting to liberate South Africa from apartheid rule. More recently, the hunter group in Sierra Leone, the *Kamajors,* turned into a militia and fought on the side of government against the rebel Revolutionary United Front (RUF). Similarly, the Hutu extremist militias, the *Inmterhanwe,* were foremost in the Rwanda genocidal conflict.

France, Belgium, and the late President Mobutu of Zaire (now Democratic Republic of Congo, DRC) intervened to stop the Tutsi-led Rwanda Patriotic Front (RPF) which helped Yoweri Museveni to power in Uganda, from infiltrating Rwanda to launch a military offensive in October 1990 to overthrow the Hutu government of late President Juvenal Habyarimana. Efforts toward peace were truncated by Habyarimana himself. The suspected plane crash that led to the death of Habyarimana opened the floodgates for the Tutsi extremists to unleash terror on the Hutus, defeating the remnants of Habyarimana's army, the Forces Armées Rwandaises (FAR), extremist Hutu militias *Interahamwe* and *Maimai.* The outcome was the genocide, which led to some 800,000 deaths. This led the mass population of Hutu refugees, the remnant of FAR soldiers, and the extremist Hutu *Interahamwe* militias to escape, with sophisticated weapons, into the DRC. The Tutsi later joined the Kabila alliance forces—Alliance des Forces Démocratiques pour la Libération du Congo (AFDL) (Nzongola-Ntalaja, 2002)—to flush out the dictator next door in Zaire (now DRC).

While Kabila was using the militias to overthrow Mobutu's government, the *Interahamwe* militias were also using the occasion to establish their base in the DRC. In the process the Kagame-led Tutsi government decided that the easiest way to exterminate the Hutus was to pursue them inside DRC with Ugandan support. Angola, Zimbabwe, Namibia, and Chad began to show interest in the DRC for economic, political, and of course, georegional strategic interest. When Kabila overthrew Mobutu he became a problem to the peace process as the Tutsis also tried to maintain their influence as having been the force that brought him to, and kept him in, power. His death changed the course of the peace process. But the DRC is yet to experience peace.

Across the river Congo, the Marxist-Leninist President Sassou-Nguesso plunged the Republic of Congo in civil war from 1993 to 1999. This case captures the general scenarios for the rise of militias in Africa. The 1992 elections led to the rise of private militias, formed by the political power contenders. The election, which brought Pascal Lissouba to power, pitched him against his rival, Bernard Kolelas. The two rivals raised Kolelas' *Ninjas* and Lissouba's *Mambas.* These were militias that carried out violent confrontations in the summer of 1993. And by December 1995, when a peace accord was concluded, about 2,000 deaths had been recorded and 100,000 people were displaced.

Even when Kolelas, by the peace accord, became the mayor of Brazzaville by submitting all his forces in support of the president, the "militias were not disbanded and the weapons that remained in the possession of 'soldiers' could immediately be remobilized, leasing the distrust between the war leaders and (fragile) balance of terror intact" (ACP-EU, 2002: 66-69). The outcome was the upsurge of the second phase of the civil war in 1997 when former president Sassou Nguesso, with the backing of France, raised a well-trained and -armed militia, the *Cobras*, to shoot his way back to power. Kolela teamed up with President Lissouba to become the prime minister. This enhanced chances of fighting Sassou-Nguesso. But it was rather too late.

Though they were able to surmount the military support of other neighboring countries in the region like Mobutu's Forces Armées Zairoises (FAZ), Rwandan *Interahamrawes* and Israeli military advisors who encircled Sassou-Nguesso's residence, the latter got his support from Gabon and Angola. Arms were distributed in the streets to children recruited to swell the ranks of *Cobra* militias (ibid.) Finally, Sassou-Nguesso ousted Lissouba and established a police state that was ruthless in destroying towns and cities where his opponents were based. Nevertheless, convulsive ethnic, regional, and personal tensions are still rife. And Sassou-Nguesso may still "fallback in a form of a withdrawal to his northern stronghold" (ACP-EU, 2002: 69) in order to survive. The menace of militias can inevitably create an "economy of affection" (Hyden, 1988) rendering the state completely incompetent in harnessing the essential bureaucratic rationality for economic development.

## SUDAN: MILITIA, GENOCIDE, AND DEMOCRACY

Democracy in the first instance predicates the creation and maintenance of institutional mechanisms for nonviolent resolution and management of conflict. Militias in Sudan embarked on ethnic cleansing in the Darfur region, heavily backed by the government of President Lt-Gen. Omar al-Bashir.[34] Its leaders and members have been supplied with arms, communications equipment, salaries, and uniforms by government officials and have participated in joint ground attacks on civilians with government troops, often with aerial bombing, and reconnaissance support from government aircraft. Instead of being disarmed, members of government-backed militias are absorbed into police, and paramilitary forces operating in Darfur.[35]

Since February 2003, the government of Sudan has used militias known as "*Janjaweed*"[36] as its principal counterinsurgency ground force in Darfur against civilians from the Fur, Zaghawa, Massalit, and other ethnic groups from which two rebel groups known as the Sudan Liberation Army/Movement (SLA/M) and the Justice and Equality Movement (JEM) of Professor Hassan Tourabi are drawn. The government-backed *Janjaweed* militias are derived from the "*Abala*," camel-herding nomads who migrated to Darfur from Chad and West Africa in the 1970s, and from Arab camel-herding tribes from North Darfur.[37] With government aerial support, arms, communications, and other backing, and often alongside government troops, the *Janjaweed* militias have been a key component in the government's military campaign in Darfur; a campaign that has resulted in the murder, rape, and forced displacement of thousands of civilians.[38]

Hundreds of villages in Darfur have been totally or partially burned and destroyed by bombing, and ground attacks. More than a million people have been forced from their homes and more than 158,000 people have fled Darfur for neighboring Chad. The vast majority of displaced civilians remain in Darfur, where most are settled in camps, and on the outskirts of towns, dependent on international humanitarian assistance that the Sudan government has blocked. In these areas under government control, displaced civilians continue to be preyed upon by the *Janjaweed* militias who are based in camps and villages in the rural areas they control, from which they have forcibly displaced most of the original inhabitants.

Despite the humanitarian cease-fire agreement signed by the government of Sudan and rebel groups on April 8, 2004, the violence has not ceased. Attacks on civilians have continued, including incidents of government bombing of both civilians and military targets. Evidence of *Janjaweed* raids on civilians and their livestock within Darfur and across the border into Chad, and rebel attacks on various targets including aid convoys, is in abundance.[39]

In the initial months of the conflict, Sudanese officials denied that the *Janjaweed* militias existed. More recently, statements by government officials have acknowledged the existence of militias but have refused to admit the government's responsibility for arming them. On April 7, Dr. Sulaf al-Din Salih, the commissioner-general of the Humanitarian Aid Commission, stated "We asked all the people of Darfur to help in protecting themselves against the rebellion. This is standard practice which we do in this country," [40] but he did not acknowledge a government policy of recruitment, arming, and coordinating the *Janjaweed* militias. On May 14, 2004, Sudanese Foreign Minister Mustafa Ismail continued to deny government support for the *Janjaweed* and publicly refused to disarm them while the rebels remained armed.[41] On July 5, 2004, the Minister of the Interior (and the President's Representative for Darfur) Abdel Raheem Muhammad Hussein continued in the same vein, noting "we will not appease the Americans by capturing tribal leaders as every Darfur tribe has a militia."[42] Further government statements reported by *Reuters* news agency of July 5, 2004, had focused on the need to disarm all "outlaw groups," without specifying that the government-backed militias would be included in this category.

These statements continue to obscure and minimize the primary role played by the Sudanese government in instrumentalizing and using the militias as a mainstay of their military force in Darfur. Despite the government's denials, evidence from official documents proves that the *Janjaweed* are an integral part of the government's military force and counterinsurgency strategy in Darfur, a force and a strategy that have been responsible for war crimes and crimes against humanity.

Human Rights Watch obtained copies of Sudanese government documents that describe an official policy of support to the *Janjaweed* militia.[43] These documents, which originate from the offices of the civilian administration in Darfur, implicate government officials ranging from a deputy minister from the central government to the highest levels of the Darfur civilian administration—the governor or "*wali*"—to provincial commissioners and local officials in a policy of support to the *Janjaweed*. The documents illustrate the involvement, at the highest levels, of the state bureaucracy in the recruitment and arming of militia and the authorization of their activities that have resulted in crimes against humanity and war crimes.

The documents include orders for additional recruitment of militia, provision of military support to allied ethnic groups, and, in one case, provide relative impunity for abuses committed by *Janjaweed* militia members against civilians. In a clear indication of official support for known *Janjaweed* militia leader Musa Hilal, a directive dated February 13, 2004 from the office of a sub locality in North Darfur is directed at all security units in the locality. The document urges the recipients to "allow the activities of the *mujahedeen* and the volunteers under the command of Sheikh Musa Hilal to proceed in the areas of [North Darfur] and to secure their vital needs." The "*mujahedeen*" are typically members of the Popular Defense Forces, a paramilitary unit organized by the government of Sudan that has frequently been used to fight its so-called holy war in southern Sudan.[44] The reference to "volunteers" refers to militia members under the command of Musa Hilal.

The document continues, in a directive: "We also highlight the importance of non-interference so as not to question their authorities and to overlook minor offences by the *mujahedeen* against civilians who are suspected members of the rebellion...." The document then qualifies the impunity perpetrated by the fighters (*mujahedeen*) in requesting that security units "ensure that what happened in the area of Kutum, which reflected a distorted version of events that raised questions about the intentions of the fighters and resulted in false media propaganda, is not repeated."

The reference to the events in Kutum is clearly to the events of early August 2003, one of the first publicly reported incidents in which *Janjaweed* and government forces were accused of collaboration and responsibility for atrocities.[45] After the SLA forces occupied and then withdrew from Kutum town on August 3, 2003, at least 42 civilians were reported to have been summarily killed by *Janjaweed* militia deliberately targeting individuals based on ethnicity.[46] The Governor of North Darfur publicly denied allegations that the *Janjaweed* were supported by government forces.[47]

Several other documents from North and South Darfur states authorize "mobilization" (i.e., recruitment) of new militia members (often referred to as "volunteers") and the provision of military support to their camps and groups by government officials.

## North Darfur

Documents from North Darfur officials, including the office of the commissioner of Kutum, one of the largest towns in North Darfur, are explicit. Despite a public declaration on February 9, 2004 by Sudanese President Omar El Bashir that the war was over and there would be an "end of all military operations in Darfur," specific orders were issued from officials in Darfur calling for increased recruitment and military support to "allied" or "loyalist" tribes. Human Rights Watch obtained a directive dated February 2004, from the office of the Commissioner of Kutum Province in North Darfur bordering Chad.

The memorandum is marked "highly confidential" and is addressed to all those in charge of "mobilization" or "recruitment" in the provincial localities. The document refers to the "President of the Republic's directives declaring…an end of military activities in major areas of operations in Darfur and the withdrawal of all outlawed groups from the areas they used to occupy in the northern part of the state, and to guarantee the avoidance of a repetition of this, we recommend the following…." It then notes six steps in follow-up of the presidential statement. Rather than ending military operations, however, the document recommends: "Increase in the process of mobilizing loyalist tribes, and providing them with sufficient armory to secure the areas." This directive coincides with a marked increase in *Janjaweed* militia activity along the Chadian border, including cross-border incursions into Chad and attacks on refugee settlements along the border.[48]

An eyewitness who was in Musa Hilal's main camp in Mistriya, near Kebkabiya, in early 2004 confirmed this pattern of government support to the militias and told Human Rights Watch that government helicopters came to the camp three times per week and brought weapons, ammunition, letters, and provisions, including food.[49]

## South Darfur

Two of the documents authorizing recruitment and military support to the *Janjaweed* are from the office of the governor of South Darfur, the highest-ranking official in the state, who is directly appointed by the president of Sudan. A document dated November 22, 2003, describes the visit of the highest ranking state official in South Darfur, Governor Adam Hamid Mussa, and deputy Minister of the Interior from Khartoum (from the national government), Colonel Ahmad Haroun, to a *Janjaweed* camp in Qardud on November 18, 2003, where they requested that leaders "recruit 300 knights [armed horsemen or *Janjaweed*] for Khartoum." Governor Mussa was removed from his position by President El Bashir on June 24, 2004, apparently due to increasing international criticism of his role in channeling government support to ethnic militias.[50]

In another document from the office of the governor of South Darfur dated March 2, 2004, a directive is issued to Said Adam Jamaa, the Commissioner of Nyala, the largest town in and the capital of South Darfur, to form a security committee and increase the level of recruitment to ensure that the activities of the outlaws [i.e., rebels] are not brought into the state. Among the named members of the security committee are known tribal leaders responsible for mobilizing militia members from their communities. These individuals include:

Mohammed Adam Saliko, a *Janjaweed* leader of Saada ethnicity reported to be in charge of the al-Qardud training camp in South Darfur, who was rewarded by the governor of South Darfur in late 2003 with a place on the list of individuals permitted to go on the *hajj* or annual pilgrimage to Mecca; Mustafa Abu Nouba of the Southern Rizeigat ethnicity; and Mohammed Yacoub, an *omda* or leader of the Turjum ethnicity.

The document continues by requesting the Commissioner of Nyala to "swiftly deliver provisions and ammunition to the new camps to secure the south-western part of the state." This March directive directly coincides with reports of increased recruitment and military activity in South Darfur in March 2004, following SLA attacks in the Buram area.[51]

The document from the office of the commissioner of Kutum province, North Darfur State, dated February 12, 2004, also appears to validate claims that the Sudanese government has a plan to resettle lands from which the original inhabitants have been displaced. The memorandum recommends certain measures to guarantee the avoidance of the return of "outlaw forces from the areas they used to occupy" in North Darfur. The memorandum is addressed to those in charge of "orientation and mobilization branch at province localities" and recommends: "(1) Designing a plan for resettlement operations of nomads in places from which the outlaws withdrew, based upon field trip and evaluation operations." The same memorandum refers also to other measures that are consistent with a plan to move new persons into land that had been emptied of previous occupants and destroyed: "(2) Rehabilitate water resources, and open schools in these areas."

Human Rights Watch recently gathered new testimony in Chad indicating that resettlement activities in Darfur may be aimed not only at nomadic communities in Darfur, but also at Chadian Arab nomads, who in some locations are being encouraged to cross the border into Darfur and resettle land previously occupied by Darfurian farmers.

Another alarming feature of Sudanese government policy as recently stated by Sudanese Minister for the Interior Major General Abdel Rahim Mohammed Hussein on July 2, 2004, is the intention to create 18 "settlements" to host more than one million displaced persons, a plan which would "facilitate offering services and protection of the villagers who were previously living in numerous scattered villages."[52]

These statements raise the concern that rather than returning to their homes and lands, displaced civilians will be forced to remain in camps or permanently resettle in new locations, effectively consolidating the ethnic cleansing that has taken place.

The "highly confidential" February 2004 memorandum from the office of the Commissioner of Kutum also confirms the use of *Janjaweed* camps sited near major towns to "protect civilians." It specifically recommends: "(3) Opening of new camps for volunteers to protect civilians in major cities, and to conduct security missions among the citizens." Janjaweed militias have moved into rural areas in many areas of Darfur and have set up military camps outside the villages and towns from which they conduct reconnaissance missions and raids on villages.

*Janjaweed* patrol the areas around the major towns and villages, including the internally displaced people camps, and have also been given responsibilities for manning checkpoints along the main roads. Displaced persons venturing outside the camps have been subjected to serious abuses including rape, torture and robbery.[53] New *Janjaweed* camps have been reported from all three states in Darfur, including at Saraf Omra in North Darfur; Mercoondi in South Darfur; and Um Dukhun, Buram, and Abugradil in West Darfur. These are in addition to more than 12 existing *Janjaweed* militia camps in the three states.

Despite the April 8, 2004 cease-fire agreement signed by the government of Sudan and the SLA and JEM rebel groups, violence against civilians continues. On the contrary, the security situation appears to be deteriorating: Human Rights Watch has documented ongoing attacks on civilians by government forces and *Janjaweed* in North and West Darfur, a proliferation of armed groups along the Sudanese-Chadian border, and attacks on government-held towns and at least two confirmed incidents of kidnapping of aid workers by rebel groups.[54] In response to international demands that the government of Sudan protect civilians from the continuing insecurity, President El Bashir recently called for 6,000 new police to be recruited.[55] However, there are increasing allegations that instead of being disarmed and disbanded, *Janjaweed* militia members are being incorporated into these new police and military forces.

## MILITARIZED ETHNOKLEPTOCRACY

Ethnicity is not a backward or primordial phenomenon. Rather, it is a social construct created by rational human beings at specific times in their history. And ethnicity is created for specific purposes and is adapted and changed to fit changing needs. Ethnic consciousness has a strong correlation with the anxiety that often accompanies periods of change like democratization in Africa. During periods of change ethnic mobilization is most likely to be volatile or conflictual. It may even become very violent or militarized.

Nonetheless, ethnicity often provides a means to retain one's dignity and survive in hostile environments where one's culture, language, and beliefs are constantly denigrated. Each of these groups may become more cohesive due to their anxieties about their place in the new dispensation, especially when one attempts to assess the changes and adaptations, using factors such as electoral behavior.

The reemergence of multiparty politics in Africa in the 1990s ignited serious political power struggles between stakeholders. Power brokers preyed on their ethnic identities and differences to gain political leverage. The deeply engrained pattern of social inequality and exclusion within African societies surfaced. The overall syndrome of systematic exclusion from livelihood resources (jobs, security, freedom, and land), exclusion from public welfare schemes, from political participation, and, moreso, from the state as a collective social and cultural construct had reared its ugly head during the single-party days. This time, the syndrome exploded in violent clashes for political inclusion to share the spoils of political office before the doomsday comes. Many textbook examples abound. In Kenya between the Kikuyus and the people of Migori District of Nyanza Province in 1997, the civil wars in Somalia, Sudan, Ethiopia, Angola, the Congos, Sierra Leone, Burundi, Rwanda, just to cite a few, are violent crises due to the politicization and misuse of ethnic identities and disparities by those in possession of military and political power (Nyang'Oro, 1993).

In sum, the resurgence of the military and militia as a power factor in African democracies simply validates the hypotheses that: (1) democracies born in violence are more prone to periodic violent challenges than those born peacefully; (2) periodic violent challenges in democracies leave them less, rather than more, stable; and (3) when democracies break down they usually do so when a culture of violence is created. Second, the resurgence of militias in African politics cannot be separated from the basic material conditions that bring peoples of different ethnic and political backgrounds together. These material conditions include security, social relations of production, and political power. Thus, the menace of militias could be both functional and dysfunctional. No African state can feign to ignore its existence. And unless the state refocuses its energy toward expanding the political and economic space, it will be difficult invoking and enforcing a law against their existence. While the state and the militias dance around each other national security is precarious. The way out is for the state to pursue subsistence democracy—good governance for human security and development.

## References

ACP-EU. 2002. *The Courier*, January-February.

Ake, C. 1992. In J. Ihonvbere. (ed.) *The Political Economy of Crisis and Underdevelopment in Africa: Selected works of Claude Ake*. Lagos: Jad Publishers.

Elaigwu, J. I. 2001. "Ethnic Militias in Nigeria." Paper presented at a National Conference on *Ethnic Militias and National Security*, National War College, Abuja, Nigeria.

Huntington, Samuel P. 1957. *The Soldier and the State: The Theory and Politics of Civil-Military Relations*. New York: Vintage Books.

Hyden, G. 1988. "The Post Colonial State: Crisis and Reconstruction," *IDS Bulletin*, 19, 4.

Luttwark, Ed.N. 1969. "The Grand Strategy of the Roman Empire from the First ..." München. Münchner Beiträge zur Papyrusforschung und antiken Rechtsgeschichte 50.

Mbaku, John.1994. *Journal of Political and Military Sociology*. 22, Winter: 241-284.

McNamara, R.S. 1968. *The Essence of Security*, New York: Harper & Row.

Macrae, R. 2002. "Human Security in Globalised World" In R. Macrae and D. Hurbert (eds.), *Human Security and the New Diplomacy; Protecting People, Promoting Peace*. Montreal: McGill Queen's University Press.

Mentan, T. 2004. *Dilemmas of Weak States: Africa and Transnational Terrorism in the Twenty-First Century Africa*. London: Ashgate Publishers.

Nzongola-Ntalaja, G. 2002. "Regional Security in the Great Lakes and the Crisis in the Democratic Republic of Congo: Implications for Security and Development." Paper Presented at a one-day international seminar organized by the Centre for Advanced Security Studies in Africa, CASSIA, Abuja, April 26. CASSIA Seminar Paper Series).

Nyang'Oro, Julius E. (ed.).1993. *Discourse on Democracy: Africa, in Comparative Perspective*. Oxford: African Books Collective Ltd.

Obasi, N. O. 2002. *Ethnic Militias, Vigilantes and Separatist Groups in Nigeria*. Abuja: Third Millennium.

*SIPRI Yearbook*. 2003. *Armaments, Disarmament and International Security*. Oxford: Oxford University Press.

*SIPRI Yearbook, 2005,* Africa's Military Expenditure (estimates 1995-2004).

| Region | 1995 | 1996 | 1997 | 1998 | 1999 | 2000 | 2001 | 2002 | 2003 | 2004 | 1995-2004 |
|--------|------|------|------|------|------|------|------|------|------|------|-----------|
| Africa | 8.8 | 8.5 | 8.7 | 9.3 | 10.3 | 10.8 | 11.0 | 11.6 | 11.7 | 12.6 | + 43 |
| North | (3.4) | 3.5 | 3.7 | 3.8 | 3.9 | 4.3 | 4.4 | 4.8 | 4.9 | 5.5 | + 65 |
| Sub-Saharan | 5.5 | 5.0 | 5.0 | 5.5 | 6.3 | 6.5 | (6.6) | 6.8 | 6.8 | (7.1) | + 29 |

**Source:** *SIPRI Yearbook 2005*, appendix 8A, table 8A.1 and table 8A.3.

Figures are in US $b., at constant 2003 prices and exchange rates. Figures in italics are percentages. Figures do not always add up to totals because of the conventions of rounding.

**Africa:** Algeria, Angola, Benin, Botswana, Burkina Faso, Burundi, Cameroon, Cape Verde, Central African Republic, Chad, Congo (Republic of), Congo (Democratic Republic of, DRC), Côte d'Ivoire, Djibouti, Equatorial Guinea, Eritrea, Ethiopia, Gabon, Gambia, Ghana, Guinea, Guinea-Bissau, Kenya, Lesotho, Liberia, Libya, Madagascar, Malawi, Mali, Mauritania, Mauritius, Morocco, Mozambique, Namibia, Niger, Nigeria, Rwanda, Senegal, Seychelles, Sierra Leone, Somalia, South Africa, Sudan, Swaziland, Tanzania, Togo, Tunisia, Uganda, Zambia, Zimbabwe.

# Notes

1. Department of Defense, Foreign Military Sales, Foreign Military Construction Sales and Military Assistance Facts as of September 30, 1998 (Washington, DC,1999).

2. Stockholm International Peace Research Institute, *SIPRI Yearbook 1999: Armaments, Disarmament and International Security*. Oxford: Oxford University Press.

3. Demilitarization for Democracy, "Fighting Retreat: Military Political Power and Other Barriers to Africa's Democratic Transition," July 1997.

4 U.S. Department of Defense, *Foreign Military Sales, Foreign Military Construction Sales and Military Assistance Fact as of September 30, 1998. Washington, DC, 1999.*

5. Bureau of Intelligence and Research, Bureau of Public Affairs, U.S. Department of State, "Arms and Conflict in Africa." Washington, DC, July 1999.

6. U.S. Department of Defense, *Foreign Military Sales, Foreign Military Construction Sales and Military Assistance Facts as of September 30, 1998.* Washington, DC, 1999.

7. Data cited are from U.S. Arms Control and Disarmament Agency, *World Military Expenditures and Arms Transfers 1997* (Washington, DC: ACDA, 1999), Table III; and Richard F. Grimmett, Conventional Arms Transfers to Developing Nations, 1991-1998 (Washington, DC: CRS, August 4, 1999), p. 58.

8. Brian Wood and Johan Peleman, *The Arms Fixers: Controlling the Brokers and Shipping Agents*, a joint report by the British Security Information Council, the Norwegian Institute on Small Arms Transfers, and the Peace Research Institute Oslo. (Oslo: PRIO, 1999), p. 2.

9. U.S. Department of Defense, *Foreign Military Sales, Foreign Military Construction Sales and Military Assistance Facts. Washington, DC: 1981, 1990, and 1997* editions.

10. U.S. State Department, *Congressional Presentation for Foreign Operations, FY 1986*, p. 333.

11. U.S. Department of Defense, *Foreign Military Sales.*

12. Human Rights Watch, "Clinton Administration Policy and Human Rights in Africa," March 1998.

13. David Schearer, "Africa's Great War," *Survival*, International Institute for Strategic Studies, 41, 2, Summer 1999, p. 92.

14. U.S. State Department, *Congressional Presentation for Foreign Operations, FY 1999*, p. 79.

15. U.S. State Department, *Congressional Presentation for Foreign Operations, FY 2000*, p. 96.

16. See the International Crisis Group's "Congo at War: A Briefing on the Internal and External Players in the Central African Conflict," November 1998, for further detail on international involvement in the war.

17. See Schearer, "Africa's Great War."

18. U.S. Department of Defense, *Foreign Military Sales.*

19. Human Rights Watch, "Angola: Arms Trade and Violations of the Laws of Wars Since the 1992 Elections," November 1994.

20. Donald McNeil, "A War Turned Free-for-All Tears at Africa's Center," *The New York Times*, December 6, Week in Review, p. 5.

21. Al Venter, "Arms Pour Into Africa," *New African*, January 19, pp. 10-15.

22. Ibid.

23. Kathi Austin, "Hearts of Darkness," *Bulletin of Atomic Scientists*, January/February 1999.

24. Reuters and CNN reports, March 8-10, 1999.

25. U.S. Department of Defense, *Foreign Military Sales.*

26. U.S. Department of Defense, ACSS Program Outline, July 1999.

27. U.S. Department of Defense, *Report on Training of Special Operations Forces*, April 1, 1998, and *Foreign Military Training and DoD Engagement Activities of Interest, FY1998 and FY1999*, April 23, 1999.

28. Research estimate by Demilitarization for Democracy. See Lynne Duke, "Africans Use Training in Unexpected Ways," and Dana, Priest, "Special Forces Training Review Sought," *Washington Post*, July 14-15, 1998.

29. Ambassador Marshal McCallie, Special Coordinator for ACRI, quoted in "U.S. Diplomat Pleads with ACRI," *The Independent*, January 14, 1999.

30. Daniel Volman, "Africa Policy Report: The Development of the African Crisis Response Initiative," April 23, 1998.

31. Ibid.

32. Department of Defense, "ACSS Program Outline," July 1999.

33. Clarissa Kayosa, "Open Letter on the Africa Center for Security Studies," Demilitarization for Democracy, September 1999.

34. See, among others, Human Rights Watch (HRW) reports: "Darfur in Flames: Atrocities in Western Sudan," Vol.16, No.5 (A), April 2004; "Darfur Destroyed: Ethnic Cleansing by Government and Militia Forces in Western Sudan," Vol.16, No. 6 (A), May 2004; Report of the High Commissioner on the Situation of Human Rights in the Darfur region of the Sudan, E/CN.4/2005/3, U.N. Office of the High Commissioner of Human Rights, May 3, 2004; "Darfur: Too Many People Killed for No Reason," *Amnesty International*, February 3, 2004.

35. "Presidential Political Decree to Resolve the Darfur Conflict," June 20, 2004, Embassy of the Republic of Sudan website at http://www.sudanembassy.org/default.asp?page=viewstory&id=280, and Joint Communiqué between the Government of Sudan and the United Nations on the occasion of the visit of the UNSG to Sudan, July 3, 2004.

36. The term "Janjaweed" has become the source of increasing controversy, with different actors using the term in very different ways. Literally, the term is reported to be an amalgamation of three Arabic words for ghost, gun, and horse that historically referred to criminals, bandits, or outlaws. In the wake of the conflict in Darfur, many "African" victims of attacks have used the term to refer to the government-backed militias attacking their villages, many of whom are drawn from nomadic groups of Arab ethnic origin. Victims have also used other terms, such as *fursan* and *peshmarga* to describe these government-backed militias. The Sudanese government and members of the government-backed militias themselves reject the name "janjaweed" and appear to use it to refer to criminals and outlaws, see "Sudan Arabs Reject Marauding 'Janjaweed' Image," *Reuters*, July 12, 2004. Other terms used by the Sudanese government include "outlaws" and "Tora Bora," to refer to the rebels, and "knights," "mujaheeden" or "horsemen," which appear to refer to members of its own militias.

37. Darfur has been the site of intermittent intercommunal conflict between groups of nomadic camel and cattle-herders and sedentary agriculturalists due to desertification and increasing competition for land and water resources. The Janjaweed are clearly also stakeholders in the Darfur conflict. Many of the members of the Janjaweed have been recruited from specific nomadic groups of Arab ethnic origin who have been involved in clashes with the so-called African farmers in previous years. The willingness of some members of the nomadic groups to take part in the conflict as an auxiliary force is no doubt linked to their interest in acquiring land and livestock. See also HRW, "Darfur in Flames," at footnote 1.

38. The Sudanese government's use of militias or proxy forces is not new. Numerous ethnic militias have been supported and used as proxy forces in southern Sudan throughout the conflict of the past two decades.

39. A Human Rights Watch report on recent attacks and violations of the ceasefire in Darfur and Chad is forthcoming.

40. IRIN, "Interview with Government Humanitarian Aid Commissioner on the Darfur Crisis," April 7, 2004 at www.sudan.net.

41. Agence France Presse, "Sudan Will Not Disarm Militias While Rebellion Rages: Foreign Minister," May 14, 2004.

42. "We Will Not Appease the Americans by Capturing Tribal Leaders," *Al Wan*, July 5, 2004.

43. On file with Human Rights Watch. These documents cannot be reproduced in full due to security concerns, however all of the documents bear official stamps, seals, and/or letterhead of the respective offices of origin that correspond with those seen on other documents from the same sources. Human Rights Watch has reproduced parts of these documents exactly as they are written in the original.

44. The presence of (People's defense Force (PDF) among the Sudanese government forces in Darfur has been noted by several sources. Some of the Janjaweed militia were allegedly trained at PDF camps in 2003. See for instance, "Militias Ravage Darfur in Gangs of Hundreds," IRIN, March 10, 2004, see http://wwww.relief-web.int/w/rwb.nsf/3a81e21068ec1871c1256633003c1c6f/f2f40c858beed2084 9256e530027080d?OpenDocument.

45. "Sudan Rebels Accuse Pro-government Militias of Killing 300 in Darfur," *Agence France Presse*, August 11, 2004.

46. "Immediate Steps to Protect Civilians and Internally Displaced Persons in Darfur," *Amnesty International,* August 29. 2003. A survivor of the Kutum massacre has stated that over 60 individuals were killed.

47. Ibid.

48. "Sudan-Chad: Cross-border Conflict Escalates," IRIN, March 16, 2004, see http://wwww.reliefweb.int/w/rwb.nsf/3a81e21068ec1871c1256633003c1c6f/e0f1adb1bfd2b0d985256e590069c777?OpenDocument.

49. Human Rights Watch interview, June 2004. Further details are confidential in order to protect the security of this witness.

50. The new governor of South Darfur is Alhaj Atta el-Mannan Idris, a former commissioner of South Darfur state and currently secretary general of the National Congress Party for Khartoum state. He is reputed to have close links to Vice-President Ali Osman Mohammed Taha.

51. *Agence France Presse*, "Sudan Turns Down Request for Aid Agencies to Extend Operations," March 15, 2004.

52. *Agence France Presse*, "Sudan to Set up 18 'Settlements' for Million Darfur Refugees: Report," July 2, 2004.

53. See HRW, "Darfur Destroyed," May 2004; "UN Agencies Report Mixed Progress on Enhancing Humanitarian Access," *UN News Service*, July 12, 2004.

54. See Human Rights Watch report on ceasefire violations and other abuses, July 2004.

55. "Presidential Political Decree to Resolve the Darfur Conflict," June 20, 2004, see footnote 2. See also: "Sudan: Threat of Forced Return Looming in Darfur," IRIN, July 12, 2004. As noted in the recommendations of the UN Office of the High Commissioner of Human Rights, May 7, 2004, and the conclusions of the EU General Affairs Council, July 12, 2004.

# Chapter 5

# Democracy Besieged by Africa's Crises

Why are the democratic prospects of African countries so poor? After all, in most African states a high level of popular support exists for the concept of democracy. In practice, popular support for democracy is a necessary, but not a sufficient, condition for democratic institutions to emerge. Other factors are necessary. Hypothetical support for representative government, absent tangible support for liberal political norms and values and without the foundation of a pluralistic civil society, provides neither sufficient stimulus nor staying power for democracy to take root. That reality was borne out over the past generation in numerous countries where authoritarian regimes were displaced by newly democratic multiparty regimes but democratization failed or is failing because of shallow foundations and a retreat to geriatric autocracy.

The building blocks of a durable modern democratic political culture are not institutional in nature. The building blocks are not elections, parties, and legislatures. Rather, the building blocks of democracy are supportive cultural values. That is to say, the long-term survival of democratic institutions requires a particular political culture. Four cultural factors play an essential, collective role in stimulating and reinforcing a stable democratic political system: political trust, social tolerance, a widespread recognition of the importance of basic political liberties, and popular support for gender equality and empowerment.

Paradoxically, a more democratic Africa may also be a repressive one. It is one thing to adopt formal democracy but quite another to attain stable democracy. A successful democracy cannot be legislated. The Western world is placing a very large political wager that the formation of democratic institutions in Africa can stimulate a democratic political culture. On the contrary, political culture shapes democracy far more than democracy shapes political culture. Therefore, the West and international financial institutions (IFIs) may need to compromise their democratic ideals with a healthy dose of pragmatism. Democracy is an evolutionary development rather than an overnight phenomenon. In fact, it is a fruit of the people's struggle.

Democratic government and civil society are central accomplishments and lasting challenges in modern societies. According to the prevailing consensus and the constitutional order, democratic government is accepted to be the legitimate and effective vehicle for political integration and conflict resolution. A sufficient measure of "civility" within a society is expected, both regarding social interaction based on norms of mutual recognition and societal engagement in achieving "civility" as a common good.

Can African states prove their validity when taking into consideration new regulatory problems and conflicts associated with the globalization or transnationalization (in the least) of social dynamics? They must prove their strength for the new democracies of transition societies and developing countries, whose economic and cultural history differs from that of Western democracies—the origin of liberal democratic developments. Worldwide economic interdependence, global ecological hazards, and migratory pressures question the ability of nation-states to take action and fragment (national) states. How does (and must) democracy adapt? How important is political governance with the help of civil society in achieving self-organization? How is democratic participation of the population/public achieved? How do types of violence and types of control develop? This range of questions roughly outlines the issues besieging liberal democracy in Africa today.

## CRISIS OF CONSTITUTIONALISM

Constitutionalism is the idea often associated with the political theories of John Locke and the "founders" of the American republic, that government can and should be legally limited in its powers, and that its authority depends on its observing these limitations. This idea brings with it a host of vexing questions of interest not only to legal scholars, but to anyone keen to explore the legal and philosophical foundations of the state. How can a government be legally limited if law is the creation of government? Does this mean that a government can be "self-limiting," or is there some way of avoiding this implication? If meaningful limitation is to be possible, must constitutional constraints be somehow "entrenched"? Must they be enshrined in written rules? If so, how are they to be interpreted? In terms of literal meaning or the intentions of their authors, or in terms of the, possibly ever-changing, values they express? How one answers these questions depends crucially on how one conceives the nature, identity, and authority of constitutions. Does a constitution establish a stable framework for the exercise of public power which is in some way fixed by factors like the original meaning or intentions? Or is it a "living tree" that grows and develops in tandem with changing political values and principles? These and other such questions are explored below.

In some minimal sense of the term, a "constitution" consists of a set of rules or norms creating, structuring, and defining the limits of governmental power or authority. Understood in this way, all states have constitutions and all states are constitutional states. Anything recognizable as a state must have some acknowledged means of constituting and specifying the limits (or lack thereof) placed upon the three basic forms of government power: legislative power (making new laws), executive power (implementing laws), and judicial power (adjudicating disputes under laws). Take the extreme case of an absolute monarch, late Gnassingbe Eyadema of Togo, who combined unlimited power in all three domains. If it is widely acknowledged that he had these powers, as well as the authority to exercise them at his pleasure, then the constitution of the Togolese state could be said to contain only one rule, which granted unlimited power to Eyadema. He was not *legally* answerable for the wisdom or morality of his decrees, nor was he bound by procedures, or any other kinds of limitations or requirements, in exercising his powers. Whatever he decreed was constitutionally valid.

When scholars talk of constitutionalism, however, they normally mean something that rules out a case like that of Eyadema. They mean not only that there are rules creating legislative, executive, and judicial powers, but that these rules impose limits on those powers. Often these limitations are in the form of individual or group rights against government, rights to things like free expression, association, equality, and due process of law.

Constitutionalism can therefore be defined as adherence to the letter and spirit of the constitution. It upholds the supremacy of the constitution and requires that government officials must obey and operate within the framework of the law. It is important that a country not only should have a good constitution but that the principles of constitutionalism are adhered to. As Okoth-Ogendo has argued, since the 1960s in Africa, there appears to be a commitment to the idea of constitution, but at the same time, there is a rejection of the classical notion of constitutionalism (Okoth-Ogendo, 1991). In any case, constitutionalism has to be understood in the context of power relations (Mandaza, 1991). Scholars have argued that there is a new concept of constitutionalism, which should rest on accountable/responsive state and collective rights and freedoms (Shivji, 1991).

It has also been argued that this new constitutionalism has become an integral part of the African political reform process (Ihonvbere, 2000). According to Ihonvbere, this new trend has been encouraged by several factors. First, there is an increased support for democratization and civil society by sub regional, continental, and international organizations such as the Economic Community of West African states (ECOWAS), the Southern Africa Development Community (SADC), the Organization of African Unity (OAU), the Commonwealth, the European Union (EU) and the United Nations. Second, there is a new acknowledgment all over Africa of the salience of pluralism and its centrality to the democratic process. Third, new coalitions and networks are emerging all over Africa as platforms for training new leaders, demystifying dictatorships, and articulating alternative agendas for democratization. Furthermore, at the end of the Cold War, there are no more superpowers that use all the resources at their disposal to maintain unpopular and illegitimate regimes. Moreover, there appears to be a consensus all over the world that military regimes are not only an aberration and unacceptable but must be resisted. Recently, the Assembly of the Heads of State of the OAU decided that they would not admit military rulers in their meetings. The Centre for Democracy and Development (CDD) aptly captured the new trend when it stated:

> At every level on the continent, the idea has taken root that the Leviathans of Africa must no longer function as "virtual democracies" (Joseph, 1997) but must be refashioned to reflect the realities of their multifaceted societies. This has been reflected in the constitutional Conferences in Benin, Mali, Togo, Niger, the Democratic Republic of the Congo, and ... in the early 1990s, in the successful constitutional arrangement of South Africa, and in the process-based constitutional commissions in Uganda and Eritrea...Today, the struggle for constitutional reform in Kenya, Tanzania, Zimbabwe and Nigeria typifies the second liberation/independence struggle in the continent. The struggle has been led predominantly by civil society in Africa, since the political parties have proved either incapable or unwilling to push for constitutions that will promote just and equitable societies, being instead distracted by a chance to exercise power. (CDD, 2000: 33-34)

All these conferences were held in Francophone Africa. However, there remains a flaw that can be exploited very easily by the military and incumbent regimes. The Côte d'Ivoire example is eloquent. The coup-prevention strategies implemented for decades by the civilian regime in Côte d'Ivoire did not institutionalize civilian control of the military. Rather, the evidence indicates that military professionalization, political insulation, and regime legitimization in the socio-economic and political spheres were ominously lacking in the strategies adopted by that country. Coup-prevention strategies in Côte d'Ivoire involved unscrupulous ethnic manipulation, politicization, and cooptation of military officers into the "inner circles of power" by late President Houphouet Boigny. These strategies contributed significantly to the 1999 military coup in Côte d'Ivoire. *Coups d'état* in such states are very likely due to the lack of constitutionalization of reciprocal obligations in civil-military relations.

Much of Africa's experience with modern governmental systems has known little else but presidents, prime ministers and supreme one-party or military leaders. These have been so powerful that their claims to democracy compel proof. Many African leaders accepted and participated in the democratic process after the collapse of the military and single- party systems of government as a means to an end. Democracy was perceived to be a vehicle or conduit pipe for personal power and gain. The situation is compounded by poverty. Most politicians in Africa see the state as the primary source of accumulation of wealth. This economic interest motivates the drive toward the monopolization of power by a ruling party. Multiparty frameworks are seen as obstacles to the accumulation of wealth by the chief (thief?) of State and his cronies. In this context it is easy to understand how incumbent governments use governmental resources like constitutions to exclude their political opponents from power. Transport, the public media, constitutions, and public security legislation are also used to take undue advantage of financially enfeebled and institutionally weak opposition parties during elections whose results are even proclaimed by French President Jacques Chirac from Paris before the vote-counting is done in Cameroon. This congratulatory message was sent to Paul Biya following the October 11, 2004, presidential election. And the drama about the congratulatory message of Chirac to Mr. Biya before the votes were even counted confirms that many "African democrats" and their foreign sponsors are not yet at ease with the verdict of the ballot box.

The legitimacy of any constitution-making process is fundamental. Legitimacy is also dependent upon an unequivocal commitment by the ruling party to that constitution (Ebrahim, 2002: 17). However, this principle will invariably be fashioned by the domestic social and political realities within which the process takes place. Some African countries have experienced constitutional instability since independence because constitutions have lacked moral authority. All too often, when a constitutional review commission is set up, governments have tended to appoint commissioners who are sympathetic to the government of the day. If the general public takes the view that the commissioners are sympathetic to, or are cronies of, the ruling party, they will shun the constitution-making exercise as a government stage-managed charade. Beyond this point, when a constitutional review body submits its findings and recommendations, sitting governments have chosen to accept only those recommendations that they find to be politically expedient for their survival in government. In some cases, governments have been known to ignore original submissions that normally form the blueprint around which the evolving constitution is to be finalized (Monze, 2003: 5). Other presidents discard the constitution as soon as it is promulgated and rule by decree.

The well-known doctrine of "separation of powers" between legislative, executive, and judiciary is vital for any true democracy. There should be at least an impartial Constitutional court in defense of the integrity of the judiciary. In the context of the criticism of a judge who ruled against President Mandela in South Africa in a certain matter, a frank-speaking advocate said:

> The country can ill afford at this stage of its development to allow politicians to use the judiciary as an instrument to achieve their political objectives. The events in Zimbabwe show very clearly that complacency in this regard can lead to anarchy and the destruction of the democratic system. Those who doubt this are reminded that today the politicians will target white Afrikaner judges who were appointed during the apartheid era; next they will target white liberal judges who were appointed during the apartheid era; and thereafter they will target all white judges irrespective of when they were appointed. Finally they will target all judges. If men and women of principle fail to protect the institution today, it may be too late when they realize the need to do so. (Mtshaulana, 1999: 541)

Constitutionalism will be inherently flawed without an overriding respect for its purposes, including respect for the rights of the people. Because of corruption, nepotism, and the high stakes involved in transferring or maintaining power, the political process is too often devoid of any of the basic agreement on the nature of politics that is vital for democratic continuity.

We often hear of attempts to "Africanize" democracy in Southern Africa. For example, in August 1997 a Zimbabwean senior minister said that foreigners masquerading as champions of democracy in Africa are in fact seeking access to wealth rather than entrenching human rights. He claimed that democracy had no roots in the history and experience of local (especially rural) people, except for learned academics who were imposing an interpretation of the worldview among the people. He insisted that Africans can never run a democracy better than the Americans or the British; just as well they cannot run a chieftainship like Africans. So this political adventurism will only encourage dissent and instability within African society. While it cannot be denied that the lack of Western democratic tradition makes some of its principles difficult to understand or implement, these principles are more conducive to protecting basic human rights than autocratic regimes, and are not supposed to be in any way "culturally relative" in principle.

Policies allowing the establishment and semiautonomy of traditional villages to preserve African identity could reduce alienation of rural people to their government if they fostered communication, and offered respect for the right of their people to basic freedoms: recognition of differing political opinions, and accountability and responsibility of their leaders. Without these principles, claims to "democracy" would be nothing more than a sham. For example, the end of military rule in Nigeria is no guarantee of democracy, because it is very likely that the military will remain powerful enough to remove (or accept endless bribes from) presidents it doesn't like, as it did in removing General Babangida.

In sum, at independence, the constitutions adopted by most African countries embodied the rights and freedoms associated with liberal democracies. However, over time as single-party regimes or military dictatorships took hold, they were generally replaced, revised, suspended, or simply ignored. In recent years constitutionalism has been revived as part of the process of political liberalization, and a number of African countries have either revised or adopted new constitutions to limit hitherto excessive executive powers and provide for rights and liberties in line with international human rights conventions. Throughout the continent, emphasis on constitutional conferences or on public discussion of constitutional provisions reflects attempts to craft documents that have public relevance and support. Although in some instances the process of constitution-making or amending remained firmly in the grasp of the incumbent political elite, in others attempts were made to reflect a broader range of views. Few African countries, however, have enjoyed a process as participatory as South Africa's, and few have invested as much in trying to make constitutional provisions known to the majority of citizens.

Although some of the new constitutions retain repressive provisions, most embody democratic principles. Doubts, however, remain over their actual enforcement. To be truly meaningful, constitutional provisions need to be translated into legislation that is effectively implemented, and leaders have to accept that they are bound by the rule of law. This remains a challenge in many instances. Given the persistence of a political culture of arbitrariness, the tendency for high-level public authorities in many countries to behave with impunity, and the significant shortcomings of the judiciary and law- enforcement systems, citizens do not yet repose much confidence in constitutional and legal arrangements to protect them from persecution and aggravation.

## RESILIENT CRISIS OF THE PATRIMONIAL STATE

The resilience of the patrimonial state (Chabal, 1997) refers to the economic causes of the African crisis. The political systems hastily put in place at independence were similar to those of the colonial metropolis. However, the reality of postcolonial Africa is that, whatever the constitutional niceties of the newly independent countries, politics was very rapidly organized around the practices of patrimonialism—that is, the establishment of patron/client networks fed by resources from the state. Indeed, the very legitimacy of postcolonial regimes hinged on the extent to which the political patrons were able to fulfill their obligations to their clients.

The patrimonial state is not, of course, a system of economic management that is conducive to development as we define it, although in economically propitious circumstances it can create the conditions for stable polities. This is because its prime economic logic is to display the ostentation and feed the patron/client networks required for holding power rather than to accumulate in order to invest productively, which is the foundation of capitalism.

Trade is even more central to growth. But a patrimonial state cannot achieve this goal of creating wealth through trade. The *Economist, (2003),* in its front-page story "The Cancun Challenge" wrote:

> A new analysis by the World Bank, published in its Global Economic Prospects on September 3rd, suggests that an ambitious, though achievable, reduction of trade barriers in the Doha round could boost global income by between $290 billion and $520 billion a year. Well over half of these gains would go to poor countries. By 2015, the World Bank reckons, a successful Doha round could lift 144m people out of poverty.

This prediction has no prospects of being materialized. The patrimonial state is not credited with the pursuit of trade and productive economic ventures. The economic circumstances of the last 30 years, however, have been such as to prevent any virtuous transition from patrimonialism. In the absence of substantial wealth creation, African patrimonial states are simply unable to continue to feed the networks that linked those in power with the rest of the population.

The marginalization of the African continent from the global economy has been reflected in its declining share of world trade and direct foreign investment. The relevant data (World Bank, 2000) have been systematically collected and presented by a consortium of African and international agencies in *Can Africa Reclaim the 21st Century?* Most African countries have now undergone between one and two decades of externally supported programs aimed at generating more efficient and productive market economies. The African Growth and Opportunity Act, enacted during the Clinton administration has been broadened placing the expansion of trade and investment at the center of U.S.-Africa policy. In brief, on May 18, 2000 President Clinton signed into law the historic Trade and Development Act of 2000, containing the African Growth and Opportunity Act (AGOA). The Act provided unprecedented opportunities and aimed to:

— Promote increased trade and investment between the United States and sub-Saharan African countries by providing eligible African countries with unprecedented liberal access to the U.S. market. Essentially all products of these eligible countries will have quota free/duty free access to the almost 10 trillion dollar United States market.

— Promote economic development and reform in sub-Saharan Africa, moving across a wide range of industries, granting tangible benefits to entrepreneurs, farmers, and families.

— Promote increased access and opportunities for U.S. investors and businesses in sub-Saharan Africa.

The African Growth and Opportunity Act offered a wide variety of benefits to businesses, workers, manufacturers, and farmers in eligible countries. It is important to remember that the Act can only offer opportunities! African countries are encouraged to seize the opportunities provided in the Act and to create enabling environments to strengthen prospects for expanded trade and investment.

Urgent attention is needed to enable the many studies that highlight the political impediments to economic growth in Africa. A leading student of these efforts, Nicolas van de Walle (2001: 235-286), has investigated "the failure of African economies to renew with sustained economic growth over the last twenty years." Here are the main causes he identifies in his study:

> The central argument of this book is that . . . the real constraints on policy are to be found within the state itself. Three kinds of factors are emphasized in particular: clientelism, low state capacity, and the ideological preferences of decision makers. . . . Second, I argue that the aid relationship between Western donors and most African regimes has exacerbated these domestic obstacles to reform. Neo-patrimonial rulers could not have resisted the pressure of international markets for two decades had they not had the assistance of the international community; large amounts of aid to the state coupled with imperfect conditionality of reform program lending have allowed African governments to get away with partial reform.

The study by Van de Walle is not only a sweeping portrayal of the failure to transform Africa's low-performing economies, it also makes a strong case that the factors most responsible for the disappointing outcomes are largely unchanged. The wave of democratic transitions since 1990, he argues, has not altered the exercise of power or the "toothless conditionality" of external donors. It is difficult to reconcile the Van de Walle critique with the promises currently being made by African governments and major international donors. The criteria for granting aid and loans have been refined, over and again, and applied by the U.S. Agency for International Development and other agencies. The conclusions formulated by Van de Walle confirm earlier studies of the ineffectiveness of the conditionalities regime by such scholars as Thomas Callaghy and Beatrice Hibou. Other factors and considerations usually intervened to influence the allocation of grant funds and distort their utilization (Callaghy and Ravenhill, 1993; and Hibou, 1996).

In the face of dwindling resources, African politicians still seek to borrow abroad in order to maintain the patrimonial structure on which their political legitimacy depends. Bereft of resources, the holders of state power resort increasingly to thievery and predatory autocracy characterized by coercion. The attendant result is that they both lose support and undermine the very legitimacy of the political system in place. For the patrimonial state to continue, the exercise of power is becoming much more nakedly violent and, inevitably, opposition to the state itself is taking on an increasingly violent hue--a spiral of force of which Côte d'Ivoire is only one of the most extreme cases. In some terminal cases, such as Zaire in those days of Marshall Mobutu or Liberia in those days of Charles Taylor, the nation-state ceases to exist.

Corporate interests and activities in Africa have also contributed to exploitation, conflict, and poverty for ordinary people while enriching African and foreign elites-the emergent transnational capitalist class. Russell Mokhiber and Robert Weissman in a ZNet Commentary of March 30, 1999, decried:

> such suspect friends of Africa as Chevron, Mobil, Exxon, Enron, Caterpillar, Bristol-Myers-Squibb, Bank of America, the Gap, Texaco, Amoco, Citicorp, Kmart, and Coca-Cola. These companies are among the members of US Africa, the corporate lobby for NAFTA for Africa. It is no accident that oil companies are so prominent among the NAFTA for Africa supporters bill in the U.S. Congress. The legislation would further open up African countries to exploitation by multinational resource corporations, and prevent countries from taking steps to control the drilling, mining, harvesting and use of resources within their own borders.

The basic structure of the African trade bill is to condition some minor new aid and trade benefits in African countries opening their economies to foreign investment and adopting the recessionary "structural adjustment" policies of the International Monetary Fund. The conditionalities in the bill include: compliance with programs of and obligations to the IMF, joining the World Trade

Organization, removing restrictions on foreign investment, minimizing government market interventions, and privatizing many government operations.

The debate that followed over the African trade bill in the U.S. Congress was different than the previous one in at least one critical respect: Representative Jesse Jackson, Jr., D-Illinois, has instilled a genuine pro-Africa bill into the debate. Jackson—who abandoned his support for the NAFTA for Africa bill after he learned how harmful it would be, and began calling the legislation the Africa Recolonization Act—introduced the African HOPE (Human Rights, Opportunity, Partnership, and Empowerment) Act. Sixty members of Congress, including Democratic Minority Whip David Bonior, D-Michigan, cosponsored the HOPE bill, which stands as a viable alternative to the Growth and Opportunity Act. The idea is that when African elites league with American corporate interests to spoliate the continent their predatory activities ignite resentment among most Africans. Thus Bob Geldof (2004) is right when he says:

> ... imposing ... cultural beliefs on other people, whether by economic muscle or cruise missile, so that they can be more like us is a farce, particularly when the obvious external purpose is regional control of resources and political influence.

## CRISIS DUE TO DERELICTION OF POLITICAL ACCOUNTABILITY

Political party finance and related corruption pose one of the greatest threats to democratic and economic development worldwide. Corruption in politics, particularly during election periods, compromises a critical asset of democracy: the faith and support of ordinary citizens in the political system. When political parties fail to appeal to voters through the development of party platforms or suffer from weak institutional capacities, they often turn to vote-buying as a means to securing support. This in turn creates competitive election spending, driving up the cost of getting elected. As a result of high campaign costs, political parties become increasingly dependent on monied interests or, in the case of incumbents, on the wrongful use of state resources. Consequently, the basic underlying principles of democracy—such as one-person, one-vote, and government accountability—are undermined and public confidence in the political process is eroded. In some cases, already limited public funds are diverted for private gain.

Over the past several years, party financing scandals have shaken countries in every region of the world, drawing increased international attention to the problem. In response, government officials and activists have launched public awareness campaigns and introduced legislative initiatives designed to restrict spending or improve disclosure about the sources of party funding and the expenditure of campaign funds. The success of these efforts varies and typically depends on a combination of legislation, enforcement regimes, and sustained political will for reform, and public pressure to demand more accountability in politics. In Africa, despite growing awareness about the negative impact of political corruption, solutions to the problem have yet to fully emerge.

Accountability is the hallmark of a democratic system. The process can be divided into two stages. The first stage makes a public servant accountable to the politician; the second makes politicians accountable, through the representative system, to the public at large. Accountability involves supplying the public with relevant information. There are a number of facets to the concept of accountability that can broadly be broken down to legal, political, administrative, and financial accountability issues.

The main reason why the patrimonial system spun out of control is because of the lack of political accountability in postcolonial Africa. The transfer of power that followed decolonization established formal systems of political accountability—broadly, parliamentary democracy—with no historical roots in the continent. The democratic political framework was an artificial construct, hastily put in place by the departing colonial powers and readily embraced by the nationalists because it was the price to pay to be entrusted with control over the postcolonial state. Of course, when parliamentary democracy works it does provide an efficient system of political accountability. However, it was naïve to assume that the hurried establishment of parliamentary democracy in former colonies with no actual experience of such a form of government would result in a functioning system of democratic political accountability.

The experience of postcolonial Africa is, without a doubt, varied and complex but, by and large, it is one in which rulers have been able to flout the constitutional mechanisms of political accountability put in place at independence, as the checkered history of Nigeria and Ghana amply demonstrates. They inherited the colonial state, a highly bureaucratic and coercive state bereft of democratic tradition, and with it the machinery of force. Their legitimacy originally stemmed from their success as nationalists, not from their democratic credentials. As time passed, nationalism became increasingly irrelevant, the patrimonial state weakened, and its legitimacy faded. The failures of government led to increasing demands for more accountability.

Political accountability, insofar as it existed under the patrimonial state, took the form of a certain redistribution of state resources by those in power to their national, regional, or ethnic folks. Where there were sufficient resources to lubricate the system of patronage, clients and their dependents accepted the politics of the authoritarian one-party state or military rule as reasonably accountable. As the economic crisis grew more severe and resources dwindled, patron-client relations began to dissolve. In the absence of any other form of political accountability, rulers sought to keep power by force. The recourse to coercion invalidated the legitimacy of the fragile edifice of postcolonial political accountability.

> The predicament of postcolonial Africa from the 1970s was thus severe: How could Africans generate new forms of political accountability in an environment marked by the collapse of the patrimonial

state, the abuse of power, and a growing economic crisis? They could not. To recognize the difficulties, however, is not to say that change in the 1990s is impossible. The current move toward greater democratization is thus partly fueled by the very strong desire of Africans for political systems in which rulers will, again, be accountable to those over whom they rule. What it would mean for African rulers to be accountable will, then, be determined by Africans themselves.

By the 1990s, bureaucratic corruption had become a major public issue that permeated the entire bureaucracy. The extensive network of corruption in the public sector ranged from petty fixers operating at lower levels of the organizational hierarchy, to mid-level officials taking undue advantage of their positions and extending to the elite whose profit from corrupt transactions with government ran into millions of US dollars, but whose positions and powerful connections rendered them virtually untouchable by the law enforcement authorities. Dereliction of duty, bribery, engaging in frauds, illegal executions and transactions and misappropriation of public funds or property were regarded as criminal offenses of the public officials by the penal codes. The corrupt public officials preyed on powerless and uninformed citizens. But in the face of the present dereliction of accountability, African leaders have resorted to use techniques of political instrumentalization of social disorder, patronage, and naked force to survive in power.

## CRISIS OF THE POLITICAL INSTRUMENTALIZATION OF DISORDER

The paradigm for analysis is the "political instrumentalization of disorder" coined by Patrick Chabal (1997). In brief, it refers to the process by which political actors in Africa seek to maximize their returns on the state of disorder and uncertainty that characterizes most African polities. Although there obviously are vast differences between countries in this respect, all African nation-states share is a generalized system of patrimonialism (however destitute) and an acute degree of apparent disorder, as evidenced by a high degree of governmental and administrative inefficiency, a lack of instrumental institutionalization, a general disregard for the rules of the formal political and economic sectors, and a universal resort to personal(ized) solutions to societal problems.

To understand politics in such a context is to understand the ways in which individuals, groups, communities, and societies seek to instrumentalize the resources they command within this general moral economy of disorder. To speak of disorder is not, of course, to speak of irrationality. It is merely to make explicit the observation that political action operates, rationally, but largely in the realm of a world that is not ordered in the sense in which the West usually takes its own polities to be. There is, however, logic to disorder, or perhaps even chaos, even if that logic is, at first sight, incomprehensible to the outside observer.

In an ordered, regulated polity, political opportunities and resources are defined explicitly and codified by legislation or precedent. Order is secured by functioning institutions (in the Weberian sense). In a world of disorder, however, there is necessarily a premium both on the personal (as opposed to institutional) relations through which the "business" of politics can be conducted and on access to the means of maximizing the returns that the "domestication" of such disorder demands. To give an example, if the permeability of borders is arbitrary, as this is commonplace in Africa, personal access to those who control trade flows through those borders is a requisite for those who want to maximize their returns on the disorder generated by such apparent arbitrariness.

Disorder also incorporates the notion of uncertainty, a concept with which economists are familiar. Again, uncertainty is both a cost and an opportunity, against which there is a premium. In a polity of disorder, the ability to hedge uncertainty is a valuable resource. The greater the uncertainty, the more valuable the hedge is, for instance, the perennial significance that witchcraft retains as an almighty hedge in Africa. Knowledge and the control of information are important in all polities but they are critical in disordered societies, where they impinge even more directly on the management of uncertainty. Whether, for example, the ruler is unwell, or prey to new influences, will be of substantially greater significance in Africa than it would be in Europe, for it could unleash a wholesale change in the patrimonial networks extant and radically reshape the existing moral economy of disorder created by the upsurge of globalization.

First, economic globalization is the powerhouse and tool for pauperization of Africans in a variety of ways:

1. Retrenchment of workers. Retrenchment leaves hundreds of thousands of households without employment and means of livelihood. Education, health, social services, and development are stifled as African countries sink deeper into the vicious circle of debt.

2. Opening up of Africa's markets to foreign goods. This imposed *free- market* ideology automatically kills local industries. This Goliath/David "free and fair competition" requires God's intervention to save the African David.

3. Aid: an instrument of globalization and pauperization of Africa. Projects aided are mainly irrelevant to Africa's needs. The massive repatriation of the dividends of the aid in the form of material resources and personnel contributes to the failure of aid as a solution to Africa's economic development. Aid thus becomes not a solution, but part of the problem; it simply globalizes poverty.

R. Cranford Pratt is very clear on the pauperization of Africa through deceitful instruments like aid (Pratt 1983: 55):

> Africa lays claim to be in a "global village" only in the same sense that the industrialized countries are able to reach out globally to find the resources they need and sell the products they manufacture. However, Africa's world has neither the institutions of self-rule nor the sense of community and mutual responsibility the [positive] image of a global village suggests. Rather, its world, dominated as it

is by the nation-state system, with that system in turn dominated by the rich and powerful within it, has developed neither the will nor the institutions to ensure that global economic (and hence political and cultural) independence operates with tolerable fairness.

Second, political and cultural globalization holds Africa up for easy exploitation, marginalization and destruction. In the witnessing words of Saral Sarkal (1991: 369):

> The only area in which capitalism is clearly victorious is in the political system. In contrast to the (formerly) AES (actually existing socialist) countries, where until recently there was little freedom and democracy, capitalist countries — not only the rich ones but also many in the Third World — have experienced a certain degree of freedom and free elections. We must not overvalue this fact. Of course, it has been a positive element in the life of the people concerned. But it has had little significance for other peoples. Freedom and democracy in the United States has not protected weaker peoples from aggression by democratic states. Democratically elected governments of the United States dropped atom bombs on the civilian population of Hiroshima and Nagasaki and perpetrated genocide in Vietnam. What humanity needs as a political system is much more than formal freedom and formal parliamentary multi-party democracy.

The cruelest dictatorships in African recent history have been sustained by powerful democratic countries of the North. Examples are not in short supply: Belgium in Rwanda; France, Belgium, and the United States in Mobutu's Zaire; and various Western governments and transnational corporations in Idi Amin's Uganda, Somalia, Sudan, and Nigeria under the many military juntas. In Laurenti Magesa's words "democracy should primarily be a matter of how human beings relate on the basis of justice, respect, and mutual concern" (1996: 89):

> Democracy in Africa should not be approached primarily as an idea or as a comparison between types of parties or political organisations... (and democracy should be for) the majority of people's conditions of existence and how they can improve themselves. In concrete terms, democracy in Africa is that process that enables people to devise ways and means of resurrecting themselves from the tomb of subservience, exploitation, fear, poverty and illness. If the multiparty system does this best, well and good! But all energies should not be invested in issues of democracy that are really theoretical and secondary.

It is increasingly becoming clear that the multiparty system of politics is irrelevant for democracy in Africa. It, alone, does not guarantee a just orientation in society and it must be combined with internal and external structures of justice for democracy to deserve the name. Africans are forced to copy systems of democracy that took the countries in question many long years of trial and error to adjust to their social and cultural environments. Africa is denied this necessary experience. Therefore, its effort to democratize lacks local content and thus tends to be alienating. Economic globalization brings with it the glitter of the West's consumer goods, attendant attitudes, and behavior. Electronics is a case in point.

The video machine has affected everything among big segments of the African population: from the attitude of shame attached to the black color of one's skin and texture of one's hair, through sexual behavior and even orientation, to the attitude towards one's elders and ancestors. What the TV/video has done in a decade to alienate Africa from itself is probably worse than what colonialism did in the same area in more than a century. It has no African content; it does not, in fact, portray African reality. Its viewers live and experience one strange foreign reality while actually living and experiencing a different local one.

This experience is one of disorder and alienation. African countries have suffered under the rule of kleptocrats, who implement highly inefficient economic policies recommended by the International Monetary Fund and World Bank, expropriate the wealth of their citizens, and use the proceeds for their own gratification or consumption in the thick of this disorder. The success of these kleptocrats rests, in part, on their ability to use a divide-and-rule strategy, made possible by the weaknesses in the institutions of liberal democracy. It is in such disorderly and alienating circumstances that kleptocratic policies are more likely when foreign aid and rents from natural resources provide African rulers with substantial resources to buy off opponents.

## GOVERNANCE AND STATE-BUILDING CRISIS

Governance is ultimately concerned with creating the conditions for ordered rule and collective action. In this respect, governance is about processes and refers to the development of governing styles in which boundaries between and within public and private sectors have become blurred. The essence of governance, as noted by Stoker (1998: 34-38) "is its focus on governing mechanisms which do not rest on recourse to the authority and sanctions of government" alone. As a concept "governance points to the creation of a structure or an order (or regime) which cannot be externally imposed but is the result of the interaction of a multiplicity of governing actors influencing each other." The need to create a structure or a new order often arises from changes in the operational economic, social, and political environments that constrain or challenge the manner in which authority is effectively exercised within existing traditions or "rules of the game." Governance has historically taken a variety of forms of which liberal democracy has been one out of many.

In the specific context of Ghanaian political history, the forms of governance had ranged from the authoritarian to the democratic during the colonial and postcolonial eras. And within these two polar types, there have also been a wide variety of forms. The authoritarian variant had comprised the "one-party state" and the "military council" types of regimes, while the democratic model had in the past been either "liberal-representative" or participatory. In this specific context, democratic governance has meant a popular rejection of the authoritarian types of governance and a strong preference for an admixture of both the liberal-representative and participatory models. This ideal is embodied by Ghana's current executive presidential type of regime. Certain qualities, notably principles and practices, differentiate democratic governance from authoritarian governance. The 1992 constitution of Ghana is full of the principles of democratic governance that are clearly spelled out in different chapters. The principles affirm and protect the rights and freedoms of the individual in relation to the state by limiting the powers of the latter in pursuance of the democratic ideal and economic and human development. A few of the principles are universally acclaimed as central to the practice of not only democratic governance but also good governance. These are:

- full respect for human rights
- the rule of law
- effective participation
- political pluralism
- transparency and accountable processes and institution
- an efficient and effective public sector
- legitimacy
- access to knowledge
- information and education
- political empowerment of people
- gender equality and equity
- sustainability
- attitudes and values that foster responsibility, solidarity and tolerance
- peace and stability

Assessing current practices of governance against each of these principles would indicate the values on which progress has either been made or is lacking in the establishment of a more democratic regime. In the context of a liberal democratic regime, democratic governance may be defined as the process by which the state, civil society, and private-sector actors pursue a society's interests, including present and future welfare on the basis of rules, institutions, values, and practices of democracy that set limits to state power and provide incentives for the individual, organizations and firms to influence the exercise of authority.

Good governance has been at the top of the agenda of international development agencies, alongside market reforms, since the 1980s. It featured prominently in meetings of the Global Coalition for Africa, sponsored initially by the Dutch Government and the World Bank, throughout the 1990s. Hopes for Africa's sustainable development have come to rest on several "preconditions": the emergence of more effective governing institutions, respect for the rule of law, the curbing of corruption, the transparent management of public finances, and executive agencies being held accountable horizontally (by parliaments and judiciaries) and vertically (by civil society and periodic national elections). In its comprehensive draft of July 2001, New Partnership for African Development (NEPAD) advocates "strengthening the political and administrative framework of participating countries, in line with the principles of democracy, transparency, accountability, integrity, respect for human rights and promotion of the rule of law." What remains to be demonstrated is how these long-standing aspirations will finally be reflected in actual practice. Many wonderful constitutions and codes of conduct have been devised in Africa that bear little relationship to how power is exercised.

Despite the abundance of scholarly analyses of state failure, erosion, contraction, and declining legitimacy in Africa, these studies have had little discernible impact on the policies of major donors. There is the obvious importance of building state capacity, and of the relevant needs, such as strengthening parliamentary oversight, increasing participatory decision making, combating corruption, and implementing judicial reforms. The gap between these laudatory objectives and the realities of institutional ineffectiveness in Africa, however, is considerable. Some of the pertinent studies of these phenomena include that of Pierre Englebert (2000). According to him, there is now a broad consensus that what has most distinguished Africa from the rest of the world since the mid-1970s is the weak capacity of its states to respond to environmental, external, and other supply shocks and to design appropriate policies and institutions for growth.

Where civil servants are irregularly paid and funds for normal functions are absent, government offices may exist in various localities, but nothing of consequence takes place within them. The governing structures have thus joined the hospitals and infirmaries that lack medicines and equipment and schools that lack books and chairs. In addition to the "failed or collapsed states," there are many cases in Africa of the advanced erosion or atrophy of the state.

Today, for most students of African government and politics, the African state has become a problematic entity (Reno, 1998). The evidence is extensive: citizens no longer looking to the state for basic protection of life and property but rather seeking escape from predatory state officials; the state becoming an instrument of domination by one or other ethnic group or clan; warlords bulldozing their way to control of the state; and entrenched leaders turning national armies into private militias. These and other documented trends cannot be overlooked as donor countries are asked to increase resource flows substantially, and private investors are encouraged to take up the many lagging economic opportunities in Africa.

For example, for the June 2002 G8 Summit, a briefing was prepared by Action for Southern Africa and the World Development Movement, 2002, pointing out causes and wider issues of economic as well as political problems of governance:

It is undeniable that there has been poor governance, corruption and mismanagement in Africa. However, the briefing reveals the context—the legacy of colonialism, the support of the G8 (2002) for repressive regimes in the Cold War, the creation of the debt trap, the massive failure of Structural Adjustment Programs imposed by the IMF and World Bank and the deeply unfair rules on international trade. The role of the G8 in creating the conditions for African crisis cannot be denied. Its overriding responsibility must be to put its own house in order, and to end the unjust policies that are inhibiting Africa's development.

## CORRUPTION AS INSTRUMENTALIZED (DIS)ORDER

According to a report by Elizabeth Blunt of the BBC Wednesday, September 18, 2002, corruption "costs Africa billions." In the program "Focus on Africa," she pointed out that corruption in Africa was costing the continent nearly $150bn. a year. The African regional body, the African Union (AU) had drawn up a convention to stamp out malpractices that the study said were hitting the poorest the hardest. Corruption is illegal everywhere in Africa, but everywhere it is woven deep into the fabric of every day life. Blunt gives a familiar example from the bottle of whisky slipped under the counter to speed a traveler's way through customs, to the presidents and ex-presidents living way beyond their declared means, it results in an assumption that no business will ever get done without a *present* changing hands.

The report before the meeting of the African Union during the week of September 18, 2002, in the Ethiopian capital, Addis Ababa, made no attempt to excuse these "gratifications" as part of the culture. It said that corruption was costing Africa more than $148 billion dollars a year, increasing the cost of goods by as much as 20 percent, deterring investment and holding back development.

Most of the cost, the report said falls on the poor. The African Union proposed the holding of a convention that would provide countries signing up to it with a blueprint for tackling the problem. It proposed that all public officials should declare their assets when they take office, that governments should take powers to seize bank documents where necessary, and that those convicted should have their assets confiscated.

The threat of corruption, perhaps the major affront to real democratic reform, continues to dominate the political process. Nongovernmental Organizations are mostly funded from outside the African states and therefore are unable to support political parties. Honest political parties must work from their own resources with no remuneration, while a corrupt incumbent party can use the public treasury and publicly owned media indiscriminately to strengthen itself and the single-party mentality. In the former single party system, there was no need for platforms or manifestos. Resources used for campaigning were national, not private, and thus corruption was negligible. Now, candidates resort to either dirty money from drug dealers and corrupt businessmen, the public treasury (if incumbent), or vast promises that are beyond the capacity of any single member of Parliament.

The areas in which corruption manifests itself include: procurement of goods and services, including award of contracts by the government; administration of taxes and prevention of smuggling, disposal, sale, and allotment of government property, including disinvestment of industries and other commercial units; administration of loans by public financial institutions; outright embezzlement of government funds; all kinds of shop-floor malpractices.

There is no doubt that corruption hurts the economic performance of a country. The consequences of corruption are, among others: siphoning away a large chunk of public resources that could have been productively employed somewhere in the economy; productivity or effectiveness and efficiency of the government are undermined by corruption; it reduces efficient mobilization of resources and management of development activities; gains through corruption are unlikely to be directed to investment in the industrial sector and are more likely to be either used up in conspicuous consumption or transferred to foreign bank accounts; corruption generates allocative inefficiency by permitting the least efficient contractor or most costly supplier with the highest ability to bribe those who award government constraints; bribes and payoffs, instead of expediting decisions and facilitating movement of files, do the opposite in an overwhelming number of cases because civil servants get into the habit of holding back all papers until some payment is made to them; once the system of bribery is well established, income gained from bribes is no longer a windfall but becomes a part of expected wages; and in addition to the award of contract for supplying, designing, and construction by the public sector, much of the corruption takes place in the external trade sector leading to overinvoicing and underinvoicing of imports and exports, and smuggling which in turn contributes to distortion in investment decisions and to capital flight. This is the main reason for which public servants go to their offices to wait for bribes.

## FALSE PROMISES

"Life More Abundant" was one of the slogans used by African nationalist leaders to mobilize their people in the struggle to rid the continent of colonial rule. The colonial legacy is combined with international trade and economic arrangements that do little to benefit the African people and further exacerbates the problem. IMF/World Bank policies like structural adjustment have aggressively opened up African nations with disastrous effects, including the requirements to cut back on health, education, public services, and so on, while growing food and extracting resources for export primarily, etc, thus continuing the colonial era arrangement. The following overview from Bob Geldof (2004) is revelative:

> [The] theory of comparative advantage ... says that a country produces that which it can produce cheaper than any other and sells it to others in exchange for that which they can produce cheaper

than us. The invisible hand of the market will of itself sort out any inequities in this system allowing for the appropriately correct level of development to any particular producer. The [European] colonies distorted this view by deciding that Africa's comparative advantage was its poverty, like we do today with our global brand footwear, clothing etc. As a result in Africa, existing patterns of farming were wiped away and huge plantations of single non-native crops were developed, always with the need of European processing industry in mind. There was a global transfer of foreign plants to facilitate this—tea, coffee, cocoa, rubber, and so on. The result was the erosion of the soil, forerunner of the desertification evident today. And with the erosion came steadily decreasing quantities of already scarce local food grown on marginal lands by laborers working for pitiful wages. This concentration on a few major cash crops or the extraction of an important mineral source left the countries on independence incredibly vulnerable to dramatic fluctuations in the prices of those commodities on the world market.

Adam Smith also suggested that the market was free within reason. It could never be laissez faire. Indeed he suggested infant economies be protected from the chill winds of the financial gales as we did in our development but prevented in others. The Navigation Acts were wholly anticompetitive policies—which at that time prevented American colonists from making their own woolen or iron goods, and were like their equivalent today when we [the developed world] impose on a Third World producer of pineapples who wants to sell in the EU a tariff of 9 percent for fresh fruit, 32 percent for tinned pineapples and 42 percent for pineapple juice—planting the seeds of today's disparities between Northern and Southern economies.

Bowing to pressures from international and domestic forces and pinning hopes on an obsolete "Asian model," almost the entire sub-Saharan region's 48 countries continue to implement programs to liberalize financial and trading policies and adopt programs of macroeconomic adjustment supported by the World Bank and the IMF. Prominent implementers of economic liberalization included Angola, Côte d'Ivoire, Ethiopia, Ghana, Guinea, Benin, Kenya, Madagascar, Mali, Mozambique, Senegal, Tanzania, Uganda, Zambia, and Zimbabwe. Although many of these countries accomplished significant macroeconomic reforms, there are few signs that governments are displaying similar commitment to the expansion of political freedoms. In many cases, economic progress was damaged precisely because of the lack of democratic accountability and respect for human rights and the rule of law.

With globalization and the increased power of market forces to propel change, financial and commodity volatility emerged as critical elements that African governments had to factor into political calculations. As political legitimacy is beginning to be tied directly to economic success, the fallout from Asia's economic crisis appears to translate into political fragility. With sagging economic performance, political leaders are confronted by a force beyond their control, a power more radically unyielding than the domestic political opponents they had grown used to controlling by a combination of brute force, favoritism, or political manipulation.

Uganda, Ethiopia, and Eritrea continue to build an autocratic brand of capitalism. For this they continued to be hailed as beacons of hope. Yet the dominance of ruling parties was unrelenting and opposition remained hobbled. Yoweri Museveni showed no shift from his so-called no-party system, while Ethiopia carried on detaining political challengers. None of the leaders of Ethiopia, Eritrea, or Uganda showed any signs of early departure—apparently joining the "old" leaders in Zimbabwe, Kenya, Gabon, and elsewhere in their attachment to power.

Four decades later in the early 2000s, Africa is mired in a complex of crises. According to Pierre Englebert (2002: 591-94), since 1960, Africans have seen their income rise by less than one-half of a percent per year, leaving the continent with the worst development record and the highest concentration of countries with negative growth of all the regions of the world. Today, one of every five Africans lives in a country severely disrupted by conflict, while the continent's share of the world's absolute poor continues to grow relentlessly, increasing from 25 to 30 percent in the 1990s. Africa has proportionately more armed conflicts and refugees than any other region; and many African countries cluster at the top of the "corruption scale" of Transparency International and at the bottom of the Human Development index of the United Nations Development Program. To these woes is added the catastrophic impact of HIV/AIDS, malaria, and tuberculosis on African societies.

Genuine excitement would be generated worldwide by an Africa in which governments demonstrate respect for their constitutions and laws, state officials at all levels responsibly execute the duties of their offices, public institutions make efficient use of funds provided, political violence and corruption are sharply reduced, the people's needs are dutifully addressed by public and private services, elections are fairly conducted, and the state, once again, becomes the collective property of its citizens. While none of these virtues are new, in the contemporary African context they would be revolutionary and promote popular democracy.

It was believed during the 1990s that such an Africa was being nurtured and that power embedded in institutions would thenceforward characterize governance in most states. These hopes have not been realized. While more liberties of speech, association, and movement have been accorded, these are often abruptly circumscribed when invoked to hold governments accountable, or to replace them democratically. Incremental democratization will continue to occur in disparate sites, a few emergent democracies will succeed in becoming consolidated, and such advances will be accompanied at times by improved governance. However, there is little to suggest that these advances will take the form of a wave of irresistible change in the near future.

Promises of accelerated development in the form of industrialization programs are made, where what is often needed is subsistence agriculture and less
reliance on international donor aid for developmental projects such as dams
and irrigation. There is no labor shortage, and over reliance on international
donor aid for such projects contributes to the high unemployment statistics.
South Africa has 34 percent unemployment, with an additional 11 percent
underemployed (Sender et al., 1996). False promises of "improvements" inspired
by visions of modern life create high expectations in the people, the resulting
disillusionment making ideal conditions for them to riot, asking for what they
believe is rightfully theirs. Equating political reform with immediate economic
improvement is mostly responsible.

But what else is to be expected? Poverty breeds the demand for quick and
visible solutions, and this is by no means constrained to Southern Africa. Fascist
mass-murderers like Hitler and Milosevic were elected democratically, because
they offered quick and visible solutions to the people's impoverishment, albeit
through complete centralization and scapegoatism. It is impossible for democracy to grow on the basis of such underlying conflicts.

## INTERNAL CONFLICT

Endless tit-for-tat conflict makes democratic reform seem hopeless to the
African people. It makes no difference to their suffering, for example, if their
head of state is a civilian or from the military. One drawback of the multiparty system is that parties are formed and aligned to exploit existing ethnic
or religious differences. Chaos and carnage ensue. Infrastructure is destroyed.
Food production and delivery are disrupted. Thousands are dislocated and flee,
becoming internal refugees and placing severe strains on the social systems of
the resident population. Food supplies run out. Starvation looms. The Western
media bombards the international community with horrific pictures of rail-
thin famine victims. Unable to bear the horror, the international community
is stirred to mount eleventh-hour humanitarian rescue missions. Food, tents,
blankets, portable toilets, high-protein biscuits, and other relief supplies are
airlifted to the refugees.

Factional leaders, who initially welcomed the humanitarian mission to feed
refugees, turn against the mission and refuse to cooperate with it, because its
presence accords some legitimacy and recognition to the hated regime. Factional leaders thus demand that relief organizations deal with them and not the
regime. The demands soon turn into extortion. At some point, relief supplies
are attacked and aid workers are taken hostage or killed. For instance, the conflict in Angola—referred to by many as "the world's forgotten war"—claimed
tens of thousands of lives in 1993 alone, with enormous suffering to the civilian
population. The fighting was so intense and widespread that for the first time
since 1979 the Red Cross had to evacuate most of its staff from its offices in
Huambo and Kuito. South Africa itself, perhaps the key to the region's stability,
has seen its post apartheid reforms offset by continual internal violence with

the gang wars, racial attacks, and politically motivated crime always prominent in world news. The victims in these circumstances are the suffering masses and democracy.

Civil strife, often spawned by long-standing and monumental human rights abuses, and fueled by weapons supplied from outside the continent, threatened many countries in Africa during the year, provoking large-scale forced migrations. As always, civilians—mostly women and children—bear the brunt of horrific abuses. Some of the most alarming reports came from Sierra Leone, where civilians were subjected to mutilations, rape, and systematic killings by rebel forces. Children were victims of gross violations of human rights committed by both sides of the conflict, both prior to and following the restoration of the government of President Tidjan Kabbah. Rebel forces fighting the government abducted an unknown number of children—probably in the thousands—for use as laborers, fighters, and in the case of girls, sexual prisoners. There were many child soldiers among fighters aligned with rebel forces, and despite promises by the government to demobilize all combatants under the age of eighteen, government allies continued to recruit children. Close to half a million Sierra Leoneans fled the fighting as refugees to neighboring Guinea and Liberia or to camps for the internally displaced. Refugees and the internally displaced suffered from a host of problems, including a lack of protection, high malnutrition and disease rates, and attacks by rebel forces.

Following the outbreak of fighting in Guinea-Bissau, when the army mutinied against President João "Nino" Vieira, after he had suspended and then fired Ansumane Mane as chief of staff, virtually the entire population of 300,000 of the capital Bissau was forced to flee toward the western regions of the country where they continued to live in life-threatening conditions. Gross human rights abuses in Sudan's civil war persisted, causing or aggravating a severe famine in three separate regions: the southern Bahr El Ghazal, Western Upper Nile areas, and the central Nuba Mountains. Both sides in the conflict employed abusive military strategies such as targeting civilians and their cattle. Combatants stripped assets from civilians, repeatedly displaced them, and manipulated and diverted relief goods and other food belonging to civilian populations.

In Uganda, the antigovernment Lord's Resistance Army (LRA) continues its campaign of terror, brutalizing civilians, destroying property, and abducting children in northern Uganda. The LRA attacked a school and abducted 39 girls. The majority of the populations in the north continue to live in "protected" camps, with inadequate access to housing, water, food, health care, and education. In western Uganda, the Allied Defense Forces (ADF), another guerrilla group, has also waged war against the Museveni government. The ADF was reportedly responsible for numerous abuses against civilians, including abductions of children. The ADF attacked and reportedly burned a school, killing an estimated 50 to 80 students and abducting an estimated 100 students and civilians.

Noncombatants also bore the brunt of the renewed fighting in the DRC. Both sides to the conflict resorted to extrajudicial executions and arbitrary detentions in appalling conditions. The conflict also forced thousands to seek refuge in neighboring countries. In Rwanda the government army and rebel forces each slaughtered tens of thousands of civilians as they struggled to control the northwestern part of the country. Rebel forces, including soldiers and militia responsible for the 1994 genocide, affirmed their intention of "completing" the slaughter of Rwandese Tutsi. In addition, government and military authorities took into custody a growing number of persons suspected of rebel ties that were never seen or heard from again.

In Burundi, a new constitutional arrangement between the government and the leading opposition party followed by a peace agreement and projected cease-fire led to hopes that the four-year-old civil war in that country might be brought to an end. Factions of some of the parties that signed the agreement disavowed it, however, and attacks by rebels and reprisals by the military continued, particularly in the western part of Burundi. As elsewhere on the continent, civilians bore the brunt of suffering in this conflict, through attacks by both sides and through deprivation of food, medical attention, and other services disrupted by the combat and economic decline.

The odds worsened for Angola's peace process and the country seemed dangerously close to renewed war. As a result, the chances of any turnaround regarding the plight of refugees and the internally displaced faded fast. Some 300,000 refugees in neighboring countries remained unrepatriated. The renewed belligerence caused further flows of refugees into the DRC, Namibia, and Zambia. By September Angola had an approximated 1.3 million internally displaced people. During 1998 alone, 142,000 newly internally displaced people were registered.

Lesotho was plunged into what appeared to be its worst crisis in its troubled post independence history when South African and Botswanan troops intervened to restore order after a long-simmering dispute concerning the elections. Lesotho's capital Maseru and surrounding towns were seriously damaged by looting and arson, largely carried out by civilians. Up to 100 soldiers and civilians died, and thousands of refugees were sent scurrying across the border into South Africa.

Corruption, incumbency, nepotism, unrealistic promises, and intimidation are often still regarded as vital tools for acquiring and maintaining power. This is perhaps the most unfortunate legacy of colonial rule. For continuous democracy to have a chance in the African States, institutional reform must be coupled with a respect for democratic principles such as recognition of differing political opinions, and accountability and responsibility of their leaders and human rights, so that the political process is no longer simplistically seen as a winner-takes-all war.

For some countries, rich in oil or precious minerals such as diamonds, wealth appeared rather to buttress dictatorial regimes characterized by a lack of respect for human rights than to promote development. Angola, Cameroon, Central African Republic (CAR), Chad, DRC, Republic of Congo, Equatorial Guinea, Guinea, Liberia, and Nigeria all fall in this category. The huge profits earned in royalties either reinforce autocratic governments, and sometimes rebel movements as well, or prevent the development of mechanisms for transparency and accountability, often with the connivance of foreign corporations. Wasted national wealth hampers development and massive abuse of human rights is the price local populations continued to pay for the country's "natural wealth."

In fact, in most of Africa, the transition to multiparty democracy was abrupt. Rulers were not adequately prepared to handle any wider popular political participation. Social violence therefore became politicized. Political repression and massive coercion turned pluralist politics in Africa into warfare (Ake, 1990). For instance, the last decade of the 20th century in Kenya will be remembered for the armed conflicts, massacres, displacements, uprisings, riots, and demonstrations, whose repercussions will continue to be felt. In January 1998, the world was shocked by the massacre of Kenyan men, women and children over a few days in the "valley of death," officially known as the Rift Valley. Its conscience was shaken by systematic reports of race and "ethnic cleansing." While such horrors are not new in the annals of human cruelty, they are systematically hidden and trivialized by the autocratic State authorities. Most weak states in Africa (Mentan, 2004) are highly personalized. For instance, countries such as Chad, Guinea-Conakry, Guinea-Bissau, and Congo-Brazzaville, and others, unless the leader controlled insurgencies by using his own henchmen, it would be difficult for him to control disorganized and decentralized internal guerrillas.

The opening of the political space in Africa led to far-reaching social, political, cultural, and economic changes. Political transformations and economic liberalization have increased competitive politics and economic globalization. This has created the need to exploit ethnicity for the sake of political survival. Those who hold political power tend to perceive opposing views as treacherous and treasonable. To maintain their rule, the rulers terrorize, harass, and intimidate the powerless. Leaders in a few countries in this region have eliminated real or suspect political enemies in order to reduce political rivalry. Typical examples are Samuel Doe of Liberia, Anwar el Sadat of Egypt, Blaise Compaoré of Burkina Faso and Obiang Nguema of Equatorial Guinea, among others. Those overthrown by popular revolts include Mobutu Sese Seko of Zaïre, Dawda Jawara of Gambia, Marshall-Emperor Ahmed Bokassa of C.A.R, Siad Barré of Somalia, Mengistu Haile Mariam of Ethiopia, and others.

## CRISIS IN THE POLITICS OF EXCLUSION: CITIZENSHIP AND BELONGING IN AFRICA

Citizenship is commonly understood to mean at least two things. The first refers to the legal status of being a citizen of a country, and the second entails the duties and responsibilities that come with being a member of the community. Although these two definitions do not specifically refer to rights, political, economic, and social rights are fundamental to citizenship as civil liberties are to the individual. In that regard, the reference to citizenship in this chapter subsumes the corpus of civil, political, economic, social and cultural rights that collectively define the human rights of individuals and groups in the modern state, economy, and society. Proceeding from this attributive definition, the concept of citizenship would be instructive to our understanding of the notion of "democratization of liberal democracy" only if it can be infused with a dynamic and genealogical meaning that emphasizes its essential political character too, and not just the legal one.

The citizen in the ancient Greek city-state was not simply the city or town dweller who had the right to live in a country because he or she was born there or had secured legal acceptance of that status. The citizen was also differentiated from the noncitizen by "his" active participation in the entire work of the assembly where laws were made to govern the polis and in the army that fought wars to defend the polis. Active and direct participation in the making of the law and its execution was then at the heart of citizenship. The mark of citizenship and the effective exercise of its inherent rights consisted of informed participation in deliberations or debates and dialogue on the policies for promoting and upholding the collective interest. In that debate, there was as much contestation of ideas as there were negotiations and agreements on the methods for realizing these ideas. And the success or failure of this process depended to a great extent on how it was steered by the chosen leaders of the assembly to deliver public goods in time and appropriately to respond to the challenges of the times.

In the modern state where the sheer size of population and territory makes direct and active participation in law making and execution very difficult, election of representatives have become the dominant means of exercising the political rights and obligations or responsibilities of citizenship both directly and indirectly. This modification of the method of exercising the political rights of citizenship has also affected the method of steering processes for exercising authority as well, with far-reaching implications for the relationship between the modern state and citizens under different regimes. This art of steering the public deliberation process within an institutional and normative framework to yield expected public goods and services shaped relations between the governors and the governed and determined the effective exercise of authority, power, and/or influence to serve the public interest. It is this art of steering that is now referred to as governance.

The ideas of national citizenship and a plural nation-state have been under crisis and challenge since the early 1990s, with processes of national integration disrupted and transformed. In Africa, as in other parts of the world, one particularly dramatic effect has been the upsurge of a wide array of diffuse and highly volatile forms of political, social, and cultural identity. Older languages of ethnicity have been transformed into even more vague—and sometimes more violent—discourses on belonging, "autochthony" (a widely prevalent term for a variant of indigenousness: literally a claim to have "sprung from the soil") and the exclusion of "strangers" who are often citizens of the same state.

This emphasis on more localist forms of belonging, sovereignty, and authority has implied a direct attack on the institution of national citizenship and the ideal of formal equality of all citizens before the law. These new manifestations range from debates over the "real" origins of candidates in election campaigns to violent contests in rural areas where claims of indigeneity and autochthony are often tied to access to land and resources, as well as to the reworking of the very basis of personhood and citizenship.

Influences both internal and external contribute to this trend, including the onset of democratization, economic liberalization and the "decentralization" of development strategies and institutions. The crisis of national citizenship and the weakening of the nation state, both in its redistributive capacities and as a focus of identification, and the concomitant effects on national citizenship, seem to leave a void that is filled by a variety of more diffuse forms of identity. Autochthony is thus often used as a metaphor for indigenousness, a language of the soil, with appeals to heritage and ancestral traditions, creating strong emotional appeal. The appearance of being rooted in what is "natural," however, belies the complexities of an often nervous discourse. Who is "in" today, can be redefined as being "out" tomorrow.

Côte d'Ivoire presents the dangers inherent in political exclusion. It was originally made up of numerous isolated settlements; today it represents more than 60 distinct tribes, including the Baoulé, Bété, Senoufou, Agni, Malinké, Dan, and Lobi. Côte d'Ivoire attracted both French and Portuguese merchants in the 15th century who were in search of ivory and slaves. French traders set up establishments early in the 19th century, and in 1842, the French obtained territorial concessions from local tribes, gradually extending their influence along the coast and inland. The area was organized as a territory in 1893, became an autonomous republic in the French Union after World War II, and achieved independence on August 7, 1960. Côte d'voire formed a customs union in 1959 with Dahomey (Benin), Niger, and Burkina Faso.

From independence until his death in 1993, Felix Houphouët-Boigny served as president. Massive protests by students, farmers, and professionals forced the president to legalize opposition parties and hold the first contested presidential election in October 1990, which Houphouët-Boigny won with 81per cent of the vote. Beginning in September 1998, thousands of demonstrators protested a constitutional revision that granted President Henri Konan Bédié greatly enhanced powers. Bédié also promoted the concept of *ivoirité*, which, roughly translated, means "pure Ivoirian pride." Although its defenders describe *ivoirité* as a term of positive national pride, it has led to a dangerous xenophobia, with numerous ethnic Malians and Burkinabés being driven out of the country in 1999.

President Bédié was overthrown in the country's first military coup in December 1999, and Gen. Robert Guei assumed control of the country. As a result, the majority of foreign aid to the country ceased. In what were seen as the first steps toward reasserting democracy, voters overwhelmingly approved a draft constitution in July 2000. However, the document permitted only those of "pure Ivoirian" stock to run for president, thereby excluding nearly 40 percent of the population. Guei, who had promised to stay in power only to "sweep the house clean," instead decided to run for president in the October 2000 elections. Gen. Guei ran against a civilian opposition candidate, Laurent Gbagbo. Each declared victory in an election most believed to have been rife with fraud. Popular outcry against Guei soon turned violent, forcing him to leave the country, and Gbagbo assumed the presidency. Many observers questioned his mandate, however, because the popular opposition leader Alassane Ouattara had been excluded from the election on the specious grounds that he was not a "pure-blooded Ivoirian." It was not until June 2002 that Alassane Ouattara was finally granted full Ivoirian citizenship, which would allow him to run in the presidential election of 2005. Hundreds have died in violence sparked by the dispute and the country is only being held together by foreign troops.

Assessments of democratization in Africa continue to be dominated by misleading benchmarks such as the holding of "multiparty elections" however restricted while underplaying substantive freedoms. Gross fraud, serious procedural irregularities, opposition party withdrawals, and boycotts persisted. Manipulated and flawed electoral processes that seemed designed to ensure victory for incumbents continued to be a profound source of tensions and crises. During 1998, election-related controversy led to crises in Lesotho, Togo, and Mali. Though the basic nuts and bolts of democracy were installed across the region—there were political parties, elections, parliaments, judiciaries, newspapers galore, and a growing number of electronic media—their ability to secure respect for human rights and the rule of law was another question.

In countries such as Angola, Burkina Faso, Cameroon, Chad, Côte d'Ivoire, Equatorial Guinea, Gabon, Gambia, Guinea-Bissau, Kenya, Niger, Tanzania, Togo, Zambia, and Zimbabwe, where the political landscape had historically been dominated by single-party structures, de jure and de facto, a legacy of dominant political control, restrictions on entry, and participation in political life and excessive regulation persisted, even when the one-party system had been liberalized. Promises to treat political competitors on an equal basis with ruling parties were of limited practical value, and opposition parties remained at a substantial disadvantage. Countries with a long legacy of intrusive state control would require huge effort and goodwill to disentangle the cat's cradle of laws and regulations that continued to enmesh the media and civil society and to hobble political opposition. Few, if any, governments appeared to relish such a prospect.

Government-controlled media continue to serve as propaganda tools. In most countries television and radio remain firmly under state control, and governments continue to threaten critical newspapers and independent radio stations that challenge government abuses. As a result, journalists are often constrained to practice self-censorship. Others are intimidated, assaulted, or thrown into jail, and numerous banning of newspapers and closures of radio stations occur.

In short, experience to date has indicated that democratization is a lengthy and complex process. Neither the breakdown of authoritarianism nor political transitions necessarily result in functioning democracies. Societies throughout Africa are in flux, and in some cases the norms and institutions of democracy have not yet replaced those of previous authoritarian regimes. The continued political volatility and violent conflict evidenced in much of the continent are indicative of the difficulties of institutionalizing democracy. In many instances both democratic and nondemocratic practices are likely to coexist, at least in the short term. In others, democratic progress will suffer setbacks, although even in these cases it is possible that more durable democratic structures that are embedded in social and cultural norms will eventually be formed. Building democratic societies takes time, and attention has to be paid to many issues, including the mechanisms for facilitating orderly political succession and peaceful alternation of power.

While the primary responsibility for consolidating and institutionalizing democracy obviously lies with African countries themselves, the international community has a role to play. Africa's partner countries and agencies have provided considerable assistance to political transition and to strengthening the institutions that uphold democracy, and such assistance will continue to be needed in the future. Effective international cooperation to promote economic growth and combat poverty, and concerted action to combat crime and corruption, would also help to create the conditions in which democracy can take root. Above all, commitment over the long-term, and consistency and coherence in donor policies, are important.

## References

Ake, Claude. 1990. "The Case for Democracy." In *African Governance In The 1990s: Objectives, Resources, and Constraints. Working Papers from the Second Annual Seminar of the African Governance Program*. Atlanta: The Carter Center of Emory University (March 23-25): 2-6.

Callaghy, TM and J. Ravenhill,(eds.). 1993. "Hemmed In." In *Responses to Africa's ... Responses to Africa's Economic Decline*. New York: Columbia University Press.

Centre for Democracy and Development 2000. *The Zimbabwe Constitutional Referendum*. The Report of the Centre for Democracy and Development Observer Mission, February 12-13, 2000.

Chabal, Patrick.1997. Inaugural lecture, delivered on March 12, 1997 in King's College London.

Ebrahim, Hassen. 2002. "Constitution Making in Africa-Challenges for the New Millennium," John F. Kennedy School of Government, Harvard University, May 9–11.

Englebert, P. 2002. " A Research Note on Congo's National Paradox" In *Review of African Political Economy*,29, 93/94 : 591-94.

G8. 2002. "It's the Blame the Victim Summit, *Action for Southern Africa, June 25.*

Geldof, Bob. 2004. *"Why Africa? Bob Geldof Speaks at St. Paul's Cathedral," DATA.org,* April 21.

Hibou, Béatrice. 1996. *L'Afrique est-elle protectionniste ? Les chemins buissonniers de la libéralisation extérieure.* Paris: Karthala, serie "Les Afriques."

Ihonvbere, J.O. 2000. "Towards a New Constitutionalism in Africa." London: Centre for Democracy & Development, CDD Occasional Paper Series No. 4.

Joseph, Richard. 1997. "Democratization in Africa After 1989: Comparative and Theoretical Perspectives," *Comparative Politics* 29 (April 1997): 363-82.

Magesa, L. *1998.* "Africa's Struggle for Self-Definition During a Time of Globalization." In *African Ecclesial Review,* 40, 5 & 6, October/December.

Mandaza, Ibbo. 1991. "Movements for National Liberation and Constitutionalism in Southern Africa." In G.I. Shivji, (ed.), *State and Constitutionalism: An African Debate on Democracy.* Harare: Southern African Political Economy Series.

Mentan, T. 2004. *Dilemmas of Weak States: Africa and Transnational Terrorism in the Twenty-First Century.* London: Ashgate Publishers.

Mokhiber, R. and Robert Weissman. 1999. Corporate Predators: The Hunt for Mega Profits and the Attack on Democracy. Monroe, Maine: Common Courage Press. Online, http://www.corporatepredators.org.

Monze, L. 2003. "Constitutions in Zambia have been imposed on people-Rev. Ndhlovu," *The Post,* Thursday, March 20.

Mtshaulana, P. M. 1999. "History and Role of the Constitutional Court," *President of the Republic of South Africa and Others v. South African Rugby Football Union and Others* 1999 (4) SA 147 (CC).

Okoth-Ogendo, H.W.O. 1991. "Constitutions without Constitutionalism: Reflections on an African Paradox." In G.I. Shivji, (Ed.), *State and Constitutionalism: An African Debate on Democracy.* Harare: Southern African Political Economy Series.

Pratt, R.C. 1983. "Aid: an instrument of globalization and pauperization of Africa." In J. Torrie, (ed.) *Banking on Poverty.* Toronto: Between the Lines.

Reno, William. 1998. *Warlord Politics and African States.* Boulder, CO: Lynne Rienner.

Sarkal, S. 1991. "The Future of Socialism—Which Socialism?" *Alternatives,* 16:3 (Summer).

Sender, John and John Weeks. 1996. "Restructuring the labour market: The South African challenge." *An ILO Country Review.* Geneva: International Labour Office.

Shivji, G. I. (Ed.). 1991. *State and Constitutionalism: An African Debate on Democracy.* Harare: Southern African Political Economy Series.

Stoker, G. 1998. *Politics and performance: The implications of emerging governance arrangements for urban management approaches and information systems.* Cambridge: Cambridge University Press.

*The Economist,* "The Cancun Challenge." London, September 4, 2003.

Van de Walle, Nicolas. 2001. *African Economies and the Politics of Permanent Crisis, 1979-99.* New York: Cambridge University Press.

World Bank. 2000. *Can Africa Reclaim the 21st Century?* Washington, DC: The World Bank.

# Chapter 6

# Globalization and Democracy or Neomercantilist Imperialism?

There is historical evidence that is contrary to the idea that democracy and capitalism in the (neoliberal) form of private enterprise and the free market are intrinsically connected. It is also true that the marriages between free markets (capitalism, economic liberalism) and free elections (democracy, political liberalism) are those of convenience or historic accident. It is not an organic relationship as portrayed by scholars of the ilk of Dominguez and Lowenthal (1996). Liberal scholars, both political scientists and economists, have theorized that the institutionalization of democracy (political liberalization) would create the necessary or facilitating conditions of capitalist development (political liberalization) or vice versa. Thus, at the level of practice, within the context of neomercantilist imperialism in the post -World War II period, the iron fist of armed force and political repression has often been cloaked with the idea of democracy and a concern for associated human rights and good governance.

By insisting that African leaders place the interests of international financial investors above the needs of their own citizens, the IMF and the World Bank have short-circuited accountability at the heart of self-governance. This insistence has corrupted the democratic process. The subordination of social needs to the concerns of financial markets (neomercantilist imperialism) has, in turn, made it more difficult for African governments to ensure that their people receive food, healthcare, and education. These are basic human rights. The international financial institutions have thus promoted the erosion of basic human rights and the perversion of the democratic process. The erosion and perversion have made the financial institutions a clear and present threat to the well being of hundreds of millions of people in Africa through globalization policies.

Globalization is a concept or term that is currently very much in use. However, like many popularly used terms, there is no commonly agreed upon meaning for globalization. Not surprisingly, people who use the concept frequently disagree, not only over the definition of globalization, but also over their assessment of the effects of globalization—that is, whether or not globalization benefits all people, all nations, or all the regions of the world.

If one is to investigate globalization and its impact on Africa, or on North America or any other region of the world, it is necessary to come up with a general understanding of the concept of globalization. First, globalization is a process of building connections between regions of the world. People argue over how connected specific countries and regions of the world are with other countries or regions, but there is general agreement that networks of global connectivity are increasing.

Second, globalization is manifested in different arenas such as communication, culture, politics, and economics. Perhaps the impact of globalization is most dramatically demonstrated in the arena of communications. The development of the Internet, advances in telecommunications, and the explosion of international jet travel have resulted in the ability to communicate instantaneously with many parts of the world. This has also resulted in the spread of a wide variety of cultural forms and expressions. Young people in cities in South Africa, Kenya, and Nigeria, listen to the same music as young people in cities like New York, Kentucky, or Oregon. This chapter, however, will concentrate on investigating the economics of globalization or rather the current strategies of neomercantilist imperialism.

Third, globalization may lead to greater economic, social, or cultural equality around the world. On the other hand, the process of globalization may result in greater inequality. It may increase the power, wealth, and influence of individuals, institutions, corporations, and nations that are already wealthy, influential, and powerful. This chapter will help the reader to critically look at and make thoughtful judgments about the siege globalization has laid on democracy in Africa.

## GLOBALIZATION OR NEOMERCANTILIST IMPERIALISM?

The term "globalization" has acquired considerable emotive force. Some view it as a process that is beneficial—a key to future world economic development—and also inevitable and irreversible. Others regard it with hostility, even fear, believing that it increases inequality within and between nations, threatens employment and living standards, and thwarts social progress. This analysis offers an overview of some aspects of globalization and aims to identify ways in which African countries can tap the gains of this process, while remaining realistic about its potential and its risks. How has Africa, especially its poorest countries, been helped to catch up? Does globalization exacerbate inequality or does it help to reduce poverty in Africa? And are African countries that integrate with the global economy inevitably vulnerable to instability?

Globalization has gained much currency in such a short period of time, since around 1986. Though used in different ways it generally denotes a multifaceted process characterized by increased international flows of capital, goods and services, information and cultural values, ways of doing things, and an associated interconnectedness of social phenomena (Therborn, 2000), and, at a different level, economic integration. However, the term globalization explains little of what is actually going on across the world and, as noted by most contributors to a special theme of the *Cambridge Review of International Affairs* (Desai et al., 2000), serves better as an *ideology*, a means of masking what is going on or to promote a certain desired form of action or thought, than as *theory*, an explanatory device or even as a means of describing the dynamics of a supposed paradigmatic (and historical) shift. For one thing, the term entirely eludes reference to the structures of political and economic power or the practice (foreign policy) in which these structures are imposed by some states, or peoples, on others. The reality of this institutionalized practice is better described, and explained, by use of a term given to Marxist discourse but abandoned by many: imperialism. Oddly enough, this point has been grasped well by some supporters and advocates of neoliberal capitalism than by the many critics of corporate capital or neoliberal globalization.

In this connection, Martin Wolf (2002) writes of the ritualistic concern with unbridled corporate power expressed by antiglobalization critics and protesters at the meeting, in New York, of the World Economic Forum as paranoid delusion. However, in defense of the many critics and opponents of corporate global power, it could be said that if it can be demonstrated that these corporations do indeed have command of a large measure of economic, if not political, power, which is used in their interest (profits), then the concern with corporate global power of critics denotes neither paranoia nor delusion. However, Wolf is also correct in pointing out that corporations are not unchallenged masters of the universe; nor are they autonomous agents of the system or as powerful as critics claim. Indeed, the change seen over the past 20 years is market-driven globalization unleashed, consciously and voluntarily, by governments.

Even at the level of local currencies, neoliberalism is a ruin to Africa. For instance, in spite of the existence of currencies like the Communauté Financière d'Afrique CFA) Franc, globalization dollarizes the domestic currency in Francophone Africa, domestic prices and government budgets. With the ever-recurrent devaluation of the CFA currency, the urge to hold the euro, the U.S. dollar, or the British pound sterling becomes irresistible. This, in turn, causes further devaluation of the local currency. These "vanguard currencies" become the local units of account and render virtually valueless the local CFA currency units.

Globalization also has the tendency to destabilize the public finances of African states by prescribing drastic reduction in the activities of the government, the dismissal, retrenchment, and premature retirement of public employees, a drastic cut in social-sector programs, a ceiling on wages, increase in the prices of public utilities, the deregulation of the banking system, and the liberalization of capital movements, including interests, profits, and dividends. All these economic policies benefit the Euro-American and Japanese transnational corporations because of the flight of capital from Africa for "safe-keeping" in the industrialized world.

Developed countries grow rich by selling capital-intensive (thus cheap) products for a high price and buying labor-intensive (thus expensive) products from Africa and other underdeveloped countries for a low price. This imbalance of trade expands the gap between rich and poor. The wealthy sell products to be consumed, not tools for production. This maintains the monopolization of the tools of production, and assures a continued market for the product. Such control of tools of production is a strategy of a mercantilist process.

## DISMANTLING ECONOMIC FOUNDATIONS OF AFRICA'S DEMOCRACY

At first glance it may seem that the growth in Africa of export goods—such as coffee, cotton, sugar, and lumber—would be beneficial to these exporting countries, because it brings in revenue. In fact, it represents a type of exploitation called *unequal exchange*. An African country that exports raw or unprocessed materials may gain currency for their sale, but they lose it if they import processed goods. The reason is that processed goods or goods that require additional labor are more costly. Thus a country that exports lumber but does not have the capacity to process it must then reimport it in the form of finished lumber products, at a cost that is greater than the price it received for the raw product. The country that processes the materials gets the added revenue contributed by its laborers. This is why Africa continues to pay more for finished products from its raw materials because of this *unequal exchange*.

People and societies in different parts of Africa have long had contact with Asia, Europe, and in the past millennium, with the Americas. Trade, migration, and the exchange of ideas between African nations and societies with the outside world greatly impacted the history and development of Africa. Just as important, contact with African societies and peoples significantly influenced the history and development of societies and culture in Asia, Europe, and the Americas.

Societies in Western Asia have traded with societies in North and East Africa for thousands of years. Indeed, historians have recorded trade between China, South East Asia, and India with East Africa kingdoms and societies beginning over a thousand years ago. Societies in Southern and Southeastern Europe have had economic contact with societies in North and West Africa (via the trans-Sahara trade) for at least 3,000 years.

Trade benefited both partners in the exchange. Societies (at least the governing classes) in Africa, Asia, and Europe were better off economically as a result of economic contact. There was a dramatic change in the nature of contact between Africa and other regions of the world beginning at the end of the 15th century.

This was particularly true for the economic relationship between Europe and Africa. This period of time in Europe was known as the Renaissance, a period of learning and cultural change. Economically, European societies and nations were very interested in expanding trade with other regions of the world. These factors stimulated European nations, particularly Portugal and Spain, to seek ocean trade routes to Asia. In North America, Spanish sponsorship of Columbus and his voyages of exploration brought Europe into contact with the *New World*. Portuguese endeavors brought Europe into direct contact with parts of West, Southern, and East Africa, where Europeans had no prior contact.

Over the next 500 years, the nature of African economic contact with other regions of the world changed dramatically. European expansion into the Americas and Asia embraced Africa in a manner that drastically impacted many societies and people in Africa. Most dramatic was the Atlantic slave trade that forcibly removed millions of Africans to work as slaves in the farms and mines of South and North America, which in turn produced sugar, tobacco, and cotton, the profits from which fueled the Industrial Revolution in Europe. This was the beginning of the global economic system.

The next phase in the development of a truly global economic system was colonization by Europe of almost all of Africa, most of Asia, and, somewhat earlier, South and North America. As a result of the colonial experience, at the time of their political independence, the new African nations were integrated into an international economic network. How did colonial economic practice result in the integration of Africa into a global economy?

At the beginning of the 21st century, 40 years after political independence, is Africa still globally connected? If so, how has globalization affected Africa? Is there a relationship between globalization and Africa's current economic situation? These are important questions that need our attention. At independence, governments of the newly freed countries were committed to promoting economic growth and development. Import substitutions and diversification of exports were strategies that governments selected in an attempt to promote economic growth. Although these two policies are quite different, both strategies resulted in a stronger connection to or integration into the global economic system through joint economic ventures with foreign direct investment.

There are several definitions of foreign direct investment (FDI) in the literature of global economic integration. Rutherford (1992: 178; 1995: 178-79) defines FDI as investment in businesses of another country that often takes the form of setting up of local production facilities or the purchase of existing businesses. He contrasts FDI with portfolio investment that is the acquisition of securities. In various press releases by the United Nations Conference on Trade and Development (UNCTAD-www.unctad.org), FDI is defined as an investment involving management control of a resident entity in one economy by an enterprise resident in another economy. FDI involves a long-term relationship reflecting an investor's lasting interest in a foreign entity. FDI definitions differ greatly across countries. The differences are likely to be based on the criterion of the percentage of ownership of shares (i.e., control) between foreigners and citizens in a country's firms.

FDIs have been flowing to different regions of the world and countries in different proportions. The United States of America, the European Union, and Japan, have been the main FDI sources and destinations over time. The African continent has been receiving the lowest share of global FDI inflows over time. According to Bjorvatn (2000: 1), the whole of Africa receives less FDI than Singapore. This is in spite of the fact that FDI is welcome and actively sought by virtually all African countries but the expected surge of FDI into the continent as a whole has not occurred. The continent did not benefit from the FDI boom that began in the mid-1980s. Since 1970, FDI inflows into Africa have increased only modestly, from an annual average of almost $1.9 billion in 1983-87 to $3.1 billion in 1988-92, and $6 billion in 1993-97. For comparison purposes it should be noted that the global FDI flows in 1998 reached a record $644 billion (UNCTAD, *Press Release*, June 22, 1999).

The figure says much about Africa's share when we compare it with, say, the $6 billion inflow to the region between 1993 and 1997. The inflow to Western Europe in 1997 was $114,857 million and to North America the figure for the same year was $98,994 million. FDI inflows into developing countries as a group almost quadrupled from less than $20 billion in 1981-95 to $75 billion in 1991-95. Inflows to Africa in that period merely doubled. It is not an exaggeration to say that Africa's share in total inflows of FDI to developing countries dropped significantly from more than 11percent in 1976-80 to 9 percent in 1981-85, 5 percent in 1991-95 and to 4 percent in 1996-97. Its share of total outflows from the United States of America, the European Union, and Japan, the most important source regions for FDI, was even lower during 1987-97 periods as other developing regions such as Asia, Latin America, and the former communist states of Eastern and Central Europe— became more attractive as FDI receptacles. The share never exceeded 2 percent until 1996. It increased to 2.4 percent in 1997.

Africa's global FDI share is also reflected in the ration of FDI to Gross Domestic Product (GDP). In 1970 the region attracted more FDI per $1,000 of GDP than Asia, Latin America, and the Caribbean. The FDI in dollars per $1,000 of GDP in 1970 was 7.9, 6.7, and 2.7 for Africa; Latin America and the Caribbean; and South, East and South East Asia respectively. The corresponding figures for 1996 are 13.6, 24.8, and 25.7. For 1997, the figures are 14.7, 33.8 and 28.3 respectively. By 1990 Africa had fallen behind other developing areas in terms of its value of FDI inflows and the FDI/GDP ratio, and has stayed behind since then. In the 1990s, the gap increased widely when the worldwide surge in FDI flows into developing world largely bypassed the region.

It should be mentioned here that the share of FDI flowing into Africa has not been even in all countries. Egypt and Nigeria have received a lion's share of FDIs flowing into the region in terms of absolute size. The share has however declined from more than 67 percent in 1983-87 to 54 percent in 1988-92, and 38 percent in 1993-97. Looking at the figures for FDI inflow into Africa as a whole it is clear that its global share is by all standards very low. This share needs to be increased given the potential positive roles that FDI can play in the continent's development. However, Africa's ability to increase its share is questionable. It is doubtful whether the continent has enough of the FDI determinants required to attract more of the global FDI outflows.

The perceived risk of investment is being reduced by: (1) legal reforms to simplify commercial jurisprudence and improve the functioning of the courts, enforce contracts fairly and impartially, and protect property rights; (2)

regulatory reforms that provide an efficient structure of incentives, including through rationalized investment codes; (3) targeted government spending to ensure that the necessary human capital and physical infrastructure is created and extended; and (4) consistent, credible policy formulation that minimizes the likelihood of policy reversal and maximizes its predictability. To ensure the successful implementation of these policies, greater attention is being given to civil service reform. The concern here is less with African welfare than the profit from invested capital.

## FAULTY ASSUMPTIONS

It is assumed that FDI is good and necessary for the development of Africa. FDI continues to be a driving force in the globalization process that characterizes the modern world economy. The process has diminished the importance of territorial boundaries, and every part of the world is in one way or another involved in the process. The continent should therefore increase its global share of FDI. The assumption is based on the potentially positive roles that FDI can play in the development of the continent. This justifies the concern about the need for and ability of the continent to increase its global share of FDI inflows. There are some potential roles that FDI can play in host economies.

Africa, like many other developing regions of the world, needs a substantial inflow of external resources in order to fill the saving and foreign exchange gaps associated with a rapid rate of capital accumulation and growth needed to overcome widespread poverty and to lift living standards to acceptable levels. The need for external financing is nowhere more pressing than in Africa, where income levels are too low to generate adequate domestic resources for the attainment of even modest rates of investment and growth. Why is this so?

Through the 1960s and 1970s, countries were encouraged to borrow on the international markets and finance their own investments. Among the alternative means of financing these investments was FDI. It was argued that this alternative was one of the most expensive ways to finance capital accumulation. Many countries borrowed instead. As a result of this latter strategy, many developing countries, including those in Africa, accumulated huge debts. Because of these huge debts, they have less accessibility to international capital. According to UNCTAD (2000a: 4), long term bank lending has completely disappeared in Africa since the mid-1980s. Private inflows of capital into the region have mainly consisted of FDI and short term bank lending. It is now widely recognized that FDI can play a useful role in development. The usefulness of FDI is not only due to its financial contribution; rather, it is important because of other characteristics of FDI when it forms part of a package of investment options.

The reasons are readily available. FDIs can (1) create employment in host economies; (2) be vehicles of transfer of technology; (3) provide superior skills and management techniques to host economies; (4) help in the capital-formation process; (5) facilitate local firms' access to international markets; (6) use local resources more efficiently and productively; (7) increase product diversity; (8)

149

use environmentally clean technology; (9) observe human and labor rights; and (10) create a lot of linkage effects in the economy, both forward and backward.

Generally speaking, then, it can be said that FDI can be an engine of economic growth in a host economy. Such investments can sustain and improve economic development in a country or a region for that matter. Given the economic conditions in Africa and its level of development, the need for FDI in the region cannot be overemphasized. The continent needs to increase its share of global FDI inflows as one of the most likely ways to increase the needed external capital for its development.

## FDI DETERMINANTS

FDI determinants are the factors that determine inflows of foreign capital into a given geographical location, say a country or a region. They give investors the confidence needed to invest in foreign markets. The list of these determinants may be very long, but not all determinants are equally important to every investor in every location at all times.

Some determinants may be more important to a given investor in a given location at a given time than to another investor.

A given determinant may be a necessary and satisfactory factor by itself for FDI inflow in one location but not in another. For the most part, they form a complementary set. What interests us in this section is to find out the factors that would motivate or attract a multinational enterprise (MNE) to invest in a particular destination after making the decision to go multinational. These are the factors that give the investors the confidence to commit their normally massive, expensive, and scarce resources in a given foreign destination.

It is difficult to determine the exact quantity and quality of FDI determinants that should be present in a location for it to attract a given level of FDI inflows. What is clear is that every location must possess a certain critical minimum of these determinants before FDI inflows begin to take place. UNCTAD's 1998 World Investment Report (1999a) presents some host country determinants of FDI. These include:

Policy Framework for FDI:
- economic, political, and social stability
- rules regulating entry and operations (of FDIs)
- standard of treatment of foreign affiliates
- policies on functioning and structure of the markets
- international agreement on FDI
- privatization policy
- trade policy (tariffs and non-tariff barriers and coherence of FDI and trade policy
- tax policy

Economic Determinants or Business Facilitation:

- investment promotion (including image-building and investment-generating activities and investment –facilitating services)
- investment incentives
- hassle costs (related to corruption and administrative efficiency)
- social amenities (for example bilingual schools, quality of life
- after-investment services

UNCTAD (1998) lists the principal economic determinants in host countries. It matches types of FDI by motives of the firms with those principal economic determinants. Where we have a market-seeking type of FDI, it looks for criteria concerning market size and per capita income, market growth, access to regional and global markets, country-specific consumer preferences; and structure of markets. In the case of FDI of a resource/asset seeking type, the focus would turn on raw materials; low-cost unskilled labor as well as skilled labor; technological, innovative, and other created assets (like brand names); and physical infrastructure (ports, roads, power, telecommunications).

There is another type of FDI: one that is directed at ensuring efficiency. This type looks for favorable balances in the costs of resources and assets listed above, adjusted for labor productivity as well as in other inputs such as transport and communications costs to/from and within the host economy. Furthermore, it is interested in whether or not the host economy is part of a regional integration agreement that may be conducive to the establishment of regional corporate networks.

Finally, given that FDI is increasingly geared to technologically intensive activities, technological assets are becoming more and more important for transnational corporations (TNCs) to maintain and enhance their competitiveness. A destination's possession of a strong indigenous technology base is vital for attracting high-technology FDI and for research and development (R&D) investments by TNCs (UNCTAD, 1998, Table 14.1: 91). A would-be host country, in order to attract scarce FDI, must be able to provide the requisite inputs for modern production systems.

For example, efficiency-seeking FDI will tend to be located in those destinations that are able to supply a skilled and disciplined workforce and good technical and physical infrastructure. Bjorvatn (1999) says that firms will locate their industrial activities in countries with superior quality of national infrastructure. Good quantity and quality of infrastructure in a location is among the factors that facilitate business operations. Physical infrastructure includes roads, railways, ports, and telecommunication facilities. The latter include traditional postal services and modern communication facilities such as the network Internet.

Regional trading blocks (RTBs) are essential determinants of FDI. These represent various forms of economic integration among countries. They are designed to promote cross or intercountry trade and mobility of factor services from within member countries by fostering a more market-oriented pattern of intraregional resource allocation. They have the potential to increase the size of a unified market. Common external tariffs imposed by RTBs are likely to force nonmembers to enter the market through FDI rather than through trade. This is one of the ways in which RTBs may be among the essential FDI determinants. No wonder then that the European Union as a group attracts so much FDI (See for example UNCTAD, 1998 for figures).

The importance of regional groupings as a factor in attracting FDI has also been advocated by the UNCTAD. The organization argues that countries stand to reap some economies of scale in regional groupings and that it develops complimentarity of interests between land-locked and coastal countries (see UNCTAD, *Press Release*, July5, 1999). In the African context, such economic groupings as the Economic Community of West African States (ECOWAS) and the Southern African Development Corporation (SADC) may be counted as RTBs.

Language and business culture are also determinants of FDI inflows. In a destination where a language like English is commonly spoken by the majority of the population, one would expect more FDI inflows than if the case were otherwise. Of course, we have cases where there has been more FDI inflow to destinations where language is on the surface a barrier—such as South Korea, Indonesia, Taiwan, and China—than to where language seems to be an advantage as in most African countries— Nigeria, Kenya, Tanzania, and Ghana— where English is widely spoken. Generally it can be assumed that the former group of countries possesses more of the other FDI determinants than the latter. For example, the huge market that China represents is likely to overshadow the language problem there. In that case language, like many other determinants, seems to be an important but not a necessary and satisfactory factor by itself.

Tax exemptions, tax holidays, or tax reduction for foreign investors and similar incentives would play a positive role in attracting FDIs into a given destination. Some other types of incentives that may play similar roles include guarantees against arbitrary treatment in case of nationalization; government provision of such utilities as water, power, and communication at subsidized prices or free of cost; tariffs or quotas set for competing imports; reductions/ elimination of import duties on inputs; interest-rate subsidies; guarantees for loans and coverage for exchange-rate risks; wage subsidies; training grants; and relaxation of legal obligation toward employees. But the costs of these incentives to the host economy must be compared to the potential benefits that FDI may bring. If, and only if, the benefits of the FDI projects more than offset the costs should host economies offer any incentives.

Labor availability and relatively low labor costs, high skills, and efficiency are important factors determining FDI inflow into a given destination. For example, the region covered by the 15 former communist states of Central and Eastern Europe is seen by some MNEs such as Daewoo, as a low-cost production base that can be used as an export platform to service West European markets. Relatively lower wage costs have also been used to account for increased FDIs in Asia especially in the Tigers of Asia (Hong Kong, Singapore, Taiwan, and South Korea). The labor force has to be nonmilitant. There should be generally good labor relations; low rates of industrial disputes, strikes, and lockouts; and a high level of employee loyalty in a given destination for FDIs to flow there in a substantial amount.

Investors may also be attracted by other factors such as low- cost but high-quality inputs and minimal transaction costs in their interaction with the government and other bureaucracies. The extent to which unnecessary, distorting, and wasteful business costs are reduced will most likely contribute positively to FDI inflow into a given destination.

The strength of a currency also may determine FDI inflow. A relatively weak currency would be more likely to attract FDIs than a relatively strong one. Realizing potential losses inherent in converting weak currency to hard ones, many foreign investors may simply plow back into the host economy their profits and other remittances. Currency devaluation may lead to cheap assets. Cheap assets, on the other hand, are expected to attract more FDIs especially through mergers and acquisitions (M&As).

Economic and structural reforms in a country are very important in winning foreign investors confidence to take their investment funds there. Such reforms can be very wide and far-reaching. The various reform measures may overlap with each other. Reforms, whether social, political, or economic, should aim at creating, maintaining, and/or improving the environment for business, both local and foreign. Some of the important reforms can involve the relaxation of entry restrictions in various sectors, deregulation in various industries, abolition of price controls, easing of controls over M&As and trade practices, removal of government monopoly, privatization, independence of the Central Bank, elimination of import licensing, and the removal of foreign exchange, exchange- rate and interest-rate controls. Such reforms are likely to create a business-friendly environment that is likely to attract more FDI. But the reforms may be expensive to a nation and its people. For these reforms to be justified, they must take into consideration the impact on the populace of the country concerned. Investors are more likely to choose those locations that make it easier to do business. These are likely to be found in countries with solid economic fundamentals. The 1997 figure for developed countries' share of global FDI inflow (72 percent) most likely reflects the presence of the solid economic fundamentals in the United States and some European countries.

The attractiveness of developing countries for foreign capital depends on the capabilities of these countries to apply existing technologies and not on their role in producing new ones. That is, FDI inflow to such countries in the first place will depend on, among other things, the existence of this capability. The ability to use the existing technology is yet another factor that can determine FDI inflow into a specific destination.

Nondiscriminatory treatment of investors, consistency, and predictability in government policies are also among the FDI determinants. Investors need to be in a position where they can plan their activities efficiently within the policy environment of the government. Those government policies that directly or indirectly affect investments should be reliable, accessible, up to date, and widely publicized.

Government credibility is essential if more FDI is to flow to a destination. In this connection, the system of processing and approving new investments may be a crucial determinant for further FDI inflow into the same destination. A long, bureaucratic, nontransparent and corrupt process is likely to scare away potential investors. What is needed is a relatively short, transparent, and noncorrupt process undertaken in, if possible, a one-stop shop. Some other FDI determinants include a positive economic growth in a given destination.

Economic growth in turn determines market prospects. It is more likely that FDI will flow more to destinations with promising economic growth both in the short and long run. Other FDI determinants mentioned in the literature include low indirect social costs like bribery or its absence; availability of risk capital; synergy between public and private research and development programs; and low rate or absence of criminality, alcohol, and narcotic abuse, as these affect the security of personnel and the quality of the labor force as a whole. The values, norms, and culture of the population in the host economy must be ready to support the principle of free competition. Authorities must be able to adjust policy to reflect new economic, social, and political realities of the time. Prevailing views on environmental issues and the occurrence of activism, while important, must not be fanatical and detrimental to business operations. They must be reasonable. Countries' health services, recreation possibilities, and overall quality of life, too, influence FDI inflow.

A country's membership in a binding multinational investment agreement and institutions concerning FDI can reduce the perceived risk of investing there. When the risk of investing in a location is reduced, we expect to see an increase in investments there. Such agreements include several bilateral investment treaties and double taxation treaties. Among the organizations that have an impact on the flow of FDI are the World Intellectual Property Organization (WIPO); the convention establishing the Multinational Investment Guarantee Agency (MIGA); the Convention on the Recognition and Enforcement of Foreign Arbitral Awards; and the Convention on the Settlement of Investment Disputes between States and Nationals of Other States.

The presence of investment opportunities in a country, needless to say, is another important FDI determinant. The opportunities should be made known to potential investors through effective promotion, which includes marketing a country and coordinating the supply of a country's immobile assets with the specific needs of targeted investors. One cannot always expect that investors will take the trouble of finding out the available opportunities in every country. Countries generally reach out to investors.

Where the world's largest TNCs invest is sometimes determined by access to technology and innovative capacity in particular countries.

These factors, in contrast to natural resources, are called "created assets." These include communication infrastructure, marketing networks, and knowledge which can be used as a proxy for skills; attitudes to wealth creation and business culture; technological, managerial, and innovative capabilities, competence at organizing income-generating assets productively; as well as relationships, such as between firms and contracts with governments, and the stock of information; and, finally, trademarks or goodwill. Possessing the assets just adumbrated is critical for competitiveness in a liberalizing and globalizing world economy. However, the traditional factors such as access to markets and natural and other resources like low-cost labor are still key FDI determinants, especially for many firms that have not yet developed large-scale international operations.

Some of the determinants overlap. It is almost impossible to give a threshold of the determinants that should exist in a location before a given amount of FDI begins to flow there. But it is clear that a certain critical minimum of the determinants should exist before the inflows start to take place. A location that possesses an optimal quantity and quality of the determinants can be said to be an attractive destination for FDI. For a destination to attract or increase its FDI share it should possess this critical minimum of the determinants.

## AFRICA AND ITS GLOBAL SHARE OF FDI

Can Africa increase its global share of FDI inflow? This is a complex and provocative question. The discussion is based on some of the FDI determinants presented in the previous section. The extent to which the determinants are present in the region is identified. I do not pretend to address all the issues facing Africa as regards its ability to increase FDI inflow. However, I expect that the issues discussed will be considered representative. It is assumed that when a given location does not have adequate quantity and quality of FDI determinants, it can be very difficult for it to increase FDI inflows in a substantial way. In what follows, I discuss the presence of FDI determinants in Africa and the possibility of increasing its global share of FDI.

Among the features that negatively affect the flow of FDI into Africa is its image, which has not been favorable. Too often potential investors discount the continent as a location for investment because a negative image of the region as a whole conceals the complex diversity of economic performance and the existence of investment opportunities in individual countries. In a foreword for UNCTAD 1999 UN Secretary-General Kofi Annan ( UNCTAD 1999b: 1) puts it this way: "For many people in other parts of the world, the mention of Africa evokes images of civil unrest, war, poverty, disease and mounting social problems. Unfortunately, these images are not just fiction. They reflect the dire reality in some African countries—though certainly not in all."

When investors perceive the continent as a home for wars, poverty, diseases, and a generally unfriendly investment destination, the result is the diversion of these investments to other regions. It may then become very difficult for the continent to increase its global share of FDI if its current negative image continues to prevail. What is needed is for both the African continent and the international community as a whole to eliminate those negative factors that give the continent its poor image. The media should not exaggerate the reality. Instead it should give a more balanced and positive picture of the continent. War in Somalia should be reported as war in Somalia and not as war in Africa, the way war in Yugoslavia is reported as war in Yugoslavia and not war in Europe.

The promotion of peace, economic prosperity, and sustainable development for Africa's people is still a big challenge. There are many symbols of failure, despair, brutality, and people who are physically and psychologically scarred by many years of dreadful warfare across the continent. Examples include Sierra Leone, Liberia, Somalia, Rwanda, Algeria, Angola, and Mozambique.

The investment climate in such locations is not likely to attract a substantial quantity and quality of investments. To the extent that dreadful warfare persists in Africa it can be very difficult for the continent to increase its global share of FDI inflow in any appreciable number. The Economist (May 13, 2000: 17), under the heading "Hopeless Africa," points out that, " since Sierra Leone seemed to epitomize so much of the rest of Africa, it began to look as though the world might just give up on the entire continent." The country is an extreme, but not untypical, example of a state with all the epiphenomena and none of the institutions of government. The situations in Sierra Leone and other war-torn territories in Africa unfortunately have negative effects on the prospects of FDI inflow into other countries.

As pointed out earlier and evidenced in the article referred to above, unrest in Sierra Leone is reported as unrest in Africa. Alongside Sierra Leone, one can mention the seven- year civil war in Burundi, which has claimed at least 100,000 lives. One can also point to the "curtain of fire" stretching from Eritrea, through Ethiopia, Sudan, and Congo to Angola. Currently there are at least 14 conflicts that rage across the continent. A Norwegian Newspaper, Vårt Land (June 17, 2000), reported that every fifth African is living in a conflict-prone zone. It is a fact that few investors, if any, would like to operate in conflict-prone zones. This is clearly not good news if the region is to increase its global share of FDI. Parties involved in such conflicts should give peace a chance if FDI is to increase in any appreciable amounts not only in the countries ravaged by war but also in the whole of Africa.

Conflicts are a barrier to efforts at increasing a location's share of global FDI. In World Bank (2000: 59), some costs of conflict in Africa are outlined. These include social and economic costs where it occurs and in neighboring countries by generating flows of refugees, increasing military spending, impeding key communication routes, and reducing trade and investment (domestic and foreign). Conflicts divert resources from development uses. It is estimated that a total of $1 billion is used on conflict yearly in Central Africa. The figure amounts to more than $800 million in West Africa. On top of this comes the cost of refugee assistance, estimated at more than $500 million for Central Africa alone. For example, Sudan's military spending is more than three times the African average.

This may have caused investment to fall by 16 per cent of GDP. Its civil war may have reduced growth by up to 8 percent (World Bank: 2000).

Crime and violence have many direct economic and human costs that may hinder FDI inflow directly or indirectly. They inhibit development in many ways. For example, some factories may not operate more than one shift because employees cannot commute safely to work. FDI projects depending on operating several shifts may therefore not be able to do so. This may mean that they lose their profitability and competitiveness. They are therefore likely to be scared away from investing in Africa.

Other factors that may hinder more FDI inflow to Africa include the AIDS epidemic and tropical diseases like malaria. From *CNN In-Depth Specials* (July 19, 2000), we learn that of the 33.6 million people infected with the HIV virus worldwide, 23.5 million (about 70 percent) are Africans. The United Nations (2004) estimated that the number of AIDS orphans would reach 13 million by 2001. The continent has already lost 13.8 million people to AIDS, and nearly 10,500 new cases are diagnosed daily. AIDS may hinder FDI inflow in that it decimates the already scarce skilled manpower. According to *Vårt Land* (June 17, 2000), the International Labor Organization (ILO) estimated that the labor force in Africa would fall by 20 percent in the near future due to the AIDS epidemic.

The availability of a healthy labor force is a very important FDI determinant. FDI will likely be scared away from Africa if the continent's already scarce labor force is further depleted by this epidemic. Besides reducing the badly needed labor force in Africa, the AIDS epidemic makes it necessary for authorities and individuals to divert scarce and very valuable pecuniary and nonpecuniary resources like time and personnel to AIDS and AIDS-related issues. These resources could have been used to create a more enabling environment for business on the continent. They could, for example, be invested in infrastructure and education. The latter steps would in turn facilitate the efforts to increase FDI inflow. The global share of FDI inflow to Africa would most likely increase by a substantial amount if it were not for the impact of the AIDS epidemic. AIDS then threatens the economic future of the continent.

Some examples of how HIV/AIDS can threaten the economic future of Africa can be drawn from Tanzania. Statistics from The Brooke Bond Limited, a giant tea company in Southern Tanzania, show that it has been highly affected by the high incidence of HIV infection among its workforce, and the concomitant high costs associated with absenteeism, and health care. Statistics from 1992 to September 2000 show a HIV-positive rate of 70 percent among a sample of sick company employees who were tested. In 1992, about 65 percent of tested patients were HIV positive. In 1998, out of 154 patients tested, 133 or 86.4 percent were HIV positive.

In 2000, the figure was 81 percent. The statistics are silent on the actual cost of the epidemic at Brooke Bond. The costs are however likely to be high. Apart from Brooke Bond, several other companies are facing similar HIV-connected problems in Tanzania. The companies include Tanzania Electrical Supply Company (TANESCO), National Insurance Company (NIC), and Tanzania Housing Corporation (THC). In 1995, 1.5 million adults were estimated to be infected with HIV. Most infections occur among the most economically active group of adults, in the age group 15 – 45. HIV/AIDS then becomes not only a health problem but also a developmental one with great impact on life expectancy and the economy at large. The horrifying data on the ravages of the HIV/AIDS pandemic is located at: http://www.ippmedia.com/ft/2000/12/13/ft1.asp. There are numerous other factors that militate against the inflow of FDI into Africa. These include malaria and other tropical diseases, forces of nature such as floods and drought, and, on occasion, government-sponsored thuggery, not to talk of corruption.

The refugee problem also adds to the bad image of Africa. The continent is home to more than half of the world's refugee population—about 12 million, including those internally displaced. Life as a refugee is not the best one can wish for. One can suffer some psychological and emotional torture that makes one unable to work productively. That is to say, it can be difficult for most refugees to supply their labor force for productive work. The problem of refugees contributes to the shortage of the needed labor force in Africa. Refugees are a cost to host governments and organizations, such as the United Nations, that finance them. Resources expended on refugees could have been used in creating a more competitive environment for investments.

So far we have discussed factors that are internal to Africa. Some factors that are external to Africa play a part in making it difficult for the continent to increase its global share of FDI. In this connection, we can cite such factors as the legacy of colonial rule, Cold War rivalry, the debt crisis, exploitative trading relations, and too strict demands for economic reform from the International Money Fund and the World Bank.

The colonization of Africa by Europe led to the current artificial division of the continent, which has been one of the major sources of war in Africa. Countries fight with each other mainly for the purpose of controlling resources found on the other side of boundaries. The economic foundations laid by the colonial masters in Africa aimed at serving themselves. Africa was made to be a supplier of raw materials, primarily from the primary sector producing agricultural outputs and minerals. The continent was made to be a market for finished products. Such economic bases are among the factors that contribute to the current poverty level in Africa. This poverty makes it difficult for the continent to create an investment friendly environment.

The exploitative trading relations between the North and South partially account for problems in Africa. In the current trading relation, the North dictates the price of commodities in its favor and against the South. Most African countries find themselves on the losing side. They mostly experience deficits in their import-export performance. This leads to, among other things, the difficulty using domestic sources to finance their development projects. As a result, most development projects, for example, infrastructure development, are likely to be abandoned. Poor infrastructure, in turn, becomes a barrier to FDI inflow.

External borrowing may offer an alternative to financing development projects by using domestic sources. This alternative is not without potential problems for the borrowing countries. When debts are accumulated, the payment of accruing interests may oblige the borrowing countries to divert resources to the service of debt repayment instead of investing in the country in order thereby to create a more attractive business environment for investments. Meanwhile, when they fail to repay, they fall into debt crisis and this makes it even harder for them to borrow more. In this way, the debt crisis in Africa is a barrier to the continent increasing its global share of FDI.

The presence and emergence of other developing regions of the world (Asia, Latin America, the Caribbean, and the former socialist states of Eastern and Central Europe) as more attractive investment locations adds to the challenges that Africa must encounter before it can add to its global share of FDI. Several regions of the world are competing for limited investments. Only those locations with adequate FDI determinants are likely to be able to increase their global share of FDI in an appreciable manner.

However much external factors may contribute to Africa's inability to attract FDI, we must ultimately focus on internal factors that militate against Africa's participation in the global economy. These include the region's very low gross domestic product. According to the World Bank (2000) the combined GDP for the region is smaller than that of Belgium and is divided among 48 countries with a median GDP of just over $2 billion, which is the output of a town of 60,000 in a rich country. Africa accounts for barely 1 percent of global GDP and only 2 percent of world trade. Its share of global manufactured exports is almost zero.

In the World Bank (2000) report referred to above, it is indicated that Africa is regressing. Many countries are worse off today than they were at independence in the 1960s. Although the region's population could potentially represent a huge market, low levels of incomes in the region erode this potential. Mozambique, for example, had a per head income of $80 in 1998. The region as a whole had an annual GDP per capita of $800 in the same year. The low-income level in Africa, which translates to limited purchasing power, then is a barrier to market-seeking FDI.

With its rapidly growing population the continent needs to grow by at least 5 percent per annum just to maintain current poverty levels. In 1997, much of Africa had a GDP growth rate of 3 percent and for the period 1997-2006, the growth is estimated to be 4.1 percent. With population growing at a faster rate than the GDP, there is a danger of growth in poverty in Africa. This does not present a promising environment for a substantial increase in FDI.

Africa has a poor "hard" physical infrastructure, like telecommunications, power, transportation, water, and sanitation. These are very crucial for development and for a location's ability to attract and keep FDI. The discussion on infrastructure draws much from World Bank (2000). Low population density, small national markets, and a high number of small and landlocked countries, make it difficult to develop infrastructure in the continent. For example, small national markets limit economies of scale, reduce competitiveness, and increase risk.

The World Bank (2000) points out that Poland has more roads than the whole of Africa. With 10 million telephone lines in the continent—fewer than in Brazil, and with half of them in South Africa—most Africans live two hours away from the nearest electronic communication. The continent contains just 2 percent of the world's telephone main lines. According to *The Economist* (November 25, 2000), 34 countries in Africa have less than ten telephone lines per 1,000 people, compared to the average of 500 lines to 1,000 in rich countries. This outcry is found in the Magazine's article on poor telephone infrastructure in Africa titled "Call Africa, and wait and wait" (ibid: 68). The article stresses that Nigeria's 120 million inhabitants have only 4 lines per 1000 people. The introduction and rapid spread of mobile phones has changed the situation for the better. This seems to be the situation in some other African countries, such as Nigeria and Ghana, where mobile phones are available at a rapidly increasing rate. Other infrastructural facilities such as paved roads, railways, ports, and telecommunications are equally inadequate and, in some cases, nonexistent.

Another issue of concern about infrastructure in Africa is its cost. From the World Bank (2000) we learn that the continent has the highest transport cost of any region. The continent is isolated from major maritime and air routes and is served by peripheral, high-cost routes. Freight costs for imports are 70 percent higher in East and West Africa than in developing Asia. For land-locked Africa the cost is more than twice as high as in Asia. Internal transport in Africa is also costlier. For example, in the mid-1990s, road transport costs in Côte d'Ivoire were two to three times those in Southeast Asia. These high costs are attributed to, among other things, lower road quality, higher fuel taxes, higher imported vehicle costs, and costly bureaucratic procedures. The cost of telephone calls among African countries can be fifty to one hundred times the cost of calls within North America.

No doubt, physical infrastructure is among the very important FDI determinants. Its value lies in its consumption, not its production. It is an input that is crucial to all other production. Its poor quality results in low competitiveness because cost, quality, and access are important determinants of competitiveness. Poor infrastructure leads to weak market integration and slower growth. From the above, it should be clear that Africa's prospects of increasing its global share of FDI inflow are not bright.

A modern communication and information technology infrastructure like the Internet is yet to be common in the region. The gap created by the digital divide between Africa and the developed world is extremely huge. This is a negative in terms of the ability to increase FDI in the region, especially in this e-commerce age. Ample resources will be required if this infrastructure is to be provided at acceptable standards. There must be exponential increases in access to electricity for more Africans, for instance.

NCTAD (2000b) correctly points out that the African continent has many challenges to overcome before it can more fully exploit the advantages of e-commerce. These include the low level of economic development and small per capita incomes, the limited skill base with which to build the e-commerce services, the number of Internet users needed to build a critical mass of online consumers, and the lack of familiarity with even the traditional forms of electronic commerce such as telephone sales and use of credit cards. Remedying the above depends on the provision of adequate telecommunications facilities in most areas of the continent as discussed in the World Bank report of 2000.

## OPPORTUNITIES AND POTENTIALS IN AFRICA

Despite the problems that make it difficult for Africa to increase its global share of FDI, the region still has some opportunities and potentials to increase the share if decisive actions are taken. A more complex and encouraging picture is slowly emerging in Africa. There are some factors that give rise to optimism that Africa may be on the right track to create an FDI-friendly environment.

The presence of these factors alone does not automatically guarantee an increased FDI inflow; the factors must be optimally balanced. Additional actions geared to proper promotion of investment opportunities in the region should be taken. Those encouraging factors that create an enabling environment for FDI should be made known to potential investors. This is because the investors have been mainly hearing about the negative factors presented in the previous section and may not be aware of these new realities. We discuss below some of these encouraging factors.

Most African countries have embarked on reform programs intended to regain macroeconomic balance, improve resource allocation, and restore growth. Privatization is opening the door to foreign and domestic business and better services. It should be noted that privatization is essential for FDIs that choose mergers and acquisition as their entry mode. Currently there are new windows of opportunities opening up for Africa. If the continent exploits these opportunities properly, its chance of increasing its global share of FDI inflows is likely to brighten.

The first window is the current greater political opening in the continent with a sharp rise in political participation. This opens up spaces for greater public accountability and pressure from civil society for better management of public resources. There is more focus on proper management of the economy today among African leaders than in the past. They seem to have the maturity to address the weaknesses of past policies.

The second window is the end of the Cold War. After World War II, Africa became a strategic and ideological battlefield where external powers sought reliable allies rather than effective development partners. The end of the Cold War signaled a reduction in external support for peacekeeping and aid flows due to waning geopolitical competition. But it also opened a window for donors and recipients to attend to issues pertaining to the effectiveness of different development strategies.

The third window is globalization and new technology. This offers greater opportunities for Africa. World markets are far more open now than ever before. The pool of capital seeking diversified international investment is growing rapidly, partly due to the demographic transition in industrial countries. Advances in the area of information technology offer huge potentials for Africa.

The region has several economic groupings or integration that may represent different continuum of RTBs. These include The Economic Community of West African States, Common Market for Eastern and Southern Africa (COMESA), and Southern African Development Community. If these groupings are properly arranged and the potentials that they represent are properly exploited, they can attract more market-seeking FDI.

The fact that at least 17 countries had broad-based privatization programs in place by the end of 1999 adds to the possibility of Africa increasing its global share of FDI. The privatization of state-owned enterprises signals increased investment opportunities. In most cases, the privatized enterprises are sold to foreign investors due to lack of capital on the part of the local population. The case of Tanzania where most of the privatized enterprises are sold to foreign investors may be a good example. In this connection it needs to be pointed out that it has been shown that Africa has the highest rates of return for capital investments in some cases UNCTAD (1999b).

Profitability is of prime interest to foreign investors. What may be the least known fact about FDI in Africa is the high rate of profitability for investments there and that in recent years it has been higher than in most other regions. UNCTAD (1999b: iv) reports that "from the viewpoint of foreign companies, investment in Africa seems to be highly profitable, more than in most other regions." For example, Japanese TNCs had the following percentage of profitability in the following regions in 1995: West Asia (12.6 percent), Latin America and the Caribbean (7.7 percent), Africa (5.6 percent), South East Asia (2.9 percent), Pacific (1.9 percent), North America (1.1 percent) and Europe (0.8 percent).

One can find a similar trend when one looks at the rates of return on U. S. FDI in Africa (see UNCTAD, 1999b: 19, for details). These details do not include South Africa. For example, for 1997, the rate was 25.3 percent compared to 16.2 percent for Asia and the Pacific. The figure for Latin America and the Caribbean for the same year was 12.5 percent. For the developing countries and all countries, the rate of return was 14 percent and 12.3 percent respectively. In fact, between 1983 and 1997, it was only in 1996 that the rate of return in Africa for U.S. FDI was below 10 percent (See UNCTAD, 1999b:18 for rates of return year by year from 1983 to 1997). Since 1990, the rate of return in Africa has averaged 29 percent. Since 1991, it has been higher than in any other region, in many years by a factor of two or more. The net income from British direct investment in Africa (not including Nigeria) increased by 60 percent between 1989 and 1995.

When looking at these relatively very attractive rates of return and profitability in Africa it becomes a paradox that the continent has not witnessed a proportional FDI inflow. Ordinarily, one would expect that investments would flow to Africa in great numbers so as to benefit from these high rates of return. But the opposite is the case. It seems that the logic of capital is preempted in Africa. Capital does not seem to flow to Africa despite the continent's promise of relatively high rates of return. Among the possible explanations of this paradox may be the assumption that these rates of return for capital investment are not widely known among the investor community.

Where the rates are known, they may reflect the risks of investing in the continent due to the absence of some other FDI determinant. It is possible that the high rates of return, from the point of view of potential investors, do not sufficiently offset the risks of investing in the continent. This may make investors turn away from Africa as a profitable investment destination. If the high rates of return for capital investment in Africa are made widely known among the investor community and other risks of investing in the continent are substantially reduced, one can expect to see an increased FDI flow to Africa.

Africa has enormous untapped potential and hidden growth reserves. For example, the continent is home to the world's largest reserves of a number of strategic minerals, including gold, diamonds, platinum, cobalt, and chromium. The mining and petroleum sectors have, for this reason, great potential for attracting more FDI into the region if appropriate steps are taken. It is worth noting that contrary to common perception, FDI in Africa is no longer concentrated in natural resources. Services and manufacturing are key sectors for FDI. In Nigeria, manufacturing attracted almost 50 percent and services close to 20 percent of the total FDI stock in the country at the beginning of the 1990s. Mauritius has been attractive as a location for manufacturing plants, including plants for electronic equipment, since the 1980s. All these give cause for optimism about Africa's ability to increase its global share of FDI.

We have reason to believe that the perception of Africa among investors may be changing for the better. When one peruses "Corporate view of Africa 1999" as presented in *Focus* on the new Africa booklet that accompaniesUNCTAD,1999b, one finds that the view of Africa held by corporate leaders of such MNEs as Barclay's Africa, Citibank, Coca-Cola Africa, Nestle, Norvatis Agro AG, Shell, Standard Chartered Bank, Unilever, and Vodafone Group International includes an acknowledgment of the impressive rates of economic growth in some key African economies, growing political stability and financial prudence, great opportunities to market products to over 600 million consumers, long term perspective and sustained efforts by TNCs, and great confidence in the underlying potential of Africa. To the extent that such positive corporate views of Africa will be widely shared by the investment community, it can be a good sign for more FDI inflow to Africa.

The international community has made some efforts to promote FDI into Africa. Such efforts include measures to accelerate foreign debt relief as a means to support economic growth in the region. Official development assistance (ODA) has a significant role in help to build infrastructure and support domestic development generally. UNCTAD undertakes investment policy reviews in Africa, and in collaboration with the International Chamber of Commerce (ICC) it has launched a project on investment guides and capacity building. The Multilateral Investment Guarantee Agency carries out assessments of institutional capacity for a large number of investment promotion agencies (IPAs) and assists them to formulate effective strategies for attracting FDI, primarily through its Promote Africa field functions. All these seem to be opportunities that, if well exploited, can help the continent to substantially increase its global share of FDI inflow.

Several trends are reinforcing traditional impulses for foreign direct investment, such as access to natural resources, markets, and low-cost labor. With the rise of globalization, technological progress allows for the separation of production into more discrete phases, often across national barriers. Information and communication technologies, together with improved logistics, allow for production to be close to markets while taking advantage of the specific characteristic of individual production locations.

## STRUCTURAL ADJUSTMENT LOANS OR USURY IMPERIALISM?

While providing economically troubled countries with loans, the IMF and the World Bank require the countries to make fundamental changes in their economic and social policies. These conditions come in the form of structural adjustment programs (SAPs), which are designed to ensure that the recipient country pays back its loans to the IMF and other international lenders. These policy prescriptions are typically designed to promote exports, reduce government spending and the government's role in the economy, increase taxation, and devalue currency.

Governments must meet these requirements by slashing basic services and reducing worker protections such as minimum wages and benefit packages. Countries must undertake a variety of measures to promote exports, at the expense of production for domestic needs. Some of the loans require the imposition of "user fees" charges for the use of government-provided services like schools, health clinics, and clean drinking water. Critics note that for very poor people, even modest charges may result in the denial of access to services. Mandated reductions in government spending frequently reduce the services available to the poor, including health and education services. Structural adjustment policies have also called for the sell-off of government-owned enterprises to private owners, often foreign investors. The result is that these countries have been precluded from developing consumer-friendly enterprises in the typically monopolistic sectors of the economy such as utilities, transportation, and communication.

However, many believe that SAPs have been a positive force in development and have prevented many loans from being wasted by government inexperience and corruption. A study of 1980s adjustment programs in 42 countries found substantial success — with steadier growth rates, lower inflation, and improvements in current accounts and trade regimes. And although times were hard for many countries, both the bank and the receiving countries increasingly agreed on the need for reform and the realization that money is only as beneficial as the policies it supports. In recent years, the World Bank has brought forth new commitments to mitigate social costs of adjustment through better design of programs, especially for governmental social spending.

There is no question that this debt burden is a persistent problem especially for the poorest countries. The total debt is substantial (see: ftworlddebt.htmlftworlddebt.html) and the cost of servicing these debts is a substantial drain on the economies of these countries. In 2001, the IMF and the World Bank approved debt-reduction packages for 23 poor countries, 19 of which are in Africa (see: ftimfhin.htmlftimfhin.html). Totaling $34 billion, these packages will halve the debt owed by these countries, according to the International Monetary Fund. The measures form part of the Heavily-Indebted Poor Countries (HIPC) initiative. With other measures the effect will be to reduce the debts owed by these countries, by about two-thirds on average. Similar to SAPs, this relief is delivered only to those countries that have demonstrated the commitment and capacity to use the resources effectively. These principles reflect the IMF goal that debt relief actually makes a difference in the lives of the poor.

But many antidebt global activists christened Jubilee 2000 argue that these measures are not enough. Instead, they advocate a 100 percent cancellation of all debts to the poorest countries and additional debt relief for other depressed economies. They further maintain that there should be no conditions attached to debt relief. They argue that because the HIV/AIDS crisis is ravaging poor African nations, there are no resources with which to pay debt. They further maintain that cancellation of such debts will not render the World Bank or IMF insolvent. But the IMF responds that total debt cancellation for those countries alone would come at the expense of other borrowing countries, including those non-HIPCs that are home to 80 percent of the developing world's poor.

Another method of raising capital for economic projects is through borrowing money from abroad or international loans. Beginning in the late 1970s, many African governments began to borrow money for economic-related projects. Some of the borrowed capital was used for development of new industries or for up-grading existing industries to make them more productive. Some of the borrowed money was used to develop or improve economic infrastructure that in turn would help facilitate industrialization. For example, loans were used to develop hydroelectric power through the damming of rivers. Electricity generated could be used in expanding industrial and agricultural production. A third target for borrowed monies was the social sector, particularly education and healthcare. An educated population is essential to economic development. Schools can provide the skills necessary for an industrialized economy.

Where did the loans come from? There were three main sources of loans to African countries over the past three decades.

First, there is the World Bank, which is headquartered in Washington, D.C. The World Bank is not like an ordinary bank because it is not privately owned. Its depositors, who are comprised of the nations of the world, own it. Richer countries in the world are expected to make deposits in the Bank, just as individuals make deposits in a regular bank. The World Bank uses deposits to make loans to countries that need assistance in social and economic development projects, just as regular bank uses money deposited by members to use as loans to other members. The World Bank has been a major lender to African countries, particularly through its "branch" bank, the African Development Bank. However, some World Bank loans have been controversial. Some critics of World Bank policy point out that at times the Bank will loan money only for projects that the Bank and its major depositors (the more wealthy nations) think are important. These projects are not always the first choice of the African governments.

They may feel that the money would be better spent on alternative projects; however, because they need capital for development, the governments may accept loans for projects that have a lower priority. Some economists also criticize the World Bank because of the *conditionalities* they set for making the loans. *Conditionality* is a big word, but it has a simple meaning. The World Bank requires that governments wanting to borrow money have to make certain policy changes before they can borrow money from the World Bank. Some of these conditions have nothing at all to do with the project for which the money is being borrowed. Rather, the conditions set are related to general economic and political policy. In the 1980s, the World Bank introduced a general set of conditionalities that was called economic structural adjustment. African governments wishing to borrow money had to implement the previously mentioned structural adjustment programs, popularly referred to as *SAPs*. The World Bank argued that SAPs would lead to greater economic efficiency and help stimulate economic growth.

However, critics of SAPs argue that these conditionalities have caused suffering and have not resulted in economic growth. One SAP condition, for example, was that governments spend less money on social services, arguing that individuals should be responsible for paying a larger share of the cost of education and health care. However, the majority of people were not able to increase their contribution to schooling and health care. As a result, in many African countries there has been a decline in school attendance and in the availability of health care for the average citizen. How important are education and health care to economic productivity?

Foreign governments are a second source of loans to African countries. These loans are called bi-lateral loans since they come from agreements between two governments, the lending government and the government that receives the loan. Some developed nations have special governmental agencies that are responsible for making loans and grants to less well off countries. The United States Agency for International Development (USAID) is the U.S. agency responsible for international loans and grants. In Canada, the Canadian International Development Agency (CIDA) carries out this function. Like the World Bank, USAID and CIDA often attach conditionalities to their loans and grants.

Private transnational banks are third sources of loans to African governments. Their headquarters are located in the United States, Western Europe, and Japan. Before the late 1970s, few private banks were willing to loan money to governments. However, their attitude toward loaning money to African governments changed. What led to this change? Additional data for answering this question can be retrieved from the following online source: ../exploreafricapics/gascrisis.jpg../exploreafricapics/gascrisis.jpg.

Although the U.S.A. has been a major petroleum producer, by the 1970s, she was dependent on the importation of petroleum to meet its need for gasoline. Western Europe and Japan, the other major industrial regions of the world, were nearly totally dependent on imported petroleum. Where did America, Japan, and Europe import their petroleum from? Primarily from western Asia (sometimes referred to as the *Middle East*: Saudi Arabia, Kuwait, Iraq, Iran, United Arab Emirates) parts of South East Asia, North Africa (Libya, Algeria), West Africa (Angola, Nigeria, Gabon), and Latin America (Mexico, Venezuela). What do all these countries have in common? Prior to the discovery of petroleum, these countries were all poor, economically underdeveloped countries. With petroleum, they had the potential for economic growth and development. However, up until the 1970s these countries had little control over the price for petroleum, which was controlled by transnational oil companies whose headquarters were in America and Europe. Since the major markets for petroleum were in these regions, it was in the best interest of the companies to set prices at a level that would be profitable for them, but that would be low enough to keep industries dependent on oil profitable and the car-driving public happy.

The once-poor oil-exporting countries recognized that the transnational companies and the industrial countries were benefiting much more than they were from this arrangement. To address what they considered to be an issue of fairness, the oil exporting countries formed the Organization of Petroleum Exporting Countries (OPEC). By the late 1970s, OPEC decided that their governments should be directly involved in setting the price of oil. If the transnational oil companies refused to accept this new system, then the OPEC countries would simply drastically cut the production of petroleum. What happens to the price of a popular product if it becomes scarce? Or as economists put the question, what happens when *demand* for a product outstrips *supply*? The price of the demanded product increases. This is exactly what happened in response to OPEC's policy! In the late 1970s, the price of petroleum more than tripled in a short period of time as gasoline became scarce, resulting in long lines at gas stations in North America and Europe.

Now, what does this have to do with loans to African countries? Some oil exporting countries became fabulously wealthy in just a short period of time in the 1970s. Most OPEC countries used their new wealth to stimulate economic development in their countries, and they also invested heavily in the expansion of education, health care, provisioning of safe water, electrification, and housing. However, even with these needed investments, there were profits left over. If we as individuals or families have money beyond what we immediately need, one of the things that we often do is put the money in a savings account in a bank. This is exactly what happened in the case of excess oil profits. Oil-exporting countries made huge deposits in large transnational banks. Nations, like individuals, do not deposit money in a bank just for its safe keeping; deposits grow with interest.

Banks are, of course, in the money-making business. Banks make a profit through providing a number of different services, but the most profitable part of banking is the making of loans. The flood of OPEC money placed some large transnational banks in an unusual situation: they had too much money! The traditional customers of large banks, large industries, were not in the position to borrow the huge amounts of money necessary to keep the banks profitable. These banks had to find or create new customers for large loans if they were to remain *solvent* (not go bankrupt).

The rapid increase in oil prices did not affect just rich countries. Most African countries are not oil producers. Moreover, like the economies of Europe, African economies were oil dependent, but they were far less able than European countries to deal with the increase in oil prices. In the early 1980s, in part as a result of oil prices, many African economies had stopped growing. They were in desperate need of capital to cover the cost of oil imports and to help their weak economies. At the same time that OPEC countries and international banks were seeking new areas to invest money and to make loans, African countries were in need of new and substantial sources of capital. As a result of this *mutual interest* during the 1980s, transnational banks loaned African governments huge amounts of money. This is a clear example of economic integration into circuits of usury imperialism.

Many African governments borrowed heavily from the World Bank through bilateral agencies and private banks. Borrowing money is sometimes necessary for poor countries. Money is desperately needed in order to maintain basic government services. However, money borrowed to provide services is not easily repaid because it is not used to produce new wealth with which the loan can be repaid. Governments face a dilemma. They need to borrow money to provide important basic services such as education and health care, but they know that it will not be easy to repay this money because education and health care are not directly productive. Schools and clinics cost money, but they do not produce profits from which loans can be repaid. Faced with this dilemma, many African governments borrowed money knowing that it would be difficult to repay the loans.

Not all loans to African governments were targeted at providing services. Some loans were directed at creating wealth and productivity. Loans, if carefully planned, can provide needed capital for economic growth and diversification. However, during the 1980s when transnational banks were anxious to loan money, they did not always think carefully about the *viability* of the projects they were funding. Moreover, some African government officials were so anxious to access capital that they did not always think carefully about the potential success of a project. This combination of anxious and willing lender and anxious and willing borrower resulted in some unwise loans.

In addition to international investment and international loans, there is a third source of capital for African countries. Exports provide the primary source of international capital for most African countries. Exports are paid for in an international currency (foreign exchange). The most commonly used international currencies are the U. S. dollar, the Japanese yen, the euro, and the British pound sterling.

These international currencies are accepted anywhere in the world. Zambia, for example, is paid in U.S. dollars for the copper it exports. Zambia can use dollars earned through export to either invest in new projects at home or pay for goods and services it needs to import. If Zambia could have used money earned from copper exports just for investment in its own economy, it would most likely have experienced stronger economic growth. Zambia, like other African countries, has other obligations that have to be paid for with the money earned through the export of copper. First, international debt repayments have to be made in an international currency.

There is another important use of money earned from exports. No country in the world produces all the goods and services needed by its citizens and its economy. To meet these needs, countries import goods and services from other countries. African economies, owing to the history of colonialism and the way in which they have been integrated in the global economy, are not self-sufficient and are dependent on imports from richer and more economically developed countries. Imports have to be paid for with international currency. Consequently, in addition to making debt repayments, African countries have to use the money earned through exports to pay for the imports that they need.

There is one more important issue to look at related to the nature of international trade and African economies. You will remember the term *"mono economies"* is used to describe most African economies. This means that most African countries are dependent on a single export. Most economies lack diversification. The nature of international trade in the current global economy serves to further disadvantage African economies. Over the past 20 years due to competition from other areas of the world, the market value of African-produced cocoa, coffee, cotton, peanuts, and tobacco has declined. Yet at the same time, the cost of imported industrial goods has continually increased. Consequently, African countries exporting agricultural goods have to dramatically increase their exports in order to pay for the same amount of industrial goods.

Julius Nyerere, late president of Tanzania, gave a concrete example of this changing relationship between the value of exports and imports. He pointed out that in 1962 when Tanzania became independent, it took two tons of sisal (a plant from which heavy duty rope is made); at that time Tanzania's leading export, to pay for the import of one tractor. By 1980, Tanzania had to sell six tons of sisal to purchase the same tractor. Without economic diversification, mono economies may become increasingly disadvantaged by economic globalization.

Today, the African continent harbors 33-35 of the world's 50 poorest countries and 51 out of the 87 countries under the control of the IMF/World Bank. Africa is perhaps the only continent in the world that, if the on-going globalization should continue, will surely experience an increase in absolute poverty in the not-too-distant future. The retrogression will occur as long as the existing payments for debt servicing continue to be in excess of the possible inflow of foreign capital, in the form of foreign investment and foreign aid. There is no doubt that the creditor countries, through their instrumentalities of the IMF/World Bank, will continue to prevent the African debtor countries from embarking upon independent economic, social, and political policies. The African economic situation will worsen as long as a majority of these governments continue the privatization of public enterprises in a weak, private-sector environment dominated by foreigners. As long as the African governments, in response to the "market," embark upon the dismissal of public-sector employees, drastic cuts in social-sector programs and wages of their employees, they will continue to lag behind. The adverse effects of inflation and devaluation will continue to pauperize the continent. Evidence is not far to seek.

In West African countries, for instance, the devaluation of their currencies by about 25-30 percent in the late 1980s and early 1990s reduced the real value of wages and government expenditure by up to 50-60 percent. They have since continued a downward process. The consequence is that even though earning average wages, the wage earners' purchasing power and their general standard of living had considerably fallen, and, too, their attendant demand for goods and services. Even though the productive capacity of most industries had considerably fallen, there are unsold stocks in the warehouses of the industries. The effects on government finance have also been deleterious.

One direct effect of the devaluation of the currencies is the influx of second hand goods into African countries. And second hand clothes, second hand footwear, second hand vehicles and vehicle spare parts are the only goods that the African wage earners can readily buy. Because of the increased costs of production at home and the dumping of inferior or second hand goods from abroad, African industries have been collapsing one by one in rapid succession. Even public-sector parastatals and institutions cannot be maintained at their predevaluation standards because of the increased costs of imported and local inputs, hence the present urge to privatize them. Devaluation has also adversely affected agricultural production. The production and the export of cotton, groundnuts, palm produce, and rubber have similarly been adversely affected.

This means that increasing globalization is leading to the disintegration of African economies in the global economy. Consequently, the experience of most African countries is the dumping into their markets of goods and services from the advanced industrialized economies, and the raping of their industrial environment. The use of African countries as dustbins for second hand and inferior goods and for untouchable rubbish, such as toxic or radioactive wastes, which richer and industrial countries are increasingly unwilling to keep in their countries, is a particularly destructive aspect of globalization. Such toxic wastes have been deposited in Nigeria and had been the subject of controversies.

The African continent as the laggard and the dustbin continent is not a new phenomenon. The London weekly *Economist* of the February 8, 1992, reported that in a memorandum, written by a chief economist of the World Bank, is a suggestion that the Bank should encourage the migration of dirty industries into the least developed countries of Africa and Asia, which are vastly under polluted and that health-impairing pollutants be concentrated in countries where wages were low as the lives of poor people are worth less than those of the rich. *The Economist* concluded that the economic dumping of toxic wastes in the poorest countries is highly defensible. An OECD study in 1995 calculated that while a human life was valued at about $1.5 million in West European countries, it was worth only about $100,000, which is 1/15, in the poorest countries.

In sum, with companies now able to move capital and production at will around the world, most of the key decisions about trade and investment are taken by private business. A hundred of the most powerful transnational corporations account for about one-third of all foreign direct investment. Both directly, and through the chains of sub-contracting and distribution which they control, they have a major impact on jobs and incomes world wide. By the end of 1993, the sales of foreign affiliates of TNCs totaled $5.8 trillion, exceeding the $4.7 trillion of exports of goods and services. About one-third of all international trade took place between affiliates of the same company (intra-firm trade). In 1993, FDI grew twice as fast as trade, and, since 1991, it has exceeded domestic investment in both transition and developing countries.

Both the accumulated stock of FDI and its annual growth are very unevenly distributed. Companies based in developed countries accounted for 97 percent of the total stock of FDI. Three-quarters of this is invested in developed countries. In 1993 and 1994, transnational investment in developing countries grew rapidly, but over 80 per cent of the increase went to China alone. Of the remainder, the vast bulk went to nine countries (Singapore, Argentina, Mexico, Malaysia, Indonesia, Thailand, Hong Kong, Taiwan, and Nigeria). The 47 poorest countries in the world received only 0.7 per cent of total world investment by TNCs. Africa is not even considered as a good partner in trade and investment.

One of the effects of structural adjustment is that African countries must increase their exports. Usually commodities and raw materials are exported. But poor African countries lose out when they,

- export commodities (which are cheaper than finished products),
- are denied or effectively blocked from industrial capital and real technology transfer,
- and import finished products (which are more expensive due to the added labor to make the product from those commodities and other resources).

This leads to less circulation of money in African economies and a smaller multiplier effect. Yet this is not new. Historically this has been a partial reason for dependent economies and poor nations. This was also the role enforced upon former countries under colonial rule.

## AFRICA'S DEBT—WHO OWES WHOM?

Different sources have given different figures regarding what the depth of the African debt really is. Thus figures should always be treated with caution. It is estimated that the debt of all developing countries jumped from $610 billion in 1980 to $2 163 billion in 1995 and to $2 465 billion by the end of 1998. As for Africa, since the early 1980s, it external debt burden has become increasingly onerous and unmanageable. According to the Drop the Debt Campaigners, African current external debt is $333 billion. The inability of Africa to service its debt is vividly reflected not only in massive build up of arrears but most important by the frequency of rescheduling (Rugumamu, 2001).

Between 1970 and 1987 interest rates shot from 3.7 per cent to 10 per cent, with maturity periods shortened by 35 per cent and grace periods for repayments shortened by 36 per cent. The oil shocks of 1973-74 were followed by those of 1979-80 coupled with the depression in non-oil-commodities markets. For Africa, these trends coincided with the weakness of its commodity markets in the 1980s, rising import prices, declining export volumes due to currency devaluation, inadequate incentives, and other policy errors (such as the adjustment programs) that exacerbated Africa's debt burden. Structural adjustment programs that have been designed to rescue debtors have deliberately squeezed out every possible penny from the ailing economies in order to pay the bilateral and multilateral debt—not in full of course (Danso, 1990).

For African countries seeking financial assistance, the IMF and World Bank provide it but apply a neoliberal economic ideology or agenda as the preconditions to receiving the money. For example,

- They prescribe cutbacks, "liberalization" of the economy, and resource extraction/export-oriented open markets as part of their structural adjustment.

- The role of the state is minimized.
- Privatization is encouraged as well as reduced protection of domestic industries.
- Other adjustment policies also include currency devaluation, increased interest rates, "flexibility" of the labor market, and the elimination of subsidies such as food subsidies.
- To be attractive to foreign investors, various regulations and standards are reduced or removed.

This debt is an efficient tool. It ensures access to African raw materials and infrastructure on the cheapest possible terms. Dozens of African countries compete for shrinking export markets and export only a limited range of products because of Northern protectionism and their lack of cash to invest in diversification. Market saturation ensues, reducing African exporters' incomes to a bare minimum while the North enjoys huge savings. This trend of pushing Africa spiraling to the bottom of poverty is because the IMF/World Bank cannot accept that investing in a healthy, well-fed, literate population is the most intelligent economic choice any country can make.

Africa is center stage in the struggle for human and economic rights. It is home to the world's gravest health crises, including the HIV/AIDS pandemic and chronic famine. Even though Africa has only 5 percent of the developing world's income, it carries about two-thirds of the debt—over $300 billion. Because of this, the average African country spends three times more of its scarce resources on repaying debt than it does on providing basic services. In addressing Africa's struggle for relief from its onerous external debt, advocates of global justice have raised a critical question: Who owes whom?

On the eve of Black History Month, Wednesday, January 28, 2004, at 2:00 p.m. at the Rayburn House Congressional Office in Washington, DC, the American Friends Service Committee, an international social justice organization, launched its Life over Debt campaign to have Africa's debt cancelled. The Life over Debt campaign reaches out to local U.S. communities—especially minority communities—to build understanding of the dilemmas Africa faces and to highlight shared experience and common ground. Through building a caring and active constituency the campaign sets out to increase America's commitment to helping address the African debt crisis.

Participants at the Black History Month deemed the African debt predicament "unacceptable to spend more on debt servicing to wealthy nations and institutions than on basic social services when millions of people lack access to primary education, preventative health care, adequate food and safe drinking water. It is not just morally wrong, it is also poor economics."

That is why on the eve of and during Black History Month the group called not just for reflecting on Africa in terms of the history for the African Diaspora, but also for Africans in Africa today. Given the potential for history to influence or control the perception of the world, it is important to reflect on how the past injustices have impacted the current debt crisis.

Current World Bank and IMF debt relief initiatives do not adequately address Africa's debt crisis. Not only is relief insufficient for countries included, but also there are countries excluded from the program that have legitimate cases for debt cancellation. To demonstrate this, the Life over Debt campaign focuses on five sub-Saharan African countries with very different cases for debt cancellation.

Debt relief program poster children dependent on commodity exports are not out of the woods:

- *Uganda* was the first country to complete the debt relief program, but as coffee prices plummeted it has seen its debt increase again—demonstrating the current relief efforts are not sufficient.
- *Mozambique*, with a history of apartheid-caused war, was forced by loan conditionalities to cut support for an infant cashew roasting industry that could have helped stabilize the economy when the raw cashew prices collapsed.

Designated as having "sustainable debt" by the World Bank—yet who owes whom?

- *South Africa* has $25 billion in foreign debt that is considered sustainable even when it is one of the most unequal countries in the world with 20 percent of adults HIV infected. A large percent of the debt is odious and illegal with an estimated $11.7 billion from interest on loans from the apartheid era.
- *Angola* is wealthy from oil and diamond exports and considered to have sustainable debt, but the country ranks near the bottom of the United Nations human development index, 161 out of 173 countries. The majority of the $10 billion debt is owed to countries involved in the cold-war era decades of war.

Classic Case of "odious" Debt

- *Democratic Republic of Congo* was promised 80 percent debt relief ($10 billion) but it is one of the strongest cases for full cancellation. Former dictator Mobuto Sese Seko was granted loans that disappeared into foreign banks with few traces. For additional information, one may contact the American Friends Service Committee or visit its web site at www.afsc.org/Africa-debt.

There are several reasons for the increase in Africa's debt. One is that when the money was originally lent to African countries, export revenue for raw materials and crops in most of these countries was more than adequate for the repayment of interest on loans and their currencies were tied to the gold standard. However in 1971 the International Financial Institutions demolished the gold standard and floated the world's currencies. The abolition of the gold standard was a rash and foolish move. When the gold standard was in existence every country knew what its currency was worth. It could devalue it at its peril, but that was the choice of an individual country.

Ever since the gold standard was dropped, no African country has been able to predict what its currency would be worth from one day to the next. Currencies are bought and sold on the international stock market. Small countries, having far less currency, are more vulnerable to the buying and selling of investors, who can reduce the value of their currencies by anything up to 90 percent overnight, just by selling it. Countries such as the US and Britain with strong currencies are not as susceptible to these massive fluctuations. The abolition of the gold standard resulted in massive devaluation of many currencies of African countries.

Another reason for the increase in African debt is that the price of commodities has fallen constantly over the years, making it harder and harder for these countries to repay their loans. As many countries struggled to repay mounting interest out of diminishing export revenue, in many cases they have been obliged to take on further loans. These further loans were tied to the strict conditions of structural adjustment programs: programs imposed on the receiving African countries, obliging them to cut back on health care, education, sanitation and housing programs, thus further worsening the plight of their citizens.

Summarily, developing countries as a whole have increased their share of world trade from 19 percent in 1971 to 29 percent in 1999. But, while the newly industrialized economies (NIEs) of Asia have done well, Africa as a whole has fared poorly. The composition of what countries export is also important. The strongest rise by far has been in the export of manufactured goods. The share of primary commodities in world exports—such as food and raw materials—that are often produced by the poorest countries of Africa, has declined.

Capital movements sharply increased private capital flows to developing countries during much of the 1990s. In other words: (1) the increase followed a particularly "dry" period in the 1980s; (2) net official flows of "aid" or development assistance have fallen significantly since the early 1980s; and (3) the composition of private flows has changed dramatically. Direct foreign investment has become the most important category. Both portfolio investment and bank credit rose but they have been more volatile, falling sharply in the wake of the financial crises of the late 1990s.

There has been remarkable movement of workers from one African country to another or to the North, partly to find better employment opportunities. The numbers involved are still quite small, but in the period 1965-90, the proportion of labor forces around the world that were foreign born increased by about one-half. Most migration occurs between developing countries. But the flow of migrants to advanced economies is likely to provide a means through which global wages converge. There is also the potential for skills to be transferred back to the African countries and for wages in those countries to rise.

Spread of knowledge (and technology) through information exchange is an integral, often overlooked, aspect of globalization. For instance, direct foreign investment brings not only an expansion of the physical capital stock, but also technical innovation. More generally, knowledge about production methods, management techniques, export markets, and economic policies is available at very low cost, and it represents a highly valuable resource for the African countries.

Inevitably, globalization is increasingly polarizing African societies in the same way that the unequal gains of the 19th century Industrial Revolution gave rise to social discontents and to communism or socialism in many countries. In many African countries today, an increasing number of urban professionals, upper-class, and upper-middle-class elites go about with pagers, cellular telephones, and watch CNN, BBC, and other foreign satellite dish programs.

All this luxury living is taking place in countries where more than three-fourths of the population do not have access to portable water, electricity, or fuels, and where an increasing number of high school, college, and university graduates are roaming the streets in search of unavailable jobs. The uneven spread of economic opportunities within African countries, brought about by globalization, is obviously increasing discontent and marginalization, especially among the youth, the urban poor, or among other disadvantaged groups. The result is increased crime rates and social upheavals that, at times, have led to rebellion against the governments or to inter-ethnic rivalries and wars.

The rise of inter ethnic violence in Africa has been frightening. In many African states today, for instance, ethnic groups are individually complaining about marginalization by the governments. Some even call for either the dissolution of the country or national conferences to discuss and determine the basis of continued association and to settle the mode of sharing the wealth (or the poverty) of the country. Globalization is threatening the very existence of many African countries.

Thus globalization is a two-edged sword. It has brought benefit to some, but misery to an increasing number of others. It has concentrated wealth in the hands of a diminishing few while denying access to such wealth to teeming masses in Africa. For instance, when a public monopoly is sold, it simply creates a private monopoly. Monopolies are not usually very economically efficient, partly because they lack the stimulus of competition. Therefore, to promote economic efficiency, an adequate legal and political framework that means more government regulation rather than less as globalization, in its neomercantilist form, decries must accompany privatization.

Mercantilists believe that the wealth of a nation depends upon the riches and bullion it could command. To attain this state, mercantilists promote the development of trade mechanisms (ships), taxation, selling of expensive goods, while protecting their economies against expensive imports but encouraging the import of cheap goods. Through such trade mechanisms, the following relevant kinds of balance-of-payment relations can be seen to explain present-day neomercantilism: The focus of the external sector is placed on export orientation.

Export in value terms is seen to be a function of nominal protection of profitable goods, whereas import of cheap raw materials, intermediate technology, and commodities is encouraged. To correct trade deficits, government financial resources using general tax revenues, or official development resources, or inflight of capital in high-interest-bearing assets, are activated. Thus, the level of deficits determines the exchange rate, interest rate, and protective levels at home against the competitiveness by other nations.

Trade relations in a globalizing order show all these to exist. For the developing countries like those in Africa, there is a continuation of worsening terms of trade of commodities, lost sectorial competitiveness and food self-sufficiency, flight of capital, and extensive external-sector volatility. On the other hand, industrialized economies are trying to protect their agricultural and manufacturing sectors against the external flow of goods, such as in textiles and automobiles in the U.S.A. and in general terms within the European Union and Japan. This is tantamount to selling expensive and buying inputs of production cheap.

Overall deficits in industrialized economies are being mitigated by taxation and by flight of capital from developing countries. Thus under such a neomercantilist order, the drive to secure external sector balances at home under exchange rate flexibility and perfect capital mobility causes industrialized economies to adopt monetary policies. The interest rate and exchange rate volatility of monetary policies prove to be permanently disequilibrating for the developing countries. The developing countries of Africa in particular have been historically selling cheap and buying expensive from the industrialized economies. Thus, both export orientation and capital transactions in the overall balance of payments prove to be permanently de-equalizing. These neomercantilist policies of globalization cannot be a midwife to democracy. Rather, these policies serve as pillars of imperialism.

The relationship between the West and Africa needs to get away from the idea that the West is "helping" a helpless Africa out of the goodness of its heart. In fact, part of Africa's predicament is a direct result of unwise or unfair economic decisions by Western nations and institutions. Rectifying these economic distortions should not be a question of charity, but a question of justice. Foolish, unproductive loans to regimes that were bad investment risks need to be written off, through an international bankruptcy court, so that African nations can start with a clean slate. Meanwhile, African agriculture needs the tools to protect it against the distortions caused by the dumping of subsidized produce from Western nations.

## References

Ake, Claude. 1990. "The Case for Democracy." In *African Governance in the 1990s*, Working Papers From the Second Annual Seminar of the African Governance Program, The Carter Center of Emory University, Atlanta, Georgia, March.

Bjorvatn, K. 1999. "Infrastructure and Industrial Location in LDCs." Discussion Paper, Norwegian School of Economics and Business Administration, November 1999.

Bjorvatn, K. 2000. "FDI in LDCs: Facts, Theory and Empirical Evidence." Manuscript, Norwegian School of Economics and Business Administration.

Danso, Alex. 1990. "Causes and Importance of the African Debt Crisis." In *The World Guide 1999/2000*. Oxford: New Internationalist Publications.

Desai, Meghnad, James Petras, Henry Veltmeyer, Robert Scrire, Leslie Sklair, Ghautam Sen, and Deepak Lal. 2000. Essays in *Cambridge Review of International Affairs*, 14,1, Autumn-Winter.

Dominguez, Jorge and A. Lowenthal. 1996. *Constructing Democratic Governance in Latin America and the Cartibbean in the 90s*. Baltimore: John Hopkins University Press.

*The Economist* (May 13, 2000:17).

————— (April 22, 2000).

Haaland, J. I. and Wooton, I. 1998. "International Competition for Multinational Investment." Discussion Paper No. 1937, Center for Economic Policy Research, London. Online: http://www.ippmedia.com/ft/2000/12/13/ft1.asp.

Rugumamu, S . 2001. "Africa's debt bondage: A case for Total cancellation" In *Eastern Africa Social Science Research Review, 17,1,* January 2001, pp:31-53.

Therborn, Goran. 2000. "Globalizations: Dimensions, Historical Waves, Regional Effects, Normative Governance," *International Sociology*, 15, 23, pp: 151-179.

UNCTAD, Various Press Releases at www.unctad.org.

UNCTAD. World Investment Report 1998: Trends and Determinants, Washington, DC.: United Nations.

UNCTAD, 1999a. World Investment Report 1999: Foreign Direct Investment and the Challenge of Development. Washington, DC: United Nations.

UNCTAD, 1999b. Foreign Direct Investment in Africa: Performance and Potential. Washington, DC.: United Nations.

UNCTAD, 2000a. Capital Flows and Growth in Africa. Washington, DC: United Nations. UNCTAD, (2000b). Building Confidence: Electronic Commerce and Development. , Washington, DC. and Geneva: United Nations.

UNCTAD, 1999a. World Investment Report 1999: Foreign Direct Investment and the Challenge of Development. Washington, DC: United Nations.

UNCTAD, 1999b. Foreign Direct Investment in Africa: Performance and Potential. Washington, DC: United Nations.

UNAIDS. 2004. Report on the global AIDS epidemic, July, Washington, DC: United Nations.

*Vårt Land*, June 17, 2000.

Wolf. M. 2002. *Financial Times*, February 5.

Chapter 7

# Globalization in Siege
# of Democracy in Africa

The Greek philosopher Plato famously did not like democracy. He saw the
death of his mentor, Socrates, decided by an ignorant and fearful mob of
Athenians, as the logical consequence of giving power to the masses. While
Plato's solution to the problem—his utopia of a state guided by philosophers
depicted in *The Republic*—obviously wouldn't cut it either in theory or in practice, he had a point.

What kind of democracy was Plato referring to? Roughly speaking, there
are two fundamentally distinct kinds of democratic government: the simple rule
of majority, despised by Plato but simplistically endorsed by many in the world
today; and a constitutional democracy, in which the decisions of the majority
of the moment are constrained by a set of rules aimed chiefly at protecting the
rights of minorities, including freedom of speech and action.

Globalization has caused anxiety and uncertainty among the less-developed
countries; the reason being that it is still unclear as to what this new political
economy portends for these countries. Also at the heart of this unease is what
seems to be the profound political and social consequences of globalization for
the Third World countries, especially those in poverty-stricken Africa. Would
they be able to cushion themselves against the painful effects of globalization?
One of the key demands of this new political economy is that there should be
no political interference in economic activity and investment decisions.

Thus globalization presents the less-developed countries with what seems
to be an intractable conundrum. While touting democracy as a condition for
economic success, the neoliberal ideology that underpins globalization removes
the economy from the political agenda through its advocacy of laissez-faire economic policies that preclude government involvement in investment decisions,
hence shielding private capital and the bourgeoisie from social and political
scrutiny.

## DEMOCRACY WITHIN THE GLOBAL NEOMERCANTILIST
## EMPIRE?

In the 1980s, the idea of democracy was advanced in the form of (1) the
return to power of civilian elected and constitutional regimes, and the restora-

tion of the electoral mechanism in the transition from one regime to another; (2) the decentralization of government services and some powers; and (3) the strengthening of civil society within the framework of government initiated political and social reforms (Reilley, 1995).

Globalized capitalism has besieged the democratic process in Africa. Liberal democracy exists in tension with capitalism. The reason is simply that democracy begins with the premise of equality among citizens, while capitalism inevitably produces economic inequality that translates into differences of political power. However, liberal democracy can and does coexist with capitalism elsewhere, notwithstanding this tension.

Capitalist globalization, however, especially in its present form, makes the practice of even liberal democracy increasingly problematic. Huge transnational corporations are able to make resource allocation decisions that cannot be controlled by even the most powerful liberal democratic African national government. That is, no matter what popular mandate such governments may have, there is little they can do to control the global decisions of the major corporations. Indeed, most liberal democratic governments are at the service of the global capitalist system, whose prosperity is wrongly viewed as a prerequisite to national economic health.

Two things relate globalization to conditions for democracy in Africa. First, the attractive promise of globalization is to generate increased economic growth and development through a regime of freer trade and international investment that will help alleviate the suffering of the lower classes in Africa. The expected increase of revenue from trade and investment is to help governments finance programs for the lower classes thereby reducing the levels of social unrest and class polarization, which are two conditions that are not conducive for democratic transformation.

The second factor is that transnational companies that are, in fact, the primary beneficiaries of globalization are also its main movers and shakers. The ability of Africa to build the necessary economic infrastructure for democratic consolidation depends on how much of the gains from trade and foreign investment is left by the transnational companies. However, the transnational companies are not the only major actors whose decisions or policies in the new era of globalization can promote or diminish the chances of consolidating democracy in Africa. There is also the official role of the developed states of Europe, North America, and Japan. The objective of democratizing Africa will be amply served if developed states shift emphasis away from aid to trade as a true instrument of economic development. This brings to mind the important issue of protectionism against goods manufactured in Africa.

## DEMOCRACY VERSUS PREDATORY AUTOCRACY: HEGEMONY, TERROR, AND INTIMIDATION

What defines the new imperialism in its most recent offensives is not only unilateralism in the projection of state power, but an increased use of its repressive apparatus with an aggressive reliance on military force in defense of the empire. However, naked power is always destabilizing. To secure the conditions of order, which are needed by the powerful, a degree of consensus or hegemony is also needed, and duly manufactured. Until recently (viz. the war against international terrorism), such a consensus was generally sought on the basis, and in terms of, a battle of democracy against international communism. At issue in this ideological struggle was the idea of democracy that decision-making power is exercised, directly or indirectly, by the people; that the holders of power represent the people and are held accountable to them; and that politics take the form of dialogue and negotiation of conflicting interests rather than violent confrontation—channeling of grievances and demands through forms of peaceful and civil struggle (UNRISD, 2001).

In this context, it was even asserted and argued (by ideologues and scholars alike), despite historical evidence to the contrary, that democracy and capitalism in the (neoliberal) form of private enterprise and the free market were intrinsically connected; that the marriage between free markets (capitalism, economic liberalism) and free elections (democracy, political liberalism) was not one of convenience or historic accident but organic (Dominguez and Lowenthal, 1996). Thus, liberal scholars, both political scientists and economists, have theorized that the institutionalization of democracy (political liberalization) would create the necessary or facilitating conditions of capitalist development (political liberalization) or vice versa. Thus, at the level of practice, within the context of Euro-American imperialism in the post-World War II era, the iron fist of armed force and political repression has often been cloaked with the idea of democracy and a concern for associated human rights.

However, democracy in this (liberal) form has proven to be a two-edged sword. Samuel Huntington—a well-known but best forgotten conservative but trilateralist political scientist and author of *The Clash of Civilizations*—recognized as early as 1974, the year to which the capitalist counteroffensive (and the conservative counterrevolution in development theory and practice) can be traced, that democracy provides conditions under which forces of opposition and resistance can expand and prosper and be mobilized against the system (Huntington, 1975).

The issue, from Huntington's view, was the generation of pressures and demands for inclusion that exceeded the institutional capacity of the system and that cannot be accommodated or contained. Thus, in the shared context of conditions under which the globalization project was launched and policies of structural adjustment were implemented, a redemocratization process in Latin America and elsewhere in the Third World generated widespread forces of opposition to, and resistance against, the projects of globalization and imperialism.

How have the guardians of economic and political order responded to the threat of organized and mobilized forces of resistance and opposition? There is a widespread belief inside and outside Africa that the promotion of multiparty democracy will provide a "quick fix" for political, security, and economic problems in Africa. Prodemocracy activists have a worthy, but naive belief in the power of the word "democracy" and in the efficacy of the multiparty system as a form of political and economic management. Just chanting the word democracy has achieved nothing in Africa. Where democratic governments have been elected, they have faced the same appalling problems of unequal terms of trade, massive foreign debts, run-down agricultural systems, dependence on a limited range of export crops or minerals, and crushing poverty for the majority of their populations.

Democracy is the process and act by which government is made accountable by stakeholders through rules and institutions that allow for open competition and participation in government (Olukoshi and Bangura 1989: 3-7).Forceful arguments for this view are located at: http://unpan1.un.org/intradoc/groups/public/documents/IDEP/UNPAN006523.pdf. Democracy is not just an object but a process of social emancipation. It entails struggles against economic exploitation, political domination, ideological alienation, ethnic marginalization, and social disinheritance of the broad masses (Syahuka-Muhindo 1995: 493). Indeed, democracy is perpetually at war with poverty engendered by exploitation, domination, alienation, marginalization, and disinheritance. This idea is developed online at: http://unpan1.un.org/intradoc/groups/public/documents/IDEP/UNPAN006523.pdf.

Poverty brings about instability and insecurity, which breed underdevelopment. The reverse is also true. Democracy must deliver on the bread-and-butter issues; otherwise, the continent could slide back into situations where the politics of poverty gives rise to the poverty of politics.

Governance, conflict management, and state reconstruction are interrelated issues. Governance is the institutional capability of public organizations to provide the public with goods demanded by citizens or their representatives in an effective, transparent, impartial, and accountable manner, subject to resource constraints. Conflict management refers to the capacity of society to mediate the conflicting though not necessarily violent interests of different social groups through political processes. State reconstruction combines national and supranational competencies for resolving violent conflicts, sustaining peace, and undertaking economic and political postconflict reconstruction. Since the 1990s this nexus of governance, conflict management, and state building has moved from relative obscurity to being a central issue on Africa's development policy agenda. Why?

The first impulse has come from within Africa, where the political landscape has been changing rapidly. After years of authoritarian regimes and political and economic decline, there has been resurgent popular demand for multiparty elections and accountability in public resource management. Since the early 1990s, 42 of 48 sub-Saharan African states have held multiparty presidential or parliamentary elections. Though these elections have not always been completely fair, they have often generated high voter turnout, sometimes more than 80 percent. This trend has been bolstered by the end of the Cold War, which has made donors less inclined to favor trusted allies over competent development partners. New aid relations emphasize ownership, accountability to domestic stakeholders, and good governance. Moreover, a number of African countries are ready to undertake "second generation" reforms, which require building social consensus and bargaining among social groups.

Globalization also explains the increased importance of these issues. Like other countries, African states face growing pressures both to decentralize and to adapt to emerging global governance structures and standards. These extend beyond trade to encompass many areas once considered within the purview of national policy. Globalization also brings risks of increased economic instability, which can lead to social conflicts. All these factors have increased the importance of sound governance and institutions for mediating conflicts and promoting social cooperation.

This chapter analyzes African postindependence performance in governance and conflict management and highlights opportunities for resolving conflicts, building peace, promoting social cooperation, and improving governance in the 21st century. A first theme of the chapter is that it is wrong to think that ethnic diversity dooms Africa to endemic civil conflicts. Poverty, underdevelopment, unemployment, and political exclusion are the root causes lurking behind social fractionalization and factionalization. But socially fractionalized societies like most in Africa require careful management. Thus African countries need to seek inclusive, participatory, and democratic polities compatible with their ethnic diversity. Under the right conditions diversity can promote, rather than impede, social cooperation and stable growth. Active and collaborative involvement by regional institutions and international donors is also critical for resolving conflict and building peace in Africa.

A second theme involves options for improving institutions for national economic management. Africa has seen many such initiatives as part of reform programs, but success has been limited. One reason for past failures is that externally inspired technocratic measures to streamline and strengthen the bureaucracy have not been matched by complementary action by incumbent regimes, or by measures to generate demand for good governance by local constituencies. This too is changing. A new breed of African reformers now places far more emphasis on transparency and on measures to empower the users of public services, in part through decentralization. Such measures have significance beyond their immediate impact, helping over time to develop the civic organizations and the capacity needed to sustain a robust democratic system.

Together these two themes point to the following implication: political and economic governance are inseparable, and together they underpin sustainable development. Especially with the spread of modern communications, a corrupt, ineffective state is unlikely to meet the popular and economic demands of the 21st century. As East Asia's experience suggests, states that successfully manage and develop their economies are likely to strengthen their legitimacy. Indeed, African countries with well-managed economies saw an increase in stability, political rights, and civil liberties in the 1990s. Conversely, states in conflict perform poorly on political criteria and have weaker economic policies and institutions.

Well-functioning states share certain characteristics. Not all of these are necessarily preconditions for development. Many countries, including many industrial ones, fall short on a number of relevant attributes. Nor is there a single model toward which all African countries should aspire. Successful options include "consensual democracy" in Japan, unitary liberal democracy in parts of Europe, and federalist democracies and confederacies in other regions. All of these approaches preserve political competition through popular participation in regular elections, but they differ in many ways.

Yet while the diversity among successful democracies suggests a variety of functional institutional arrangements, effective public institutions generally have some common fundamental characteristics. The first is the capacity to maintain nationwide peace and law and order, without which other government functions are compromised or impossible. Second, states must secure individual liberty and equality before the law, a process still working itself out in the West and elsewhere. This has been a major institutional inadequacy in many African states. Secure property rights and transparent adjudication of disputes arising thereof are critical in shaping investment decisions. Third, the state needs workable checks and balances on the arbitrary exercise of power. Public decisionmaking must be transparent and predictable. Oversight mechanisms should guard against arbitrariness and ensure accountability in the use of public resources, but need not eliminate the flexibility and delegation needed to respond quickly to changing circumstances.

Once this institutional infrastructure is in place, the public sector has an important role in financing and providing key social, infrastructural, and dispute resolution services. Effective states raise revenue and supply these services in ways that contribute to development. Where corruption is detected, legal and administrative sanctions are implemented, regardless of the social and political status of perpetrators. A free press and public watchdog organizations guard against abuse of power and reinforce checks and balances for effective service delivery. The political process is broadly viewed as legitimate and provides an anchor of predictability for private investment and economic development more broadly. Besides enhancing individual liberties, a participatory civil society, free speech, and an independent press are indispensable for promoting productive and healthy investment.

It would be naive to expect these characteristics to be adopted automatically as the political platform of the leadership of any country. Governments the world over are susceptible to factional contests for political power, motivated by incentives other than those that encourage good governance. But without political stability and checks and balances on power, public responsibility for key services and social legitimacy for government are in jeopardy and economic development may not be achieved. Without these foundations of good political and economic governance, African development will be sluggish or stalled.

Perceptions of African governance have been bedeviled by a tendency toward sweeping generalization and unwillingness to acknowledge not just failures but also mixed outcomes and some successes. Any review of the governance track record of African governments since independence thus confronts the challenge of both describing general patterns and highlighting variations across countries.

By definition, colonial rule tended to be unaccountable to Africans and overly reliant on the military to suppress dissent. Its departure was rapid and unanticipated by both colonizer and colonized. Part of the early caution about the departure of colonialists was perhaps a response to the recognition that local skills were inadequate and the institutional foundations of incoming African governments were poor. For example, when Congo gained independence in 1969, it had just 16 postsecondary school graduates, for a population of 13 million.

The constitutional innovations introduced at independence partly sought to promote long-repressed local values. But these were unavoidably blended with the formal structures of national governance introduced by European colonialism. With notable exceptions like Kenya and Zimbabwe, British colonialism bequeathed to its former dependencies the legacy of "indirect rule," which provided considerable autonomy to "traditional" rulers—whether these were genuinely traditional or not against the backdrop of English common law.

In contrast, former French colonies inherited a metropolitan-centered system of direct rule extending to the remotest rural cantons, circles, and communes. Belgian administration in Burundi, Congo, and Rwanda was comprehensive and highly autocratic. Until its cataclysmic end in 1974, Portuguese colonialism in countries like Angola, Guinea-Bissau, and Mozambique abjured local participation in governance, much less indigenous representation. This complex patchwork of old and new state institutions produced a varied but generally disappointing record in national governance. But there were exceptions— like Botswana, Côte d'Ivoire (until the 1980s), Kenya, and Mauritius—where public institutional capability was considerable. Overall, the political transition between the 1960s and the early 1990s can be divided into three phases:

Guarded experimentation—1960s to early 1970s: Former British colonies inherited variants of the Westminster system, with competitive parties, independent judiciaries, and cabinet governments based on a merit-recruited, politically neutral civil service. Former French-ruled states got a powerful presidential system wielding strong executive authority. Under this system the comparatively weak office of the prime minister headed the public service and was answerable to a chamber of deputies elected on a run-off constituency majority system. But confronted by the divisive, ethnic-driven politics of redistribution in the 1960s, innovations were made to introduce all-purpose nation building ideologies. Single parties emerged encompassing dissidents and competitors, sometimes using patronage to consolidate power—and not always peacefully. Thus conceived, national unity was expected to facilitate faster, friction-free growth.

Though many presume that economic and institutional decline set in almost immediately after independence, which was not the case. With limited aid, African economies grew by more than 5 percent a year between 1965 and 1973. Primary school enrolments rose sharply, and new universities, infrastructure, and public service training programs were developed. At the same time, driven by the development orthodoxy of the day, the supposed scarcity of indigenous entrepreneurs, and the fear of commercially dominant expatriate minorities, many countries laid the foundations for increased state control and centralization of resource allocation in a broad range of economic activities.

Military rule, dictatorships, and economic regress—mid 1970s to 1990s: After military takeovers in the early 1960s in Congo-Brazzaville, Dahomey (Benin), and Togo, the first gush of military coups in 1965-66 in Burundi, Central African Republic, Congo-Kinshasa, Ghana, Nigeria, and Upper Volta (Burkina Faso) opened the way to autocratic military rule. External involvement played a major role in such cases. Many proved disastrous from an economic and institution-building point of view, as evidenced by Ethiopia (1974-91), Ghana (1966-69 and 1972-83), Mali (1968-91), Nigeria (1983-98), Somalia (1969-91), Uganda (1971-79), and Zaire (1965-97). By 1990, half of Africa's states had military or quasi-military governments. In parallel with authoritarian military governments came a trend towards single-party rule under autocratic civilian leaders, largely pursuing interventionist economic policies, in some cases under the banners of socialism or Marxism. Especially when combined with external shocks, the resulting economic decline and politicization of the bureaucracy eroded much of what remained of institutional governance capacity and undermined many of the accomplishments of the 1960s.

Political and economic liberalization—late 1980s and 199's recurrent balance-of- payments crises and economic regress, together with pressure from donors, led a number of African governments to adopt structural adjustment policies in the 1980s, opening up markets, encouraging deregulation and private initiative, and reducing state economic intervention. The popular processes that led to the collapse of Benin military government in 1989, the fall of the Berlin Wall in late 1989, and the release of Nelson Mandela from prison in early 1990 increased demands for constitutional reform. Under popular pressure, some francophone states (Benin, Congo-Brazzaville, Mali) held national conferences that replaced authoritarian constitutions with French-style democratic ones. Especially after 1989, popular discontent with military or autocratic regimes found vent in mass demonstrations in favor of individual freedoms and multiparty government. Most remaining African governments conceded the principle of democracy in the first half of the 1990s. By 1999 nearly all countries had held multiparty elections with varying degrees of credibility.

# DEMOCRACY AND LIBERTY

From the time of Herodotus democracy has meant, first and foremost, the rule of the people. This view of democracy as a process of selecting governments, articulated by scholars ranging from Alexis de Tocqueville to Joseph Schumpeter to Robert Dahl, is now widely used by social scientists. Elections—open, free and fair—are the essence of democracy, the inescapable *sine qua non*. Governments produced by elections may be inefficient, corrupt, shortsighted, irresponsible, dominated by special interests, and incapable of adopting policies demanded by the public good. These qualities make such governments undesirable but they do not make them undemocratic. Democracy is one public virtue, not the only one, and the relation of democracy to other public virtues and vices can be understood only if democracy is clearly distinguished from the other characteristics of political systems.

This definition also accords with the commonsense view of the term. If a country holds competitive, multiparty elections, we call it democratic. When public participation in politics is increased, for example through the enfranchisement of women, it is seen as more democratic. Of course elections must be open and fair, and this requires some protections for freedom of speech and assembly. But to go beyond this minimalist definition and label a country democratic only if it guarantees a comprehensive catalog of social, political, economic, and religious rights turns the word democracy into a badge of honor rather than a descriptive category. After all, Sweden has an economic system that many argue curtails individual property rights; France until recently had a state monopoly on television; and England has an established religion. But they are all clearly and identifiably democracies. To have democracy means, subjectively, "a good government" renders it analytically useless.

Constitutional liberalism, on the other hand, is not about the procedures for selecting government, but rather about goals of the government. It refers to the tradition, deep in Western history, that seeks to protect individual autonomy and dignity against coercion, whatever the source—state, church, or society. The term marries two closely connected ideas. It is liberal because it draws on the philosophical strain, beginning with the Greeks, that emphasizes *individual liberty*. It is constitutional because it rests on the tradition, beginning with the Romans, of the rule of law. Constitutional liberalism developed in Western Europe and the United States as a defense of the individual's right to life and property, and freedom of religion and speech. To secure these rights, it emphasized checks on the power of each branch of government, equality under the law, impartial courts and tribunals, and separation of church and state. Its canonical figures include the poet John Milton, the jurist William Blackstone, statesmen such as Thomas Jefferson and James Madison, and philosophers such as Thomas Hobbes, John Locke, Adam Smith, Baron de Montesquieu, John Stuart Mill, and Isaiah Berlin.

In almost all of its variants, constitutional liberalism argues that human beings have certain natural (or "inalienable") rights and that governments must accept a basic law, limiting its own powers, that secures them. Thus in 1215 at Runnymede, English barons forced the king to abide by the settled and customary law of the land. In the American colonies these laws were made explicit, and in 1638 the town of Hartford adopted the first written constitution in modern history. In the 1970s, Western nations codified standards of behavior for regimes across the globe. The Magna Carta, the Fundamental Orders of Connecticut, the American Constitution, and the Helsinki Final Act are all expressions of constitutional liberalism

## THE RISE OF ILLIBERAL DEMOCRACY

From Gabon to Togo, from Sierra Leone to Zimbabwe, we see the rise of a disturbing phenomenon in international life—illiberal democracy. It has been difficult to recognize this problem because democracy right from the colonial era has meant liberal democracy —a political system marked not only by free and fair elections, but also by the rule of law, a separation of powers, and the protection of basic liberties of speech, assembly, religion, and property.

In fact, this latter bundle of freedoms—what might be termed constitutional liberalism—is theoretically different and historically distinct from democracy. Liberalism, either as a conception of political liberty, or as a doctrine about economic policy, may have coincided with the rise of democracy. But it has never been immutably or unambiguously linked to its practice. Today the two strands of liberal democracy, interwoven in the Western political fabric, are coming apart in Africa. Democracy is flourishing; constitutional liberalism is not. For instance, Ethiopian "elected" government turns its security forces on journalists and political opponents, doing permanent damage to human rights as well as human beings.

Naturally there is a spectrum of illiberal democracy, ranging from modest offenders like Cameroon to near-tyrannies like Equatorial Guinea and Togo, with countries like Burkina Faso and Congo Brazzaville in between. Along much of the spectrum, elections are rarely as free and fair today, but they do reflect the "reality of popular participation" in politics and support for those elected. And the examples are not isolated or atypical. Freedom House's 1996-97 survey, Freedom in the World, has separate rankings for political liberties and civil liberties, which correspond roughly with democracy and constitutional liberalism, respectively. Of the countries that lie between confirmed dictatorship and consolidated democracy, 50 percent do better on political liberties than on civil ones.

In other words, most of the "democratizing" countries in Africa today are *illiberal democracies*. In the case of Francophone Africa Fomunyoh (2001: 39) notes that they fall into four categories as they wobble along: (1) countries that are on the path to democratic consolidation; (2) countries in which democracy is making faltering progress; (3) countries in which the future of democracy remains uncertain; and (4) countries in which the democratic gains of the 1990s are eroding.

# WHAT DEMOCRACY? FOR WHOM IN AFRICA?

The model of democracy for which Africans are yearning is one applicable in time and space consonant with their historical aspirations. But the assault of globalization on Africa has established a period marked by the failure of most Africans to think. It is also one that inhibits Africans to even conceptualize about the historical possibilities of social transformations in terms of how to reach a stage of society where a man or the humanity of women is not contested.

The human desire to live a life devoid of all forms of arbitrariness—whether class, gender, race, communal exclusivity and soon—is no longer problematized. And it is taken for granted. Many have given up all struggles for any search for alternative policy solutions and truths, which would lead to a construction of humane communities. The international financial institutions are the real thinkers.

This amounts merely to the celebration of the present. And, in this era production is no longer the determining aspect of social life. The markets and stock exchanges are. It is an era when it is said to be possible for the state to withdraw from social provisioning because the market can fill the vacuum created by its withdrawal. To the extent that markets can create conditions for development and human welfare, the state in its current form can only confine itself to management of law and order and repressive collection of taxes.

In this regard, it no longer requires social policies for purposes of legitimating itself, as it was previously. Rather than the state playing statistics, it is now the transnational capitalist class doing so, while the middle classes play the stock market and the lower classes wait for fortunes from bingo and beauty contests: The best person wins! It is an era when consumer dominance is said to be the new logic of society and not real societal needs, and individuals are integrated into this consumer society through seduction or repression. It is an era marked by the dominance of the "supermarket ideology," which goes as far as redefining "love" in terms of the relationship between a person and his or her car, "revolution" as a new brand of soap, a microwave, or a washing machine, "freedom/Uhuru" as possession of a cellular phone, "democracy" as acceptance and tolerance of real differences by agreeing to disagree, "partnership" as exploitative relationship between man and woman, the poor and the rich, oppressor and oppressed, boss and worker, etc, "participation" as acceptance of decisions from the powers that be under duress, "knowledge" and "truth" as the power to cheat and deceive.

In fact, vices have been turned into virtues and the wicked and villains have become heroes while the Masalakulangwa and Robin Hoods (those seizing from the rich and giving to the poor) of the world have become objects of ridicule and cynicism. African countries entered this era through the implementation of the structural adjustment programs spearheaded by the International Monetary Fund (IMF) and the World Bank. These programs stressed the efficiency of free market allocation of resources and emphasized deregulation and export orientation so as to achieve international competitiveness based on comparative advantage. The SAPs were deemed to be a means to overcome the crisis facing African countries since the 1970s.

SAPs championed the notion of "globalism" or "one world," in which a single market for goods, capital, services, skills, and technology prevails. The causes of the crisis were attributed to the predominance of welfare-oriented policies pursued by governments and the neglect of pure economic concerns. The perception that states are the driving force of economic growth was replaced by the perception of an increased role for market forces in the allocation of resources and a much-enlarged role for the private sector in production and the management of the economy. SAPs, it was alleged, were the preconditions for growth and implicitly for poverty reduction because the benefits of growth would trickle down to the poor.

These international financial institutions specifically demanded that the African countries introduce external sector reforms to bring domestic prices into line with world market prices through liberalization of imports and exports and devaluation of currency. Beyond this, they were supposed to liberalize internal trade markets by removal of price controls, deconfinement of industrial products, liberalization of interest-rates, and the like. They were further demanded to introduce management reforms so as to bring expenditures into line with real resources, in terms of control of growth of money supply, cuts in government spending for social and productive services provisioning through "cost-sharing" measures, elimination of subsidies, and so on.

Together with these was the restructuring of the public sector through removal of protection, subsidies, and support for parastatals, privatization of public enterprises and civil and parastatal service reform (retrenchment of workers, socalled downsizing), and the restructuring of agriculture (by introduction of individualization, titling and registration of land), and others. The fragile governments were required to create "enabling environments" through tax exemptions and holidays and protection of their interests. With these notions of globalization, even the very history of processes that sparked the spiral of the international crisis was thrown overboard.

What emerged was the dominance of a universalistic cult (something of an intellectual movement) of a program of desired ends rather than an empirically supported understanding of more general trends with regard to the various activities internationally. By the late 1980s and 1990s, the euphoria of the 'globalization' was at its zenith: It had become the stock-in-trade of journalists, media pundits, policymakers, politicians, corporate elites, and many an academician. The expectations were that in a globalized world there will be a single society and culture occupying the planet. This society and culture will probably not be harmoniously integrated, although it might conceivably be. Rather it will probably tend toward higher levels of differentiation, multiplicity, and chaos. There will be no central organizing government and no tight set of cultural preferences and prescriptions. In so far as culture is unified, it will be extremely abstract, expressing tolerance for diversity and individual choice.

Importantly, territoriality will disappear as an organizing principle for social and cultural life; it will be a society without borders and spatial boundaries. Thus, the process conceptualized by right-wing utopianism.

Indeed, globalization is the name that has been given to the social, economic, and political processes that have, taken together, produced the characteristic conditions of contemporary existence. In particular, globalization refers to the ways in which previously distant parts of the world have become connected in an historically unprecedented manner, such that developments in one part of the world are now able to rapidly produce effects on geographically distant localities. This in turn has made it possible to begin to imagine the world as a single, global space linked by a wide array of technological, economic, social, and cultural forces.

Globalization in those terms can be grasped only as a salvation to the bourgeois image from its critics and the defeat of all pro-people and welfarist policies, which stood for the interests of those in the twilight zone--the poor and the marginalized. Theoretically, globalization was a real expression of the rise of the "new capitalist classes" since the 1970s, based in the media, finance, advertising, academia, merchandizing, international stock-exchange, etc., who emerged via new speculative forms of accumulation based on finances and plunder of natural resources, rather than productive investments of the formerly productive "old capitalist classes."

Through the operation of corporate and finance capital that was highly mobile, the whole world was turned into speculative markets, whereby they entered any country and left at any time regardless of the long-term goals. Their main preoccupation was the purchase of equity and bonds through stock exchange and financial markets--the buying and selling of rights, whether investments in liquid assets or existing assets that were being privatized. With the world of computer dominance, the world financial markets became hooked up around-the-clock trading, with takeover specialists busy buying and selling off corporations, regardless of what they were producing or the fact that millions of workers were becoming unemployed.

These new forms of accumulation had no interest in investment and development of new industries, but in commercial real estate and "mercantilist" forms of profit making. Developments in communication technology, it was claimed, had disembodied experience. The "new middle classes" completely recast even the notion of work as the activity that provides individual motivation, social integration, and systemic reproduction. Instead what became central was the consumer conduct and freedom in the market as the cognitive and moral focus of life, which had the efficacy to integrate society and manage its system. In this regard, even the "grand narratives" to legitimate power, which were necessary in the past, had become obsolete.

Legitimization of state through social policies, as an instrument of power, had been replaced by the seduction of the consumer by the market, and where this failed, by repression. In this respect, it was necessary to agitate for the withdrawal of the state from the social provisioning sphere on the pretext that markets were playing that important role, hitherto considered to be its role, given that there was no need to justify the state and its activities as true and moral. At the ideological level, these aspects related to globalization and their attendant inequalities were reinforced by the new developments as a result of the Human Genome Project. With the developments in genetic science, it became possible to reduce human beings to a biological expression of one's DNA. DNA was increasingly demonstrating that there are innate differences in abilities as a result of genetic and biological inheritance.

Therefore, hierarchization and differentiation or differences in power, wealth, knowledge, and skills are part of human nature. This has implications on how Africans look at themselves as people in a predetermined form--from issues of racial and ethnic differences and intelligence to homosexuality, free market entrepreneurs, and male dominance. By the early 1990s, globalization had even created the illusion that it was possible for everyone to be self-employed, if given the skills of entrepreneurship. It promised great opportunities to African countries and the people, and the economists assured Africans about this.

Africans were told that as the free markets worked their magic--with the reforms of privatization, deregulation, and flexibility, the benefits would trickle down to the poor in the long run. The reality has been different. Even the IFIs have admitted that there has been no convergence of per capita income levels between the North and the South. They have shown that the number of low-income countries has actually risen from 52 in 1965 to 105 in 1995, the majority being African. That is not all: they further admitted bluntly that capital has gained in comparison with labor, and profit shares have risen everywhere.

By the mid-1990s, the antiglobalization drama—which started in Seattle (against the World Trade Organization) moved to Davos (against the Trilateral Commission and the World Economic Forum) and to Washington, DC (against the World Bank and the International Monetary Fund), and took place at the threshold of the millennium--was not anticipated at all. For those who were celebrating "globalization," such anticipation amounted to a midsummer night's dream. This road show marked an open revolt against an open international economy in the advanced countries, in favor of protectionism from a broad political spectrum—environmentalists, trade unionists, and many other civil activist organizations.

In April 2001, the police fired 7,707 teargas canisters against the antiglobalization protesters in Quebec, Canada. This was to be repeated in Gothenburg, Sweden, where police used live ammunition against the people, and in Barcelona, Spain, where police attempted to provoke people into violence. In Genoa, Italy, one demonstrator was killed and 600 were injured or beaten by the police. The use of excessive force against those who oppose globalization has been on the rise.

Here, the immediate questions that arise are: What is new about globalization? Aren't the elements identifying it a mere relabeling of what was termed colonialism/neocolonialism or imperialism in the past? Given the debates surrounding the whole question of globalization and its consequences, are there any quantitative or qualitative indicators to measure the degree of this process or lack of it? In which way, for example, can ordinary people realize what globalization is, judging by their own standards, if they are not told about it given that what they face is reinforced marginalization, further hierarchization and inequalities, the heightening of tension, and the deepening of immerseration--things that have existed in the history of capitalism?

Why is it that some of the basic experiences have to be requalified, even if not rationally explained, as globalization? Given that there is already ample evidence that globalization in one way or another has been responsible for the erosion of the welfare of peoplein Africa, job destruction, and mass unemployment, and has thrown people into deeper immerseration tensions, is that not the uncritical acceptance of globalization an attempt to turn vices into virtues?

Globalization in African countries resulted in the states becoming completely dominated by the multilateral and transnational institutions, increasingly becoming powerless institutions as far as powers to control the movement of financial and money capital were concerned. In reality, the paradox of the SAPs, like the globalization process, is that the tendency of the state to intervene in economic affairs has tended to increase over the years on behalf of finance capital and against the disempowered "wretched of the earth."

This is regardless of the political, economic, and ideological rhetoric. This tendency has tended to increase when its effectiveness has been on the decline. Part of the reason is that SAPs measures that seek to reduce public expenditure, human development, and welfare are incompatible with democracy and human rights. People tend to resist some of the measures, as it has been the case in most African countries. Practically, this has necessitated the expansion of state bureaucracy and enhanced the repressive role of the police and the military, with a weakening power in the economic sphere.

## POLITICS OF DEMOBILIZATION

It is in this context that one can understand why the IFIs have become obsessed with the question of good governance, democracy, and capacity building in recent years. They express the need for strong states that can facilitate the integration of the African countries in the capitalist global economy. That is, states that can make effective interventions in terms of adjustments to cope with inflation, trade policies, tax incentives, export subsidies, privatization, sectoral policies (in terms of master plans and integration of activities), research policies, regulations, and controls.

The motto is the "rule of law," regardless of whether the laws are just or unjust. It is essentially an attempt by the IFIs to make sure that the new type of African state is able to effectively control the rebellious populations and restructure the balance of class forces, so that transnational and multinational capital is able to operate without any major hindrances. This explains why democracy, good governance, and a clean human rights record became conditionalities of support from the IFIs by the end of the 1980s. Within this context, it was reduced to consolidation of market economy, privatization of state enterprises, multi-partyism, the emergence of NGOs, and the irresponsibility of the state in social provisioning, a democratic constitution, and "laissez-faire" state, without any historical references in regard to how the transition would lead to the process of emancipation of the ordinary people.

Liberalization of the economy and the opening up of the markets for international capital through denationalization and privatization or decapitalization (an unpatriotic thrust) reducing public expenditure on social services (an antipeople move against education, health, and public goods in general) and multipartyism became the main thrust of donor policies by late 1980s and early 1990s as far as African countries were concerned.

In the context of demolishing the single-party state systems that existed in Africa, there was hardly any revisiting of the experiences of multipartyism of the early days of independence, for example, which led to authoritarian regimes in the case of Senegal, Botswana, Nigeria, and others. With the euphoria of multipartyism, it was assumed that the "democratization" process would lead to more liberating practices in African countries, because the West and the IFIs had pronounced it.

The fact that the same "democratic" West until 1970s tended to rationalize repression in Africa for political, ideological and economic reasons was completely forgotten. For example, while the heads of state of the Front-line States termed apartheid a crime against humanity, the West never accepted this: they preferred the term gross violation of Human rights, in the Ronald Reagan formulation. Some of the same powers had supported the regimes of Ahmed Bokassa (Central Africa), Idi Amin (Uganda), Mobutu Sese Seko (Zaire), and many others, for the same economic, political, security, and ideological reasons!

The history of the emergence of party politics (whether multiparty or single party) itself was never taken into account. What was ignored was the fact that democracy as a mode of politics has always existed historically. Parliamentary parties emerged in Europe after 1870s, with the defeat of the working-class movements (specifically the Parisian Communards in 1871) and the vanguard single-state parties in 1917 with the Russian Revolution (specifically in its Stalinist variant). Both modes of politics have been in a crisis for a long time, even before their introduction to Africa. The crisis of the parliamentary forms was fully demonstrated by the U.S. elections of November 2000 in the State of Florida. This attests to the fact that the American system is not the best model for democracy. Such aspects were not taken into consideration--that is, the actual interests safeguarded by multipartyism.

Furthermore, in the demolition of single-party systems, no account was taken of the critique of statism (of both single and multiparty) and proposals for political changes from the social movements that began in the late 1970s and early 1980s as a result of the crisis and the implementation of the SAPs; a critique that was accompanied by the reevaluation of African societies in the form of championing for the autonomy of the "civil society." It manifested itself into the demands for autonomous civil movements (for workers, peasants, women, students, professionals, youths, etc.) as a form of people restructuring relations among themselves and also the same people and the states, by way of limiting the oppressive powers of states. This critique that aimed at transforming the extreme statization of all aspects of social, economic and political life of societies, rather than a destruction of the states, was sidelined and forsaken with the introduction of multipartyism from above. Thus, struggles for broad democracy were derailed by the late 1980s.

Instead, the whole question of democracy was reduced to multipartyism and the existence of a pluralist system. This system, according to this logic, would transform the state into some form of an intermediary network through which groups could compete for power and influence policy and decision making. Even the civil society/state relationship discourse was radically transformed to one that supported liberalization and the operation of market forces in response to what was termed an "informal" or "second" economy. The World Bank and the IMF promoted this conception of civil society, backed by scholarly works of both Western and African origin.

The belief that civil society organizations reconceptualized as nongovernmental organizations, NGOs in Africa have an important role to play in political, economic, and social development was concretized. This was in response to real struggles taking place at international and local levels. At the international level, the events in the late 1960s and 1970s, with the crisis of welfarism, saw popular protests in the West and other countries spearheaded by women's rights, antiracism, antiwar and nuclear disarmament and environmental protection movements. The peace and antiracist movements revealed that sciences and the state were war machines; the women's movement exposed the patriarchal nature of societies and their institutions; and the environmental movements sounded the survival-threatening global impacts of human social and economic activity.

The women's movement had an imprint in all these resistance movements, and even exposed their patriarchal nature. The major outcome of these movements was an enormous deepened grasp of the various ways in which the bureaucratic environment worked to keep members of the various social groups from acting in concerted ways. The entire system regulating the relationships between men and women and people and the environment appeared as a constraint in the attempts to grasp the processes taking place during this period of crisis of the welfare institutions. These movements arose because of crises engineered by capitalist transformations in economic forms of organization, crisis of ecology, crisis of institutional racism, and sexism.

The women's movement had a far-reaching impact upon both substance and concepts worldwide. It helped to shape the views and studies of the family institutions and to show that the views and studies of the family and gender were not necessarily the same thing. The antiracist and peace movements helped in the elaboration of issues related to war and peace, national and international relations, imperialism as an object of study, and nationality and ethnic relations.

The post-1970s movements in Africa, within this international context, saw a full-scale reappraisal of social conditions, and political commitment to the liberation and empowerment of women, both as an end in its own right and as a means to improving society as a whole. National and international bureaucracies were forced to adopt the women agenda, as a result of these struggles. The United Nations declared the period 1975-1985 a Decade for Women, Peace, Equality, and Development. This resulted in the confrontation of ideas and actions regarding the notions of underdevelopment, women's roles in development, the impact of division of labor, the conditions of women, oppression and sexual inequality, sources of oppression and sexism, patriarchy, class, caste, and racial inequalities.

At the end of the decade in 1985, Third World women made one voice on the international scene in the Copenhagen and Nairobi conferences. Third World women were of the view that the simple division of subjects on the basis of sex analysis was limiting: instead, direction should be toward examining gender as a social construct reflecting real conditions of oppression and exploitation. Issues that came out in the Nairobi Conference included even those that divided women—gender, class, status, age, kinship affiliation, racism, and colonialism. Third World women identified their problems in terms of development, "nation building," internal gender struggles, and liberation struggles.

Third World women saw their work as political, challenging the new growing patriarchal system imposed on their societies through colonialism and Western religions and educational influence. Here there was no question of political indifference: One could not afford to be indifferent to the way society is organized, nor close one's eyes to the issues of oppression or be one-sided. They posed the questions of social justice and equality of rights more sharply. The slogan was: "The personal is political!"

National governments and international agencies, including the United Nations, responded to these issues by attempting to incorporate and neutralize these issues. Donor agencies started setting up "Women-in-Development" (WID) projects, as a form of sponsorship of their development strategies, with a huge expertise that in turn generated a bureaucratic discourse on women in development. This was meant to move the movements from the liberationist and emancipatory tendencies and concerns, away from the concerns of ordinary women and men.

But practically, the antiwelfarist development strategies of SAPs, which all the donors were sponsoring, and were harming especially women and children, militated against these attempts to co-opt these endeavors. Thus real democratic struggles that sought new historical visions and modes of politics that aimed at defending women, youth, children, workers, poor peasants, and the marginalized minorities were derailed by reducing politics to the number of parties and confining politics to the practices of the parties and the state by late 1980s.

For the IFIs and their supporters in Africa, the problem was not lack of mass democracy; rather it was that of how to put forward a defense of capitalism by trying to justify economic liberalization and commercialization of public and civil institutions and its consequences as far as the majority of the people are concerned. SAPs, if anything, merely restructured capital (private and public), which benefited from the *statist* model of the 1960s and 1970s around newly deregulated branches (mainly import-export activities and the plunder of natural resources).

For the working people this meant further marginalization, aggravation of tensions, and more hierarchization. The practical problem for the IFIs and their local transnational capitalist class or supporters was how to win popular support for the SAPs' measures and the market order. These measures are essentially antipeople and antihuman rights. The popular democratic opposition to SAPs, which started in the 1980s, seemingly was in some instances threatening to destroy the fundamental basis of the liberal order and the institutions of privatization and market forces. For the Western world, this was support for totalitarianism and against political and civil liberties, as it was against economic freedom for private capital.

Thus multiparty democracy, reduced to the number of parties, the right to govern after garnering more votes (regardless of the manner in which one got the votes), had become the anchorage of legality and legitimacy in a world that worked hard to make the states irresponsible and remove the notion of the public and public interests. Of course, this was a way of submitting people to the belief of the values of the economy--the "return of individualism" (self-help, self-employment, cost-sharing, etc.) and the destruction of all philosophical foundations of welfarism and collective responsibility toward poverty, misery, sickness, misfortunes, education, and so forth.

Both single-party and multiparty democracy systems have been in a crisis for a long time. Why has this been the case? In practice, in multiparty states, parties have always been quasistate institutions competing for the distribution of positions. This distribution is often regulated by the constitution and operates on its basis and the prevailing system. The institutions are not those for the reconstitution/reconstruction of the state so that it becomes responsive to popular needs and popular control. In this system politics exists only in the party and the government, and parties acquire statelike structures as tools of political organization within a state project.

The ultimate aim of the parties is to occupy the statehouse or the treasury. Parties in opposition merely end up working to replace the one in power rather than address real issues, because they also regard the state as the only terrain and reference of politics. As demonstrated in the history of the Western world in terms of safeguarding the so-called economic freedom, the struggle for or against democracy and human rights has always been in terms of how to institute/elect regimes that would not set out to destroy the fundamental basis of market economies and the functioning of capital in general. The biggest fear in such democracies has always been the rule of the majority. Thus in these countries, the problem has always been how to safeguard economic liberty in a mass democracy situation (if this cannot be prevented). In other words, how to make the modern state that claims to represent the interests of all remain legitimate in the face of mass opposition.

What this amounts to is the fact that single-party or multiparty regimes all over the world have made some totalitarian demands on their members, groups, sections of groups, classes, and even individuals in the name of the so-called interests of the country or government. And the struggle since the emergence of the modern state has been in terms of whether the state can dominate the civil society or the civil society dominates the state, not as dichotomies, but as mutually exclusive entities.

In this regard, one should not wonder that with the protests against globalization, demonstrators are accused of being "enemies of the poor" by the ideologues of the financial and corporate gurus. In 2002 The International Chamber of Commerce and the UN general secretary in a Geneva Business Declaration suggested that activist pressure groups should place emphasis on legitimizing themselves. Where this does not happen, rules establishing their rights and responsibilities should be considered. Business is accustomed to working with trade unions, consumer organizations, and other representative groups that are responsible, credible, transparent, and accountable, and consequently command respect. What one should question is the proliferation of activist groups that do not accept these self-disciplinary criteria. There is democracy in action! Corporate-led globalization hates democracy. No wonder the WTO planned its November 2002 conference to be held in Qatar, in the middle of the desert, away from the protestors.

The one-party system has its problems too. In the single-party state system, parties tend to see themselves as the exclusive and only source of progressive politics, and therefore reduce politics to organizations and building of parties, while condemning people outside the parties to nonexistence politically. In this system, all other sites of politics (the farm, the factory, the school, the homestead erroneously labeled household by Westerners of African countries, the sports grounds, the media, the theatre, and others) fall under the guidance of the party. The party becomes an organ of management and therefore oppressive and authoritarian on the pretext that it is the only derivation of truth. The masses become mere nonthinking beings or at best a bunch of ignorant riffraffs, incapable of self-emancipation.

In other words, both single- and multiparty forms of democracy have historically been oppressive. They have at one point or another discriminated and disenfranchised some people (blacks in America up to the 1960s, women in the West until early 1920s, workers, etc.). The champions of multiparty politics did not take these facts into account. They took the system for granted.

All they have been doing all along is to pitch the merits and demerits of multypartyism against those of the single-party, by indiscriminately citing examples from Ancient Greece, Washington, DC, and other places. This cult of the "universal" has ignored the fact that democracy is a historical mode of politics within the context of redefining relationships among the people and between the people and the state. The reason is that the oppressors are singled out as the enemies and the masses as those in the oppressed camp, even if these are also differentiated.

## BEYOND MULTIPARTYISM: NEED FOR SOCIAL MOVEMENTS

Multiparty politics in Africa in general need a serious critique. Most parties that have emerged/exist so far are elite parties. They are not organic parties of mass or community character ideologically or practically. There is an acceptance of the universal concept of liberal democracy and human rights among most of these parties, whereby democracy and human rights are viewed in terms of forms of rule and governance that includes the right of representation, organization, and expression. It is individual rights that override in this conception, rather than peoples' rights as individuals and communities. It is a matter of winning through the ballot box by any means necessary--foul or fair.

This democracy which was introduced from above in the early 1990s has resulted in the sowing of more seeds of discord given that it defends politics of exclusion and inclusion, corruption, privileges, and denials. The winning and losing of votes is based on mobilization, power to buy votes, and coerce or cheat, which include mobilization of even forms of identities, imagined or real, prejudices and discriminations. The simple game is that people who are in power will definitely exclude and marginalize people who voted against them.

Thus the issues of "Who originates from where among those in power" or "which party represents which people" become the real stuff in politics. It is a war of one against all; and the winner takes or remains in power. Self-censorship is imposed on the people in that critical minds and people who interrogate the unfairness and injustices perpetuated by the system are misconstrued to belong to this or that party, and in the process are persecuted; while those who toe the line or display a sense of loyalty are rewarded. Genuine knowledge, fidelity to truth, and critical intellectual faculties are banished and mediocrity is enthroned.

Citizenship, rather than nationalism, patriotism, and pan-Africanism become the real stuff. Thus Kenneth Kaunda in Zambia or Jenerali Ulimwengu in Tanzania, or Alassane Ouattara in Côte d'Ivoire, for example, are declared stateless by a stroke of a pen. Citizenship, religious and "ethnic" issues are politicized than ever before, and, in the process, some people or communities are made scapegoats while real oppressors, thieves, pillagers, and killers are left to go scot-free with impunity. The result is reinforcement of discriminatory tendencies. While the state is ideally supposed to be an arbiter in resolving contradictions in a society, in the current African situation it tends to identify itself with certain groups vis a vis others, thus representing sectional interests—those of the powerful and wealthy—the transnational capitalist class.

In African countries, these states were born out of military conquest and occupation after 1884, and therefore they had no room for prescriptions from the people because they were based on discriminatory and oppressive practices. Political parties, as statelike structures working hard to occupy the state, like the colonial state itself, have tended to put a wedge between politics and economics by insisting that the only place for conducting politics is in the government and the parliament, despite the fact that women declared as far back as the 1970s that the personal is political! They have always been scared of the emergence and consolidation of independent labor, peasant, women, youth, and peoples' movements that seek to defend the weak, the poor, and the environments for the mutual survival of mankind.

The tendency for these parties has been to distance themselves from such organizations and such activities, except when it is to their advantage. What can be said is that the state and the political parties are part of the problem and the major obstacle to evolution of real democratic transformations. Real democratic transformations require one to transcend the simplistic formal democracy—that is, existence of multiparties and regular elections, as prescribed by the donor and international relations perspectives, to include the question of promotion of social justice, equity, and equality (i.e., social democracy). It has to involve the restructuring of relations and redressing imbalances (both historical and contemporary) among the people in all their manifestations, including gender, ethnic, class, racial, and so on. It has to be redefined to include the question of poverty eradication (not alleviation) and access and control of productive resources that enable people to reproduce as well as ensure more equitable social development.

For democracy to make sense, it has to be linked with those who are victims of the prevailing circumstances. It must be seen to be taking into account issues of social justice and social democracy. It has to be directed to the questions of redressing imbalances, inequalities, and exploitation rather than simply setting up "democratic institutions" and "good governance"—a movement from the authoritarianism of one state party to that of many state parties.

It is in this respect that one can empathize with the words of the Kenyan moral philosopher, the late Odera Oruka, who pointed out in the early 1980s that the average man and woman in Africa is a citizen of an "Uncivil Republic," who does not have the right to liberty that embraces "freedom of thought and opinion, freedom of speech and assembly and freedom of emigration." These do not exist for the average man or woman in Africa. Those who live below the economic baseline of humanity are denied the right to liberty.

The average person in the uncivil republic has no complicated thought and opinion. They have but one concern: they are hungry and jobless. This is what people want to express but they cannot express because they lack the means and the right to liberty. Those who stand up to speak for them are easily silenced or wiped out by the tools of state terrorism. Oruka was to further point out that all rights to work, minimum standards of life, fair wages, social security, freedom from hunger, and freedom to join trade unions and other associations are absent. Instead, the only rights guaranteed are the rights to property, which are meaningful to the few who are wealthy. The rights being protected by multipartyism are those of the wealthy and powerful.

Multiparty politics are doing more harm by reinforcing the politics of "them" and "us." We need a conception of democracy and human rights and its organizational forms that stand for peace, justice, equity, and equality. This democracy should aim at treating/resolving differences between workers and bosses, peasants and merchants, students and teachers, men and women, youths and elders, Moslems and Christians, Africans and Asians/Arabs/Europeans, majority and minority, people and state. It has to address issues such as: In which way is production organized? Who is producing, and who is appropriating the surplus? What forms of accumulation are taking place? What kinds of social relations exist among individuals, groups, and organizations as far as the control of resources is concerned? Only in this way can we prevent the consolidation of unpatriotic territorial jingoist politics, clothed in unanimity regarded as a basis of so-called national unity, peace, and stability, which is essentially false; a unanimity that blocks the possibilities of resolution of problems.

What we need are serious public collective mutual debates for self-questioning and self-criticism organized to resolve Africa's problems. People need to come together and talk instead of the violent confrontations between parties being witnessed currently. What is required is a space for people to dialogue under circumstances whereby everybody has the right to talk and is called upon to discuss the crisis confronting Africans. This means the ending of divisions between the parties (political interests) and the trade union, cooperatives, student organizations, women's movement, youth movements, environmental movements, and activist organizations (supposedly nonpolitical interests), which distract people from effectively participating in political processes.

In this regard, only social movements (territorial and panterritorial), and especially those grounded on the foundations of peace, equality, equity, democracy, stability, and pan-Africanism can articulate emancipatory democratic politics. For such movements to exist, there must be an emergence and consolidation of politics in civil society (grassroots-based movements and people's organizations) leading to real transformations of the state structures from engines of repression to those of mobilization for development.

Political parties are not civil society organizations because their objectives are directed toward the control of state power (state entryism), rather than its transformation. Civil society organizations that can become effective are those that are activist and rooted in society and are socially accountable. In this regard, most NGOs, except for the activist ones with a social transformational mission and vision, are not civil society organizations. This is because they tend to be controlled or co-opted by governments and international agencies. There are some that have even become corrupt. In so doing they have abdicated their responsibility to civil society. Civil society implies self-organizations, which defend the interests of the majority of the people who are poor and marginalized and promote civil liberties and social transformation.

Those organizations/movements recognize the fact that the state in its current form in Africa cannot guarantee social welfare to the people, unless it is reorganized so that it becomes responsive to the ordinary people's needs, and not those that refuse to transcend the assumptions so fashionably current that There Is No Alternative (TINA, according to Margaret Thatcher) for the dominant discourse—an inevitability of some sort. Democracy in the present African conditions can refer only to two things: First, the extent to which the people's will enters decisions that will affect their life chances; and second, the extent to which their means of livelihood are guaranteed.

In political terms the first demand does not suggest capture of "state power" by the people (workers and peasants), but it does imply ascendancy to state power by a national democratic alliance in which the popular classes hold the balance of power. The second demand implies equitable (not equal) distribution of resources. Neither liberal democracy imposed "multi-partyism" through AID or through the mouth of the cannon nor "market forces" can guarantee these two conditions. It appears, therefore, that the issue is neither liberal nor "compradorial" or parasitic democracy but social democracy.

A comprador, in the original sense of the word, was the Chinese manager or the senior Chinese employee in a foreign commercial establishment. The compradors served foreign economic interests and had close connection with imperialism and foreign capital in fostering alien bureaucrat-capitalism, pillage, and mindless exploitation of the Chinese workers.

The liberal "democratization" taking place in Africa is such that the popular masses who initiated the process of democratization got usurped or their movement got hijacked by their class enemies, the comprador class or parasitic bureaucrat-capitalists. This usurped democratization explains why the much vaunted "liberal democracy" has remained a sham throughout the continent, a mere stratagem used by the West to reproduce itself ideologically in Africa today.

In this regard, there is nothing more erroneous than to think that democracy merely involves the issues of "good governance," structural adjustment or "rule of law" as Africans are made to believe currently. Real democratic politics must address the issues of redressing imbalances, inequalities, relations of domination and exploitation. Democracy as a mode of politics is historically a process of peacefully dealing with/resolving differences and overcoming obstacles to the attainment of nonarbitrary forms of societal organization—the actual goal of human activities. Therefore democracy must be linked to the question of social justice, the only sure guarantee of peace and development.

# References

Fomunyoh, C. 2001. "Democratization in Fits and Starts," *Journal of Democracy*, 12, 3: 37-50.

Huntington, Samuel (19xx). *The Clash of Civilizations and the Remaking of the World Order*. New York: Simon & Schuster.

Reilley, Charles. 1995. *New Paths to Democratic Development in Latin America: the Rise of NGO-Municipal Collaboration*. Boulder, CO: Lynne Rienner Publishers.

Petras, James and Henry Veltmeyer. 2002. "The Age of Reverse Aid: Neoliberalism as a Catalyst of Regression," *Development and Change*, Vol. 33, No. 2, April.

Petras, James and Henry Veltmeyer (2001). *Globalization Unmasked: The New Face of Imperialism*. London: ZED Press.

Chapter 8

# Transnational Crime versus Democracy in Africa

Organized crime and democracy are antithetical. That is to say the guiding principles of one do work against the guiding principles of the other. In organized crime there are lords and patrons. Organized crime has a legal system that disregards human rights in favor of power and control. Organized crime is much like the feudal class systems. It is this class system that the champions of democracy seek to escape when they frame constitutional governments.

Democracy, on the other hand, is a belief in the sovereignty of a nation and its entire people. The legal system of any democracy upholds the rights of all individuals, not just the powerful and wealthy. The principles of democracy promote individual freedom; democracy upholds the potential of mankind; and most of all, inherent in democracy is the belief that men are capable of governing themselves.

There are those who say the battle against organized crime will be the battle of the 21st century. When political contributions in the millions are allowed, who is to say exactly where those dollars start out? Skillful public relations firms are paid huge amounts to plan the strategy of a political campaign and the public falls prey to media manipulation of the persona of the candidate. Is this democracy? Uncertainty looms over democracy when it comes to transnational criminal syndicates like terrorists, drug pushers, and the like.

In his classic study of African organized crime, James Opolet (1979) suggests that an appropriate definition of organized crime on the African continent is a criminal conspiracy to quickly and easily make a profit through the exploitation of political instability, disorganized and under funded law enforcement, pervasive institutional corruption, and the exploitation of entrepreneurial opportunities. He identified three types of organized criminal entrepreneurs. First, there are established business and commercial leaders and high-ranking public officials who use their governmental and economic positions to personal advantage. Second, there are less respectable, "shady," businesspeople who maintain working relationships with government officials and criminal entrepreneurs. And lastly, there are "criminal operators" engaging in drug trafficking, poaching, smuggling, and robbery (ibid.). Implicit in the definition given by Opolet and typology of illicit entrepreneurship are difficulties in the economy and the organization of law enforcement and criminal justice coupled with illicit market opportunities that give rise to a set of social conditions conducive to the creation of organized crime syndicates.

Conflicts and inefficiency in law enforcement, along with political corruption and economic dislocation, are major predisposing factors toward the creation of organized crime syndicates in Africa. But one crucial impetus overrides all others in establishing a genesis for criminal organizations, the need for an illicit market. The market for illicit goods and services that supports the activities of African organized crime syndicates is supported by several factors unique to the African situation. First, Africa has commodities that are in high demand outside the continent, such as ivory and coffee beans. Second, Africa has shortages of essential goods which can be obtained from outside sources, such as sugar, soap, and motor vehicle parts (Kibuka, 1979).

The ease of modern transportation in the late 20th century has made the smuggling of goods out of Africa and into Africa much easier, as smuggling activities are subsumed in normal commerce and tourism activities. The core of syndicate activity in Africa revolves around black-market business crimes, crimes that invite participation by highly educated, but frequently unemployed or underemployed young people.

The attractiveness of black market entrepreneurship is enhanced by the fact that even those young people who are employed often find these are jobs that fail to guarantee financial security (ibid.). In economies marked by high levels of surplus labor, unemployment, poverty, and an egregious maldistribution of wealth and power, crime creates opportunity, and opportunity creates organized crime.

A highly diverse array of crime syndicates, handling a variety of goods and services, dominates the African scene. West African diamond and cattle smugglers, Ugandan and Kenyan coffee smugglers, and Somali poaching bands represent just some of the variety of criminal entrepreneurship found on the African continent (Opolet, 1979).

New syndicates, created in recent years, have often organized around money laundering and the drug trade. In many ways drug trafficking has been the key developmental variable in modern African organized crime. It has both augmented and reorganized traditional smuggling and poaching operations, and has created an anomaly on a continent where the indigenous drug market has been decidedly weak and unprofitable.

## TRANSNATIONALIZATION OF CRIME

Globalization is the result of advances in technological, transportation, information, communication, and financial systems that are worldwide in scope and transcend national borders. It has not only facilitated the transfer of goods, people, and money through the global economy, but has also masked the transportation of illegal items and aliens. Globalization also assisted in transforming organized crime from a domestic to a transnational phenomenon, and from a law-and-order problem to a national and international security threat.

Criminals organize themselves internationally into syndicates operating transnationally and exploit the free movement between states to traffic drugs and weapons to new consumer markets. Conditions of poverty in cities where survival takes precedence over the rule of law, and in which street gangs are seen as a way of life, lead to the development of gangsterism into powerful transnational crime organizations. It is these organized crime groups that take countries such as Italy, Hong Kong, Brazil, and Colombia by storm.

Evidence indicates that organized crime grows quickly and flourishes in periods of political transition that were normally preceded by periods of violence. The state then focuses its resources in areas of reconstruction and development only, leaving gaps for the emergence of crime syndicates. The collapse of communist rule in the Soviet Union is one example where thousands of criminal organizations quickly emerged. The present emergence and operations of international crime syndicates in South Africa support this argument (Williams, 1997: 13). More than a century ago, the growth of organized crime in Sicily was the result of weak government and strong ethnic and family bonds.

Globalization results in the long term in irreversible contraction in the domain of state authority. States have in effect lost control of markets as reflected in the development of parallel, informal economies, the rise of grey and black-markets, and the inability of states to prevent the flow of illicit products across their borders or to prevent illegal migration. This is also reflected in the growing occurrence of theft of intellectual property, the growth of transnational software piracy, and counterfeiting of products and currencies. One can thus understand why international arms embargoes have never been nearly effective enough to achieve the desired results.

The current global migration has reached unprecedented levels as people are driven by the desire to escape poverty in search of a better life. Factors contributing to this migration are mainly poverty, famine, conflict, and repression, while attracting factors are mainly economic opportunities in industrial countries as well as transnational family and ethnic networks. Traffickers are earning a fortune by moving desperate migrants illegally across international borders. Among these illegal migrants there are inevitably members of criminal organizations who bring their criminal skills, knowledge, affiliations, and contacts with them.

The best-known criminal organizations with migrating elements are Chinese, Nigerian, Italian, and Russian syndicates. The ethnic networks are an important resource for many transnational crime organizations as they provide cover, recruits, and transnational linkages to facilitate criminal activities. Some of these illegal migrants are sold by traffickers to provide cheap labor while women and young girls are sold for prostitution. The illegal migrants bring about additional demands for state provision and services that must then be shared with the citizens of the host country.

Financial infrastructure links countries, banks, and stock markets, curren-cies, and investment portfolios in a global exchange mechanism that operates 24 hours a day, using "megabyte money," which is not under government control. This global financial infrastructure offers a golden opportunity for criminal activities. No regulatory measures have been developed to match this increased volume of financial business. This financial system makes it possible to trade anonymously to move money rapidly and easily, and to obscure both origin and ownership, making it impossible to detect illegal money.

A global world has created opportunities for criminal organizations to advance their illicit activities. International borders and sovereignty of states do not hinder criminal activities; criminal groups are able to slip through border controls most of the time. Transnational crime organizations operate across frontiers. They exploit the limitations of government law-enforcing agencies in operating only within the borders of the country. Different states are used in a number of ways by criminal organizations, in promoting their activities. The following kinds of states and their roles are briefly discussed below:

- *Home States* are those from which transnational crime syndicates operate. Here a favorable environment exists as a result of the weakness of the state. The criminal organization has succeeded in ensuring that the state authori-ties willingly cooperate or collude in their activities. These states will then be used as sanctuaries or safe havens.

- *Host States* are those in which transnational crime organizations have lucra-tive markets or other targets for their activities. Syndicates operate effec-tively with low risk in those host states, where they normally mask them-selves in ethnic networks providing cover and recruitment. Such networks are difficult to penetrate because of language and cultural barriers.

- *Transshipment States* are located as major transit routes for certain illicit commodities such as drugs, arms, or illegal aliens. Those states are particu-larly vulnerable to operational corruption.

- *Service States* are those with financial sectors that are structured in ways that enable crime syndicates to further their activities, especially with the movement and protection of their financial assets. States that offer offshore banking are normally used as Service States.

- It is also clear that some states may be used to fulfill simultaneous roles, that is, a combination of the above-mentioned roles.

Globalization has brought about the transformation of the globe from the communist-capitalist superpower era to the new era where the interstate trade, transportation, communications and information and technology revolution has accelerated. No state at present can afford to remain isolated from these developments (Shaw, 1998). The negative part of globalization is its openness to misuse by criminal syndicates. States throughout the world are fighting a losing battle as the crime syndicates grow stronger, adjusting and adapting their operations according to developments in global trends.

## AFRICA'S VULNERABILITY

For decades the African continent has been plagued by wars, famine, diseases, and until recently the AIDS epidemic. The security of this continent is now seriously affected by the new global epidemic of narcotics trade. Transnational crime organizations have also succeeded in establishing a firm network of criminal activities in a number of countries.

Ghanaian and Nigerian syndicates are known to obtain their drug consignments from Colombia. In the East African states this trade is conducted from Asia. It is from these regions that much of the world's illicit opium crops are refined into heroin and then smuggled into Europe. It has also been confirmed that drugs from India and Thailand destined for the Persian Gulf are channeled through East Africa. In the case of Zanzibar, the United States of America and the United Kingdom have agreed to assist the authorities with the necessary intelligence on traffickers, together with special equipment for the airport, in order to fight this problem.

North Africa is also known as a center of traffickers in mandrax (methaqualone) while Central African airports of Bangui (Central African Republic), Kigali (Rwanda), and Kinshasa (Democratic Republic of Congo) play a decisive role as transit areas to Western Europe. The Southern African states have not remained unaffected by trafficking activities. Between Johannesburg and Lusaka (Zambia) and the Republic of Congo the drug trafficking is facilitated by a small clandestine network. In Namibia, a new route for illicit drugs through Southern and Western Zambia has been opened since 1990. Zimbabwean passports are known to have been stolen or faked for use in drug trafficking trips.

Africa, especially Southern Africa, is facing the daunting challenge of transnational crime that has rapidly spread and entrenched itself in the region. This is already having serious social and security implications for the Republic of South Africa (RSA) and its neighbours. Authorities in these countries need to launch combined exerted efforts to curb this problem. Regional structures such as the Southern African Development Cooperation must focus on this problem in establishing a joint task force that deals specifically with transnational crime.

The end of apartheid and the introduction of a new democratic political dispensation in South Africa have exposed the RSA to the growing global narcotics trade. The newfound democracy triggered an unprecedented interstate movement of people in the region. Among these people, elements of unemployed and criminals engaged themselves in cross border smuggling, gunrunning, and drug peddling.

The new political order opened up new trade links with other countries, resulting in more regular international flights from various destinations around the globe. This increased freedom of movement was quickly exploited by crime syndicates as the RSA was seen as a new market for illicit trade. Already record quantities of cocaine and other narcotics have flooded into the country; this trend is certain to continue and worsen if left unchecked.

Transnational crime syndicates frequently operating between Swaziland and Lesotho, as well as the RSA, usually involve drug, diamond, and illegal weapon smuggling, car and stock theft. Stock theft has often resulted in tension between the RSA farmers and citizens of Lesotho. Illegal immigration is also a common problem caused by nationals from these neighboring states. The South African Police Service (SAPS) and South African National Defense Force (SANDF) in cooperation with their neighboring counterparts have been deployed on numerous occasions to trace the stolen stock and vehicles from Lesotho and South Africa.

The transnational crime situation in the RSA is no different from that of Lesotho and Swaziland. The main problem in the RSA is illegal immigrants. Illegal weapons trade has flourished, especially from Mozambique, with the ultimate destination being Gauteng and Kwa Zulu-Natal provinces. The drastic downscaling of border control operations by the SANDF due to financial constraints has led to an increase in the number of illegal border crossings. It is evident that some customs officials and the Department of Home Affairs officials are being corrupted and bribed by crime syndicates to turn a blind eye to illegal immigration. A number of arrests and prosecution for false identity documents and passports support this.

As is the case with some customs officials, it is now also more evident that transnational crime organizations have already succeeded in infiltrating some law-enforcement agencies. A number of immigrant women from Thailand, who were illegally imported to operating as sex workers in Johannesburg, have recently been arrested together with a number of members of the South African Narcotics Bureau (SANAB) as accomplices to this criminal activity.

The corruption of politicians and bureaucrats undermines the state's legitimacy and credibility and also subverts the security of the state concerned. It can be recalled that in 1996 a plot to assassinate the former Gauteng premier Mr. Tokyo Sexwale was uncovered, because of his repeated condemnation of the drug trade. This was one method used by crime syndicates to intimidate authorities who are committed to curb their illegal activities.

## TRAFFICKING IN HUMAN CASH CROPS

Child trafficking is the recruitment, transportation, transfer, harboring, or receipt of a child for the purposes of sexual or labor exploitation, forced labor, or slavery. It is a human rights tragedy estimated to involve thousands of children in West Africa and over a million children worldwide. This trafficking of girls is for domestic and market work and the trafficking of boys is for agricultural work. Hundreds of children are trafficked annually in Togo, sent from, received in, or transited through the country. They are recruited on false promises of education, professional training, and paid employment; transported within and across national borders under sometimes life-threatening conditions; ordered into hazardous, exploitative labor; subjected to physical and mental abuse by their employers; and, if they escape or are released, denied the protections necessary to reintegrate them into society. Their stories disclose an appalling chain of events that the Togolese government has thus far failed to break.

According to The Synergy Project (2002) joint estimates developed by UNAIDS, UNICEF, USAID, and the U.S. Bureau of the Census, the total number of living children under age fifteen whose mother, father, or both parents have died of AIDS in sub-Saharan Africa is 11 million. The abuses documented by Human Rights Watch fall squarely within the definition of child trafficking in the United Nations (UN) Protocol to Prevent, Suppress and Punish the Trafficking of Persons, Especially Women and Children, Supplementing the U.N. Convention Against Transnational Organized Crime (2000), known as the Trafficking Protocol. Togo has signed but not ratified both the Trafficking Protocol and the Optional Protocol to the U.N. Convention on the Rights of the Child on the Sale of Children, Child Prostitution and Child Pornography (2000). It has ratified both the Convention on the Rights of the Child (1989) and International Labor Organization (ILO) Convention No. 182 on the Prohibition and Immediate Action for the Elimination of the Worst Forms of Child Labor (1999), the latter of which obliges states that are parties to the Convention to take "immediate and effective measures" to eliminate child trafficking "as a matter of urgency." At the regional level, Togo has participated in multilateral negotiations toward a regional antitrafficking protocol for West Africa and has signed numerous declarations of commitment to eradicate the practice.

Togo's trade in children is illustrative of a larger, regional phenomenon involving at least 13 West African countries. Based on the testimony of children and local experts, Human Rights Watch documented four routes of child trafficking into, out of, or within Togo: (1) the trafficking of Togolese girls into domestic and market labor in Gabon, Benin, Nigeria, and Niger; (2) the trafficking of girls from within Togo to other parts of the country, especially the capital, Lomé; (3) the trafficking of girls from Benin, Nigeria, and Ghana to Lomé; and (4) the trafficking of boys into labor exploitation, usually agricultural work, in Nigeria, Benin, and Côte d'Ivoire.

Children interviewed by Human Rights Watch in (2002) from both West Africa and Kenya (2001) came predominantly from poor, agricultural backgrounds and had generally little schooling before being trafficked. Most were promised that by going abroad they would gain some formal or vocational education, which they could then use to earn money for themselves or their families. In numerous cases, children were recruited by traffickers after running out of money to pay for school; despite a statutory guarantee of free primary education in Togo, school fees range from 4,000 to 13,000 CFA francs (U.S. $6-$20) per year.

Many of the children interviewed were trafficked following the death of at least one parent. Others had parents who were divorced, or at least one parent living and working away from home. A growing cause of orphanhood in Togo, human immunodeficiency virus/acquired immune deficiency syndrome (HIV/AIDS) was identified by some experts as a possible factor in susceptibility to child trafficking.

Girls interviewed by Human Rights Watch were typically recruited into domestic or market labor, either directly by an employer or by a third-party intermediary. Most recalled some degree of family involvement in the transaction, such as parents accepting money from traffickers, distant relatives paying intermediaries to find work abroad, or parents handing over their children based on the promise of education, professional training, or paid work. Following their recruitment, the girls' journey away from home in many cases involved an intermediate stop where they could be left to fend for themselves for weeks or months at a time, before being transported to a country or city of destination by car or boat. Human Rights Watch documented numerous cases of girls taking boats from Nigeria to Gabon, a perilous and sometimes fatal journey. In one case, a boat capsized off the coast of Cameroon and nine girls died.

On arrival, girls were deposited in the homes of employers where they performed long hours of domestic and market work. From as early as 3:00 or 4:00 a.m., children tended gardens, and transported and sold market goods and baked bread. At night, they worked as housemaids, prepared food, and cared for small children. Human Rights Watch documented astonishing cases of girls as young as three or four years old being forced to carry infants or sell merchandise. Almost no girl received any remuneration for her services. Many recounted incidents of physical and emotional abuse, often leading them to escape and live in the street. Officials from the NGO *Terre des Hommes* told Human Rights Watch they had interviewed numerous trafficked girls who experienced sexual abuse in the home, and that some had tested positive for HIV. One child told Human Rights Watch she was forced to sleep in the same bedroom as a male boarder and was afraid she would be raped.

Boys interviewed by Human Rights Watch were for the most part recruited into agricultural labor in southwestern Nigeria. A small number worked on cotton fields in Benin, and one child was recruited into factory work in Côte d'Ivoire. Traffickers tended less to make arrangements with the parents of the boys than to make direct overtures to the boys themselves—tempting them with the promise of a bicycle, a radio, or vocational training abroad. Contrary to expectation, they were taken on long, sometimes perilous journeys to rural Nigeria and ruthlessly exploited. Most were given short-term assignments on farms where they worked long hours in the fields, seven days a week.

Boys worked from as early as 5:00 a.m. until late at night, sometimes with hazardous equipment such as saws or machetes. Some described conditions of bonded labor, whereby their trafficker would pay for their journey to Nigeria and order them to work off the debt. Many recalled that taking time off for sickness or injury would lead to longer working hours or corporal punishment.

## TOGOLESE GOVERNMENT RESPONSE

Despite these obligations, Togo has made insufficient progress in reducing the number or severity of its child trafficking cases, and Human Rights Watch's interviews revealed the inadequacy of Togo's system of protecting and rehabilitating trafficked children. Togo's effort to develop a tougher response to child trafficking in domestic law is on the wrong track.

Togo has repatriated and reintegrated some trafficked children (with the assistance of other countries with which it has bilateral agreements) and/or placed them in the care of NGOs. However, other trafficked children have received no targeted state help in repatriation and have found their own way home with the help of civilians or police officers. This was particularly the case for boys interviewed by Human Rights Watch who, at the end of their work term-usually about nine months-were usually given a bicycle and told to find their way home: they described riding bicycles from Nigeria back to their villages in Togo, a journey that lasted up to nine days. Some boys were stopped by soldiers and forced to bribe them in order to be let go. Some boys have died on the way home and have been buried on the side of the road. One girl was improperly detained in a penal facility on arrival back in Togo.

Numerous government and NGO representatives attested to a lack of resources for rehabilitating trafficked children, and children's testimony corroborated these accounts. Interviews with several child sex workers in Lomé's so-called *marché du petit vagin* (literally, market of the small vagina) revealed that some girls had come to Lomé under conditions of child trafficking and been forced into sex work after escaping or being abandoned. A survey in 1992 showed that HIV prevalence among sex workers in Lomé was already 80 percent.

Aside from bilateral repatriation agreements, the Togolese government's most concrete responses to child trafficking have been the creation of local "vigilance committees" to identify vulnerable children and track potential traffickers; and the drafting of a law, currently before the national assembly, that imposes a five-to-ten-year prison term on traffickers and/or a fine of up to 10 million CFA (U.S.$15,000). The draft law imposes the same penalty on parents of trafficked children who in some way or another might be regarded as complicit in the sale or handing over of their children to traffickers; this includes not only parents who are deceived by false promises of education and professional training, but also those who fail to report known trafficking cases to the police. No allowance is made for parents who resign themselves to sending their children abroad in the good faith belief that they have no alternative or that working abroad is in their child's best interests.

Child traffickers capitalize not only on entrenched poverty, but also on inadequate access to education, poor vocational opportunities, and orphanhood. They exploit a widespread practice of employing girls as domestic workers, a tradition that predates the advent of child trafficking. Their methods are facilitated by lax border patrols, haphazard reintegration of trafficked children, weak prosecutorial efforts, and in some cases corruption. In addition to holding traffickers criminally responsible for their actions, and rather than incarcerating parents who succumb to the false promises of traffickers, Togo and its neighbors must confront the social and political factors that allow such inhumanity to be inflicted upon children.

## Scale of Child Trafficking

There are no precise statistics on the number of children trafficked annually in West Africa. A figure of 200,000 is often cited as a UNICEF estimate for West and Central Africa, although a UNICEF official told Human Rights Watch that the organization could not determine who initially provided the figure. In 1999, UNICEF identified approximately 12 routes along which children are trafficked in the region, and designated 13 countries of the region as "receiver," "provider," "receiver and provider" and/or "transit/stop-over" states. Two years later, in 2001, the International Labor Organization's International Programme on the Elimination of Child Labour (ILO-IPEC) published a synthesis of 9 country studies of child trafficking in West Africa, concluding that trafficking routes flowed from countries and regions with widespread poverty, low education levels, and high birth rates to those that are less populated and more developed.

Togo, which met the profile of the ILO of a so-called sending state and was designated principally as such, was also identified in the ILO-IPEC report as a "receiving" and "transit" point as well as having a substantial internal trade (i.e., within its own borders). Official estimates of the number of Togolese children directly affected by trafficking are derived from both the number of children intercepted at Togo's borders and the number of children "rescued" and repatriated from abroad. At a regional meeting on child trafficking in January 2002, the Togolese government representative, Suzanne Aho, reported that 297 children had been trafficked from Togo in 2001. Aho later told Human Rights Watch, however, that the number of cases of child trafficking recorded in 2001 was 261, as compared to 337 in 1999; in her view, the diminution may have resulted from more traffickers escaping notice rather than from fewer actual cases (Human Rights Watch, 2002).

These figures may be underestimates, as many of Togo's trafficked children never come into contact with the authorities, and the government lacks the resources to intercept children systematically. Official estimates tend to be much lower than those put forth by ILO-IPEC, as in 1999 when the government recorded 337 cases of child trafficking and ILO-IPEC recorded over 800.

Although the UNICEF and ILO-IPEC reports did not trace the beginnings of child trafficking, the Togo study concluded that the practice as currently defined had existed "for at last ten years" in that country and had been growing rapidly since the government and NGOs first began recording cases in the mid-1990s. The study went on to associate child trafficking with modern phenomena such as improved transport, increased demand for cheap migrant labor, and increased poverty occasioned by such things as structural adjustment programs and economic crisis in the mid-1990s. At the same time, both the UNICEF and ILO-IPEC reports clearly viewed child trafficking as an outgrowth of long-standing practices such as labor migration and child labor. Noting, for example, that "the people of central and western Africa have always migrated for economic reasons," the ILO-IPEC report suggested that in some communities the trafficking of children into neighboring countries followed the migratory patterns of their parents. Of 96 children interviewed for ILO-IPEC's Togo study, most reported being trafficked into agricultural, domestic, restaurant, or market work in Nigeria, Gabon, or Côte d'Ivoire; in other countries, children reported working in these sectors as well as in plantation labor, diamond mining, and sex work.

The Togolese trade first garnered international attention in 1999, when the British Broadcasting Corporation (see *BBC News*, April 16, 2001, *National Geographic News,2001, Reuters, 2001, PANA Daily Newswire,2001, and Dow Jones International News,2001*) reported that two women had been stopped at the Togo-Ghana border with seven children who had allegedly been handed to them by their parents. Two years later, the Nigerian-registered ship *Etireno* left the city of Cotonou, Benin, allegedly with 250 children from Benin, Mali, and Togo on board, bound for domestic service and other jobs in Gabon. Though accounts of child slaves on board the *Etireno* were exaggerated—authorities later confirmed that approximately 23 children aged 3 to 14 were onboard, only 8 of them Togolese and not all destined for child labor—the incident marked a watershed in regional and international efforts to combat child trafficking. Since the *Etireno* incident, international media have documented the trafficking of Togolese girls into domestic labor in Côte d'Ivoire, Nigeria, Gabon, and Congo Brazzaville.

## Causes of Child Trafficking

Poverty and lack of opportunity are major causes of trafficking. Child trafficking typically begins with a private arrangement between a trafficker and a family member, driven by the family economic plight and the trafficker's desire for profit and cheap labor. Someone comes along and says he or she has professions or jobs for the children and the parents believe it, a village chief in Vogan told Human Rights Watch. But then the person puts them in servitude or gives the child to someone else. Human Rights Watch heard numerous accounts from Togolese villagers of deceitful negotiations between parents and child traffickers.

Parents think that in letting children go they are doing something good for them; but someone takes them and makes them domestic workers, and someone else takes all the money instead of giving them a salary. A woman in Élavagnon added that traffickers tell the parents their child is doing well and getting paid, but they do not give money to the kids and do not buy them anything.

UNICEF for West and Central Africa says poverty (Bazzi-Veil, 2000; UNICEF, 2001; Abalo, 2001, and Salih, 2001) is a major and ubiquitous causal factor behind child trafficking. In those West African countries classified as "sending" states—

Togo, Benin, Mali, Nigeria, and Burkina Faso—anywhere from 33 to 73 percent of the general population lives on less than U.S.$1 a day. The ILO-IPEC study in 2001 of 96 trafficked children also found that a large majority (87 percent) of trafficked children came from families engaged in subsistence agriculture. Of 45 parents interviewed, 70 percent of mothers and 60 percent of fathers had never attended school. Some 74 percent of households studied were polygamous. In addition, 82 percent of households surveyed had more than five children.

In Togo, annual school fees range from 4,000 to 13,000 CFA (between U.S.$6 and $20) despite a statutory guarantee of free primary education. Parents always say they can not afford school fees. They prefer that the child be with an uncle in Abidjan. The complicity of parents in these cases is a shame. In its 2001 global overview of child trafficking, ILO-IPEC remarked that children with no access to education often have little alternative but to look for work at a very early age.

For girls, trafficking is thought by some experts to build on a long tradition of parents using their daughters as domestic workers rather than sending them to school. In 2002, girls in Togo were estimated to be 20 percent less likely than boys to be enrolled in primary school, 25 percent less likely to reach high school, and more than 50 percent less likely to enter university. In 1994 the NGO Anti-Slavery International (ASI) and the Africa branch of the World Association of Orphans (WAO-Afrique) observed that in Togo it has been found that parents prefer to send girls rather than boys into domestic service, not only because household chores are traditionally seen as "women's work," but also because the girl's income helps to support the schooling of her brothers. Eight years later, in 2002, ASI suggested an evolution from this tradition of child domestic labor to the modern practice of child trafficking: "the process of recruitment is becoming more organized, as agents and traffickers trawl rural areas offering incentives to parents," the NGO noted. The result is that more children and young people in West Africa are working in households in no way related to their own, often at considerable distance.

## The Link to HIV/AIDS

Studies have linked child trafficking to the breakdown of the family unit caused by divorce or the death of a parent. The ILO-IPEC 2001 study of child trafficking in Togo found that of 96 trafficked children interviewed, almost 30 percent had experienced the death of a mother, father, or both parents. A similar pattern was found in Cameroon, where 60 percent of 329 trafficked children belonged to single-parent families. These data have led some researchers to posit a link between child trafficking and HIV/AIDS, a rapidly growing cause of orphanhood in sub-Saharan Africa.

At least 95,000 children under age 15 have lost a mother or both parents to AIDS in Togo; two-thirds of those orphans were alive as of 1999. A recent study of AIDS-affected families in Togo's Maritime region, funded by the World Bank and implemented by the NGO CARE-Togo, observed that children orphaned by AIDS spend less time in school because of an inability to pay school fees, face prohibitions from attending public school, and, in some cases, withdraw from school entirely.

Also noted was the potential for AIDS-affected children to contract HIV and other sexually transmitted infections as a result of child trafficking. A vicious circle is created because these children, left to their own resources without moral, financial, or emotional support, are vulnerable and susceptible to sinking into delinquency (theft, drugs) and prostitution only to meet the same fate as their parents, which is to die of AIDS. Efforts to protect AIDS-affected children from exploitation and abuse are often compromised by the deep stigma with which these children live (UNAIDS, UNICEF, USAID, and *Synergy Project*, 2002).

Porous borders and lax regulatory environments, traditional migration patterns, ethnic affinities, and inadequate information about trafficking and its risks—these factors help to explain why economic pressures do not lead to child trafficking in all cases of extreme poverty. There are places where people are very poor, but they don't see child trafficking as a solution. There are regions where there is a very strong tendency toward migration and those where there are traditions of sending children to stay with uncles or aunts (CARE/WORLD BANK, 2002; Akolatse and Djonoukou, 2002; Mensah, 2002).

Especially conducive to child trafficking is the active or passive encouragement by border patrols and other law-enforcement agents. ILO-IPEC has noted that customs officials turn a blind eye to trafficking in parts of West Africa, particularly in routes through Cameroon and Nigeria. A 2000 ASI study of child trafficking between Benin and Gabon made the same point, documenting cases of traffickers giving money to police to overcome the difficulty of crossing Gabon's borders.

The many forces at the root of child trafficking help to explain why Togo's efforts to combat the practice have thus far been unsuccessful. Following the first World Congress against Commercial Sexual Exploitation of Children held in Stockholm, Sweden, in 1996, Togo developed a National Plan to Fight Against Child Labor and Child Trafficking, calling for the creation of a database on traffickers; improved legislation to protect children; exchanges of information on trafficking with Benin, Ghana, and Burkina Faso; improved cooperation among police, customs, and immigration officers; improved educational opportunities for girls and street children; awareness-raising campaigns; and the rehabilitation and reintegration of trafficked children. While some of these measures have begun to be implemented, the Togolese government has thus far been unable to infiltrate the private arrangements between parents, children, and child traffickers, much less to address the social and economic circumstances at their root.

Human Rights Watch interviewed 41 girls and 31 boys who were trafficked when they were between the ages of 3 and 17. Of the girls, 13 were trafficked internally—that is, from one part of Togo to another—and 24 were trafficked externally to Gabon, Benin, Nigeria, or Niger. The remaining four girls were trafficked to Togo from Benin, Nigeria, or Ghana. All of the boys were trafficked from the interior of Togo to parts of Nigeria, Benin, or Côte d'Ivoire. Of the 72 trafficked children 10 were recruited and transported from home but were intercepted before arriving at their destination.

In interviews with trafficked children, Human Rights Watch found a link between lack of schooling and vulnerability to child trafficking. Though almost half of the children interviewed were 16 or older at the time of the interview, few had attended secondary school, which is normally commenced at age 15. Among the general population, it was estimated in 1993 that 34 percent of boys and 12 percent of girls in Togo enrolled in secondary school. In numerous cases, children said they were recruited by traffickers after running out of money to pay for school.

As in the ILO-IPEC study, Human Rights Watch found significant differences in the experiences of trafficked girls as compared to trafficked boys. While most girls interviewed reported working in domestic or market labor, boys reported working in agriculture and, in one case, in a furniture factory. In addition, whereas a number of girls said they were trafficked within Togo, all of the boys reported having been trafficked from Togo to other countries. Finally, while most girls interviewed by Human Rights Watch fled their traffickers following prolonged periods of physical and mental abuse, most boys were released after a period of time and told to find their way home to Togo. When people talk about "liberal democracy" they immediately think of "democracy for whom?"

It's really important to say whose interests democracy serves – the interests of the rich and powerful or the interests of working and poor people. The struggle for democracy is the one that puts the needs, interests, and voices of all working and poor women, children, and men at the center of the process. This is popular democracy.

When one looks deeper into popular democracy, several principles and processes emerge as essential for understanding and organizing in our current moment—equality, participatory decision-making, struggle, and liberation.

Equality means the equal sharing and access to all the resources and goods and services to satisfy people's material, intellectual, cultural, and spiritual needs. It also means that all people are valued and treated equally and have equal rights regardless of race/ethnicity, nationality, gender, sexuality, age, disability, and so on. Going from the extreme polarization of today's wealth and poverty to equality among all peoples is an ongoing process as well as an essential principle of popular democracy.

Participatory decision-making involves full bottom-up and active participation in making decisions that affect the lives of all in society, especially of working and poor people. The involvement of those most adversely affected is key to this process. The selling, buying, and enslavement of children is thus incompatible with liberal democracy.

# TRANSNATIONAL DRUG TRAFFICKING

Just as corporate entities build power and influence through acquisition and partnership with other companies in the legitimate business world, criminal groups are building alliances with counterparts in other nations. Colombian drug traffickers are linking up with African crime groups to provide couriers for European deliveries, which are routed through Eastern Europe or the former Soviet Union to minimize detection. Proceeds from these crimes may be laundered through four different countries before reaching their final destination in an offshore haven in the Caribbean. Local law enforcement, whether in an African nation or one of the member countries of the Organization for Economic Cooperation and Development (OECD), is hard-pressed to track suspects and evidence through this convoluted maze. Only bilateral and multilateral efforts can work effectively to inhibit organized crime that is invading every part of the continent. The international community has a large stake in assisting the ability of the following nations to address their rising political and economic power:

- *Nigeria:* illicit drugs: a transit point for heroin and cocaine intended for European, East Asian, and North American markets; safe haven for Nigerian narcotraffickers operating worldwide; major money-laundering center; massive corruption and criminal activity, along with unwillingness of the government to address the deficiencies in its anti-money-laundering regime make money laundering a major problem

- *Benin:* Illicit drugs: transshipment point for narcotics associated with Nigerian trafficking organizations and most commonly destined for Western Europe and the USA; vulnerable to money laundering due to a poorly regulated financial infrastructure

- *Côte d'Ivoire:* illicit drugs: illicit producer of cannabis, mostly for local consumption; transshipment point for Southwest and Southeast Asian heroin to Europe and occasionally to the USA, and for Latin American cocaine destined for Europe and South Africa; while rampant corruption and inadequate supervision leave the banking system vulnerable to money laundering, the lack of a developed financial system limits the country's utility as a major money-laundering center

- *Togo:* illicit drugs: transit hub for Nigerian heroin and cocaine traffickers; money laundering not a significant problem

- *South Africa:* illicit drugs: transshipment center for heroin, hashish, marijuana, and possibly cocaine; cocaine consumption on the rise; world's largest market for illicit methaqualone, usually imported illegally from India through various East African countries; illicit cultivation of marijuana; attractive venue for money launderers given the increasing level of organized criminal and narcotics activity in the region

- *Amsterdam:* illicit drugs: major European producer of illicit amphetamine and other synthetic drugs; important gateway for cocaine, heroin, and hashish entering Europe; major source of America-bound ecstasy; large financial sector vulnerable to money laundering

- *Philippines:* illicit drugs: exports locally produced marijuana and hashish to East Asia, the USA, and other Western markets; serves as a transit point for heroin and crystal methamphetamine
- *Switzerland:* because of more stringent government regulations, used significantly less as a money-laundering center; transit country for and consumer of South American cocaine and Southwest Asian heroin
- *London:* illicit drugs: gateway country for Latin American cocaine entering the European market; major consumer of synthetic drugs, producer of limited amounts of synthetic drugs and synthetic precursor chemicals; major consumer of Southwest Asian heroin; money-laundering center
- *Hong Kong:* Illicit drugs: strenuous law-enforcement efforts, but faces serious challenges in controlling transit of heroin and methamphetamine to regional and world markets; modern banking system provides a conduit for money laundering; rising indigenous use of synthetic drugs, especially among young people
- *Spain:* illicit drugs: key European gateway country for Latin American cocaine and North African hashish entering the European market; destination and minor transshipment point for Southwest Asian heroin
- Additional originating countries with no known drug trafficking: are Burkina Faso and Kuwait.

The "dirt and diamonds" in Elf trial indicates how high this organized crime can eat into the heart of a government. According to *Nzoom* of April 2, 2003, 37 defendants were asked to explain dirty dealings within France's political and business elite involving the embezzlement of some $U.S. 200 million and former French oil giant Elf Aquitaine. The fruit of an eight-year investigation, the trial exposed the use of cash sweeteners to secure contracts for the then state-owned Elf in oil-rich countries, and how some of that cash slipped into the pockets of certain executives.

The trial also raked up well-known sleaze like the kickbacks from an illegal arms deal secured via a now infamous liaison between then Foreign Minister Roland Dumas and a woman who dubbed herself "The Whore of the Republic." The trial was overshadowed abroad by the start of a U.S.-led war on Iraq, but keenly watched in France where the affair stirred up charges of endemic corruption a decade ago during the last years of the late President François Mitterrand.

Elf is now part of French oil major TotalFinaElf, which negotiated multibillion-dollar deals with Saddam's Iraq. It was France's biggest company and controlled by the state at the time of the alleged siphoning off of huge sums of cash into offshore bank accounts between 1989 and 1993. With the prosecution documents running to 44,000 pages—peppered with evidence of luxury villas and jewelry—the trial ran for several months, following the longest investigation in French judicial history.

This case had ramifications as far away as Venezuela, Uzbekistan, Angola, Gabon, Cameroon, and Congo-Brazzaville, as well as Spain and Germany, where judges believe Elf paid bribes linked to its 1992 purchase of the eastern German Leuna refinery complex. The prosecution argued that politicians in Elf's African strongholds were given cash for every barrel of oil extracted. Anti-corruption magistrate Renaud van Ruymbeke also investigated charges that Elf paid tens of millions of dollars of bribes to win a contract in Nigeria in 1995.

The trial was a high drama in addition to past courtroom showdowns between Dumas and Deviers-Joncours and the Hollywood-style capture of Sirven at his Philippines hideaway in 2001 following his four years on the run. On being seized, Sirven removed the chip from inside his mobile phone and swallowed it, to prevent investigators from tracking down the last few people he called as police narrowed in on him.

One major weakness in the illicit market, however, is the apparent absence of a strong, high-profit, consumer-driven illicit drug market. Drug use as a social problem is a relatively new phenomenon in Africa, and one that seems to postdate the establishment of drug trafficking syndicates (Duke, 1996; Farah, 1996). With the notable exceptions of *khat* chewing among the Sufis in Eastern Africa and the use of cannabis products, in both the Northern and Southern African regions, there is little historical evidence of the widespread use of psychoactive substances on the African continent (Asuni and Pela, 1986). For example, a study of 300 university students in Benin City, Nigeria, in the mid-1980s, found ready availability and widespread use of indigenous psychoactive substances such as coffee, cola nuts, cannabis, alcohol, and cigarettes (Nevadomsky, 1985).

In addition, this study found some utilitarian use of diazepam and diazepoxide by students during examination periods. But even with these substances, recreational use was rare, and any use outside of the pressures and stresses of the university system was very uncommon. Students possessed a passing knowledge of cocaine. But even that knowledge was very suspect, with researchers finding that students frequently confused cocaine with codeine. Cocaine use was not in evidence and the drug itself was not reported to be readily available (Nevadomsky, 1985).

The study found no instances, whatsoever, of heroin use, despite the already well-developed role of Nigeria as a transshipment point for Southwest and Southeast Asian heroin bound for the United States (Nevadomsky, 1985). A similar study among 14-25 year-olds found that alcohol, tobacco, indigenous stimulants, cannabis, and sedative-hypnotics were the most commonly used psychoactive substances in Nigeria. The study concluded that heroin and cocaine use was almost entirely unknown (Pela, 1989).

## MONEY LAUNDERING

The UN Global Program on Money Laundering (GPML) states that in today's globalized economy, organized crime groups generate huge sums of money by drug trafficking, arms smuggling, and financial crime. "Dirty money," however, is of little use to organized crime because it raises the suspicions of law enforcement and leaves a trail of incriminating evidence. Criminals who wish to benefit from the proceeds of large-scale crime have to disguise their illegal profits without compromising themselves. This process is known as money laundering.

Since this term was coined to describe the notoriously sneaky activities of the entrepreneur criminal syndicates that mushroomed in the early part of the 20th century in the United States of America, the term "money laundering" has established itself in criminal justice systems all over the world. It is therefore often assumed that there is consensus over its definition and the meaning of concepts such as "dirty money," "illicit transaction" and "legitimate assets."

The primary objective of the laundering process, it is often asserted, is to convert money derived from an illicit transaction, which is therefore "dirty," into some other legitimate asset, thereby concealing the predicate transaction. International law has therefore urged governments to criminalize the money conversion (laundering) process. Countries are required to penalize the laundering of funds derived from activities that happen within their territory, as well as funds originating from beyond their borders. In addition, attention should be paid to proceeds generated by local crime and transmitted to foreign countries. In fact, several grey areas continue to afflict the criminalization of money laundering around the world.

Uncertainty is centered around the lack of uniformity on which predicate transactions are illicit, with the exception of activities recognized by international criminal law, such as drug trafficking. Controversy about whether the basic transaction from which money was derived was unlawful or criminal stifles the transnational enforcement of criminal law. It is easier to describe money laundering than to define it. Money laundering comprises all activities to disguise or conceal the nature or source of, or entitlement to, money or property that has been acquired from serious economic crime. For instance, a minister from Equitorial Guinea, who was under investigation for money laundering in the US, was reported to have acquired residential property in Cape Town, South Africa ( See *This Day*, Cape Town, South Africa, June 28, 2004).

A starting point in identifying money laundering trends is to locate the predicate activity areas from which proceeds for laundering are derived. Potentially, there are as many activities relevant to the inquiry as there are varieties of economic crime. Practical reasons make prioritization necessary. In the absence of objectively acceptable criteria, or a quantification of the magnitude of different kinds of crime, this is a difficult exercise. Some guidance may be derived from the perceptions of law enforcement authorities, insofar as they have been codified in international conventions. The American origin of the term money laundering is intricately connected to organized crime in the spheres of alcohol trafficking and prostitution. When it was introduced into international criminal law, money laundering control was directed at drug trafficking. In many ways, syndicated drug trafficking is still regarded as a core predicate activity for money laundering.

*Drug trafficking* is identified most readily with money laundering in all parts of Southern Africa. *Dagga* (marijuana) and mandrax sales feature prominently among the sources of illegal funds, but they are by no means the only ones familiar to crime syndicates. Significant sums are also generated from sales of cocaine, heroin, and ecstasy. Since the early 1980s the drug industry has been known to influence trends in "downstream" crimes, notably vehicle theft, smuggling, corruption, housebreaking, armed robbery, and murder.

## Money Laundering and Legitimate Economic Activity

The affinity of money laundering to legitimate economic activity is particularly in evidence in respect to the transnational transmission of funds. One can expect the direction of such transmissions, as well as the scale, to be influenced by similar factors to those that encourage or discourage legal business. At a general level, studies of the alternative remittance system called *hawala* are relevant to the analysis of money laundering in the region.

The system has been observed to be in much use in the Middle East, South East Asia, the USA, Western Europe, and, to a certain extent, in China. The primary incentive for informal fund transfers is cost effectiveness. As commentators on the *hawala* have observed, this is attributable to low overheads, exchange rate speculation, and integration with existing business activities. The second reason is efficiency. A *hawala* remittance takes place in one or two days, at most, compared with longer periods—sometimes weeks—when formal transmission methods are used. For example, an international wire transfer or the transmission of a bank draft via a courier service between North America and South Asia, involving at least one correspondent bank and delays due to holidays, weekends, and time differences, can take several weeks.

*Hawala* is also competitive because of its reliability. At its most efficient level, it has been able to eliminate disadvantages associated with formal international transactions, which can be complex and involve the client's local bank, the latter's correspondent bank, the main office of a foreign bank, and a branch office of the recipient's foreign bank. Details of such transactions can be obtained from the website: http://www.interpol.int/Public/FinancialCrime/MoneyLaundering/hawala/default.asp.

The fourth reason is the lack of bureaucracy. Alternative remittances are attractive to those without official documentation, fixed addresses, or bank accounts. It tends also to be the vehicle of choice to any who do not trust banks, regard bank charges as excessive, or simply prefer anonymity. The fifth reason is tax evasion as nonformal remittances provide an unscrutinized and thus tax-free channel.

To what extent is the *hawala* in use in Southern Africa? The absence of an empirical survey makes this question difficult to answer. It is clear, however, that factors associated with *hawala* exist in certain parts of the region. There are even circumstantial indications of the use of similar remittance systems in Tanzania, Malawi, South Africa, and Zimbabwe and the contiguous East African countries of Kenya and Uganda. Anecdotal evidence abounds about the transmission of disposable funds between countries in the region that occasionally circumvents the formal system. It has emerged that, since the 1980s, significant quantities of money have been transmitted and used in South Africa. Source countries noted include Angola, the DRC, Malawi, Mozambique (from the 1970s, especially around the advent of Frelimo rule), Zambia, and Zimbabwe.

The trend does not seem to have abated, even with the advent of the Prevention of Organized Crime Act (1998) and the Financial Intelligence Centre Act (2001) in South Africa. Part of the reason is that the factors that encourage the trend have remained virtually intact. In certain cases, developments in the source countries have increased the flow. Asset flows to South Africa are influenced by the following:

- *The scope for investment in residential property.* With the exception of Botswana, Lesotho, Swaziland, and Zimbabwe, the average price of good-quality residential property in South Africa is relatively lower than in other parts of the region. This oddity is probably attributable to the creeping dollarization of economies in Southern Africa. In addition, the prevailing security of property rights in South Africa is rather less fragile than it is in some other parts of the region.

- *The existence of educational facilities.* South Africa has a variety of institutions offering tertiary education and training in English, which is internationally marketable. On account of shifts in funding policies, some institutions are desperate for patronage by foreign students. This creates a niche that can be exploited by illicit investment in education.

- *Imbalances in the availability of essential commodities, such as medical drugs, construction equipment, and materials.* This provides opportunities for the conversion of illicit funds into re-salable assets in countries such as the DRC, Zambia, and Zimbabwe.

- *The abundance of hard currency* and the ease with which it can be obtained beyond the borders of South Africa, which is in turn attributable to *the lack of faith in state capacity or efficiency.* This translates into a lack of faith in local currencies, low use of local financial institutions, and a predatory relationship with the local economy. The ubiquitous *bureaux de change* open up numerous opportunities for the acquisition of hard currency in an unregulated manner, or by false pretences. These practices have been reported in Malawi, Mozambique, Tanzania, Zambia, and Zimbabwe on a continuing basis.

- *The presence in South Africa of a relatively developed financial system and safe investment climate/environment.* This factor is self explanatory and related to the last factor.

The presence of migrant communities across national borders enriches the environment for the transmission of resources between the respective countries, often informally and with no recourse to the financial institutions and regularly in violation of currency movement control laws. An example is the spread of the Lundas in Angola, the DRC, and Zambia, the Tutsi in Rwanda, Uganda, and the DRC; the Venda in South Africa and Zimbabwe; and the Chewa-speaking communities on either side of the Malawi/Zambia border. In addition, dual nationality eases movement between the countries and makes it difficult to regulate currency transmission.

## Effects of Money Laundering on the Economy

According to Fedelis Tembo, Senior Internal Auditor, Government of Zambia,

> money laundering is a tool used by people involved in illegal activities, such as drug trafficking, organized crime, tax evasion, political bribery, and corruption. The events of September 11 2001, have added another dimension to the problem of money laundering and brought to light the convergence between money laundering and terrorism.

Money laundering can have a wide range of adverse effects on the economic, political, and social structures of a country. Because laundered money passes through the financial system, money laundering may also detrimentally affect the financial system as a whole and banks in particular. Money launderers use front companies to mingle the proceeds of illicit activity with legitimately acquired funds and in the process obscure their illegal gains. They may have access to huge illicit funds, allowing them to subsidize these front companies and to offer products and services at below-market rates. This gives such front companies an advantage over their competitors, who have to rely on legitimate sources of funding.

The magnitude of money laundering is difficult to estimate, but may be between 2 and 5 percent of the world gross domestic product. *The Economist Magazine* (June, 21, 2001) reported that the International Monetary Fund (IMF) estimates that U.S.$ 500 billion to U.S.$ 1.5 trillion is laundered through the banking system each year.

Banks and other financial institutions provide a conduit through which money flows. The financial system is the focal point of anti-money-laundering initiatives because dirty money is most easily identified when it first enters the financial system. It is the responsibility of each central bank to ensure that the financial system does not become a conduit for laundering money.

Money laundering can result in unexpected changes in money demand and increased volatility of international capital flows, interest rates, and exchange rates. The unpredictable nature of money laundering, coupled with the attendant loss of policy control, may make sound economic policies difficult to implement.

## National and Bank Risks

Money laundering can make government tax collection difficult and may reduce tax revenues. The negative reputation resulting from these activities may also diminish legitimate opportunities for sustainable economic growth while attracting international criminal organizations.

Banks are the target of money laundering activities because of their capability of handling huge cash transactions, of transmitting funds efficiently, and also because of their assumed trustworthiness in keeping information on the financial activities of customers confidential.

Bank vigilance involves the identification of unusual funds, unusual transactions, and noting of individuals who open and maintain accounts on a regular basis. Failure to maintain this vigilance and act upon it can lead to banks being liable to criminal prosecution, supervisory fines, and other penalties. In fact, the political costs of organized crimes like money laundering are staggering. The pervasive corruption and penetration of organized crime into the political process are inhibiting the development of new laws needed as a foundation for a democratic free market economy.

An often highly corrupted tax authority and the links of government personnel to organized crime deprive the state of needed revenues. Substantial numbers of citizens have lost faith in the integrity and capacity of the legal process, and in the ability of their new governments to deliver on basic obligations, such as payment of wages and retirement benefits, and provision of health care.

## ARMS TRAFFICKING AND INSECURITY

According to *Africa News* of May 7, 2001, "The present members of the UN Security Council combined supply 85 percent of the arms which find their way into the illicit market through middlemen." Arms transfers and trafficking remain one of sub-Saharan Africa's major security problems. Africa continues to have the greatest number of armed conflicts of any continent. Hostilities have affected Angola, Burundi, Cameroon, Chad, Côte d'Ivoire, Democratic Republic of Congo, Djibouti, Eritrea-Ethiopia, Guinea, Guinea-Bissau, Kenya, Liberia, Nigeria, Cameroon, Republic of Congo, Rwanda, Senegal, Sierra Leone, Somalia, Sudan, Tanzania-Zanzibar, Uganda, and Zimbabwe. The influx of light weapons financed by cash, diamonds, or other commodities did not cause Africa's wars. But it has prolonged them and made them more lethal and not conducive for the survival of democracy.

These conflicts in sub-Saharan Africa cumulatively have claimed at least 7 to 8 million lives. Also, by 2001, more than 3.5 million of the more than 14 million refugees and asylum seekers in the world were in Africa. Of the approximately 21 million internally displaced people in the world, more than 10 million are Africans.

Nations and manufacturers eager to dispose of arsenals of arms made superfluous by post-Cold War political developments and technological innovations continue to view Africa as an attractive market in this era of the free market. The inability of the international community to control arms transfers and trafficking contributes to the persistence of these devastating conflicts. African leaders also have acknowledged that their porous borders and ineffective national legal codes governing firearms commerce also play a role in the continued vulnerability of the continent to opportunistic arms merchants.

Apart from undermining the promise of African democratization and development, armed conflicts contribute to political decay, facilitate state collapse, cause widespread human rights violations, generate refugees and internally displaced persons, and exacerbate famine conditions. Conflicts also divert scarce resources away from social services, disrupt trade, discourage tourism, and contribute to the breakdown of family structures.

The pervasiveness and persistence of conflict also have grave psychological consequences as children are traumatized or become accustomed to a culture of violence. A recent study published by the Coalition to Stop the Use of Child Soldiers claims that 120,000 minors, out of a worldwide total of 300,000, are participating in various African wars. Angola, Burundi, the DRC, Ethiopia, Liberia, Rwanda, Sierra Leone, Sudan, and Uganda are thought to have some of the largest numbers of underaged or child soldiers. With the exception of the more conventional Eritrean-Ethiopian conflict (1998-2000), efforts to end Africa's conflicts have yielded no lasting successes. One obstacle is war-profiteering by soldiers and guerrillas. The arms market continues to offer many opportunities to those who possess assets other than hard currency to finance weapons purchases. Diamonds, other gemstones, and minerals enable cash-poor governments and insurgents the ability to acquire arms.

In the DRC, for example, soldiers from Rwanda, Uganda, and Zimbabwe enrich themselves by plundering natural resources such as diamonds, columbite-tantalite (coltan), and ivory. Insurgent groups such as the Congolese Liberation Front (FLC) and the *Mai Mai* engage in similar practices. In West Africa, the sale of conflict diamonds smuggled out of Sierra Leone fueled the Revolutionary United Front (RUF) insurgency and enriched the guerrillas' regional patrons like Foday Sankoh, Charles Taylor, and Blaise Compaore. Diamond smuggling and arms trafficking funded by oil revenues yield substantial profits to arms merchants willing to sell to one or both parties to the Angolan civil war.

International efforts to control the bartering of natural resources such as diamonds and other precious stones, coltan, timber, and other commodities for weapons have done little more than drive much of the illicit trade deeper into the shadows. On the positive side, insurgents in Sierra Leone, the DRC, and Angola may not be smuggling out as many diamonds as they previously were able to, and the cost of the weapons they purchase probably also has risen. Sadly this has not been enough to put a crimp in the illicit commodities for arms trade.

## The United Nations and Arms Trafficking

Arms transfers and trafficking have continued to spiral, in part, because the international community has not effectively enforced UN sanctions, and has criminalized embargo violations, penalized financial institutions that act as conduits for weapons purchases, failed to promote indigenous controls over African arms production and sales to countries under UN arms embargoes, or taken actions against countries that serve as arms transshipment points. Numerous international and regional programs aspire to reduce the flow of weapons into sub Saharan Africa. These initiatives have succeeded only in documenting the devastating impact that arms transfers have on Africa.

The UNO has imposed arms embargoes against Liberia and Somalia and against various insurgent groups, including the Revolutionary United Front (Sierra Leone), National Union for the Total Independence of Angola (UNITA), and Hutu and ex-FAR extremists in Central Africa. The United Nations has perhaps made its greatest effort to enforce its arms embargo against UNITA by essentially freezing its bank accounts, restricting the travel of UNITA officials, and limiting UNITA's ability to market diamonds.

Despite these measures, UNITA continued to wage a fierce guerrilla war. None of the embargoes has been enforced effectively despite repeated violations acknowledged by the UN and revealed by nongovernmental organizations such as Amnesty International and Human Rights Watch. Similarly, the expired one-year (2000-2001) arms embargo against Eritrea-Ethiopia failed to deter weapons deliveries of heavy and light equipment to either party. Beyond arms embargoes, the UNO and some member states, notably Canada and Great Britain, advocated a "name and shame" policy.

According to UN Secretary General Kofi Annan the "public identification of international arms merchants" is the single most important tool in combating the arms trafficking problem. On September 24, 1999, the UN Security Council held its first ministerial meeting on small arms; this led to a Security Council presidential statement urging member states to curb arms trafficking. The UN's "name and shame" strategy has had no impact on weapons flows. Neither the UN nor any of its member states has focused on Africa's role in arms trafficking.

In particular, there has been no UN action against countries like Burkina Faso, Kenya, Tanzania, and Uganda; all are major transshipment points for arms shipments to West, Central, and Eastern Africa. The UN Register of Conventional Arms, which has been in operation since 1993, has received data about weapons sales from 153 nations. However, the response by African states is among the lowest in the world.

## African Union and Arms Trafficking

In July 1999, the Organization of African Unity issued a declaration on the Illicit Proliferation, Circulation and Trafficking of Small Arms and Light Weapons that called for a coordinated African solution to the arms trafficking problem. In collaboration with the Pretoria-based Institute for Security Studies, the OAU devised the Initiative on Small Arms Proliferation and Africa, designed to raise awareness of the small-arms proliferation problem and to facilitate an in-depth discussion of the menace it poses. Several sub regional initiatives aim to control arms trafficking but they lack the investigative capabilities and legal authority to enforce strictures against arms trafficking. Mali, working through the Economic Community of West African States such as Benin, Burkina Faso, Cape Verde, Côte d'Ivoire, Gambia, Ghana, Guinea, Guinea-Bissau, Liberia, Mali, Mauritania, Niger, Nigeria, Senegal, Sierra Leone, and Togo), devised the West African Small Arms Moratorium that imposed a renewable three-year (1998-2001) voluntary ban on the manufacture, import, and export of weapons throughout member states. Because of a lack of resources for enforcement, this moratorium failed to impact significantly on arms trafficking activities in Liberia and Sierra Leone. Weapons sales to other West African countries also continued unimpeded.

There are at least 8 million small arms in West Africa, according to some estimates, with more than half in the hands of insurgents and criminals. Criminal elements in Ghana alone reportedly possess some 40,000 small arms. The Southern African Development Community Committee on Small Arms seeks to control weapons flows to Africa by encouraging all states to observe and enforce UN arms embargoes and to criminalize their violations. SADC has yet to persuade its members (Angola, Botswana, Lesotho, Malawi, Mauritius, Mozambique, Namibia, South Africa, Swaziland, Tanzania, Zambia, and Zimbabwe) to undertake such actions.

## Trafficking Networks

Arms trafficking is a complex and convoluted business. A single sale of weapons may involve an array of brokers, banks, transportation companies, and transshipment points. The availability of false end-user certificates enables traffickers and their clients to circumvent UN arms embargoes. The following case study may illustrate the multifaceted nature of the arms trafficking problem and its deleterious impact on African society. "Gun Runner Extraordinaire." Victor Butt, a Russian national based in United Arab Emirates, has come to symbolize the arms trafficking problem in sub-Saharan Africa. He owns at least five airlines that fly sixty-aircraft and employ some 300 people. Over the past several years, Butt repeatedly has demonstrated an ability to deliver weapons and other military supplies to clients throughout Africa according to the U.S. Department of State Bureau of Political-Military Affairs report issued July 9, 2001.

Currently, he operates in Angola, Cameroon, DRC, Kenya, Libya, Republic of Congo, Rwanda, Sierra Leone, Sudan, and Uganda. International efforts to arrest Butt or curtail his operations have thus far been unsuccessful. Butt and other arms traffickers transport weapons and other military supplies through Africa by a variety of routes, sometimes directly, often through one or more transshipment points. These nodes comprise an elaborate network of options for arms dealers who wish to keep their activities private.

Some of the more frequently used African airfields transited by Butt and others include Entebbe, Goma, Kigali, and Luanda. African seaports used by arms traffickers include Aseb, Beira, Conakry, Dar-es-Salaam, Djibouti, Durban, Luanda, Merca, Mombasa, Monrovia, and Nacala. After arrival, arms are forwarded to their destination by road, rail, air, or ferry. For example, shipments through Dar-es-Salaam normally are sent by rail to Mwanza, a port on Lake Victoria, and then loaded onto a ferry for Port Bell in southern Uganda or other regional destinations.

## Guns, Insecurity and Instability.

According to the United Nations International Regional News (*IRIN*) of December 5, 2004, over the last 50 years the use of small arms has cost some 2 million lives in the Great Lakes and Horn of Africa, where in some countries guns are as abundant as goods are in supermarkets and where there is a general climate of violence. The consequences for societies of the proliferation of illicit light small arms are dramatic.

Besides the violent resolution of differences and the concomitant increase in crime, this phenomenon has deeper implications. The insecurity created by the presence of such weapons in civilian hands stymies peaceful development and foreign investment in these countries. The circulation of illegal small arms also helps to intensify conflicts and make them last longer.

Many of Africa's pastoral groups are threatened by the proliferation of small arms that makes conflicts with their neighbors more lethal. A typical example concerns the Karimojong in northeast Uganda, who for centuries relied on traditional weapons when engaged in cattle rustling and clan warfare. Such fighting claimed relatively few lives and was settled eventually by elders. By the late 1990s, there were an estimated 30,000-40,000 AK-47s in the hands of Karimojong and neighboring pastoral communities. Ownership of such a weapon conferred political, social, and economic status. Oftentimes, an AK-47 was part of a bride price. Not surprisingly, cattle rustling and clan warfare became more lethal. Efforts by the Uganda People's Defense Force (UPDF) to disarm the Karimojong led to occasional clashes.

The proliferation of AK-47s not only has intensified conflict but also has undermined the authority of the elders. As a result, Karimojong society not only is less cohesive but also has become part of the arc of conflict that stretches from the Horn of Africa to East, Central, and Southern Africa.

The proliferation of illegal firearms in Kenya has reached crisis proportions. A recent study of Kenya by South Africa's Institute for Security Studies indicates that black marketers sell some 11,000 guns annually, most of which enter

Kenya from Ethiopia, Somalia, Sudan, and Uganda. According to Kenya's chief licensing firearms officer, "Seventy-five percent of the country is awash with illicit arms."

As a result, gun-related incidents rose by 200 percent in 1995 (most recent available figures) over the previous year. Conditions in Nairobi, a city of some 2.8 million people, are particularly worrisome. Guns are increasingly used in carjacking, kidnappings, rapes, muggings, and robberies. Police suspect those organized crime elements or retired or serving soldiers or police are responsible for at least some of these incidents. Reportedly, Somali gun dealers in the East Leigh section of Nairobi regularly rent weapons for an afternoon to anyone who can pay their fee.

In mid-2000, the Kenya Police reported that they were recovering between 1,800 and 2,000 unlicensed guns per month in Nairobi. One year later, there still were an estimated 5,000 illegal firearms in circulation in Nairobi, or one illegal weapon for every 560 Nairobi residents. This figure does not include unrecorded sales that are undoubtedly much higher. Gun-related crimes probably would continue to escalate as the police lack the resources to stem the flow of weapons into Nairobi.

In West Africa, Nigeria is a significant actor both as a producer and consumer of weapons. Press reports indicate South African and Russian arms manufacturers visited Nigeria in early 2001 to tender proposals to rehabilitate and expand Nigeria's Defense Industries Corporation (DICON). Press reports also suggested an eagerness to acquire arms that may have involved at least one unorthodox and politically suspect arms transaction. Nigerian police, in late May 2001, seized a shipment of weapons at the port of Apapa that allegedly originated in Pakistan and were purchased, with the assistance of unnamed Indian agents, by several retired Nigerian generals with links to the late General Abacha.

The intensification of hostilities along the Guinean-Liberian-Sierra Leone border some years back heightened demand for arms in that already saturated area. Liberian dissidents operating across the Guinean border received arms and ammunition delivered to the port of Conakry. Several reports suggested Liberian timber exports increasingly were used to finance and smuggle weapons, further facilitating Charles Taylor's ability to evade UN sanctions directed against Liberia's exchange of conflict diamonds for arms. At the end of the day, neither African or non-African nations nor the international community has been willing to levy painful political, economic, or legal penalties against individuals or countries to dissuade them from selling arms to or within Africa. Such limitations make it unlikely that the arms trafficking problem in Africa will be significantly ameliorated anytime soon.

Indeed, corruption and criminal activities like arms trafficking deter foreign investors who need stable investment environments, reducing economic growth and depriving the state of revenues needed to repair depleted infrastructures and create new economic opportunity. Thousands of millions of dollars in assets have been laundered overseas by sophisticated criminals, depriving the state of assets needed to pay salaries and pensions. Many would-be investors have decided that there are easier and safer places to put their money than in Africa raked by instability and fratricidal wars. For those who did invest, the high level of corruption becomes an added concern, especially for American businesses that must comply with the Foreign Corrupt Practices Act. That law criminalizes a variety of practices, including bribery, that are commonplace in the African region.

## TRANSNATIONAL TERRORISM IN AFRICA

Transnational terrorism has emerged with an intensity and diversity of activities unmatched by other transnational crime groups in the international arena (Mentan, 2004: Ch.6.). In Africa, crime groups number in the thousands. Rather than the rigid hierarchical structure of the prototypical organized crime family, the terrorist groups are based on network structures, often using violence as part of their business strategy. Unlike other countries where established crime syndicates have specialized in particular goods and services, terrorism as organized crime has infiltrated a full range of illicit activities.

These groups have also penetrated deeply into the legitimate economy, including many companies that used to belong to the state and have been privatized. The networks exploit the traditional market in illicit goods and services that includes prostitution, gambling, drugs, and contract killings, supply of cheap illegal labor, stolen automobiles, and extortion of legitimate businesses. It has also branched out to include such diverse activities as the illegal export of oil and raw materials, and the smuggling of weapons, nuclear materials, diamonds, and human beings.

These groups are often comprised of unusual coalitions of professional criminals, former members of the underground economy, and members of the elite and security apparatus. Their ranks contain highly trained specialists (such as statisticians and money launderers) not readily accessible to transnational crime groups in other parts of the world. The actions of the transnational terrorist group, al-Qaeda, in the African region raise two questions: Does Africa threaten to become a hotspot of international terrorism? And, how can terrorist attacks in Africa be prevented in future?

According to the rash conclusion of some development specialists, poverty is the main cause of terrorism. If this were in fact the case, sub-Saharan Africa would provide ample fertile soil for terrorist cells to take root and spread. That both processes are thus far not discernible adds credence to the thesis that the causes of terrorism are complex.

Terrorism is founded on the interaction of a lack of economic perspectives, social deprivation, a loss of cultural identity, political repression, and a dysfunctional state. But these factors alone do not lead inevitably to terrorism. If they did, Africa would qualify as the hot spot of international terrorism. Instead, rather than being directed outward, it appears that the potential for violence arising from the interplay of these factors in sub-Saharan Africa is, for the most part, directed inwards against one's own society in the form of increasing violent crime, civil war, and plundering warlords.

Clearly (international) terrorism requires two additional factors: a mobilizing, unifying idea, such as that offered by Islamic fundamentalism; and appropriate agitators, who abuse this idea in order to organize a powerful terrorist force against a common external enemy. This raises the question of the spread and strength of Islam in sub-Saharan Africa. Experts on Islam differentiate between numbers of centers of Islam in the region, including the West African Sahel zone, the tropical zone along the Gulf of Guinea, the Sudanese Nile region, Ethiopia, the East African coastal strip, the area inhabited by the Somaal, and the Cape region. In all of these regions, the spread of Islam took a different path in which the relative importance of specific elements of the religion depended on the historical and social context.

Nevertheless, the majority of these areas appear to share two common features. Islam did not develop into an exclusive state religion, and the interpretation of the Islamic legal code (shariah) appears to have been moderate across the board. This does not mean that Islam is not a political force in these regions. On the contrary; in West Africa, for example, spiritual leaders and traditional Islamic leaders have played, and continue to play, a central role in exercising political power and maintaining clientele systems. Even the long-standing practice of a moderate interpretation of Islam is subject to change. A radicalization has taken place with the introduction of shariah in several Nigerian states, rigid adherence to shariah in Somalia, and extremist tendencies among Muslims in South Africa. The reasons for this are in part rather varied. In the case of Nigeria, it appears that aggressive missionary work in the north by Saudi Wahabis has played a decisive role in escalating the conflict between Christians and Muslims, a conflict that flared up again during the Miss World competition in 2004.

Still, despite all the differences, these processes of radicalization have one thing in common. Where Muslims are in the minority, they generally belong to the losers of the social and political change that Africa has gone through over the past years. That is especially the case in the coastal states of West and East Africa. In West Africa, democratization has removed Muslim leaders and their followers from the levers of power; in East Africa the social advancement of the Muslim minority has trailed that of the region's already low average.

The partial loss of power for Muslims in West Africa stands in fundamental conflict with claims to power based on tradition. The social conflicts in the coastal states of West Africa are increasingly developing along a north–south divide that is largely congruent with the geographic division between Christians and Muslims. This is particularly noticeable in Nigeria, Ghana, and Côte d'Ivoire.

Nevertheless, in the short term it is unlikely that extremist Muslims in sub-Saharan Africa will become an important and integral part of al-Qaeda's terrorist network. In contrast to North Africa, membership is likely to be limited to a few individuals. Al-Qaeda's call after the Mombasa attacks on African Muslims to join their cause was met with decidedly more indignation than approval, with two important exceptions. First, the Somalian group al-Ittihad al-Islamya is considered a part of al-Qaeda. It is suspected of carrying out the attacks in Mombasa—even if some observers doubt that this group is still operational. Second, there are extremist elements in South Africa that could develop into terrorist cells.

The possibility, however, of the development of a genuine African variant of terrorism cannot be ruled out entirely. The necessary ingredients—lack of economic perspectives, social deprivation, and a loss of cultural identity, political repression and dysfunctional states—are virtually omnipresent in sub-Saharan Africa. All that is needed is a mobilizing idea and agitators in order to direct the violence bred by these factors externally. Indications of this sort of process already exist.

In the Democratic Republic of Congo it has become conventional wisdom to interpret the country's miseries as the result of policies of the industrialized countries. They are charged with preventing the development of the country in order to keep the price of raw materials down and using states such as Uganda and Rwanda in order to ensure access to these resources by force. With the attacks in Kenya and Tanzania, the perception that Africa has once again, following the end of the Cold War, become a victim and the theatre of a conflict between external parties—namely the terrorist network of al-Qaeda and the alliance against terrorism—is likely to strengthen the already widespread tendency to believe in conspiracy theories. Africans are increasingly going to wonder if the war on terrorism is "their" war.

In the next couple of years, the importance of Africa in terms of international terrorism will focus on two factors. First, the weak and desolate states of Africa provide an excellent space to draw back to and their informal economies offer superb conditions for money laundering and parking capital. Second, ineffective state security apparatuses create a convenient environment for carrying out attacks.

Sub-Saharan Africa is home to more failing states than any other region. Somalia, Liberia, Sierra Leone, and the DRC are in the final throes of a process of state disintegration. Guinea, Chad, the Central African Republic, the Republic of Congo, Sudan, and Angola are also in the advanced stages of this process. But even in more or less functioning states such as Kenya, Tanzania, Mali, Zambia, Cameroon, Malawi and, until recently, Côte d'Ivoire, the state is hardly capable of effectively maintaining a monopoly of violence and controlling the entire territory of the country. Border areas and the slums of the big cities are already de facto zones outside the state's control. The training and equipment of security forces are entirely insufficient and corruption and criminalization of the police is far advanced. The shadow economy of these crumbling states makes capital transactions and trafficking in weapons, raw materials, and consumer goods possible, without which terrorist networks would be unable to function. Although rumors that al-Qaeda is profiting from the diamond trade in Sierra

Leone and precious gems trafficking in Tanzania have yet to be proven, they are entirely plausible.

Kenya is an excellent example of the consequences of eroding state power. For years the northeast of the country, which borders Somalia, has been essentially cut off from the rest of the state. Safe travel in this part of the country is possible only in militarily protected convoys. The security forces have withdrawn to isolated forts, leaving control of the area to gangs and Somali warlords. In the poverty-stricken areas of Nairobi, power basically rests in the hands of militias run by religious sects and ethnic leaders.

Well-supplied with weapons from Somalia, they carry out gang robberies. Police officers rent weapons and vehicles to criminal groups and occasionally participate in robberies. Income from criminal activities ensures their physical survival and provides them with the hope of social advancement. Under these conditions, the Kenyan security forces would not have been able to prevent the attacks in Mombasa even if the government had been sufficiently informed of the danger and had taken the situation seriously. The government is currently incapable of controlling the trading of goods and the movement of people across the Somali–Kenyan border even if it were determined to do so.

The incapacity of the majority of African security forces to protect targets threatened by terrorism is in stark contrast with the great variety of such potential targets including embassies, the numerous agencies and projects of international development organizations, subsidiaries of American and European companies, and international tourist hotels. The U.S. embassies and offices of the development organization USAID already resemble 'wild west' forts of the 19th century. Oil and mining companies have resorted to protecting their property with private, paramilitary security services.

Americans, Europeans, and Africans who can afford to are increasingly withdrawing to heavily guarded and elaborately protected gated communities. Still, barriers cannot be efficiently erected around all threatened establishments. This is especially the case for geographically isolated institutions, which would be too costly to protect. Examples include development projects in remote areas and tourist hotels in national parks.

How should Western industrialized countries respond to these dangers? To a certain extent, the problem will solve itself. As the impression of a general insecurity in Africa grows, which is now strengthened even further due to the increased danger of terrorist attacks, tourists and corporations are increasingly turning their backs on the region—with the exception of South Africa and along the Gulf of Guinea where oil exploration still attracts considerable investment. This intensifies the existing economic misery in the majority of these countries. Of course, development and African experts react to the growing danger of terrorism almost reflexively by warning that the causes of terrorism must be fought. But even if the international donor community was to devote a great deal more of its resources to economic and social development, fighting poverty, and cultural dialogue, it would still be decades before African states obtained a level of development that would make violent solutions to conflicts unlikely.

Moreover, wealth does not prevent the creation of terrorist cells, as the example of Saudi Arabia shows. The problem of a growing terrorist threat in Africa also requires measures that will have an effect in the short term. Among the possibilities could be a reversal of the trend of withdrawing militarily from the region. The USA already appears to be moving in this direction. However, the fact that neither the substantial presence of French troops in Djibouti nor the intelligence efforts of the German navy off the coast of Somalia and East Africa were able to prevent the attacks in Mombasa raises doubts about the appropriateness of this suggestion. And an attempt to combat terrorist cells in Somalia with an intervention of Ethiopian troops had only limited success. Of greater importance for the short-term fight against terrorism in Africa would be state capacity building, in particular in terms of concentrating on the reform and support of the security sector in general and the police in particular.

Terrorist organizations operate much like the Mafia, living and operating in a criminal environment. Most Americans focus on the Middle East as the bull's eye of terrorist activity in the world. But Africa is both agent and victim of terrorism. As agent of terrorism, it continues to fester as a breeding ground for al-Qaeda and other terrorist organizations. Terrorists fleeing from Afghanistan and elsewhere in Southwest Asia are finding safe haven to the south. There, operating in vast, open spaces with long, porous borders, these groups are able to recruit and train members and bankroll their operations.

Besides, Northern Africa serves as a *transit route* for terrorists headed to Europe. East Africa, particularly Somalia, has become a hotbed of al-Qaeda elements.

Western Africa has witnessed dramatic rises in anti-American and extremist Islamic rhetoric, particularly in northern Nigeria. In addition to al-Qaeda and other less-known insurgent groups, Africa is home to Lebanese Hezbollah, the worst terrorist organization in the world. Hezbollah finances much of its activities through Sierra Leone's diamond trade and through arms and narcotics smuggling and human trafficking.

The continent is also a victim of terrorism. Africa witnessed terrorism against U.S. targets long before September 11, 2001, most notably when al-Qaeda operatives launched simultaneous attacks against the U.S. embassies in Nairobi, Kenya, and Dar Es Salaam, Tanzania, in 1998. Additional attacks in Mombassa in November 2002 demonstrated that terrorist cells were still active. Members of the Algerian terrorist group *Salafist Group for Call and Combat* kidnapped European tourists, reportedly using the ransom money they collected to purchase weapons, ammunition, and equipment in 2003.

While sub-Saharan Africa is showing many factors that led to the rise of international terrorism in the Middle East and Central Asia, the emergence of a genuinely African type of international terrorism is rather improbable—at least for the foreseeable future. The main terrorist threat in Africa arises from the incapability of African states to control their territory and to protect potential targets of terrorist assaults. Africa cannot win the fight against terrorism without determined investments in state capacity building, especially in the security sector, by its American and European partners. Such assistance can, however, be misused for undermining political liberalization and democratization in Africa and, by that, could reinforce political factors which contributed to the emergence of international terrorism in other regions. Alertness and a differentiated approach can at least minimize this risk.

The African Charter of Human and Peoples' Rights (Banjul Charter), in force since October 1986, has been ratified by almost all African states and can be expected to inform the development of constitutional human rights law in Africa. This exposes Africa to potential conflicts between two or more competing legal regimes. Article 12 of the Convention against Transnational Organized Crime, for example, requires states to enact domestic laws that grant wide powers of confiscation, freezing, or seizure of property or proceeds derived from organized crime. This would include the power to seize property where illegitimately obtained property has been intermingled with that derived by legitimate means. In either case, the onus will rest with the alleged offender to show that the property seized derived from lawful activity. It is important to note that article 7(1) read with articles 3 and 14 of the African Charter protects the right of property, the right to have one's case heard before a court, and the right to be presumed innocent until proven guilty. To some these contradictions are latent in the Algiers Convention when read with associated African positions. For example, Article 3(1):

> the struggle waged by peoples in accordance with the principles of international law for their liberation or self-determination, including armed struggle against colonialism, occupation, aggression and domination by foreign forces shall not be considered as terrorist acts.

This sits uncomfortably with the Grand Bay Declaration on Human Rights signed by the OAU in the same year (1999), Article 8(q), which defines terrorism (for whatever motives) as a violation of human rights. In the end it would be a Pyrrhic victory if terrorism were defeated at the cost of sacrificing Africa's commitment to those values reflected in the Banjul Charter. Africa's challenge is to implement agreements and legislation that effectively combat terrorism while conforming to the requirements of international human rights law and international commitments to enhance the continent's credibility in its bid to empower its people for democracy and development.

Summarily, the increasing visibility, assets, and political influence of organized criminal groups in Africa have become a matter of mounting international concern in recent years. Transnational crime groups control thousands of millions of dollars in assets. Their huge economic clout facilitates corruption domestically and internationally. They undermine African governments. They undermine attempts of developing African countries to build democracies.

Transnational organized crime will be a defining issue of the 21st century for policymakers—as defining as the Cold War was for the 20th century and colonialism was for the 19th. No area of international affairs will remain untouched, as the social fabric and political and financial systems of many countries deteriorate under the increasing economic power of international organized crime groups.

Illicit trade in nuclear materials threatens the security of nations. Large-scale arms smuggling may spark or fuel regional conflicts. Drug trafficking and illegal-alien smuggling are expected to exact an ever-higher human cost in larger numbers of source and destination countries. The proliferation of international prostitution and pornography rings has serious social and health consequences. The illicit timber trade and trafficking in rare species and nuclear wastes have already done grave damage to the African and global environments.

The massive profits of the diverse transnational organized crime groups, laundered in international financial markets, are undermining the security of Africa's financial systems. Meanwhile, the competitiveness of legitimate businesses is being undercut by organized crime's involvement in industrial and technological espionage.

There is no form of government immune from the development of transnational criminal organizations, no legal system capable of fully controlling the growth of such crime, and no economic or financial system that is secure against the temptation of profits at levels far greater than those possible from legal activities.

The consequences are most devastating, however, in African states where people are attempting to establish democracy, self-determination, and the rule of law. Nations in this situation are found in many parts of the globe, but in this book we are concerned with African states. Many of these countries are now contending with stagnant economies, weak governments, and limited uncorrupted law enforcement capacity. They are fertile grounds for organized crime.

Organized crime in African states has emerged with an intensity and diversity of activities unmatched by other transnational crime groups in the international arena. In these states, crime groups number in the thousands. Rather than the rigid hierarchical structure of the prototypical organized crime family, the groups are based on network structures, often using violence as part of their business strategy, like the strikes on Dar es Salaam and Nairobi by terrorists in 1998. Unlike other countries where established crime syndicates have specialized in particular goods and services, organized crime in Africa has infiltrated a full range of illicit activities. These groups have also penetrated deeply into the legitimate economy, including many companies that used to belong to the state and have been privatized.

Organized crime exploits the traditional market in illicit goods and services that includes prostitution, gambling, drugs, and contract killings, supply of cheap, illegal labor, stolen automobiles, and extortion of legitimate businesses. It has also branched out to include such diverse activities as the illegal export of oil and raw materials, and the smuggling of weapons, nuclear materials, and human beings. These groups are often comprised of unusual coalitions of professional criminals, former members of the underground economy, and members of the ruling Party elite and security apparatus. Their ranks contain highly trained specialists (such as statisticians and money launderers) not readily accessible to transnational crime groups in other parts of the world.

Organized crime has penetrated these states, from the municipal to national level, by financing selected political campaigns and the election of their members to parliament. Criminal groups have co-opted officials of African governments. In some cases, the groups have supplanted the state by providing the protection, employment, and social services no longer available from the struggling new government.

Organized crime and endemic corruption threaten stability and the transition to a liberal democratic system. The indigenous crime problem within these countries is significant, but widespread criminal activity throughout the region worsens the situation. Criminal links operate across the continent and increasingly groups interact with their counterparts around the world.

Many of these states lack institutional capacity to address organized crime. Most of the expertise and the institutions to deal with the problem do not exist. In the early years of impoverishing structural adjustment programs, organized crime and corruption grew unimpeded by laws or personnel capable of addressing them. Economic development often floundered without appropriate legal structure and the presence of established enforcement mechanisms. Resources continued to flow to the elite as a result of high-level corruption, leaving the mass of the citizenry impoverished and without faith in their new governments. Criminal groups in tandem with corrupt officials picked the national pockets with impunity; robbing ordinary citizens of the assets they were to have inherited through privatization.

Corruption and criminal activity also deter foreign investors, reducing economic growth and depriving the state of revenues needed to repair depleted infrastructures and create new economic opportunities. Thousands of millions of dollars in assets have been laundered overseas by sophisticated criminals, depriving the states of assets needed to pay salaries and pensions. Many would-be investors have decided that there are easier and safer places to put their money than Africa. For those who did invest, the high level of corruption became an added concern, especially for American businesses that must comply with the Foreign Corrupt Practices Act in Africa.

The hijacking of the privatization process by organized crime and corrupt officials has resulted in economically polarized African societies in many of the states. Instead of an emerging middle class, there is now a small, extremely rich, new elite (transnational compradoral capitalist class), and a large, impoverished population. This is particularly problematic in societies where citizens are educated in an ideology committed to social equality. Although economic inequality existed, it was more hidden from view than that of the new parasitic elites who flaunt their wealth both domestically and overseas.

The political costs of organized crime are staggering. The pervasive corruption and penetration of organized crime into the political process are inhibiting the development of new laws needed as a foundation for a democratic, even free market, society. An often highly corrupted tax authority and the links of government personnel to organized crime deprive the state of needed revenues. Substantial numbers of citizens have lost faith in the integrity and capacity of the legal process, and in the ability of their "new democratic governments" to deliver on basic obligations, such as payment of wages and retirement benefits, and provision of health care.

Just as corporate entities build power and influence through acquisition and partnership with other companies in the legitimate business world, criminal groups are building alliances with counterparts in other nations. Colombian drug traffickers are linking up with Nigerian crime groups providing couriers for European deliveries, which are routed through Eastern Europe or the former Soviet Union to minimize detection. Proceeds from these crimes may be laundered through four different countries before reaching their final destination in an offshore haven in the Caribbean. Local law enforcement is hard-pressed to track suspects and evidence through this convoluted maze.

Only bilateral and multilateral efforts can work effectively to inhibit organized crime that is invading every part of the world. It is clear that despite the challenges posed by crime groups around the world, the international community has a large stake in assisting the ability of African nations to address their rising political and economic power.

The new found strength that organized crime has gained through international alliances is also its weakness. Networks of these enterprises are brutal, but fragile. Though groups may exploit gaps in legislation and enforcement abroad, they can also be severely weakened when law enforcement and prosecutors in many nations coordinate their efforts and strategies. If united in common cause, governments can prevail against criminal groups to protect democracy and the African public.

## References

Asuni, T. and O. A. Pela. 1986. "Drug Abuse in Africa," *Bulletin on Narcotics*, 38, 1 & 2: 55-64.

Bazzi-Veil, L. et al. 2000. *Étude sous-régionale sur le trafic des enfants à des fins d'exploitation économique en Afrique de l'Ouest et du Centre.* Abidjan: UNICEF West and Central Africa Regional Office, (WCARO), 2000, p. 9; United Nations Development Program's *2002 Human Development Report*, retrieved from www.undp.org/hdr2002/complete.pdf on August 6, 2002. Poverty rates tend to be much higher in rural areas, as in Togo where the general poverty rate is 35 percent but the rate in rural areas is 78 percent. Abalo, "Trafic des enfants au Togo," p. iii. The links between poverty and child trafficking have been the subject of numerous studies and journalistic accounts. Poverty has been said to force families to find ways to reduce childcare costs; tempt children into seeking a better life abroad; and draw rural families to higher wages in urban areas. It has also been said to compel farmers to employ their children in the fields, leading to high rates of school drop-out and heightened vulnerability to recruitment by trafficking intermediaries. Poverty is also thought to contribute to the employment of girls as domestic workers, itself a potential forerunner to child trafficking.

*BBC News* and other journalistic reports *see*, for example, "West Africa's Little Maids," *BBC News*, April 16, 2001, at http://news.bbc.co.uk/hi/english/world/africa/newsid_1279000/1279776.stm (accessed May 29, 2002); H. Mayell, untitled, *National Geographic News*, April 24, 2001; "Togo Hands Suspected Child Traffickers to Benin," *Reuters*, May 7, 2001, at http://global.factiva.com/en/arch/print_results.asp (accessed April 8, 2002); R. Mulholland, "Legal Inquiry Underway in Benin," U.S. Fund for UNICEF, May 10, 2002; "UN Plans Active Part in Eradicating Child Trafficking," *PANA Daily Newswire*, May 31, 2001, at http://global.factiva.com/en/arch/print_results.asp (accessed April 8, 2002); "West African Domestic Servants Face Slavery," *PANA Daily Newswire*, June 11, 2001, at http://global.factiva.com/en/arch/print_results.asp (accessed April 8, 2002); "Immigrant Ship Leaves Togo, Heads For Nigeria," *Dow Jones International News*, June 23, 2001, at http://global.factiva.com/en/arch/display.asp (accessed April 8, 2002).

*CARE/World Bank Study.* In this study, 100 of 214 students were orphans, of whom more than half had lost at least one parent to AIDS. These statistics are more explanatory when read together with the following documents:

A.Y. Akolatse and K.T. Djonoukou. 2001. "Analyse de la situation des orphelins, veuves et familles affectées du SIDA dans la Region maritime en vue de la réalisation d'un programme de prise en charge," *IDF/RIPPET Project*. Lomé: CARE/World Bank, 2001, p. 37. In a different study, the World Bank found that orphans in Togo, defined as children who have lost either a mother or both parents, were about 20 percent less likely to attend school than children with two parents. The vulnerability of AIDS-affected children to hazardous and exploitative labor has been documented in other parts of Africa. *See* for example Human Rights Watch, "In the Shadow of Death: HIV/AIDS and Children's Rights in Kenya", *A Human Rights Watch report*, vol. 13, no. 4(A), June 2001; UNICEF East and Southern Africa Regional Office (ESARO), "Child Labor in the Shadow of HIV/AIDS." Nairobi: UNICEF-ESARO, April 2002; *Synergy Project*, "Children on the Brink 2002." In the 2001 CARE/World Bank study, one Togolese therapist is quoted as saying that "AIDS is a new sickness that causes fear. It is a sickness of gypsies and prostitutes." Fidèle Avajon, director of an NGO that used to work with AIDS orphans, told Human Rights Watch that "families don't accept easily that someone among their relatives died of AIDS. We had families where we knew someone died of AIDS, and we tried to help. But the family refused our help because they didn't want to admit the death was from AIDS." Arsène Mensah, program coordinator of the NGO Aide Médicale et de Charité, attributed the stigma to early information campaigns saying "AIDS is death. If a family knows that someone in the family has AIDS, they withdraw from that person," he said. "People are still afraid of being contaminated." *See* Akolatse and Djonoukou, "Analyse de la situation des orphelins," p. 30; Human Rights Watch interview with Fidèle Avajon, director, Association pour une Meilleure Intégration Sociale, Lomé, May 7, 2002; Human

Rights Watch interview with Arsène Mensah, Aide Médicale et de Charité, Lomé, May 7, 2002.

CIA *World Fact Book 2002*, March 19, 2003. Information Drawn From the Suspicious Activity Reporting System, *SAR Bulletin*, Issue 4, January 2002, United States Department of the Treasury, Financial Crimes Enforcement Network, Alert to financial institutions, Case #3. http://www.ustreas.gov/fincen/sarbul0201-f.pdf.

Duke, L. 1996. "Drug trade moves in on S. Africa." *Washington Post*. September 1: A33.

Farah, D. 1996. "Tracing Colombia's Nigerian Connection." *Washington Post*. June 21: A32.

*Human Rights Watch* interview with Suzanne Aho, Lomé, May 6, 2002.

Kibuka, E. P. 1979. "Crime in African Countries," *International Review of Criminal Policy*. 35: 13-23.

Mentan, T. 2004. *Dilemmas of Weak States: Africa and Transnational Terrorism in the Twenty-First Century*. London: Ashgate Publishers.

Opolet, J.S.E. 1979. "Organized Crime in Africa," *International Journal of Comparative and Applied Criminal Justice*. 3, 2: 177-183.

Nevadomsky, J. 1985. "Drug Use Among Nigerian University Students: Prevalence of Self-Reported Use and Attitudes to Use," *Bulletin on Narcotics*. 37, 2 & 3: 31-42.

Pela, O. 1989. "Patterns of Adolescent Psychoactive Substance Use and Abuse in Benin City, Nigeria," *Adolescence* 14, 95: 569-574.

Salah, R. et al. 2002. "Child Trafficking," p. 4; UNICEF-WCARO, Workshop on Trafficking in Child Domestic Workers, p. 30. Other documents to complement Salah's study are: Bazzi-Veil, "Trafic des enfants en Afrique de l'Ouest et du Centre," p. 8; Boonpala and Kane, "Trafficking of Children," pp. 20-21; ILO-IPEC, Synthesis report, pp. 13-14, 31; Abalo, "Trafic des enfants au Togo," p. xix; U.N. Office for Drug Control and Crime Prevention, "Trafficking for forced labour," public service announcement, retrieved from www.odccp.org/multimedia.html on June 27, 2002.

Shaw, M. 1998. "Organized Crime in Post-Apartheid South Africa," *ISS Papers, 28, Institute* for Security Studies, Halfway House, January 1998.

*Synergy Project*. 2002. "Children on the Brink 2002: A Joint Report on Orphan Estimates and Program Strategies," Washington, D.C.: USAID, July.

UNAIDS, UNICEF, USAID and *Synergy Project*. 2002. According to reports from these three organizations and the U.S. Bureau of Census, the total number of living children under age fifteen whose mother, father or both parents have died of AIDS in sub-Saharan Africa is 11 million. *The Synergy Project*, Children on the Brink 2002: A Joint Report on Orphan Estimates and Program Strategies. Washington, D.C.: USAID, July 2002. WHO/UNAIDS, "Togo, Epidemiological fact sheets on HIV/AIDS and sexually transmitted infections," p. 3; Human Rights Watch interview with Apelète Devotsou, National AIDS Program, Lomé, May 6, 2002.

Williams, P. 1997. "Transnational Organised Crime and National and International Security: A Global Assessment." In V. Gamba (ed.) Society Under Siege: Crime, Violence and Illegal Weapons, TCP Series: Volume 1, Institute for Security Studies, Halfway House, September 1997, p. 13.

Chapter 9

# African Democratic Alternative: Toward a Conceptualization

Markets have escaped the boundaries of eroding national frontiers and become global. But governing organizations have not. This has created a perilous asymmetry. Global economics operate in an anarchic realm without significant regulation and without the humanizing civic institutions that within national societies rescue it from raw social Darwinism. National boundaries have become too porous to hold the economy in, but remain sufficiently rigid to prevent democracy from spreading out.

What have been globalized are economic vices such as crime, drugs, terror, hate, pornography, and financial speculation. The civic virtues of apostles of liberal democracy have not been globalized. The result has been a growing tension between the beneficiaries of globalization and just about everyone else (Chossudovsky, 1997: chapter 11). The globalized economy is one in which the primary global agents are corporate, and the primary conceptual framework is no longer tied to 19th-century concepts of national boundaries. This chapter seeks to examine these transnational institutions and processes and ask whether they enrich or undermine democratic practices in Africa.

## GLOBALIZING DEMOCRACY?

President Olusegun Obasanjo (2004) of Nigeria admitted that,

> Reassuringly enough, there is today in Africa demand for a new approach to governance. The clamour today for democracy and good governance in Africa stems from two broad reasons. First, the denial of fundamental human rights, the presence of arbitrariness and the absence of basic freedoms for the individual have in the main remained familiar traits of a majority of governments in Africa. The strain of these styles of governance has prompted a demand and a clamour for new approaches to the resolution of various national questions. In consequence, Africans are clamouring for greater responsiveness on the part of their political leadership, respect for human rights, accountability and a two way flow of information between the people and their leadership. They are also clamouring for an adequate legal system and for the laws and the independence of the Judiciary and a free press, which together

can serve as a bulwark against the oppression of government, and especially a corrupt or unpopular government.

President Obasanjo has made the point. Global capitalism is much more concerned with expanding the domain of market relations than with, say, establishing democracy, expanding elementary education, or enhancing the social opportunities of society's underdogs in Africa. Because globalization of markets is, on its own, a very inadequate approach to world prosperity, there is a need to go beyond the priorities that find expression in the chosen focus of global capitalism.

As George Soros (2000) has pointed out, international business concerns often have a strong preference for working in orderly and highly organized autocracies rather than in activist and less-regimented democracies and this can be a regressive influence on equitable development. Further, multinational firms can exert their influence on the priorities of public expenditure in less secure Third World countries by giving preference to the safety and convenience of the managerial classes and of privileged workers over the removal of widespread illiteracy, medical deprivation, and other adversities of the poor. These possibilities do not, of course, impose any insurmountable barrier to development, but it is important to make sure that the surmountable barriers are actually surmounted.

The modern world is now undergoing a "third wave" of democratization in which the spread of democratic norms and practices is replacing authoritarian ones in many countries around the globe. The major question that has continued to perplex scholars is how, exactly, do countries make the transition to democracy, or become more democratic? Can globalism be governed? Or, as a first step, can we start by building a global civil society? Until recently, one could look in vain for a global "we, the people" to be represented. That is now changing. There is internationalism, a forming crystal around which a global polity can grow. Effective global governance to temper the excesses of the global market does not yet exist; however, international activism by nongovernmental organizations has made some surprising gains. People who care about public goods are working to recreate on a global scale the normal civic balance that exists within democratic nations. Consider the following:

- A young woman named Jody Williams, with celebrity help from a princess (sadly deceased), creates a worldwide civic movement for a ban on land mines that actually enacts a treaty.
- A Bangladeshi visionary, Mohammed Yunus, develops an idea for microfinancing, which makes miniloans to women in third world societies, which at once jump-starts enterprise and liberates women from traditional servitude.
- Striking fear into retired tyrants everywhere, European public opinion and spirited English law lords make possible the arrest of a Chilean ex-dictator. Ill health got Augusto Pinochet temporarily off the hook, but the Chilean

Supreme Court has lifted his immunity and the tocsin has sounded. Dictators are no longer safe in their retirement havens.

- Women's groups from around the world meet in Beijing in a demonstration of international solidarity that asks nothing of national governments and everything of civic institutions that are powerfully reinforced by their actions.

- Multiplying coalitions of workers, environmentalists, students, and anarchists use the Internet to fashion a decentralized, nonideological resistance to the International Monetary Fund, and the World Trade Organization, effectively capturing media attention by taking to the streets in Seattle, Washington, D.C., London, and Prague.

- Hundreds of NGOs gather in new international organizations like CIVICUS, the World Forum on Democracy, and Transparency International, and begin to develop the kind of civic networking across nations that corporations have enjoyed for decades, courtesy of the World Economic Forum at Davos, Switzerland.

- President Bill Clinton offers the corporate leaders at Davos a "wake-up call" reminding them that there are "new forces seeking to be heard in the global dialogue," progressive forces that want to democratize rather than withdraw from the new world order.

What is afoot here? Davos is a good place to begin. For nearly 30 years, the world's multiplying multinational corporations, transnational banks, and speculators have met every February in the Swiss ski resort to network, strategize, and acquire legitimacy by mixing with invited statesmen and intellectuals. Davos has been a fit symbol for an international arena in which the "three-legged stool" of government, civil society, and the private-market sector on which stable democracies are said to rest has been transformed into a tottering toadstool held up by a thick and solitary economic stem.

The asymmetries resulting from the rapid globalization of markets in the absence of any commensurable globalization of political and civic institutions are largely ignored by elected officials, even those of the center-left. Ripped from the box of the nation-state, which traditionally acted as its regulator and civilizer, capitalism turns mean and anarchic. The market sector is privileged; the political sector is largely eclipsed (when not subordinated to the purposes of the market); the private is elevated above the public, which is subjected to ruthless privatization at every turn. Liberty itself is redefined as the absence of governmental authority and hence an exclusively market phenomenon, while coercion and dependency are associated with government even when (especially when) government is democratic.

The difficulty African nation-states have with globalization comes not just from the force of what is happening in the international arena but from ideological developments within nation-states. The push toward privatization is bipartisan. This is not decentralization—the devolution of power down the democratic public ladder to provinces, municipalities, and neighborhoods—but de-democratization, the shifting of concentrated power at the highest levels from public to private hands. Power shifted from authorities that were hierarchical but also public, transparent, and accountable, to authorities that remain hierarchical but are private, opaque, and undemocratic. In the unfettered high-tech global market, crucial democratic values become relics. Indeed, because globalization is correctly associated with new telecommunication technologies, the globalized and privatized information economy is constructed as an inevitable concomitant of postsovereign, postmodern society.

## GLOBALIZATION FOR CAPITAL, NOT FOR PEOPLE

The world's giant transnational corporations, and the governments and multilateral institutions that cling to them, are globalizing the wrong things, things that are of benefit to them and no one else. For example, the globalization of crime is commonplace. The late President Mobutu (1988: 25) who plundered Zaire (Democratic Republic of Congo) for decades was asked who introduced corruption in his country. He retorted: "European businessmen were the ones who said: 'I sell you this thing for $1,000, but $200 will be for your (Swiss bank) account.'" It was through this transnationalization of crime that Mobutu came to have more money than his country's foreign debt.

These transnational corporations are refusing to globalize the things that would benefit all of Africa. Finance-sector liberalization has opened borders to the free flow of capital, so that an estimated U.S.$1.5 trillion churns through world currency markets each day. But 90 percent of this is speculative, of benefit only to the giant hedge funds and banks and, as the peoples of Asia found during the financial crisis of 1997, prone to fly out of a country with little warning but much damage.

World Trade Organization agreements have promoted free trade. But, while southern economies have had to open up to northern companies' investment, goods, and services, Europe and the USA are allowed to maintain enormous barriers to the South's main exports, including textiles and agriculture. The last round of free-trade talks will cost the least-developed countries $600 million by 2004, according to the United Nations Development Program.

Neoliberal, market-first economic policies have spread to governments in every corner of the world. But the means by which these policies have been forced on the South —through the IMF structural adjustment program—have generated economic stagnation, poverty, and inequality. Sub-Saharan Africa, for example, spends more on servicing its $300 billion debt than it does on health and education for its children.

Culture, ideas, theories, and communication have also become interlinked and interdependent. But the culture is a facile, junk-food Hollywood monoculture pumped out by the giant news and entertainment companies, such as Disney, Time Warner, and News Corporation. And the ideas and theories are all too frequently nothing more than advertisements and PR campaigns, whether in politics, economics, or social theory.

Wealth, meanwhile, is not being globalized; quite the opposite, it's being concentrated. The world's three richest men, Bill Gates, Warren Buffet, and Paul Allen—own assets equivalent to that owned by the 600 million people in the world's 48 least-developed countries. Technology, similarly, is not being spread; it's tightly controlled. Ninety percent of the world's patents are held in the North, primarily by high-tech companies such as Microsoft, Monsanto, and Merck. The WTO's agreement on trade-related intellectual property rights will ensure it stays that way—it was, after all, written by the Intellectual Property Committee, a coalition of 13 US technology companies.

Even the Internet, globalization's icon, is only increasing inequalities between rich and poor. Half the world's population have never made or received a phone call, let alone surfed the Net; lacking the money for even basic needs, they are not exactly in the market for PCs or Internet service providers. And while capital can roam the globe, most of the world's people cannot. The borders remain closed to them.

Far from being a liberating process for the world, globalization has only enhanced the power of the transnational corporation and the wealth of its share-holders. According to the UNDP, 500 corporations now control 70 percent of the world's trade and 80 percent of its foreign investment. Fortunately, there is not just one process of globalization. There are two. When thousands protest outside the World Economic Forums (WEF) today, they noisily and vigorously reject one, and just as determinedly uphold another.

The globalization we reject, which is dominant but failing, is the globalization of capital, of corporate power. The second globalization, the rising one, the one Seattle11 (S11) is part of, is driven by awakening people's movements all over the world which are rejecting corporate domination and advancing new models of economic and social development of their own. This is the globalization that raised its voice in Seattle against the WTO; in Washington against the World Bank and the IMF; in Chiang Mai, Thailand, against the Asian Development Bank; and in Melbourne against the WEF. This is the globalization of solidarity, of people's power, indeed, of democracy.

## MEDIA CONCENTRATION VERSUS DEMOCRACY

Nowhere are the asymmetries of the new globalism more evident than in media mergers like Disney/ABC, Viacom/CBS, Verizon (Bell Atlantic/GTE), and AOL/Time Warner/CNN/EMI. These mergers present a challenge not just to economic competition in the domain of goods, labor, and capital, but to democracy and its defining virtues. These include free and autonomous information (guaranteed by the independent existence of plurally owned media), social and political diversity (guaranteed by genuine pluralism in society), and full participation by citizens in deciding public policies and securing public goods (guaranteed by a robust public domain). When the U.S. Congress passed the Telecommunications Act of 1996—the first major piece of legislation dealing with new media since the Federal Communications Act of 1934—it effectively ceded the modern information economy to the private forces that control global markets.

The new monopolies are particularly insidious because while monopolies of the 19th century were in durable goods and natural resources, and exercised control over the goods of the body, new information-age monopolies of the 21st century are over news, entertainment, and knowledge, and exercise control over the goods of the mind and spirit. When governments control information and news, we call it totalitarianism; when monopolistic corporations control them, we call it free market strategy.

The impact on diversity is misleading because sources of content and information delivery appear to be multiplying. Superficially, this trend is pluralist and empowering. AOL and Time Warner cover different consumer bases, and the new partners, Steve Case of AOL and Gerald Levin of Time Warner, both promise to pursue "open access" on cable so that the owners of "pipes" that carry content do not become monopoly gatekeepers. But it is hardly clear between AOL and Time Warner who actually represents the pipes and who the content. AOL controls online content but as a Web server is also a monolithic Web portal. Time Warner wanted the deal to get its content on the Web; it is a content provider but, via hard cable installations, also controls pipes. AOL wanted the deal to get its Net services on fast hard-wired cable (it currently depends on snail-speed telephone lines). To suggest there is no real overlap, to suggest there is other than one audience and one information market, is to badly misunderstand the technology and to muddy the real issues of monopoly and globalization in the new information society.

Indeed, the whole point of "convergence" or "splitting" is to eliminate the features that separate hardware and software, the carriers and the content, until there is a seamless stream of information and entertainment entering your home: one medium, one content, one audience. Telephones, computers, televisions, VCRs, DVDs, video stores, and content companies are the segmented way of the past. The new media company must control them all; in an economy that demands integration and convergence, this means they must control (own) one another.

Monopoly is not an accidental outcome but a necessary condition of doing business in this new world. Vertical integration is a condition of synergy. When Bill Gates insists his integration of an Internet portal into his Windows operating system is a 'natural' extension of his original product, he is being truthful. But the truth he tells is that convergence means monopoly, and synergy means vertical integration; that a capitalism still defined by real diversity, genuine competition, differential markets, and multiple firms is an anachronism—these are practices of the industrial past that have no place in the postindustrial information-economy future.

Now this may all represent a new and powerful logic of an information economy that dictates its own imperatives. But no one has spent much time trying to think about how this new economic logic in which private monopoly is a public good impacts the traditional logic of the democratic society, which holds that private monopoly is a public bad. There were good reasons for thinking that many newspapers and magazines were better than a few when the founders wrote the First Amendment. There were good reasons for thinking that broadcast media were public utilities over which the public had special claims when legislators wrote the U.S. Federal Communications Act of 1934. There were good reasons for thinking that diversity of content and pluralism of culture were integral virtues of a democratic society when America embraced multiculturalism in the 1980s and 1990s.

Does a change in private technological and economic logic mean that the public logic of democracy must accommodate itself uncomplainingly to that change? Or is it technology and the information economy that need to be reassessed and revised to meet public goals and common goods as a democratic people? Should private logic dominate public logic in democracy? Are Steve Case, Gerald Levin, and Ted Turner appropriate unelected representatives to shape Africa's destiny as an information society? Will their decisions become de facto legislation for the rest of the world? These troublesome questions cannot be answered in the context of national politics. The real challenge is whether one can address the erosion of democracy in the asymmetrical setting of global markets, where such civic and political tools as are available within nations have gone missing.

Is the outlook not quite as pessimistic as the diagnosis suggests? Is there no emerging African alternative to global markets in new transnational civic organizations and social movements, and are there no other political strategies that can oppose privatization within African nations and then help them reassert control over the global economy through traditional "concert of nations" approaches? After all, the IMF and the WTO are not supranational organizations, but the tools of groups of powerful nations. They will bend to the will of democratic African governments, if these governments can once again represent the public interests of their sovereign peoples and can find ways to cooperate.

## TRANSNATIONAL CIVIL SOCIETY?

The marketplace functions effectively within nation-states because it is only one of three sectors. The private-business sector is not only balanced by the public-government sector, but the two are in turn mediated by a civil society that, like government, is public and composed of communities and other collective associations, but like the market is voluntary and free. Within nation-states, it is not the market alone but this stable tripod of governmental, civic, and private institutions that generates liberty and produces the pluralistic goods of free society. Rip the market from its nesting place in nation-states, however, and you have wild capitalism—wild not in itself (it is supposed to be aggressively competitive) but because in globalizing it slips the civilizing embrace of its nation-state hosts.

The turmoil in Seattle, in Washington, D.C., and London arose from frustration. The protectionist backlash bespeaks a deep insecurity in the face of a world out of control—an exaggerated nightmare of a world in which American soldiers serve under foreign command, Islamic fundamentalists conspire to wage terror on the American heartland, jobs hemorrhage abroad, immigrants inundate the nation and rend its fragile unity. Far from suggesting common cause between American protestors and the wretched of the earth elsewhere, however, this backlash can look like an American version of the politics of fear.

Yet the democratic world really is out of control because the instruments of benign control—democratic governing institutions—simply do not exist in the international setting, where markets in currency, labor, and goods run like engines without governors. Happily, the rising internationalism of transnational civic institutions and social movements promises a measure of countervailing power in the international arena and serves as an alternative to the reactionary racist politics of a Pat Buchanan or a Jean-Marie Le Pen.

These civic efforts—the work of citizens rather than governments, or the work of governments reacting to citizens (and not just theirs)—embody a global public opinion in the making, a global civic engagement that can alone give the abstraction of international politics weight. The outreach of citizens and civic groups can make entities like "Europe" more than a mere function of economic and security concerns. Coteries of NGOs, the shifting voice of global public opinion, and the emergent hand of the international rights movement may not be the equal of multinational corporations or international banks, but they represent a significant starting place for countervailing power. They put flesh on the bare bones of legalistic doctrines of universal rights. But rights depend on engaged citizens and a civic space where their activities are possible. These new transnational civic spaces offer possibilities for transnational citizenship and hence an anchor for global rights.

## A CONCERT OF NATIONS?

Even so, these transnational civic projects should not fool anyone into thinking that Amnesty International or Médecins Sans Frontières are the equivalent in clout of an AOL or Time Warner or the IMF. International markets spin out of control not just because the economy has been globalized, but because, nation by nation by nation, people have conspired in the transfer of sovereignty from popular hands that are transparent and accountable to private hands that are neither. One remains transfixed by privatization on the Thatcher/Reagan/Blair/Clinton model, and so one is unable to avail oneself of the many potential control mechanisms already in place.

One bemoans the absence of governance and international regulation over free markets, though in truth the international institutions most often vilified are ultimately instruments of sovereign nations acting in concert. Their subservience to multinational corporations and powerful banking and financial interests reflects not just some historically inevitable erosion of sovereignty but the willed sellout of sovereign peoples to the myths of privatization. As international civil society grows stronger, it can become a source of countervailing democratic pressure on African governments.

Technically, like the United Nations, the WTO is itself a creature of nation-states. Like the IMF and many other market institutions, it could be regarded as the exoskeleton of international governance. But privatization—globalization's nasty twin—has robbed the nations that nominally control it of their democratic will, and they appear to be servants rather than masters of the new global corporate sovereigns. With animals running the zoo—those who seek such public goods as environmental protection, transparency, accountability, labor safety, and the protection of children—look in vain for keepers and finally settle for theatrics, raising a ruckus rather than effecting a change.

Were they to agree on policy, the leading industrial nations could probably work their will at the IMF and the WTO. Ironically, although global markets do erode national sovereignty, a reassertion of national sovereignty as a consequence of domestic political campaigns aimed at challenging privatization could go a long way toward controlling global markets. Currently, the WTO treats national boycotts of imported goods as illegal, even when they are motivated by legitimate safety or environmental or child-labor concerns. Its members can change these provisions. African nations worry with reason that imperial world environmental and safety and minimum wage concerns are a way of putting a human face on protectionism. By imposing impossible-to-meet standards, the United States can win back jobs from developing nations. But if imperial world governments agreed to pay the price of meeting those standards, they would win the support of Third World governments in regulating global capitalism and improving standards worldwide.

National sovereignty is said to be a dying concept, but it is a long way from dead. Sovereign nations remain the locus of democratic society and the only viable powers capable of opposing, subduing, and civilizing the anarchic forces of the global economy. International civil society, the emerging global alternative to world markets, needs the active support of sovereign states for its fragile new institutions to have even a modest impact. Working together as they began to in Berlin and Warsaw, progressive forces within the democracies can increase the voice of civil society in how the world is organized and governed.

## NEOLIBERALISM, ACCOUNTABILITY AND TRANSPARENCY IN AFRICA?

Accountability is defined as the degree to which political leaders are responsive and responsible, and the degree to which public policy reflects citizen preferences. Within the United Nations System-wide Special Initiative on Africa (UNSIA), launched in 1996, the Economic Commission for Africa (ECA) and the United Nations Development Programme (UNDP) are mandated to lead consultations on governance, to organize co-ordinated and collaborative programs for implementation, and to mobilize resources and political support for good governance.

At the First Annual Africa Governance Forum (AGF I), which took place in Addis Ababa July 11-12, 1997, participants agreed to pursue collaborative and coordinated programs in support of good governance and to organize such a forum annually. These forums would, inter alia, discuss best practices in various areas of good governance through consultations among African governments, international partners, and civil society oganizations; and report and discuss the status of ongoing governance programs.

AGF I generated debate on a wide range of programs that reflect key areas of governance in Africa. These include leadership building, transparency and accountability, civil society empowerment, institutions of political transition, and peace and stability. Discussion during AGF I, as well as in postforum consultations, emphasized the need to focus AGF II on a single priority area of governance so as to have significant impact on the tenor of debate and the scope of national programs presented for support. Further, it was agreed that "Accountability and Transparency" would be the sole agenda item for the Second Annual Africa Governance Forum. AGF II has been made possible from the support of the governments of Norway and Switzerland and the European Commission.

The Concept Paper that followed the discussions poses a number of key questions that inhere in this pivotal theme, examining relevant practices, processes, and methodologies applied by African governments in their striving for accountability and transparency. It offers an operational definition of the concept in accordance with United Nations decisions and resolutions. It also provides an exposition of critical issues, institution, and processes that underpin the performance of governments in their management of public affairs and in their relationship to other segments of national society, as well as external actors, both public and private.

More specifically, the paper analyses the functional relationship between political and financial accountability in governance on the one hand and, on the other, economic and social development. Additionally, the document sets out elements of a framework and program for national accountability and transparency that may be adapted, as appropriate, to specific national situations. Finally, it shows how these elements may relate to changing the attitudes and practices of external players, such as multilateral and bilateral donors, international development agencies, nongovernmental organizations, and multinational corporations.

What is the conceptual status of "good governance?" At the minimum, liberal and radical paradigms would agree that governance refers to the institutions and relations to do with political power: the way political power is exercised and legitimized. In other words, governance is constructed primarily on the terrain of power. Thus articulated, the values and principles by which governance would be judged and characterized relate to forms of governance, such as democratic governance or authoritarian governance or dictatorial governance.

The good governance discourse, however, does not admit of the relationships of power. Rather it presents itself as a moral paradigm, distinguishing between the good, the bad, and the evil. What is good and bad governance thus turns out to be a moral judgment, on the one hand, and relativist and subjectivist, on the other. The result, I want to suggest, is that "good governance" has no conceptual or theoretical value in understanding a phenomenon with a view to change it. Rather, it is, at best, a propagandist tool easily manipulatable by whoever happens to wield power. And this is exactly how it has been deployed in the dominant, neoliberal discourse.

One of the political conditionalities imposed on African governments by the international financial institutions and the donor community is good governance. This has become a flexible tool in the hands of global hegemonies to undermine the sovereignty of African nations and the struggle for democracy of the African people. For the people are no longer the agencies of change but rather the victims of "bad governance" to be delivered or redeemed by the erstwhile donor community.

The instrument of this deliverance is supposedly the policies and political conditions—multiparty, governance commissions—that must be put in place for a state to qualify to receive aid. The recipients on their part reform their governance structures, with aid and technical assistance from the same donor community, to satisfy their, what these days are called, partners.

How this consultancy of AGF1 and AGF II represent the struggle of the people of Africa to construct a democratic state and polity, it is difficult for one to tell. And this is because, one is not even sure if good governance means the same thing as democratic governance of, for, and by the people of Africa. After all they were never consulted on the appointment of the advisors. What about the Commission for Human Rights and Good Governance created in every African country as a showcase to solicit aid?

This beggarly attitude explains why good governance reforms are conceived according to the dictates of donors. Structures parallel to existing ones are put up as a result of donor pressure. The desirability and viability of such structures is hardly assessed within the African countries concerned. One of the effects of setting up such structures is to undermine time-tested traditional state structures. Worse, reforms from the top instigated by donor conditionalities undermine the right of the people themselves to struggle for and conceive their own institutional reforms and set their own priorities.

Furthermore, such top-down reforms conceived, prioritized and financed by the erstwhile IFIs and donors undermine the very basis of democratic governance, that is, accountability to the people. The governors are accountable to the donors and their consultants and advisors on good governance rather than the people. Where is then the so-called democracy, trumpeted so much, and in whose name political power seeks legitimacy?

## ACCOUNTABILITY AND TRANSPARENCY: A THEMATIC REVIEW

What do accountability and transparency mean? Simply put, accountability is the obligation to render an account for a responsibility that has been conferred. It means that those individuals and organizations charged with the performance of particular actions or activities are held responsible. This responsibility is judged or measured in terms of clearly articulated codes of conduct.

Transparency or openness means the ready, unobstructed access to and availability of data and information from public and private sources that is accurate, timely, relevant, and comprehensive, as well as tolerance for public debate, public scrutiny, and public questioning of political, economic, and social policy choices.

What are the dimensions of public accountability? It has a number of dimensions including the following key elements:

- **Political accountability**: This means making authorities answer to the people for actions they take or fail to take in discharging their official duties. Observance of a constitution is an important test of political accountability under a system of democratic governance. Checks and balances are a potent mechanism for guarding against abuse of power.

  A constitution is in essence a solemn pact between the people and the state, which provides the basic foundations for the legitimacy of government and the people's rights to demand a clear, straightforward report of what the government has done in carrying out the responsibilities conferred on it by the citizens at large. Fair, competitive, and free elections that provide the possibility of changing governments offer one means of enforcing political accountability. Elections also foster broad-based and mass participation in this rendering of a comprehensive account.

- **Administrative accountability**: This refers to the vertical reporting relationships that inhere in classical administrative structures of governance, usually known as the bureaucracy or the civil service. Clear definitions of norms, rules, roles, and responsibilities—the division of labor—provide yardsticks against which to gauge administrative performance. The armed forces constitute a significant and special component of the governance structure. They, too, must be held accountable to civilian authority that is constitutionally established and politically legitimate.

  These two accountability systems at the macro level may be complemented by mechanisms and institutions at the micro level through decentralizing government, enhancing competition, and fostering participatory arrangements that promote horizontal accountability to interest groups, users' associations, and other forms of civil society and community-based organizations.

  Developing action models for monitoring and evaluation helps to institutionalize input for accountability, the process by which it is carried out, and the transparency of the outcome over and above the usual heavy bureaucratic reliance on written rules, standard operating procedures, and accepted routines.

- **Financial and budgetary accountability:** This dimension of accountability refers to the ability to account for the allocation, use, and control of public monies and public assets and properties from beginning to end in accordance with legally mandated and/or professionally accepted rules, principles, and practices for each phase of the monitoring process through the final audit.

What is the relationship among accountability, transparency, and good governance? Accountability and transparency strengthen the legitimacy of government, public officials, and their policies and decisions in the eyes of the people. They contribute to giving individuals and groups the sense that they as citizens are truly in charge of their government.

Disputes between individuals, organizations, classes, and regional or ethnic groups often break out over issues of the distribution of power and wealth. In many African countries, the public sector and the government still pervade economic and social matters, quite often including the production and delivery of economic and social goods and services. In such a context, political power is an important channel for accessing and controlling economic and social resources. Political competition between individuals or groups is more likely to become or to remain orderly and peaceful when the allocation of budgetary resources is made in an open and accountable manner. The same holds true for the process of choosing among economic and social options.

Full, proactive and honest disclosure of temporary economic setbacks and financial difficulties strengthens public understanding and patience, thereby protecting the democratic process against demagoguery and other forces likely to undermine democratic governance. A transparent electoral process increases the likelihood that election results will be readily accepted by all competing parties. It thus leads to more stable government. Efficient or effective government will depend on the institutions, quality, and substance of governance. And this in turn will depend on the competence, integrity, honesty, legitimacy, and accountability of those who govern.

What is the relationship between political and financial accountability, on the one hand, and socioeconomic development, on the other? The interests of the people are more likely to influence a government's agenda and decisions where political and financial accountability exist than where they are absent— simply because economic, financial, and social resources of the country are more likely to be allocated in the most economically efficient, socially beneficial, and environmentally friendly manner. The poor, including such underprivileged groups as rural women, can exercise greater leverage on public policy and budgetary choices as political accountability expands beyond urban-based elite circles.

At the microaccountability level, development programs and projects, as well as government agencies, are more likely to respond to the public interest and to monitor the quality and timeliness of their performance where their beneficiaries and stakeholders have mechanisms through which to make their voices heard.

Financial accountability reinforces the trust and confidence of both the national taxpayer and the external aid donor, thereby creating a climate for better revenue collection and therefore higher overall resources for the development process, as well greater external moral and material support. Economic reforms are more likely to be regarded as legitimate and therefore easier and faster to implement, politically and socially, if there is full confidence that the adjustment process is transparent and that both public and private officeholders meet the highest standards of accountability for inputs, the process itself, and its results.

A well-paid, efficient, and highly motivated civil service is indispensable for sound public policymaking and implementation. Lack of administrative accountability renders technical expertise ineffective and unrewarding; at the same time, it corrodes the moral backbone of public administration. A corrupt bureaucracy undermines the effectiveness of democratic institutions and overburdens the private sector. Petty corruption, for instance by the police or customs officials, can be as damaging to the legitimacy of democracy as grand corruption.

What happens when accountability and transparency break down throughout a system? A worldwide phenomenon, corruption generally refers to the abuse of public office for private gain. It is worth noting, however, that the private sector is far from immune to corruption. Moreover, much corrupt activity, both within and between countries (frontier corruption), occurs at the interface between the public and the private sector. Corruption does not necessarily involve money or in-kind payments; nepotism—favoritism shown to friends or relatives in conferring privilege—is one of the most common forms of corruption.

Several theories have been advanced to explain or, at times, justify corruption. Economists emphasize outright measurable profiteering behavior through a variety of mechanisms, one being the principal-agent-client model, another, the arm's-length principle. Some theories point to contextual factors, including culture and social values, conflicting signals, and loyalties arising from societies undergoing significant transitions, whether economic, political, or sociopsychological—often all at the same time. Other theories use individual and psychological variables as predictors of corruption and corrupt behavior.

Corruption entails a number of categories of costs to society, among them: losses in economic efficiency, distortions of incentives and distribution, loss of political legitimacy by government institutions, dilution of the work ethic, and damage to the moral fabric of society. Fighting corruption is not a simple proposition. First, the optimum level of corruption may not be zero. Patronage, for example, exists to some degree in all democracies, notably after a general election, and is not necessarily an evil. Often, it helps consolidate hard-won gains, especially after a fundamental transition from one system of governance to another, giving recognition and responsibility to significant actors in the change process who might not otherwise participate in the new political order.

While a multitude of solutions and measures may be combined in anticorruption policy and program packages, the exact mix and effectiveness of each will vary with individual country or sector circumstances. From a general public policy point of view, it is worth recalling that corruption tends to increase with monopoly and discretionary power, but correlates negatively with accountability. Any policy package to fight corruption must include a two-pronged strategy: (1) economic and social reforms; (2) building and strengthening institutions and institutional capacity.

Institutional capacity-building to tackle corruption requires: (1) strengthening civil society and the mass media, through multiplying the mechanisms available to voice public opinion; (2) strengthening government watchdog agencies, such as the offices of the inspector general, comptroller/auditor general, and mediator/ombudsman. Measures need to be taken to ensure that these offices have adequate human, financial and logistical resources, both quantitative and qualitative, appropriate work procedures and investigative powers, and adequate independence; and (3) strengthening the agencies and departments in charge of the electoral processes, so as to safeguarding the integrity and credibility of elections and of democracy itself.

Political will is critical to the effectiveness of any anticorruption measures. However, in itself, political will does not suffice. It must be supported by appropriate institutions. The national and local leadership must also be seen to be honest and determined to weed out corruption. One issue is whether to focus "on revamping the system" or "catching individual culprits." The ultimate objective is to dismantle any system of incentives that entices individuals, groups or organizations into corruption.

## Accountability and Transparency Practices and Issues in Africa

It remains a historical and contemporary truism that global hegemonic power, or imperialism, is an antithesis of democracy. In league with local reactionary classes or transnational capitalist classes and groups, imperial powers have played a major role in suppressing democratic struggles of the African people (Shivji, 2002). Neoliberal politics, thrust down the throats of African people, is a corollary of the economic policies of the structural adjustment programs based on the Washington Consensus (entrenched rights for banks and multinational corporations), mindlessly propagated and imposed by the World Bank and IMF.

There is nothing intrinsic about African cultures that predisposes the continent to corruption or creates a vacuum of transparency and accountability in governance. However, corruption and lack of accountability can create enormous damage in Africa—economic, social and psychological—as the continent adopts economic and political reform measures to democratize and to benefit from globalization.

Since the early years of independence, notably over the last decade or so, African countries have made significant efforts to put in place, maintain, and nurture systems, structures, processes, and practices to uphold accountability and transparency in the management of public affairs. They have also sought to guard themselves against both petty and grand corruption. Given Africa's diversity—including differences in such factors as political systems, emergence from situations of civil war, urban/rural balance, functional and legal literacy, and development of communication networks—the record is a mixed one.

But reform efforts at the national level, coupled with the strength of civil society organizations (many of them traditional) at the local level, provide ample ground for optimism. Each country, at its own pace and within its particular circumstances, taking advantage of experiences throughout the region at various levels, will seek home-grown answers to some of the issues discussed later in this chapter. What structures, processes, and practices of accountability exist in Africa?

## ALTERNATIVE CONCEPTUALIZATION OF DEMOCRATIC INSTITUTIONS AND CULTURES

Although the recent history of African countries varies, the single-party political systems that most countries have experienced since independence have entrenched nondemocratic principles and practices that now need to be overcome if democracy is to be institutionalized. While the mechanics of multiparty elections can be put in place relatively quickly, developing accountable, credible, and durable institutions that uphold democracy is a much longer-term and difficult process. The challenge therefore is not only to hold routine general elections, but it is to produce structural reforms of the polity to empower citizens. This is particularly the case since,

> [t]ied as it is to literacy and an internalised discourse that state structures are, as they say, by and for the people, democracy cannot be willed into being in the nation-states that resulted from the independence struggles of Africa. A state that was founded on colonial imposition, structured as a bifurcated one —that is, with 'citizens' being the elite minority, and 'subjects' the teeming populations held under customary laws—could not pretend for ever that its structures had any organic handle on 'the people' and their self-understanding. Following this logic, it is consistent that African countries fail in their attempt at forging democratic societies, insofar as they retain the structures pointedly forged by the contingencies of colonial rule (Soros, 2000: 7).

This failure is particularly challenging in countries that lack traditions of political competition or a culture of democracy. The ability of democratizing countries to define and craft appropriate and relevant institutions that promote participation and inclusion and protect individual rights will affect how far and how quickly democracy is institutionalized. Just like democracy itself, the current situation regarding respect for constitutions, adherence to the rule of law, and the effective functioning of institutions of state and civil society is mixed. Why? There are many reasons that will be explored in the sections that follow.

## Democratic Political Culture

Do Africans understand the very term democracy in the conventional Western sense of political pluralism, representation, and competing interests? Or do they understand it as political monism or monistic democracy: that is, the centralization and control of potentially competing interests and attempts to eliminate competition among groups? Cultural patterns, once established, possess considerable autonomy and can influence subsequent political and economic events.

Political culture is therefore an essential link between democracy and economic development. For example, the rise of Protestantism (Weber, 2002) increased popular receptivity to capitalism, which as it developed eventually brought about higher levels of economic development. The resulting widespread prosperity permitted increases in interpersonal trust among citizens and, ultimately, the development of a durable set of orientations that roughly corresponds to the concept of "civic culture." This civic culture led to the development and stabilization of democratic governments.

There are two main elements of democratic political culture. One, from the civic culture tradition, emphasizes a mixture of participation in politics with more passive roles. The key tests have come to involve the degree to which citizens express support for the right to organize civic groups, work for political parties, protest, and vote. The second approach involves citizens' willingness to extend civil rights to proponents of unpopular causes. This willingness of citizens explains why tolerance is a critical element of democratic political culture. Both approaches can be summarized under these buzzwords: extensive political participation and inclusive political values.

Throughout Africa, prevailing political cultures have been conditioned by the recent past. Although most countries experienced periods of single-party rule, development of democratic political cultures will be easier in those that maintained a degree of tolerance, civil liberties, and relatively open political systems. Even in these, however, it will still take time. Democratic culture will be firmly established only once both the political leadership and the general populace believe that democracy is the most appropriate way of ordering public affairs, and adherence to formal rules replaces reliance on contacts, patronage, and connections. Experience indicates that tangible improvements in the political situation help to foster popular support for democracy. To the extent that electoral democracy is instituted but authoritarian practices persist, it will be difficult to build a political culture supportive of democratic development.

Although civic education alone will not create a culture of democracy, it is necessary to help people understand what democracy means, inform them of their rights, and empower them to participate in the political process. It is particularly important for women and disadvantaged minorities who might otherwise remain excluded. The media have a crucial role in increasing popular awareness and understanding of democracy, and throughout the continent there has been a significant expansion of private print and electronic mediums.

Also, the increased communication and access to information brought about by technological advances will facilitate the development of a political culture supportive of democracy.

In most countries, political liberalization has reduced government censorship and control of information, with the result that the sort of independent and professional media that is a hallmark of functioning democracies is starting to develop. At present, countries such as Mali, Benin, Mauritius, Botswana, and South Africa enjoy the greatest press freedom according to an assessment by the *Press Freedom Survey, Freedom House of 1999*, while the press is least free in countries such as Sudan, Equatorial Guinea, the Democratic Republic of Congo, Sierra Leone, and so on. In general, the broadcast media is subject to more legal restrictions than the print media.

## Civil Society

The word "civil" is derived from the root *civicus*, indicating a diversity of people living together peacefully (a city). The city represents a qualitative evolution from what initially was a small, primary, heterogeneous community, where everybody did basically the same thing and where solidarity was based on similarity. A city has both diversity and organic solidarity, based on mutual interdependence. This is the beginning of civil society.

Civil society, therefore, is connected to the urban community and implies the coexistence of individuals who are able to find ways of resolving differences and disputes. As such, civil society can be traced back to the beginning of the city, the metropolis, and its diversity. The idea as a concept along with the "social contract theorists" appeared in the 17th century. The basic notion is that solidarity is a contractual relationship, between individuals or between different groups, or between groups and the state. In the 17th and 18th centuries, it was fashionable to talk about the social contract and it was then that Locke, Hobbes, and Rousseau all developed their own conceptions of civil society. While Hobbes argued that once a state is formed, it is supreme, Locke, Rousseau, and other libertarians believed that the state must always be held accountable to civil society.

Conceptually speaking, civil society has the following three ancestral traditions:

- The social contract theorists (17th-20th century) Locke, Rousseau, Weber, Puttman, Fukuyama, and others, whose idea is that civil society is the product of free will, that part of that free will is the formation of the state, and that the state, therefore, has to remain accountable to civil society.
- The second tradition is based on the idea that the state is formed by the initial free will of the people, but once the state is in place it reins supreme, and everything is abdicated to the state. This notion runs all the way from Hobbes to Fascism, populism, and Arafatism.
- The third conception is represented by Marx and Gramsci, who make a distinction between the civil and political societies: whereas civil society

influences indirectly through social formation, the political community is the state, the police, the naked aspect of domination.

There is no doubt as to the importance of civil society in building popular support for democracy. Civil society countervailing forces are needed to monitor the compliance of new regimes. They can be instrumental in helping to change the way societies function, and break the patterns of clientelism and neopatrimonialism that threaten new democracies.

Civil society organizations can complement political parties in promoting understanding of democracy and participation in the political process. They can serve as a training ground for future political leaders, and promote political tolerance and inclusion. They can help to manage conflict and overcome societal cleavages, as well as to promote human rights and democratic values. Civil society organizations have a particular role to play in challenging corruption and promoting accountability and transparency.

The challenge for democratizing African countries is to create conditions conducive to the growth of the sort of civil society institutions that can effectively play these roles. This, like democracy itself, will take time. Though varying in degree, authoritarian single-party regimes generally sought to suppress or co-opt civil society and organized associational life. As a result, the civil society institutions that provide a countervailing force to government and limit the bounds of state interaction were few and fragile in most countries prior to the onset of political liberalization. Yet, in spite of weaknesses, much of the impetus for change in Africa came from civil society. In many instances, civil society organizations were the voices of conscience that kept the ideals of democracy alive. When political organizations were unable to function, they helped to create the conditions for democracy, often at great cost.

This contribution notwithstanding, in most countries the ability of civil society to support the institutionalization of democracy is somewhat ambivalent. Given their relative newness, some organizations of civil society are based on personalities, while others serve narrow interest groups. Not all nongovernmental organizations are either genuinely representative or democratic. Some, especially those that played a role in bringing about political transition, find it hard to adapt to changed circumstances. In spite of the difficulties, however, throughout the continent there has been an expansion of civic activism, and an increasing number of organizations are engaged in providing the civic education and awareness that will help democracy take root.

## Parliaments

The factors that drive a legislature's role in lawmaking and oversight processes are: the extent of its formal powers; the adequacy of the capacity provided by its procedures/structures/support; the amount of political space/discretion afforded by other power holders (executives, parties); and the goals of the members and leaders of the legislative bodies themselves.

## Formal Legislative Powers

What is the scope and extent of a legislature's power to enact laws? In some systems legislators have a monopoly on the right to introduce legislation directly, while in others legislators can only consider proposals originated in the executive. There is also variation in the range of options in shaping legislation (amendment, rejection, referral back to executive branch), in the finality of legislative passage (executive veto powers and override possibilities and requirements), and the impact of legislative rejection or inaction (including the possibility of executives ruling by decrees that have the force of law). An important subset of lawmaking powers is the extent of a legislature's influence over taxing and spending. These range from having a monopoly over the origination and passage of such measures to pro forma approval powers over these decisions made elsewhere.

Finally, there is the degree to that a legislature can influence the promulgation of administrative regulations that interpret statutes and the judicial review process which might pass on the meaning and validity of laws. Legislatures range from being relatively weak in formal powers to quite strong. Most people realize that strong formal powers do not guarantee an influential legislature. Among the other factors that shape degree of influence are those discussed later?

## Capacity

Formal powers mean little if a legislature lacks the capacity to use them. The rise of many American state legislatures as effective bodies beginning in the 1960s, for example, came with investments in capacity building. The extent of capacity can be gauged in a number of areas. There are variations in capacity for management of process (referral, dispositions, scheduling and limiting debate, etc.) and degree of internal complexity (level of effectiveness of committee system, respect for specialization/expertise, deference to committee decisions, etc.).

In addition, there are differences in the extent to which there is an adequate administrative structure to support the above activities. Is there, for example, a system to meet the unique information needs of legislators that blends the technical/analytic/policy components of decisions with the political consequences/prospects/opportunities presented?

## Political Space

When a legislature gains influence, it usually means that others have lost a measure of control. An important determinant of how much power a legislature can exercise, then, is the extent to which other important power holders—most importantly executives and parties— cede, lose, share, exchange, or let slip the power they hold. The range is wide, with authoritarian systems on one end (autocratic executives, hierarchical-disciplined parties) providing little political space, to more pluralistic and competitive systems providing more. The gradient in between is wide, and a lot of parliamentary assertiveness occurs in apparently unlikely circumstances. Uganda, for example, has a strong president, but is developing a more assertive parliament.

## Political Will

A final consideration has to do with what the leaders and members of a parliament want to do. While formal powers and the factors that drive the general limits of political space often change slowly if at all, a number of parliaments have changed markedly due to leaders and members choosing to exercise their formal powers more aggressively and to exploit openings in political space as they occur. Recent leadership efforts at parliamentary reform and assertiveness in Zimbabwe, for example, are reshaping the lawmaking process to give Parliament an earlier, more extensive, and more public say in a system where the executive originates laws and in which a single party Zimbabwe African National Union-Patriotic Front (ZANU-PF) dominates.

Both the role and function of parliaments in Africa are changing rapidly as a result of political liberalization. How parliaments discharge their responsibilities will influence the trajectory of political transition and determine how well the political system operates. In many countries parliaments and parliamentarians are increasingly asserting their independence and acting as a check on executive power. However, they face a number of constraints, not least prevailing political structures that continue to favor the executive at the expense of the legislature, and the legacy of patronage politics and the personalization of political power. For the most part, the effective functioning of parliaments is also hampered by lack of resources, insufficient technical expertise, and limited culture of democracy or experience of competitive politics.

The political environment in which parliaments function should be conducive. Otherwise, neither mechanisms nor procedures to promote accountability and increased technical capacity will result in greater effectiveness. In most African countries, political tolerance and the idea of shared responsibility for governance are only now being learned, and the role of the parliamentary opposition is still not well-understood. In many instances, while minority parties have to understand their role and undertake it effectively, the executive and ruling party also needs to recognize the legitimacy of minority parties. Clear lines of authority, separation of powers, and parliamentary independence are necessary even where the ruling party has a significant majority.

As elsewhere in the world with the exception of Scandinavia, women remain generally underrepresented in parliaments and in political life in African countries. In most cases, politics and political decisionmaking still tend to be male-dominated, and women often face considerable cultural constraints. Those countries, such as South Africa, that have made the most progress in terms of increasing the numbers of women have tended to adopt special arrangements such as quota systems, although not necessarily through legislation. However, such arrangements are at best temporary compensatory measures, and the fundamental constraints to women's participation in the political process still need to be addressed.

Political scientists often make the generalization that ineffective assemblies—serving as "rubber stamps" in approving decisions made elsewhere or "caves of the winds" given more to venting than governing—are the most common type of legislature. There is, nevertheless, a significant and growing group of legislatures that function as important governing partners because they represent constituencies, shape laws, and exercise a degree of oversight or control over the executive. Performing these functions contributes to good government by increasing its capacity to monitor and respond to public sentiments/dissatis-factions, by playing a part in passing legislation capable of withstanding critical scrutiny, and serving as a vehicle for improving the degree of probity, efficiency, and responsiveness in the administration of laws. While these functions are important singly, performing representation, lawmaking, and oversight func-tions in tandem is also important.

### Representation

Where they function, legislatures are useful nerve endings of the polity in the sense that they are often the branch of government to which popular complaints/dissatisfactions/demands for action are first articulated. This is so because legislatures typically operate with greater transparency or at least with less secrecy, in comparison with either the judicial or executive agencies.

They are diverse in their memberships (usually designed to represent a broader range of interests/characteristics/places) from which a first hearing and early support may be gained. Constituents have greater access; they are often more likely to feel that they have a claim on a representative than on other government officials. And legislative proceedings are often organized to maximize public attention to particular controversies and to offer participation opportunities ranging from contacting individual representatives to organized hearings.

Not surprisingly, a common legislative role is as an arena for the articula-tion of societal differences over policy. The richer the information environment surrounding legislatures—the vitality of the civil society and the vibrancy of member relationships with constituents—the greater the flow of these senti-ments into the consciousness of those who run the government.

### Lawmaking

Representing the public means more than articulating citizen preferences; it also involves having a say in translating preferences into policy through enact-ing legislation. The representative and lawmaking functions coexist in an uneasy but necessary relationship. Lawmaking requires reconciling of differences once articulated, as well as pressing the legislature's claim to power against the execu-tive and other powerholders, such as political parties. This requires legislative processes capable of reconciling conflicts and bringing to bear enough expertise to be taken seriously by the executive branch and other actors in the system.

In most legislative bodies, the workhorses of this portion of the process are committees. The more effective committee systems simultaneously provide arenas for expressing differences and environments, which foster compromise and decision. Where committee deliberations are important in shaping the behavior of the whole legislature, committee members have power incentives to specialize and to become both advocates of popular positions and develop negotiating skills to shape outcomes. And when a committee system is comprised of specialized bodies, capable of effectively considering legislation in their own areas, the whole legislature develops the capacity to deal with the executive branch across a wide range of topics in sufficient depth to be serious governing partners.

## The Judiciary and Rule of Law

Promoting adherence to the rule of law is a major challenge for many fledgling democracies in Africa and elsewhere. The temptation is to mistake "legal order"(what pleases the ruler(s) is law) for the rule of law (a constraint on government power).Yet it is essential for a predictable, stable environment in which citizens are both informed of their rights and have confidence that they will be protected. As events in other regions of the world have shown, without rule of law, good governance is virtually impossible. Reestablishing rule of law is especially difficult in countries coming out of conflict, while crime and corruption pose particular threats to fragile democracies.

With few exceptions, African countries need to improve their justice systems to foster public confidence. In general throughout the continent, qualified members of the legal profession are in short supply, legal access is limited, civil security and policing are ineffective, and the court system is poorly developed. In some countries concerted action to combat corruption in the legal sector is also needed.

Judicial independence helps to promote rule of law. However, this is relatively weak in the majority of newly democratizing countries where political interference remains common and many serving members of the legal profession are accustomed to unquestioning deference to the state, rather than to upholding constitutional principles and protecting the legal rights of citizens. A number of democratizing countries retain—and some still use—repressive legislation that needs to be revised to make it consistent with constitutional provisions designed to protect individual rights and freedoms.

In some countries, civil liberties have increased, but political freedom remains constrained. In others, restrictions that were eased in the early days of political transition have been imposed again. At times, laws have been passed with the specific intent of penalizing a particular individual or group of individuals, and legislation governing elections and political parties has not always been fairly applied.

## Military and Security Establishments

Given its past involvement in politics, the military is an important variable in the institutionalization of democracy in most African countries. Its support cannot be automatically assumed, and like other stakeholders it has to be brought into the process of political transition. Military and security establishments suffered from the same decline as other state institutions under single-party rule.

Over time in some African countries, professionalism and meritocracy gave way to patronage and corruption, while in others ethnicity and group identity became defining issues. There were exceptions, and in countries such as Botswana, Malawi, Zimbabwe, and Senegal the military retained its status as an independent, apolitical body, focused on its professional mission. At the other extreme, regime change through military coups became part of the political landscape, particularly in West Africa, where military governments entrenched themselves in a number of countries.

Like other institutions in democratizing countries, the military now has to adapt to new circumstances and define its role in a more open and participatory system of governance. Civilian oversight of the military is a central feature of democratic governments, but this will require that elected officials themselves behave in a democratic manner, as well as develop a greater understanding of security issues and defense policy and budgeting than has often been the case. In some countries, military establishments need to be more inclusive and broadly representative of society in terms of ethnicity and religious affiliation.

In most instances, nondiscriminatory recruitment practices, transparent systems of promotion, and clear limitations of discretionary power need to be instituted. The mission of the military also needs to be clearly understood by both the military and society as a whole. Partly as a result of past experiences, civil-military relations in the majority of African countries—even those that have not experienced military rule—are characterized by distrust, lack of understanding, and misconceptions. Engendering public confidence in the military is a significant challenge for democratically minded governments.

## Promoting Peaceful Political Succession

Democracy promotes the orderly, peaceful political succession that has not yet become the norm throughout Africa. It does not necessarily result in political alternation, although it provides the basis for it. In a number of established democracies, including Sweden, Germany, and the United Kingdom, ruling parties have retained power through successive elections. In others, such as Switzerland and the Netherlands, the same parties have been represented and the same individuals have served in consecutive coalition governments.

In the United States, although term limits apply to presidents, there are many long-serving members of Congress. However, in these countries political competition is preserved because the institutional basis for free and fair elections, and thus for the people to exercise their will, exists. Alternation of power, or the lack of it, is the free and fair choice of the electorate.

Political alternation as a result of competitive elections has been rare in Africa since the onset of democratization. Rather, the overwhelming advantages of incumbency, fragmentation of the opposition, and high cost of political campaigning have often combined to minimize genuine political contestation. Furthermore, with few exceptions, power sharing is not generally part of the prevailing political culture.

Political parties and electoral systems that facilitate political inclusion and participation are the primary vehicles for ensuring political competition and orderly political succession through the ballot box. Most countries have embraced the concept of multiparty elections. However, developing the structures that ensure a competitive political environment takes time. Important variables are the willingness of incumbent parties to allow free and fair elections and to accept the results, and the ability of opposition parties to unite their efforts.

## Political Parties

African states are not well served if majority parties are so predominant that political alternation or power sharing are essentially impossible. Throughout the continent, greater political freedom has resulted in an increased number of political parties. However, the balance of power remains heavily tilted in favor of incumbents in almost all instances. How political parties are formed and function affects their ability to effectively facilitate representation and participation in the process of governance. In many African countries, both ruling and minority parties need to learn how to function in a competitive political environment if traditions of political exclusion and patronage are to be overcome. Like political parties everywhere in the world, those in African countries will also have to ensure that women and minority groups are afforded greater opportunities for participation.

Moreover, in many cases, both ruling and minority parties need to institute more transparent and accountable operating procedures, and practice internal democracy. While the majority of democratizing countries have passed legislation to discourage party formation along specifically ethnic, regional, or religious lines, recently established parties often lack a broad-based constituency.

Given the newness of competitive politics, many political parties and candidates are still developing political organization skills, and relatively few have managed to define distinct political platforms or build support outside of urban areas. Some, though not all, have the overthrow and replacement of incumbent regimes as their overriding motive. In some instances governments also place limitations on political party activities, making it difficult for minority parties to function adequately.

Although a number of factors limit political participation and competition, access to financial resources is perhaps one of the most significant. Most political parties in Africa do not have a broad support base of individual financial and volunteer contributions to draw upon. The relative shallowness of the private sector also reduces the potential for obtaining corporate funding. Given that government contracts continue to provide a lucrative share of business in most countries, there is an incentive for private firms to support ruling parties. Parties outside of government complain that ruling parties divert public funds for campaign purposes, while ruling parties at times argue that NGOs are established to receive donor funds that are then channeled into support for opposition parties. In some instances, newly formed parties rely on a limited number of wealthy patrons, while their founders largely fund others. Political parties have also at times attempted to establish business ventures to generate resources, but this can lead to serious conflict of interest, particularly when the parties are in government.

Debates over political party funding continue throughout the continent. Although many advocate public funding of political parties, others argue that African countries cannot afford to use public funds for this purpose. In some instances there is little popular support for public financing of political parties. Additionally, unease has been expressed that governments resisting reform could use state funding to create new parties to fragment and thus weaken the opposition.

However, a number of countries have successfully provided limited public resources to political parties on the basis of seats obtained in elections. This has reduced concerns that nonviable parties would be formed around elections in order to obtain funds. Whether or not public resources are provided, greater transparency of funding procedures, together with more stringent disclosure and accounting requirements, would go a long way to addressing real or perceived problems surrounding party financing. Control and supervisory mechanisms also need to be applied to ruling, as well as to minority, parties.

## Elections and Electoral Systems

Political leaders throughout the continent have succumbed to pressure for elections, and even those who came to power through nondemocratic or extraconstitutional means have tried to legitimize their regimes through elections. The openness and integrity of the process has, however, frequently been questioned and unequivocally free and fair elections are not yet the norm. In established democracies, elections are a basic mechanism for ensuring accountability, in that the possibility of being voted out of office acts as an incentive to respect rules. In fledging democracies however, they can play a more ambiguous role, and in some instances, flawed elections have served to undermine public confidence in the electoral process.

Ensuring equitable representation and participation in the political process is a concern even in established democracies that have over time developed a variety of mechanisms and structures designed to facilitate it. To date, no perfect electoral system has been developed, and debates continue as to the relative merits of proportional representation, plurality-majority, or hybrid systems. African countries, like others elsewhere, have to adopt electoral and parliamentary systems that best meet their needs. However, if democratic politics are to be sustained and a political culture supportive to democracy built, such systems should facilitate political inclusion and encourage the formation of representative parliaments, responsive to the needs of all citizens. Transparent and honest elections, managed by competent electoral commissions, would help to build credibility in the electoral process.

Proportional representation can assure losing parties with a share of seats in parliament commensurate with the percentage of the vote won, and thus broadens the base of representation. The list system also allows members of different groups to be represented. The disadvantage is that parliamentarians do not belong to specific districts or identify with the needs of specific populations. There is also the danger of splintering of parties, many of which have narrow bases, and as a consequence, stable government is not necessarily ensured. On the other hand, plurality-majority systems have the advantages of ensuring that representatives have a responsibility to their constituents. They encourage the formation of broad-based parties, single-party governments, and a clear parliamentary opposition. They also facilitate the election of independent candidates. However, minority parties are not necessarily awarded seats commensurate with their share of the vote. Moreover, parties can rely on a regional vote, while such systems are also vulnerable to manipulation of electoral boundaries.

Whatever the electoral system, the cost of elections and election campaigns throughout the continent have to be brought to manageable levels, if elections are to be sustained without massive external support. In many African countries the costs of campaigning are very high compared to their level of economic development and available resources—indeed, they are often as high as in much richer countries. Political campaigning is often expensive because of widely dispersed rural populations, poor transportation and communications, and limited media coverage. In some cases, however, campaign costs are driven up by traditions and expectations of political patronage, which not only distort the political process, but also increase public tolerance of corruption. The high cost of campaigning also effectively undermines political competition by excluding those who are unable to access sufficient resources. These are obviously not issues for Africa alone. Countries throughout the world grapple with problems of political corruption, party contributions, and the cost of campaign financing.

In Africa, proponents of state funding of political campaigns argue that this is the surest way of ensuring a level playing field and guarding against political corruption, at least in the early days of democratic transition. Others, however, counter that African countries are too poor and have too many demands on already limited resources to provide public funding for election campaigns. It is not only a matter of whether and how to provide state funding for political campaigns, but also of establishing parameters covering both the source and amount of contributions, and the use of public resources.

A legislated upper limit on the amount that can be spent on political campaigns could help to control the cost of election campaigns and broaden the pool of candidates. Measures to ensure appropriate and frequent access to media channels by all parties would guarantee a degree of public exposure at a fixed cost. There is also need for better monitoring and accounting of campaigns. In many instances, lack of proper records and audited accounts make the actual costs of campaigns and the source of funds difficult to accurately assess.

## Political Alternation

Attempts by incumbents to remain in office are not confined to Africa. Throughout the world, those with political power want to retain it. In established democracies, observance of rules and the strength of political institutions ensure that constitutional provisions are observed and the results of competitive elections accepted. There are also opportunities for former political leaders to remain engaged in public affairs or pursue other career choices.

The entrenchment of incumbents appears to be particularly pronounced in Africa and countries elsewhere that lack a tradition of competitive politics, offer few alternatives to political power, and where democratic institutions are relatively weak. Asia and the former Soviet Union provide multiple examples of incumbent regimes either refusing to embark on political transition or trying to manipulate and control the process to remain in power. Institutional mechanisms, such as the presidential term limits that are now becoming more widespread in Africa, help to ensure political alternation. So, too, do policies that provide for leadership change within political parties.

The need for committed and competent leadership is at the heart of the debate about democratization. To a significant degree, poor leadership was responsible for the crisis of governance and resulting popular alienation that characterized many African countries in the recent past. Frequently, single-party regimes vested too much political and economic power in the head of state. Highly personalized politics, coupled with lack of mechanisms to ensure accountability, led to a culture of impunity. Once in office, leaders tended to remain there, unless they were violently overthrown or removed by a military takeover. Long-serving heads of state and political figures became a defining feature of many postindependence African regimes.

Perpetual incumbency is in part a reflection of the prevailing understanding of political authority, how it is acquired, and how it is exercised. In newly democratizing countries throughout the world this understanding is often colored by a legacy of neopatrimonial regimes. As such, public office often appears to serve a deeper "functional" or rentier purpose for incumbents, and voluntary resignation is synonymous with economic suicide and loss of the ability to play patron in a patrimonial culture. This is reinforced by the paucity of alternatives to political power in most countries. Given the still-predominant role of the government in the economy and society of many African countries, and the lack of viable alternatives, the stakes of gaining or losing political power are extraordinarily high. This notwithstanding, political leaders have a particular role in facilitating orderly succession by encouraging the development of future leaders and, by their example, promoting the turnover of leadership in government and political party structures.

In Africa, peaceful political succession in the context of competitive politics, albeit with a dominant party, has occurred in countries such as Botswana, Senegal, and Tanzania. To date, very few elections have resulted in regime change. Indeed, the defining characteristic of elections throughout the continent is that the existing political order has been retained. Elections, without the institutions and political culture that uphold democracy, can be subject to manipulation, and in some African countries have served to endorse nondemocratic regimes and prolong the tenure of autocratic rulers. In other instances, elections brought about a change in government, but the countries subsequently experienced a decline in civil liberties or, as in Sierra Leone, instability and armed conflict. Only in a few countries—Mauritius, Benin, and Madagascar—have the two peaceful transitions, generally regarded as a benchmark for democracy, been achieved. However, there are tremendous variations within the group of countries that have experienced elections without a transfer of power. The levels of political freedom and good governance enjoyed in countries such as Botswana and Ghana stand in stark contrast to those pertaining in Sudan, Equatorial Guinea, or Togo.

A central issue is whether the institutional basis for political alternation exists. Lack of genuine opportunities for alternation presents a problem to African political development and to the consolidation of democracy. It is both a cause and a consequence of the predominance of personality-driven politics. It also inhibits the development of stable political institutions. And it is often a source of the violent conflicts that engulf succession and power alternation on the continent. It breeds frustration among political reformers and opposition parties over the possibility of political change. It helps to create disillusionment with the democratization project and to induce doubts over its suitability and sustainability in African conditions. In addition, without alternation of power, it is difficult, if not impossible, to test the durability of democratic arrangements and institutions.

In order for African democratic transitions to be put on a sustained course toward consolidation, the politically debilitating cycles of perpetual incumbency and violent change in leadership have to be overcome and orderly political succession and peaceful power alternation made a regular aspect of political practice. With a new generation of elected leaders nearing the end of their constitutionally allowed terms, the issue of how to transition incumbent leaders out of power has become most salient for some democratizing countries. Other countries are faced with the more difficult problem of how to deal with leaders who came to power and served in nondemocratic regimes, and who have not embraced political transition. While some such political leaders may willingly step down, others may be reluctant to relinquish power out of fear of reprisals for previous actions. In some instances incentives to relinquish power, including amnesties, may be appropriate, while in others this could be seen as rewarding past wrongs.

Orderly political succession through the ballot box and peaceful alternation of power are the hallmarks of effective democratization. In African countries over time, a liberal constitution, an appropriate legal framework, and a vibrant civil society, as well as a political culture of trust, tolerance, and moderation, should provide a sufficient basis for regular political succession and peaceful alternation of power. But in the interim, and especially in countries where the tendency is toward confrontation rather than compromise, public discussion of how political succession could best be promoted may be useful. Dialogue and negotiation could dispel misconceptions, help decide on the desirability and feasibility of various options for accountability and justice, and generate consensus over retirement benefits for ex-leaders. Public consideration of how the issue has been addressed in other African and non-African countries could also help to focus attention on realistic and feasible solutions.

## Role and Status of Former Leaders

In Africa, elders are viewed with respect as repositories of societal wisdom. They are never reduced to ossified museum pieces (Nursing Homes) for tourists. Their place must be respected in any African democratic process. Since the onset of political transition, positive examples of peaceful political succession and of leaders relinquishing political power are increasing. In Tanzania, presidential term limits were adhered to without question by President Hassan Mwinyi. Presidents Jerry Rawlings of Ghana and Frederick Chiluba of Zambia, stepped down at the end of their terms of office. Among others, President Kenneth Kaunda in Zambia, President Aristides Pereira of Cape in Verde and both Presidents Mathieu Kérékou and President Nicephore Soglo in Benin accepted the outcomes of elections that resulted in their leaving office. In Mali, President Toumani Touré, the head of the transitional government, did not stand for election, and in Nigeria the military head of state, President Abdulsalami Abubakar, maintained his resolve to hand over to an elected civilian president. Most notably, perhaps, President Nelson Mandela of South Africa and President Ketumile Masire of Botswana—both highly popular presidents—voluntarily stepped down.

This new trend in African politics raises questions of the role and status of former leaders, as well as the support provided to them. One of the hallmarks of functioning democracies is that provision for political leaders once they leave office is both made and respected. This stands in contrast to the tendency since independence for former leaders in Africa, whether they are virtuous or vicious, and regardless of constitutional indemnities and other settlements, to suffer marginalization, vilification, humiliation, persecution, and even at times imprisonment and death by execution. With democratization, there is increasing recognition that those incumbent leaders who accept democratic change should be eligible for the same sort of benefits, privileges, and protections that former heads of state and government in other countries enjoy.

Many African countries have made constitutional and legal provisions for former heads of state. While the provisions in countries as diverse as Botswana, Central African Republic, Tanzania, Madagascar, Senegal, Mozambique, and South Africa vary, at a minimum they guarantee former presidents security, provide them with diplomatic privileges and immunities, and make some arrangement for their material well-being. There is obviously an issue as to the cost of retirement packages. Reaching agreement on the degree to which the financial and material needs of former leaders and their dependents will be met by the state is part of the democratization process. Whatever arrangements are instituted should be linked to the office, and not to individual incumbents. Moreover, stipulating such provisions in constitutions provides some protection against future reversals.

Although former political leaders in established democracies can be assured of a reasonable income from other sources after leaving office, the options for African leaders are somewhat more limited. Retirement pensions thus have to be sufficiently generous to maintain a certain standard of living for former leaders and their dependents. There have been suggestions that in some cases it may be necessary for payments indexed to inflation to be made in foreign currency by internationally respected banks, but this is obviously a matter for individual countries to decide. In addition to pensions, most countries have made some provision for the housing, representation, health care, and transportation needs of former leaders and their immediate families. Security, diplomatic privileges, and protocol arrangements are also commonly provided. These provisions are intended not only to assure political leaders that their future well-being will be protected, but also to express gratitude and respect for the function of the head of state.

In some countries, democratization has raised questions of accountability for the past actions of political leaders. These are complex issues that can affect the course of political transition, in that incumbents could be reluctant to leave office if they feel they will be punished for past deeds. At the same time, although former presidents should not be above the law, nor should they be vulnerable to arbitrary punishment or politically motivated legal action. All African constitutions limit the criminal responsibility of sitting presidents, but none rule it out entirely. Those that make provision for serving presidents to be indicted only for treason confer the broadest immunity. In most countries it is less clear whether presidents can be prosecuted for offenses committed outside the exercise of official duties while in office, or whether former presidents can be indicted for acts committed in the exercise of official duties while in office. Constitutions generally consider amnesty and pardon to be extrajudicial procedures that can be granted to former presidents in respect of acts committed during the term of office. Such measures can be useful in support of national reconciliation, particularly in the transition to democratic rule.

In addition to security and material needs, some countries try to assure former political leaders continued recognition, status, and involvement in public life. This provides an opportunity for them to contribute to the process of democratization and its consolidation in their respective countries and regions as well as on the continent as a whole. In order to avoid controversy, the formal roles retired leaders play and the status afforded to them should perhaps be constitutionally and legally determined, although in most established democracies the status of former heads of state has been resolved through practice rather than constitutional provision. Varieties of models from African as well as other countries exist for both formal and informal roles. In some instances, provision is made for former leaders to serve in official and constitution-based advisory bodies such as Benin's Council of Elders that comprises all surviving former presidents, or Guinea's constitutionally mandated Economic Council. In those Latin American countries where upper legislative chambers exist, constitutions commonly provide for former presidents to be appointed as Senators for life.

Throughout the world, former leaders take on informal roles as advisors, counselors, members of prestigious boards of corporations and large/international nongovernmental organizations. Foundations, think tanks, universities, and organizations can provide a forum for retired political leaders to write their memoirs and/ or engage themselves in a project. The options for this in Africa are relatively few at present. The international arena also provides a number of examples of very high-profile successful postincumbency engagements to draw upon—for instance, the former president of Ireland and the former prime minister of Norway both currently hold high-level United Nations posts. Some former African heads of state and senior political figures have built significant international reputations since leaving office. Others have formed their own voluntary organizations or associated themselves with established bodies. Mwalimu Julius Nyerere, General Amadou Toumani Touré, President Abdulsalami Abubakar, and Sir Ketumile Masire are all highly regarded for their international work and as elder statesmen, as was President Olusegun Obasanjo before his return to politics. Now that he has left government, there is no doubt that Nelson Mandela will also take his place as an eminent elder statesman.

While the option chosen for a postincumbency role depends largely on the temperament and expertise of the former leader, more opportunities need to be made available for them to contribute positively to the development of the continent. Possibilities include functioning in advisory capacities in regional groupings such as the Economic Community of West African States and the Southern African Development Cooperation, in keeping with the role played, for example, by elder statesmen and political leaders in promoting regional cooperation in Europe. Other opportunities exist in election observation and in economic integration affairs. Additionally, a foundation or other center could perhaps be established to serve as a clearinghouse for matching expertise and particular talents with regional or international needs, and for providing former leaders with the staff and resources to undertake assignments. The General Cooperation Agency could explore the possibilities, including the financial implications, of establishing such a center.

There is a need, more than ever before, for Africans to rid their lives of ignorance, fear, and other complexes that have turned a noble race into a slave-enduring, poverty-managing, inferiority-complex-inducing, powerlessness-adjusting, and hopelessness-accepting mentality. As long as Africans subject themselves to the business or project of integration into the heinous, inhuman, and unsustainable economic global order and its corresponding artificially constructed and antipeople democratic practices, so long shall the on-going pathetic state of Africans continue. The present pathetic state of the African, with a badly wounded, mangled, and trampled human dignity and at present classified as a third-rated people in the comity of nations, needs the attention and concern of every living African.

Africans need untainted knowledge and a clearer insight into the global arrangement of political, economic, and social institutions before they throw themselves headlong at any democratic institution on offer. The idea of imitating Western institutions or parroting after western experts in our drive to bring progress, prosperity, and social development to Africa without a good understanding of the spirit that moves the Western world is to consign Africa to the third-rated position of the world forever. We need to have known by now that aping the West or the Middle East in matters of governance and institutional arrangements of politics and economics can never emancipate Africa from its lowly and beleaguered position.

The current global democratic practices seem to favor the shenanigans of the dishonorable members of all societies. Democracy tends to give the hoodlums an easy access to plan and execute electoral fraud or electoral *coups d'état* in every country. There seems to be a real confusion among the larger population as regards the concept of democracy and the democratic practice of party electioneering. The secret powers running the affairs of this world seem to have sold a political dummy to the entire world. By equating democracy with political party activities and most disastrously around money power, they have succeeded in perverting the noble ideas behind the Greek democracy.

As it were, it seems what the world celebrates as democracy is actually the celebration of money. In other words, democracy today is the immortalization of the power of Mammon. Now, everywhere in the world and under the pretence of democracy, criminal gangs are mopping up governments. No nation seems capable of defending itself from the evil fangs of the political hoodlums as they cleverly entrench themselves in the machinery of government dictating inimical policies of greed and avarice that will eventually ruin this world.

Democratic practices and institutions as configured at present in the world have failed to prevent the parasites, psychopaths, and miscreants of the world from taking over national governments. As a result, democratic practice in every country is disenfranchising the noble people while welcoming into its fold all the privileged criminals of societies or their puppets. In every country, the true honorable people have been frightened off from partaking in the democratic processes. The premeditated and orchestrated hooliganism sponsored and organized by the godless moneymen and -women has left the coast clear for the hoodlums and dishonorable people to hijack the institutions of government for nefarious activities. The truth of the matter is that democratic practices as now undertaken in Africa and even in most parts of the world can no longer produce honorable men and women for elective offices. This fundamental problem of governance needs the attention of all supporters of democracy.

Held Together by Pins

If indeed the scenario painted above is true, what shall the awakened Africans do? There is a need for the intelligentsia of Africa to look again at the concept and practice of democracy afresh. It is glaring that the democratic institutions now under construction all over Africa under the auspices of the World Bank, International Monetary Fund, and multinational conglomerates cannot serve the human needs of Africans. These convoluted and impracticable types of democracy are other forms of colonialist impositions meant to serve the national interest of the Western nations. If so, how long shall Africa continue to play the fool?

## PATRIARCHY, GENDER, AND DEMOCRACY

According to Johan Galtung (1996: 40),

> Patriarchy is seen as an institutionalization of male dominance in vertical structures, with very high correlations between position and gender, legitimized by culture (e.g. religion and language), and often emerging as direct violence with males as subjects and women as objects. Patriarchy...combines direct, structural and cultural violence in a vicious triangle. They reinforce each other in cycles starting from any corner.

The persistence of cultural and traditional practices that ensure that women continue to be construed as property by males through the heterosexual marriage ritual in particular (which is very authentically African), and the continued use of social status laws that are couched as customary law and practice and where they serve to locate women outside the sphere of modern systems of rights and jurisprudence, are clear expressions of an archaic patriarchy that in many instances was preserved by the colonial state and jealously guarded by the patriarchs of African society today.

Almost without exception, all historical narratives about African women pose them as wives/daughters or mothers. It is rare to locate a history about Africa before colonization that posits women as autonomous beings, having an agency of their own, and exercising their rights as citizens and crafters of the African reality. The exceptions may be as queen mothers and rulers who were constantly shadowed by "wise and knowing" males.

Therefore, the claims that African societies were gender-fair and cognizant of women in their right as citizens and persons are fraught with historical contradictions and are really images of romantic notions about the past. This is not to say that all African women were slaves without any kind of mobility or social recognition. However, there is little if any countervailing evidence to show that women existed in communities that granted them their rights as thinking and knowing beings. They never got outside of the very narrow confines of their domestic/reproductive roles.

## Power and Democracy as Historically Exclusionary Practices

Power and notions of freedom and justice have remained deeply class based and androcentric. They are reflective of the opinions, options, and interests of ruling-class men. Color or location in spatial terms does not make any difference. And even when such systems aspire to be inclusive and socially expansive, they remain essentially exclusionary and patronizing of those who have been constructed as "other" in relation to power as the most critical resource in that society.

Across Africa men and women have struggled for the collective visions of freedom and justice. It is critical to acknowledge the opportunities that nationalist liberation struggles and anticolonial resistance provided to those groups that had been until then excluded from the public, for example women. The implications of nationalism as an ideology which is fundamentally sexist and exclusionary of women, particularly during the neocolonial period, must be critically evaluated. However, the very notion of the public space emerges as an expression of the development and existence of surplus pegged largely on the unpaid labor of women in the home and the unremunerated labor of enslaved communities in the wider society.

It is within this milieu of exchange that new relationships of property and power are played out in full view. These relationships are institutionalized in new structures that over time become known as the public—a space and a concept that reflect the new relations of production and civic interaction. It is here that the state and the key institutions of the society are located and dominated by men as a gender and as the owners of wealth—both material and social. Juxtaposed to the public space where men are free to roam, always of course in relation to their status, the notion of the private arises out of the definition of women as the private property of males, located in male- headed households. Even to date, women cannot form a family on their own, as a legal entity in all our societies. They have to marry men in order to create a legally and socially recognized unit called the family. Through rituals and practices that have become euphemistically understood as "cultural" and "traditional," women's capacities and abilities to labor and to reproduce are institutionalized in the patriarchal family as the private property of their fathers and husbands. It is at this interface between human creativity and the existence of surplus that the most crucial relationships of power and control become embedded, especially in relation to women.

Over time, women, like poor men and the young, become excluded from the resources that are located in the public, and a dualistic system of rules and regulations is formulated that has kept women largely in the private sector—working long hours without remuneration for their labor—which is one of the main reasons why women remain the poorest people in the world, and like the slaves, women have been excluded from the rights and civic entitlements that emerge out of the various struggles enacted in the public.

Therefore, while it is important to show the linkages between gender and poverty across the female/male divide, it is even more important to recognize that poor men have always had access to the public sphere, where they are able to engage in struggles for fairness and economic and social justice. On the contrary, women have remained largely tied to the private sphere where they continue to be treated as the slaves of men in the heterosexual family, even in the families of those men who struggle against economic enslavement.

In all societies across Africa, men have colluded to keep women out of the public sphere where rights and entitlements are located (we know that there are no rights in the family, only privileges and benevolent gestures and much violation, exclusion, and death), and even as one lauds the struggles against colonization, one often shies away from the acknowledgment that most black men colluded with the colonial state in the exclusion of black women from the cities and those sites where the possibility of becoming free was located. To date, even after almost half a century of independence, all African governments have retained the vicious sociolegal and coercive practices that exclude and suppress women and female children. These practices characterized feudal African societies and were further refined by the colonial state with the assistance of privileged African men. The present deinstitutionalization of traditional courts and traditional statuses in the political and legal systems of a country like South Africa speaks most tragically to this ongoing collusion between men of different classes and colors to exclude women from the democratic institutions and practices that women and men fought so courageously to build.

The maintenance of the public/private divide through claims of cultural authenticity and the need to hold onto so-called traditions that are basically practices and value systems that privilege men in the home and in the key institutions of African societies, has inhibited the greater participation of women in the transformation of Africa to the present day. Notions of what is political and public are still fundamentally tied to the claim that what women know and do is best suited to the production of use values for household consumption and the reproduction of the species. Even in societies where women have excelled as professionals and knowledge producers, they are faced with a continuous backlash, often premised on fundamentalist beliefs that so easily mobilize communities to participate in the undemocratic exclusion of women from their rights. One has only to look at the issue of taboos around the sexuality of women and how these taboos are perpetuated through fundamentalist claims that are centuries old and viciously misogynist. The traditions allow women to be raped and violated by claiming that women bring such violation upon themselves through the ways in which they dress and by the very nature of their female bodies as "unclean" and "sexually dangerous."

In all African societies one finds the blatant justification of the victimization of women by men in key positions—for example, within the judiciary, in organized religion, within families, and in social and cultural organizations, which deploy ancient patriarchal myths of exclusion and privatization to defend impunity. By impunity I mean the deliberate, socially sanctioned violation of rules and systems of human conduct that are the collective possession of a society, and that have been designated as the markers of human dignity. The notions of integrity and personhood lie at the core of human dignity and decency. One learns these from the moment one enters a human space. Every human being is born with the inalienable right to physical, emotional, and sexual integrity, and the nurturing process in all societies recognizes the importance not only of protecting the integrity of other human beings, particularly while they are young and vulnerable, but is also anchored on the transmission of these notions to the individual as untouchable and inalienable rights. This is why one abhors slavery and fights to the death to remain free.

Yet the very people who understand the centrality of human integrity as a civic right are often those who engage in and support practices and so-called customary laws that violate and undermine the physical, emotional, and sexual integrity of women and girls in the name of culture and male supremacy. This impunity, which lies at the heart of violation and social injustice in all societies, is embedded in the privatization of women within the key social and political, religious, and cultural institutions across this continent and the world at large.

Therefore it is critical to understand that inasmuch as the private/public divide, which has facilitated the construction of power in essentially class and masculinist terms within most societies, continues to be challenged and resisted by women's and other social movements, the major difficulty in making the political inclusive of everyone lies in the persistent exclusion of women as citizens. Unless one sees the interconnectedness of impunity as it is culturally, politically, economically, religiously, and legally framed and sanctioned, one cannot begin to respond effectively to the imperative of restructuring one's society in sustainable and democratic ways.

In other words, one has to see the culturalized expressions of impunity (through female genital mutilation, male child preferences, unfair eating practices, incest, witch-hunting, especially older women and widows, child marriages and coerced marriages, and feminized altruism) in order to debunk them and declare them criminal offenses against citizens in each and every instance. Only in this way can one begin to replace them with new democratic, life-enhancing cultural notions and practices.

Africans must reject outright (and not try to reform) those legal systems that are partial and often blatantly patriarchal: for example, the persistence of notions of male conjugal rights; refusals to recognize marital rape as a crime; allowance of polygamy and rampant sexual mobility; notions of paternity that define children as the property of the man rather than emphasizing the responsibilities and obligations of parenting in democratic family relationships; inheritance practices that allow men to inherit women as a form of property/ slaves of male-controlled families; and a myriad of injustices that are allowed to circulate and reproduce themselves through the often-deliberate misrepresentation and/or insistence by judicial officers that women cannot be considered persons in the ways that men are.

Africans must critique the exclusionary economic practices (which globalization is reinforcing and extending to every aspect of human life) that are deepening the immiseration of women and young people using the rhetoric of dog-eats-dog; dangerous claims that have become normative and naturalized as the only reality possible. How unthinkable that one could be living in a world where the narrow, sectarian claims of a voraciously greedy class could assume such public hegemony and go so largely unchallenged even by those who know that it is a blatant lie.

Africans have to make the personal political by transforming the meaning of politics from its current definition as men contesting power by any means, including and especially through the making of war and the use of critical resources at the expense of millions across this continent, while its citizens become refugees; nonpersons in flight, without any rights or securities. There is need to change to a notion and practice of politics that guarantees the rights and securities of all citizens, all the time. These past decades have brought a worsening situation in numerous African countries' fratricidal wars, as the African petite bourgeoisie finds itself less and less able to accumulate competitively with the ruling classes of the North. Africa has remained "economically marginal" in the capitalist global system. But Africa's resources and knowledge, for centuries, have fueled the "development" of Northern societies and proven to be crucial to the maintenance of their current notions of democracy.

However, for the African petite bourgeoisie, the crisis of reproduction has been intensified by the concentration of wealth globally in the hands of a smaller and smaller number of transnational corporations that are poised to take over the state in the North. They have recaptured and recolonized the state in Africa and in the rest of the South. The Multilateral Agreement on Investments agenda was precisely about that. It made capitalist privilege the ultimate priority in every sense of the word and deed. It is also clear that in the history of human existence, war has always been a means of class accumulation by those elements that occupy the state, a patriarchal state that ensures the privilege and supremacist ideologies and systems of a small group over the rights and entitlements of the vast majority.

Today there is coincidence of globalized class interests with those of an African ruling class in almost every African theater of war. The generals are consolidating their class statuses by looting national treasuries and extending the arenas of war and destruction across national and regional boundaries, as in the Great Lakes region of Africa. A restructuring of the relationships within and among the ruling factions that occupy and use the African patriarchal state is clearly visible when one looks at the ongoing devastation of the Congo and the parties involved in that debacle. In Sierra Leone, Eritrea, Ethiopia, Angola, Rwanda, Burundi, Algeria, Sudan, Liberia, and Nigeria political violence has become the everyday tragedy of this most beautiful and unquestionably most bountiful continent on earth.

That is why the normalization of war through the militarization of African societies and regions, under the guise of so-called pan-Africanist rhetoric, is totally unacceptable and must be exposed for what it really is: the plunder and accumulative rampaging of gangs of middle-class bandits who openly defy the demands of the people for accountability and democratic responsibility. At this point in time, Africans have to fight to retain the very language of anti-imperialist resistance and to keep the memory of enslavement and colonization alive because it belongs to us all—always—until our worlds are no longer determined by racism, classism, sexism, fundamentalisms, and pernicious forms of sectarian ism and communalism. Certain groups of Africans are deploying a collective memory in the justification of an openly militaristic class project that is costing the lives of millions of Africans and has laid waste to great swaths of this continent. This nationalist opportunism must be exposed and the rights and security of the African citizen must become the most important priority of all. Africa can no longer allow selfish class interests to dominate and destroy a continent that belongs to all its peoples.

Africans have to find the courage to go beyond the hypocritical rhetoric of regional integration that in actual fact only facilitates greater accumulation by both national and global capitalist forces, at the expense of the basic human and social rights that African working people have fought so courageously to attain. The interface between class, gender, and racist/communalist interests is the site where the most critical and most productive contestation has to take place. One needs to understand the phenomenon of globalization, in its multifarious forms, as a restructuring of the old, hegemonic relationships of economic and political power, which are mobilizing technology, new notions of space and communication, and the political lapse in radical politics to make up for whatever was lost to Africans during decolonization and liberation struggles across the world.

## Women's Politics as Sustainable Alternative Political Vision

For centuries women have fought private and public battles to make the world safer for themselves and for those with whom they live, and it is this fundamentally inclusive epistemology that informs women's politics across the ideological and political divide within what is called the women's movement. This is where one of the most critical political resources to a different future lies. There are some of these political gems that are so often unseen or even misunderstood by so many progressive men in the workers' and youth movement in particular.

First and most fundamentally, women's struggles against patriarchy have made visible the intersectionality of all known forms of exclusion and oppression—racism, class exploitation, sexism and chauvinism, paternalism, ableism, and heterosexism. By rejecting all these expressions of injustice, women have brought together in a social movement for rights the totality of issues that underpin patriarchy as an ideology and a system of privilege for the few over the interests of the majority. Women's struggles have, for the first time in the human narrative, made visible the interconnectedness of all systems of injustice in ways that neither the struggles of workers or of poor people in general have done.

Second, by raising the essential issues of integrity and personhood, women's politics has challenged the bifurcated nature of notions of justice and equality at every level of their societies, rupturing the public/private divide that still keeps millions of women the world over outside those civic resources and spaces where rights are embedded and secured. The notion of rights is intimately linked with the demand for the social, economic, political, and legal recognition of human value by those whose labor and reproductive capacities were appropriated and exploited by the ruling class. Men who labored without pay came together to collectively demand the right to paid work and the recognition of their labor as valuable. It is in the valorization of human labor that the right to a dignified life becomes possible, and through a publicly recognized engagement with the market and the demand that profitmaking not be allowed to keep the worker enslaved to the owners of capital, workers have been able to win the rights that define them as a class in all our societies.

Through the demand that women's rights must become human rights, women have drawn from the struggles by workers and colonized people and are insisting that the notion of human rights itself is partial and unsustainable unless and until it encompasses fully (without a single cultural compromise) the total rights of women to physical, emotional, sexual, and social integrity as complete persons in all their societies. The demand for integrity and personhood lies at the core of women's sexual and reproductive rights and this campaign has been most instrumental in taking women's unmet sexual and reproductive needs out of the private realm where they were considered "domestic matters" and locating them in the public sphere, making them a political and policy issue and requiring that the state and the major institutions of the society not only recognize these rights as legitimate and inalienable, but also provide the material and infrastructural resources to sustain them. The extension of these rights to all women in all our societies remains a major challenge that globalization as a retrogressive process is making even more difficult. In response to the specific impacts of globalization in this regard, women have formed global coalitions around the issues of sexual and reproductive rights and health, meeting in various international conferences (Beijing, Nairobi, Mexico, and at the level of the United Nations and the Economic Commission for Africa) to insist that states not only ratify the conventions and international instruments that women have formulated, without reservation clauses, but also that states, as the assumed custodians of citizens' rights and entitlements, must undertake to implement such policies in order to safeguard the sexual and reproductive rights of women in totality.

This has met with a tremendous backlash, the use of so-called cultural appropriateness and slogans of authentication that seek to fragment women's rights through the claim that sexual and reproductive rights are "Western" and "un-African." Of course we know that when women demand their rights they become inauthentic and un-African and that is exactly what we aim to do. We will subvert the archaic notions of what is African as we insist on becoming modern and free; and we will redefine and restructure relationships of power and control, surveillance, and exclusion as we claim our democratic rights to be citizens in the fullest ways. Therefore, African men can moan as much as they want—while they remain locked in backward notions of what is African and practice western modernity in every other way but toward Africa women. Patriarchal claims and threats should not stop women.

In reality, however, these claims and threats often become translated into life-taking expressions of the backlash, and the vilification of women's rights' activists and women who claim their rights is real and requires the urgent response of all progressive men in our societies. This is not a matter only for women to resolve, because fundamentally it is about old systems of male privilege from which all men benefit in one way or another. Therefore no man is exempt from the political responsibility of fighting for the sexual and reproductive freedoms of women, for women's integrity and personhood, and for their right to be total citizens in both the public and private spheres. But, in addition to recognizing and defending all women's rights, men have to begin the process of moving themselves to a new gendered and male identity by interrogating their location within patriarchal society as men. How could it be that male comrades spend their lives critiquing and resisting capitalism and fundamentalisms of every kind, except those that construct them as males in deeply essential ways? At the core of masculinity lie heterosexism and male systems of privilege that underpin impunity and supremacy—even if not used by individual males in their relationships with women.

Knowledge and understanding of patriarchy in its most intimate and most pernicious forms are essential so that men do not oppress women again. But feminist and women activists never assume that because they are able to defend themselves they do not need to restructure the societies in which they live so that all women can access their freedom and their rights. Progressive men have to do the political work of transforming maleness and masculinity. It is not enough to be a good man—you have to be a revolutionary man so that women do not have to do this work for men. Everyone has to free her-or himself.

Finally, the women's movement is without doubt one of the most vibrant and most sustainable movements globally, and through the creation of national, regional, and global coalitions and networks, women have begun to change the world in very significant ways. In Africa, women's demands for justice, peace, and equality have shaken the foundations of old patriarchal assumptions about what is normal and acceptable. Women have begun to change the character of the public through educational and professional achievement and contestation. We are changing the meaning of science and knowledge by challenging the old dogmas and paradigms that excluded our experiences and opinions. At the level of the law the changes have been astounding and absolutely marvelous. In most African societies impunity no longer rages as an absolute force, although it remains a key challenge in the transformation of those areas where women's lives are most undemocratically and most dangerously affected.

Politically, women are challenging the state and its hegemony over the meaning of citizenship; women tend to question the assumption that the male-dominated state is the best protector of common property. This is particularly common in countries like Zimbabwe, where a neocolonial state simply took over from the colonial state in terms of being the middle-man in relation to the land as a common resource. Women also demand that the state step aside and let the citizens relate directly to the land as a critical economic and sociolegal resource. The same is happening in Mauritius and in many countries on the continent.

By changing their relationships with the state and with males in both the intimate and public spheres, women are becoming postcolonial in new and exciting ways. The challenge and disruption of old patriarchal relationships that construct women as private or communal property and men as the "natural" heirs of all power in African societies speaks to the emergence of a "postcolonial" consciousness among women (and among poor men who are challenging the neo-colonial state from where they are located as workers and peasants and homeless/landless persons) which will form the core of a sustainable anti-globalization strategy in the future.

In addition to understanding how capitalism and neoimperialism work at the levels of macroeconomic strategies, cultural and technological hegemony, the military-industrial complex and the use of guns, human trafficking and drugs, Africans also need to focus on their own political traditions and the resources being generated by social movements at the national, regional, and global levels. Understanding of how the World Trade Organization and General Agreement on Tariffs and Trade work to extend and intensify capitalist exploitation and human misery is necessary. Africans need to remain vigilant about the resurrection and pernicious implementation of the Multilateral Agreement on Investments agenda. It is also essential to put more energy into the reformulation of African capacities to think, mobilize, and transform Africans and their societies in ways that will finally rid them of the scourge of human-invented systems of greed and inequality. After all, globalization is just a fancy term to describe patriarchy in its most nefarious form.

## References

Chossudovsky, M. 1997. *The Globalization of Poverty*. London: Zed Books

Furedi, F. 1994. *The New Ideology of Imperialism*. London: Pluto.

Galtung, Johan.1996. *Peace and Conflict, Development and Civilization*. London: Sage Publications, and Oslo; International Peace Research Institute.

Gibbon, P. (ed.). 1993, *Social Change and Economic Reform in Africa*. Uppsala: The Scandinavian Institute of African Studies.

Mamdani, M., 1994, "A Critical Analysis of the IMF Programme in Uganda," In Ulf Himmelstrand, Kabiru Kinyanjui, K. & Edward Mburugu, (eds.). *African Perspectives on Development: Controversies, Dilemmas and Openings*. Dar es Salaam: Mkuki na Nyota. Mobutu, S. S. *New African*, July 1988.

Mongula, B. S. 1994. "Development Theory and Changing Trends in Sub-Saharan African Economies, 1960-89." In *Ulf Himmelstrand*, Kabiru Kinyanjui & Edward Mburugu, (eds.). *African Perspectives on Development: Controversies, Dilemmas and Openings.* Dar es Salaam: Mkuki na Nyota.

Mwanza, A. M. (ed.). 1992. *Structural Adjustment Programmes in SADC: Experiences and Lessons from Malawi, Tanzania, Zambia and Zimbabwe.* Harare: SAPES.

Olakunle, George. 2000. "African Politics, African Literatures: Thoughts on Mahmood Mamdani's *Citizen and Subject* and Wole Soyinka's *The Open Sore of a Continent.*" *West Africa Review* 2, no.1. [On-line] <http://www.icaap.org/iuicode?101.2.1.3> (4 February 2001).

Olusegun Obasanjo, Speech made at the Fourth African Development Forum (ADF-IV) held in Addis Ababa from the 11th-15th October 2004 on the theme "Governance for a Progressing Africa."

Shivji, I. G., 2002, "Is Might a Right in International Human Rights? Notes on Imperial Assault on the Right of Peoples to Self-determination." In Sifuni E. Mchome (ed.), In *Taking Stock of Human Rights Situation in Africa.* Dar es Salaam: Faculty of Law, University of Dar es Salaam.

Soros, George. 2000. *Open Society: Reforming Global Capitalism.* Public Affairs, NY.

Weber, Max. 2002. *The Protestant Ethic and the Spirit of Capitalism*, Translated by Peter Baehr and Gordon C. Wells, New York: Penguin Classics.

# Chapter 10

# Conclusion: Looking to the Future

In February 1990, a new political era began in Africa with the convening of a national conference in the West African state of Benin that led to the peaceful deposition of long-time ruler Mathieu Kérékou and a transition to a constitutional democracy. Although Kerekou returned to power through competitive elections in 1996, Benin has persisted as a pluralist democracy. The same is true of several other countries in Africa, such as Ghana, Mali, and Senegal. Less than five years after this dramatic start of what was optimistically hailed as Africa's "second independence," many of the new democracies proved to be really liberalized autocracies; public institutions continue to be fragile and inefficient; and deliberately instigated violence increasingly determines political outcomes.

Africa's interminable and innumerable crises all share a similar origin. Each of Africa's crises begins when someone assumes power through an election or a *coup d'état*. The new leader then proceeds to entrench himself in office by amassing power and surreptitiously debauching all key government institutions, namely, the military, the civil service, the judiciary, the parliament, and the financial system. With all powers in his hands, he transforms the state into his personal property to benefit himself, his cronies, and tribesmen, who all then proceed to plunder the national treasury with impunity. All others who do not belong to these privileged groups are excluded, as the politics of exclusion is practiced. The tyrant employs a variety of tactics to decimate opposition to his rule such as co-optation, bribery, infiltration, intimidation, and "divide and rule."

Some of these obstacles are largely the legacy of colonial rule, which didn't imbue the weak/threshold/quasi- states with enough of a democratic tradition to ensure accountability and regime continuity. The lack of democratic tradition engendered a resort to corruption, nepotism, and entrenched power in leadership.

These practices in turn left the people increasingly cynical as to whether anything had changed, or whether Western democracy could work in Africa. Too often one heard disillusioned cries of: "Democracy has not worked in Africa." Were these cries justified or were expectations of democracy unrealistically high?

The advent of political pluralism in the early 1990s throughout most African states brought new hopes for democracy, human rights, and economic prosperity. Since 1990, the year of the resurrection of political changes in Africa, multiparty elections have been held in more than 40 African countries. Many leaders and their movements that had been in power for so long, like Kenneth Kaunda (the "father of Zambia's independence") or Dr. Hastings Kamuzu Banda (Malawi) were removed. However, the shortcomings in the first and second batch of multiparty elections show that new "democratic" institutions have created their own challenges. Violence, corruption, human rights abuses, resilience of neopatrimonialism, dereliction of accountability, the political instrumentalization of disorder and the entrenchment of kleptocratic leaders and their increasingly authoritarian stances continue, indicating that after decades of one-party and military dictatorships, change doesn't come easily.

Indeed, Africa once again has veered toward a precipice. The much-vaunted "African renaissance," a three-way equation of a flowering of democracy, culture, and economic growth, appears to be in tatters. Instead, sagging economic performance, backsliding on democracy and other human rights reforms, and increased national and regional tensions menace much of the continent. In fact, Africa is facing crises in multiple dimensions.

## ENTRENCHED LEADERSHIP

With few exceptions, the leadership elected at the first fair elections entrenched itself, disregarded democratic constitutions, and replaced them with single-party constitutions or rule-by-decree, thus in effect reenacting the ghost of authoritarianism. Political rhetoric continues, but because of the way democracy is seen and played out in these African states, little consensus mitigating raw political conflict is the order of the day. The crushing of high hopes has largely been because of the misunderstanding and abuse of democracy by political leaders, because of their false and unrealistic promises to the people, and because of the peoples' tendency to equate democracy with economic advancement.

Obviously, colonial rule didn't create any lasting democratic tradition in Africa. The one-party system was seen at the dawn of independence as a valid tool to create national unity and political stability against a background of ethnic and geographical diversity. Since independence, only a few leaders of African countries have voluntarily resigned. The rest have been overthrown by their armies, killed, or removed at the first democratic elections. Many constitutions have had loopholes and provisions to remove any limits to the number of terms in office, and this helps explain the high number of military coups, even after the euphoria of return to constitutional democracy. Nelson Mandela's refusal to stand for a second term as President of the Republic of South Africa was so outstanding, since many African leaders still see themselves as irreplaceable—vital to their country's unity.

The constitutions of Zambia and Zimbabwe allow the president to nominate up to 8 and up to 30 persons (respectively) to the National Assembly. The undemocratic nature of this practice is worsened by the "first-past-the-post" electoral system in the African Commonwealth countries. This electoral system strengthens majorities in National Assemblies, assures presidents of comfortable electoral victories, and lessens opportunities for political debate within and between states. A proportional representation system, such as in the Republics of South Africa, Namibia, and Mozambique, would promote a more multiparty system, reducing high majorities and allowing minority involvement. Giving more autonomy to local councils could also increase public participation.

The predominantly centralized nature of the African states far worsens the effects of inefficiency of the administration, fatal economic decisions, and corruption. The preference for decentralization intended here is very different from what obtains in Francophone Africa where by "decentralization" is meant deconcentration of state terror.

It is noteworthy that concentration of power without checks and balances leads easily to informal politics as against formal politics.

In simple language it leads to the rule of man, instead of the rule of law. Informal politics can be observed in any country but in Africa it seems that informal politics often takes the upper hands over formal politics. It introduces into politics the neopatrimonial or the patronage system that leads to misuse of national resources and fails to accumulate capital for investment. Even assistance projects are unable to mark nationwide impacts on the development process. These are major negative outcomes of poor governance.

## WHOSE DEMOCRACY?

There is no doubt that Africa is facing a serious dilemma with respect to democracy. Democracy has become the catchphrase for everything that is wrong with Africa. It is the magical word expected from any African government seeking foreign aid or technical support from donor agencies. Every project document must contain a paragraph or two specifying the democracy plan and programs before it can receive favorable attention. Every thinking African must be worried about the sincerity of the continent's foreign "friends" with respect to this democracy crusade. They tend to wonder for whose benefit is the advice that Africa should or must embrace the Western model of democracy. Is it for the interest of Africans or for the interest of those exploiting the riches and wealth of Africa?

Democracy is a philosophical idea and a political practice invented by ancient Greeks to regulate the civil administration of their city-nations. The Greeks designed their democratic practices, as principles for harmonious social relations and as institutional arrangements of state, to limit the role of wealth in the decision-making processes of the city-states. In its original form, it was not a particularly perfect practice because it denied slaves and women the right of citizenship.

However, the lofty universal principles it engendered have received a lot of tinkering here and there ever since across the globe. In every country where seekers after the truth of existence have shown interest in the principle of democracy, they have made attempts to uphold for everyone the basic principle of equality of persons. They have tried to ensure the rights of every citizen to participate in the affairs of the state or society to which he or she belongs, and they have initiated and tried to device justifiable and amicable strategies for decisionmaking in handling the affairs of their society (Weber, 2002). Noble thinkers have also tried to improve or devise the best approach of delegating political power in a state and of safeguarding the abuse of power by people delegated to handle the social, economic, and political affairs of the society. The attempt to devise the best approach is usually sought when the geographical spread of the state is too large to support direct participation of every citizen.

Despite the fact that every state/nation gears its democracy toward the practice of the aforementioned principles, there are as many variants of democracy as there are nations in the world. It is a known fact among students of politics that monarchical parliamentary democracy is not the same as federated republican democracy. Moreover, neither is socialist democracy the same as communist democracy. Yet each of these systems of democracy claims it is the ideal and the best form of democratic practice. At this moment in the history of the world, every enlightened African needs to critically review the thrust of the sanctimonious powers of the world as they push, shuffle, and blackmail African countries into embracing one particular form of democratic principles, reforms, and practices.

The questions that each enlightened African or Africanist scholar should be asking are: Which of the democratic practices is suitable for my country? Is it not true that the type of democracy in practice in a nation is a reflection of the nature, history, and culture of the people concerned? Is it not true that there is a history behind the monarchical parliamentary democracy of Britain? Is it not also true that both the federated republican democracy of the United States of America and the pluralistic republican democracy of the Swiss have pertinent history behind them? If these facts are true, why should Africans not allow their nature, culture, and history determine the types of democracy suitable for each household, each community, each region, each state and each nation?

Looking at several stable democracies, it is apparent that the philosophical ideal a nation wishes to pursue will definitely determine the kind of democratic practice a people will adopt. For example, if equality of persons, impartial social justice and individual freedom are ideals a nation decides to pursue and safeguard, the parliamentary democracy of Britain will definitely not be a suitable choice for these aspirations. It is a commonly known fact among the well-informed people that the British democratic practice does not hide its abhorrence for the principle of equality of persons.

The British monarchical social order built its culture around a rigid, hierarchical, and nonmixing class system where the sovereignty of the nation resides solely in the personality of the reigning king or queen. The British monarch owns all and sundry, both the land and the people on it belong to the Crown and the noblemen. The British state, contrary to popular belief and sponsored political propaganda, is run like a sophisticated Mafia, where every crucial decision of government is made in secret and the nationals are carefully kept in the dark at all times. It is also true that the British Parliament does not hide its disgust for the principle that ordinary subjects of the Crown have sufficient common sense to participate in the political affairs of Britain apart from casting the vote when those who know best about such cerebral matters call for election.

In comparison but very different in conception and practice is the democratic constitution in a republic. Essentially, democracy in a constitutional republic takes for granted the principle of equality of citizens in every respect and facet of the word as a *sine qua non*. Even though this is the conceptual frame of a constitutional republic, the contradiction arises with its design of a representative democracy that tends to accord almost a monarchical status to its political leaders. Under a constitutional republic, leadership ought to be anathema because it is totally at variance with the concept of equality of persons. Every citizen ought to have the right and the opportunity to offer him-or herself for election in order to serve the state or community. Service and not leadership ought to be the singular motive and cardinal goal of every elected representative. However, when a state elects representatives under the platform of leadership or rulership in an election, then it becomes imperative that the business of people's representatives will not be to serve but wholly to rule.

The innocuous value that seems to accept the essential role of elected representatives in the American democratic constitution as leaders or rulers inadvertently destroys equality of citizens. As a result and in practice, the people cannot expect full accountability of the tenure in office from their leaders or rulers because cultural perception of the leader-servant dichotomy expects the habit of given a full account of stewardships only from servants. Leadership connotes supremacy or superiority and it will be degrading under the present principle of political leadership or rulership in the United States of America for elected representatives of the people to give full accounts of their stewardship to their subjects. They may, if they so wish (and this could only be at the pleasure of the leaders) give a perfunctory account of their stewardship, but the electorate cannot compel them to do so in full detail. At few times when called upon to account in full, it has always taken the full weight of the Congress to squeeze out the truth from the political leaders. This practice is a fundamental flaw in the doctrine of anticlassical democracy that tends to support the inescapable role of political leadership in democracy (Schumpeter, 1965).

Political scientists have traced the root of this kind of leadership attitude in the American democracy to its historical link with Britain. History tells us that the American war of independence was in fact, among many other things, a rejection of the inherited status quo of the traditional monarchical colonial parliamentary government that consistently transfers political and economic powers among family members. Under the monarchy, the kings, the governor-generals, and the prime ministers occupied positions of personal leadership and responsibility that almost in the past tended to assume a divine authority. This hereditary traditional position wittingly throws out all ethical considerations of equality of persons, a primary requirement of republicanism. In spite of the desire of the founding fathers of America to do away with monarchy in their lives, the vestiges of monarchy still run deep and wide throughout the sophisticated democratic practices in the country.

In the last few years and because of the unique access to public and private information through the Internet, Americans and the world at large are gradually coming to terms with the fact that the much-flaunted American democracy is under the control of a few fabulously wealthy families. In other words, the democracy of the United States of America is a camouflaged monarchy under the auspices of a cabal and a clandestine oligarchy. Unfortunately, Africans who lack knowledge and understanding of the democratic and leadership fraud in America love to ogle and ape the leadership practices in the United States as they push and press their countries to adopt the U.S model of government. In conversation, these Africans routinely throw in the phrase, "even in America," as an incontrovertible statement of fact to demonstrate that the American democracy is a superior political order.

On the other hand, there is the Swiss democracy as a different example of a constitutional republic. Since 1830 Switzerland has been essentially pluralistic—a system that allows different ethnic or other groups to preserve their own customs and to hold equal power within the same society or nation. This is particularly evident in its strict abhorrence and "hostility to all purely personal power." According to Wolf Linder (1994), the Swiss were not unaware of the aristocratic and oligarchic democratic regimes around them but they wisely cling to their own popular ideals of pluralism.

Today the Swiss democratic principle of pluralism manifests itself openly from the cantonal legislatures to the Council of State where, for example, chairmen of councils do not as a rule hold office for more than one year at a time and are not immediately re-eligible as chairmen. As a result, the type of larger than life aura bestowed on the American Presidents is practically nonexistent in Switzerland.

African countries have played dice with several borrowed versions of democratic practice and they have had their fingers burned. There is nothing wrong with any version of the practice except that to lose sight of the history behind the practice and the evolutionary process that informed its design is for the borrower to curry avoidable disaster. Therefore, is it not high time that the African intelligentsia accepted democratic principle not as a principle written in stone but as an idea that is open to reviews and corrections as circumstances demand? Hence, for Africans to expect they can borrow one variant of democratic practice and transfer it wholesale from one culture to another is a demonstration of the apelike mentality.

One would like to invite all thinkers in Africa to begin afresh on a course of seminal reflections that can unravel the history and the philosophy of the lost cultures of the continent over the centuries of devastations in order to ascertain the type of democratic practice relevant to each nation of Africa. The culture of a people holds the key to their beliefs and their understanding of the meaning of life. Unless a democratic practice flows from these beliefs and understanding, it can never fulfill the physical and spiritual needs of the people concerned.

As mentioned in a previous section, the history of Africa since the period of colonization shows that the cultures of Africans have been bastardized as the foreign conquerors perverted and ridiculed the philosophy or the meaning of life, as Africans knew it. After a long association with these conquering forces, Africans are neither here nor there in the global socioeconomic and political equations. The popular belief systems in practice all over the continent are artificial and they hold no meaning to the psyche of Africans. African ancestors might have embraced these foreign faiths as a means to an end because it was the only path open to them for social elevation and social acceptance into the "civilized societies" of their conquerors. It is high time every living African woke up to the reality of a spiritual vacuum in Africa before its enemies eat or bury the continent alive for good.

In this respect, when one sees Africans reverencing, adoring, venerating, hero-worshipping, and wagging tails for the royals, nobles, moneymen and -women, military and civilian politicians, and all other dishonorable human-kinds, one is tempted to conclude that these subservient behaviors are evidences of lack of knowledge of the historical facts of human existence. Hence, societies or peoples that invest so much trust and build such great hope on the antiso-cial, histrionic and narcissistic humankinds need to know they are investing in whirlwinds. The dishonorable personalities of the world today are not worthy of such high and noble expectations. Understanding this truth calls on each and everyone to seek liberation and emancipation from the rock-bottom level of human existence that enemies have consigned Africa as a whole continent.

## LOOKING FORWARD: RESEARCH AND POLICY STRATEGIES

If there is an overriding lesson to be gleaned from a survey of democratization on the African subcontinent, it is that current, conventional policies based on neoliberalism toward the region neither maximize the concerned national interests of imperial powers nor do justice to Africans in their quest for stability, prosperity, and independent religious and cultural identities. A more sophis-ticated understanding of democratization should be a precondition for policy formulation. In this spirit, certain policy and conceptual questions surface and beg further analysis.

- What are the democratically active sectors of the population on the African sub-continent? How is their activity manifested?
- What is the nexus between democratization, ethnicity, and class in selective African cases?

- Is the conventional dichotomy between moderate and radical "friends" of the West on the subcontinent appropriate? If not, what categorization should be substituted?

- To what extent are radical transnational democratic or deviant movements influencing indigenous variants of African democratization efforts? To what extent are they operating independently on the subcontinent?

- How can dialogue and understanding be fostered between foreign agencies and representatives of democratic forces on the subcontinent in both government and in the broader civil society?

- To what extent do foreign policies of foreign bodies in the underdeveloped world outside of Africa shape perceptions of democratization in the region?

- How do foreign policies based on neomercantilist policies toward democratization on the subcontinent fit into global policies of globalization, democratization, eradication of poverty, and development? Greater understanding of the nuances of democratization is a prerequisite to the delineation of preliminary policy recommendations toward democratizing areas of the African subcontinent.

## GOING FORWARD: AREAS FOR ACTION

Four key areas for action should be:

- Giving new value to the content and relevance of politics as the realm within which key decisions affecting society are taken. Solutions to the problems and challenges of democracy would have to be sought within and not outside of democratic institutions;

- Building a new legitimacy for the State. There can be no sustainable democracy without a State that is capable of promoting and guaranteeing the exercise of full citizenship;

- The need to promote greater diversity and flexibility of economic policy options whilst maintaining macroeconomic stability. From this perspective, the discussion on the economy and diversity of forms of market organization must be part of any broad public debate; and

- Considering globalization and its impact on African States as part of the democracy debate.

The delineation of areas of action is intended to demonstrate that a government of the African people should ensure that decisions affecting everyone should be taken by everyone. Government of the people therefore should mean a State of citizens in the full sense of the term. It should be a system of electing authorities as well as a form of organization that guarantees the rights of all: civil rights (guarantees against oppression); political rights (to be part of public or collective decisionmaking); and social rights (access to wellbeing). It is the democracy of citizens as the organizing principle, not one of corporate capitalists and that

African leadership (*Financial Times*, Jun 17, 1992, p. 4) in whom the masses have "... lost confidence in (its) capacity ... to provide jobs, housing, health care and its ability to combat corruption."

## References

Schumpeter, J. A. 1965. *Capitalism, Socialism and Democracy*. London: Unwin University Books (11th Impression).

Weber, Max. 2002. *The Protestant Ethic and the Spirit of Capitalism*, Translated by Peter Baehr and Gordon C. Wells, New York: Penguin Classics.

Wolf, Linder. 1994. *Swiss Democracy: Possible Solutions to Conflict in Multi-Cultural Societies*. London: The Macmillian Press.

# Index